Microsoft®Office
PowerPoint® 2007
on Demand

Steve Johnson

Perspection, Inc.

que®

Que Publishing
800 East 96th Street
Indianapolis, IN 46240 USA

Microsoft® Office PowerPoint 2007 On Demand

Library of Congress Cataloging-in-Publication Data

Johnson, Steve, 1961-

  Microsoft Office PowerPoint 2007 On Demand / Steve Johnson

      p. cm.

  ISBN 0-7897-3643-8

  1. Presentation graphics software. 2. Microsoft PowerPoint (Computer file)

    I. Title

  T385.J647 2006

  005.5'8--dc22

                    2006032189

Printed and bound in the United States of America

First Printing: October 2006

09 08 07   4 3 2

Que Publishing offers excellent discounts on this book when ordered in quantity for bulk purchases or special sales.

For information, please contact: U.S. Corporate and Government Sales

  1-800-382-3419 or corpsales@pearsontechgroup.com

For sales outside the U.S., please contact: International Sales

  1-317-428-3341 or International@pearsontechgroup.com

Trademarks

Warning and Disclaimer

Publisher
Paul Boger

Associate Publisher
Greg Wiegand

Acquisitions Editor
Stephanie McComb

Managing Editor
Steve Johnson

Author
Steve Johnson

Technical Editor
Alex Williams

Production Editor
Holly Johnson

Page Layout
Emily Atwood
Dori Hernandez
Alex Williams

Interior Designers
Steve Johnson
Marian Hartsough

Indexer
Katherine Stimson

Proofreader
Emily Atwood
Holly Johnson

Team Coordinator
Michelle Newcomb

Acknowledgements

Perspection, Inc.

Microsoft Office PowerPoint 2007 On Demand has been created by the professional trainers and writers at Perspection, Inc. to the standards you've come to expect from Que publishing. Together, we are pleased to present this training book.

Perspection, Inc. is a software training company committed to providing information and training to help people use software more effectively in order to communicate, make decisions, and solve problems. Perspection writes and produces software training books, and develops multimedia and Web-based training. Since 1991, we have written more than 80 computer books, with several bestsellers to our credit, and sold over 5 million books.

This book incorporates Perspection's training expertise to ensure that you'll receive the maximum return on your time. You'll focus on the tasks and skills that increase productivity while working at your own pace and convenience.

We invite you to visit the Perspection Web site at:

www.perspection.com

Acknowledgements

The task of creating any book requires the talents of many hard-working people pulling together to meet impossible deadlines and untold stresses. We'd like to thank the outstanding team responsible for making this book possible: the writer, Steve Johnson; the technical editor, Alex Williams; the production team, Emily Atwood, Alex Williams, and Dori Hernandez; the editors and proofreaders, Emily Atwood and Holly Johnson; and the indexer, Katherine Stimson.

At Que publishing, we'd like to thank Greg Wiegand and Stephanie McComb for the opportunity to undertake this project, Michelle Newcomb for administrative support, and Sandra Schroeder for your production expertise and support.

Perspection

About The Author

Steve Johnson has written more than 35 books on a variety of computer software, including Microsoft Office 2003 and XP, Microsoft Windows XP, Apple Mac OS X Panther, Macromedia Flash MX 2004 and 8, Macromedia Director MX 2004, Macromedia Fireworks, and Adobe Photoshop CS and CS2. In 1991, after working for Apple Computer and Microsoft, Steve founded Perspection, Inc., which writes and produces software training. When he is not staying up late writing, he enjoys playing golf, gardening, and spending time with his wife, Holly, and three children, JP, Brett, and Hannah. When time permits, he likes to travel to such places as New Hampshire in October, and Hawaii. Steve and his family live in Pleasanton, California, but can also be found visiting family all over the western United States.

We Want To Hear From You!

As the reader of this book, *you* are our most important critic and commentator. We value your opinion and want to know what we're doing right, what we could do better, what areas you'd like to see us publish in, and any other words of wisdom you're willing to pass our way.

As an associate publisher for Que, I welcome your comments. You can email or write me directly to let me know what you did or didn't like about this book—as well as what we can do to make our books better.

Please note that I cannot help you with technical problems related to the topic of this book. We do have a User Services group, however, where I will forward specific technical questions related to the book.

When you write, please be sure to include this book's title and author as well as your name, email address, and phone number. I will carefully review your comments and share them with the author and editors who worked on the book.

Email: feedback@quepublishing.com

Mail: Greg Wiegand
         Que Publishing
         800 East 96th Street
         Indianapolis, IN 46240 USA

For more information about this book or another Que title, visit our Web site at *www.quepublishing.com*. Type the ISBN (excluding hyphens) or the title of a book in the Search field to find the page you're looking for.

This Book Is Safari Enabled

The Safari® Enabled icon on the cover of your favorite technology book means the book is available through Safari Bookshelf. When you buy this book, you get free access to the online edition for 45 days. Safari Bookshelf is an electronic reference library that lets you easily search thousands of technical books, find code samples, download chapters, and access technical information whenever and wherever you need it.

To gain 45-day Safari Enabled access to this book:

◆ Go to *http://www.quepublishing.com/safarienabled*

◆ Complete the brief registration form

◆ Enter the coupon code LEMA-NMTL-MT9X-N5MM-DZ8D

If you have difficulty registering on Safari Bookshelf or accessing the online edition, please e-mail customer-service@safaribooksonline.com.

Contents

Introduction   xv

1 Getting Started with PowerPoint   1

    Starting PowerPoint   2
    Viewing the PowerPoint Window   3
    Using the Ribbon   4   **New!**
    Choosing Commands   5
    Working with Toolbars   6   **New!**
    Choosing Dialog Box Options   8   **New!**
    Using the Status Bar   9   **New!**
    Choosing the Best Method to Start a Presentation   10   **New!**
    Creating a Blank Presentation   11
    Creating a Presentation Using a Template   12   **New!**
    Opening a Presentation   13   **New!**
    Arranging Windows   14
    Using Task Panes and Window Panes   15   **New!**
    Understanding PowerPoint Views   16
    Browsing a Presentation   18
    Getting Help While You Work   20
    Saving a Presentation   22   **New!**
    Saving a Presentation with Different Formats   24
    Getting PowerPoint Updates on the Web   26
    Recovering a Presentation   27
    Diagnosing and Repairing Problems   28   **New!**
    Closing a Presentation and Quitting PowerPoint   30

2 Developing Presentation Content   31

    Creating New and Consistent Slides   32   **New!**
    Working with Objects   34   **New!**
    Developing Text   36
    Entering Text   38
    Editing Text   40
    Setting Editing Options   41

Correcting Text While Typing   42

Resizing Text While Typing   44

Inserting Information the Smart Way   46

Inserting and Developing an Outline   48

Moving and Indenting Text   50   **New!**

Setting Tabs   52

Changing Text Alignment and Spacing   54   **New!**

Changing Character Spacing   56   **New!**

Changing Character Direction   57   **New!**

Formatting Text   58   **New!**

Modifying a Bulleted and Numbered List   60

AutoFormatting Text While Typing   62

Applying a Format Style   64

Inserting Symbols   65

Creating a Text Box   66   **New!**

Creating Text Columns   68   **New!**

Finding and Replacing Text   69

Rearranging Slides   70

Using Slides from Other Presentations   72   **New!**

3   Designing a Look   73

Making Your Presentation Look Consistent   74   **New!**

Viewing Masters   76

Controlling Slide Appearance with Masters   78   **New!**

Controlling a Slide Layout with Masters   80   **New!**

Modifying Placeholders   82

Controlling a Slide Background with Masters   84

Adding a Header and Footer   85

Inserting Slide Numbers   86

Inserting the Date and Time   88

Understanding Color Themes   89   **New!**

Viewing and Applying a Theme   90   **New!**

Creating a Color Theme   92   **New!**

Choosing Theme Fonts   94   **New!**

Choosing Theme Effects   95   **New!**

Creating a Custom Theme   96   **New!**

Adding Colors to a Presentation   98   **New!**

Adding a Background Style   99   **New!**

Modifying a Background Style   100

Saving a Template   102

4 **Drawing and Modifying Shapes** 105

Drawing and Resizing Shapes 106 **New!**
Inserting Multiple Shapes 108
Adding Text to a Shape 109
Drawing Lines and Arrows 110 **New!**
Creating and Editing Freeforms 112
Modifying a Freeform 114
Copying and Moving Objects 116
Adding a Quick Style to a Shape 118 **New!**
Adding a Quick Style to Shape Text 119 **New!**
Applying Color Fills 120 **New!**
Applying Picture Fills 122
Applying Texture Fills 124
Applying Gradient Fills 126 **New!**
Applying Shape Effects 128 **New!**
Creating Shadows 130 **New!**
Adding 3-D Effects to a Shape 132 **New!**
Adding 3-D Rotation Effects to a Shape 134 **New!**
Aligning Objects to Grids and Guides 136
Aligning and Distributing Objects 138
Connecting Shapes 140 **New!**
Selecting Objects Using the Selection Pane 142 **New!**
Changing Stacking Order 143
Rotating and Flipping a Shape 144
Grouping and Ungrouping Shapes 146
Inserting AutoShapes from the Clip Gallery 148
Adding a Shape to the Clip Organizer 150

5 **Inserting Pictures and Multimedia** 151

Inserting Multimedia Clips 152
Adding and Removing Clips 153
Organizing Clips into Categories 154
Locating and Inserting Clip Art 156
Accessing Clip Art on the Web 158
Inserting a Picture 160
Examining Picture File Formats 161
Creating a Photo Album 162 **New!**
Adding a Quick Style to a Picture 164 **New!**
Applying a Shape to a Picture 165 **New!**
Applying a Border to a Picture 166

Applying Picture Effects 167 **New!**

Modifying Picture Size 168 **New!**

Compressing a Picture 170

Modifying Picture Brightness and Contrast 171

Recoloring a Picture 172 **New!**

Cropping and Rotating a Picture 174

Creating WordArt Text 176 **New!**

Formatting WordArt Text 178 **New!**

Applying WordArt Text Effects 180 **New!**

Modifying WordArt Text Position 181

Inserting Movies and Sounds 182

Inserting CD Audio 184

Recording Sounds 185

Setting Movie and Sound Play Options 186

Playing Movies and Sounds 188

6 Inserting Charts and Related Material 189

Creating SmartArt Graphics 190 **New!**

Using the Text Pane with SmartArt Graphics 192 **New!**

Modifying a SmartArt Graphic 194 **New!**

Resizing a SmartArt Graphic 195

Formatting a SmartArt Graphic 196 **New!**

Formatting a Shape in a SmartArt Graphic 198 **New!**

Creating an Organization Chart 200 **New!**

Modifying an Organization Chart 202 **New!**

Inserting a Chart 204 **New!**

Selecting Chart Data 206

Entering Chart Data 207

Editing Chart Data 208 **New!**

Importing Data 210

Modifying the Data Worksheet 212

Selecting a Chart Type, Layout, and Style 214 **New!**

Formatting Chart Objects 216

Changing the Chart Layout Objects 218

Saving a Chart Template 220 **New!**

Inserting a Table 222 **New!**

Modifying a Table 224

Formatting a Table 226 **New!**

Adding a Quick Style to a Table 228 **New!**

Applying Effects to a Table 230 **New!**

Sharing Information Among Documents 231

Embedding and Linking an Object 232

Modifying Links 234

Inserting a Microsoft Excel Chart 236

Inserting a Microsoft Word Document 238

Inserting a Microsoft Organization Chart 239

Modifying a Microsoft Organization Chart 240

Linking and Embedding Sounds 242

7 Creating a Web Presentation 243

Adding Action Buttons 244

Adding Hyperlinks to Objects 246

Creating Hyperlinks to External Objects 248

Inserting Hyperlinks 250

Using and Removing Hyperlinks 252

Saving a Presentation as a Web Page 254

Saving a Presentation as a Single File Web Page 256

Saving Slides as Web Graphics 257

Changing Web Page Options 258

Opening a Web Page 259

Previewing a Web Page 260

Getting Documents from the Web 262

Accessing Office Information on the Web 263

Exploring XML 264

Saving an XML Presentation 265 **New!**

Opening an XML Presentation 266

8 Finalizing a Presentation and Its Supplements 267

Changing Page Setup Options 268 **New!**

Preparing Handouts 270

Preparing Speaker Notes 272

Customizing Notes Pages 274

Changing Proofing Options 275 **New!**

Checking Spelling 276

Using Custom Dictionaries 278 **New!**

Inserting Research Material 280

Finding the Right Words 281

Using the English Assistant 282 **New!**

Translating Text to Another Language 283

Changing Text to a Language 284

Exporting Notes and Slides to Word 285

Documenting Presentation Properties 286 **New!**

Checking Compatibility 288 **New!**
Saving Slides in Different Formats 289
Saving Outline Text as a Document 290
Creating a PDF Document 291 **New!**
Creating an XPS Document 292 **New!**
Selecting Printing Options 293
Previewing a Presentation 294
Printing a Presentation 296
Printing an Outline 298

9 Preparing a Slide Show **299**

Creating Slide Transitions 300 **New!**
Adding Animation 302 **New!**
Using Specialized Animation 304
Coordinating Multiple Animations 306
Animating a SmartArt Graphic 308 **New!**
Adding Slide Timings 310
Recording a Narration 312
Setting Up a Slide Show 314
Creating a Custom Slide Show 316
Creating a Self-Running Presentation 318
Working with Fonts 319
Saving a Presentation as a Slide Show 320

10 Presenting a Slide Show **321**

Starting a Slide Show 322
Navigating a Slide Show 324
Annotating a Slide Show 326
Delivering a Show on Multiple Monitors 328 **New!**
Packaging a Presentation on CD 330 **New!**
Showing a Presentation with the PowerPoint Viewer 332
Customizing the PowerPoint Viewer 333
Showing Multiple Presentations 334

11 Reviewing and Securing a Presentation **335**

Adding Comments to a Presentation 336
Editing Comments in a Presentation 338
Inspecting Documents 340 **New!**
Adding Password Protection to a Presentation 342

Restricting Presentation Access   344   **New!**
Adding a Digital Signature   346
Avoiding Harmful Attacks   348
Using the Trust Center   350   **New!**
Selecting Trusted Publishers and Locations   351   **New!**
Setting Add-in Security Options   352   **New!**
Setting ActiveX Security Options   353   **New!**
Setting Macro Security Options   354   **New!**
Changing Message Bar Security Options   355   **New!**
Setting Privacy Options   356   **New!**
Working with Office Safe Modes   358   **New!**
Marking a Presentation as Read-Only   360   **New!**
Sending a Presentation for Review Using E-Mail   361
Sending a Presentation by Internet Fax   362

12   Working Together on Office Documents   363

Configuring Groove   364   **New!**
Launching Groove   365   **New!**
Viewing the Groove Window   366   **New!**
Setting General Preferences   367   **New!**
Creating a Groove Workspace   368   **New!**
Inviting Others to a Workspace   369   **New!**
Dealing with Groove Alerts   370   **New!**
Sharing Files in a Workspace   371   **New!**
Holding a Discussion   372   **New!**
Adding Tools to a Workspace   373   **New!**
Setting Calendar Appointments   374   **New!**
Managing Meetings   375   **New!**
Working with Forms   376   **New!**
Tracking Issues   378   **New!**
Creating a Picture Library   380   **New!**
Adding a Contact   381   **New!**
Sending a message   382   **New!**
Chatting with Others   383   **New!**
Sharing Files with SharePoint   384   **New!**
Sharing Files with Synchronizing Folders   386   **New!**
Working with a Shared Workspace   387   **New!**
Publishing Slides to a Library   388   **New!**
Saving a Presentation to a Document Management Server   390   **New!**

13 Customizing the Way You Work   **391**

     Setting General PowerPoint Options   392   **New!**
     Customizing the Way You Create Options   394
     Accessing Commands Not in the Ribbon   395   **New!**
     Scanning and Imaging Document   396   **New!**
     Managing Pictures   398
     Using Multiple Languages   400

14 Expanding PowerPoint Functionality   **401**

     Viewing and Managing Add-ins   402   **New!**
     Loading and Unloading Add-ins   404
     Enhancing a Presentation with VBA   406
     Viewing the Visual Basic Editor   408
     Setting Developer Options   409   **New!**
     Simplifying Tasks with Macros   410   **New!**
     Controlling a Macro   412
     Adding a Digital Signature to a Macro Project   414
     Assigning a Macro to a Toolbar   415   **New!**
     Saving a Presentation with Macros   416   **New!**
     Opening a Presentation with Macros   417   **New!**
     Inserting ActiveX Controls   418   **New!**
     Using ActiveX Controls   420
     Setting ActiveX Control Properties   421   **New!**
     Playing a Movie Using an ActiveX Control   422   **New!**
     Changing the Document Information Panel   424   **New!**

W Workshops: Putting It All Together   **425**

     Project 1: Optimizing Presentations   425
     Project 2: Creating Better Presentations   428
     Project 3: Creating Custom Animations   431
     Project 4: Creating a Self Running Presentation with
           Narration   432
     Project 5: Creating a VBA Form in a Presentation   434
     Want More Projects   438

     New Features   439   **New!**
     Microsoft Certified Applications Specialist   444
     Index   453

Introduction

Welcome to *Microsoft Office PowerPoint 2007 On Demand*, a visual quick reference book that shows you how to work efficiently with Microsoft Office PowerPoint. This book provides complete coverage of basic to advanced PowerPoint skills.

How This Book Works

You don't have to read this book in any particular order. We've designed the book so that you can jump in, get the information you need, and jump out. However, the book does follow a logical progression from simple tasks to more complex ones. Each task is presented on no more than two facing pages, which lets you focus on a single task without having to turn the page. To find the information that you need, just look up the task in the table of contents or index, and turn to the page listed. Read the task introduction, follow the step-by-step instructions in the left column along with screen illustrations in the right column, and you're done.

What's New

If you're searching for what's new in PowerPoint 2007, just look for the icon: **New!**. The new icon appears in the table of contents and through out this book so you can quickly and easily identify a new or improved feature in PowerPoint 2007. A complete description of each new feature appears in the New Features guide in the back of this book.

Keyboard Shortcuts

Most menu commands have a keyboard equivalent, such as Ctrl+P, as a quicker alternative to using the mouse. A complete list of keyboard shortcuts is available on the Web at *www.perspection.com*.

How You'll Learn

How This Book Works

What's New

Keyboard Shortcuts

Step-by-Step Instructions

Real World Examples

Workshop

Microsoft Certified Applications Specialist

Get More on the Web

Step-by-Step Instructions

This book provides concise step-by-step instructions that show you "how" to accomplish a task. Each set of instructions include illustrations that directly correspond to the easy-to-read steps. Also included in the text are time-savers, tables, and sidebars to help you work more efficiently or to teach you more in-depth information. A "Did You Know?" provides tips and techniques to help you work smarter, while a "See Also" leads you to other parts of the book containing related information about the task.

Real World Examples

This book uses real world examples files to give you a context in which to use the task. By using the example files, you won't waste time looking for or creating sample files. You get a start file and a result file, so you can compare your work. Not every topic needs an example file, such as changing options, so we provide a complete list of the example files used through out the book. The example files that you need for project tasks along with a complete file list are available on the Web at *www.perspection.com*.

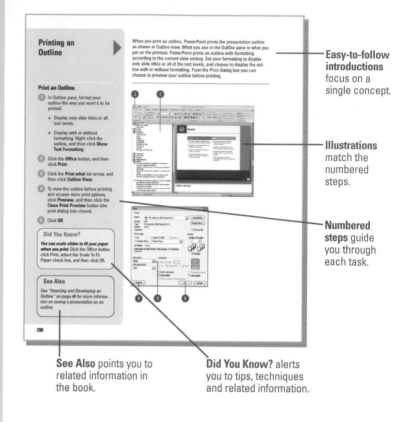

Easy-to-follow introductions focus on a single concept.

Illustrations match the numbered steps.

Numbered steps guide you through each task.

See Also points you to related information in the book.

Did You Know? alerts you to tips, techniques and related information.

Real world examples help you apply what you've learned to other tasks.

Workshop

This book shows you how to put together the individual step-by-step tasks into indepth projects with the Workshop. You start each project with a sample file, work through the steps, and then compare your results with project results file at the end. The project files are available on the Web at *www.perspection.com*.

Microsoft Certified Applications Specialist

This book prepares you for the Microsoft Certified Applications Specialist (MCAS) exam for Microsoft Office PowerPoint 2007. Each MCAS certification exam has a set of objectives, which are organized into broader skill sets. To prepare for the certification exam, you should review and perform each task identified with a MCAS objective to confirm that you can meet the requirements for the exam. Throughout this book, content that pertains to an objective is identified with the following MCAS logo and objective number next to it.

Workshop

Introduction

The Workshop is all about being creative and thinking outside of the box. These workshops will help your right-brain soar, while making your left-brain happy, by explaining why things work the way they do. Exploring possibilities is great fun; however, always stay grounded with knowledge of how things work. Knowledge is power.

Getting and Using the Project Files

Each project in The Workshop includes a start file to help you get started with the project, and a final file to provide you with the results of the project so you can see how well you accomplished the task.

Before you can use the project files, you need to download them from the Web. You can access the files at *www.perspection.com* in the software downloads area. After you download the files from the Web, uncompress the files into a folder on your hard drive to which you have easy access from your Microsoft Office program.

Project 1: Optimizing Presentations

Skills and Tools: PowerPoint options

PowerPoint comes with a varied set of features that allow you to create different kinds of presentations. However, not all features are created equal. Some features, such as hardware graphics acceleration, give you a little extra speed when you have the right hardware on your computer, but it also causes some movies not to display properly on the screen. Other features, like AutoFormat, are great when you want PowerPoint to automatically resize title or body text, but it also can be frustrating when you don't want text size to change. If you take your presentations on the road, not having the right fonts installed on the presentation computer, missing linked movies and sounds, or showing a slow large presentation can create big problems.

The Project

In this project, you'll learn how to set options to optimize PowerPoint and presentations for typical usage on any computer.

425

The **Workshop** walks you through indepth projects to help you put Microsoft Office to work.

Microsoft Certified Applications Specialist

About the MCAS Program

The Microsoft Certified Applications Specialist (MCAS) certification is the globally recognized standard for validating expertise with the Microsoft Office suite of business productivity programs. Earning an MCAS certificate acknowledges you have the expertise to work with Microsoft Office programs. To earn the MCAS certification, you must pass a certification exam for the Microsoft Office desktop applications of Microsoft Office Word, Microsoft Office Excel, Microsoft Office PowerPoint, Microsoft Office Outlook, or Microsoft Office Access. (The availability of Microsoft Certified Applications Specialist certification exams varies by program, program version, and language. Visit *www.microsoft.com* and search on *Microsoft Certified Applications Specialist* for exam availability and more information about the program.) The Microsoft Certified Applications Specialist program is the only Microsoft-approved program in the world for certifying proficiency with Microsoft Office programs.

What Does This Logo Mean?

It means this book has been approved by the Microsoft Certified Applications Specialist program to be certified courseware for learning Microsoft Office PowerPoint 2007 and preparing for the certification exam. This book will prepare you for the Microsoft Certified Applications Specialist exam for Microsoft Office PowerPoint 2007. Each certification level has a set of objectives, which are organized into broader skill sets. Throughout this book, content that pertains to a Microsoft Certified Applications Specialist objective is identified with the following MCAS certification logo and objective number below the title of the topic:

Microsoft Certified Application Specialist   PP07S-1.1
PP07S-2.2

445

Logo indicates a task fulfills one or more MCAS certification objectives.

Get More on the Web

In addition to the information in this book, you can also get more information on the Web to help you get up to speed faster with PowerPoint 2007. Some of the information includes:

Transition Helpers

- **Only New Features.** Download and print the new feature tasks as a quick and easy guide.

Productivity Tools

- **Keyboard Shortcuts.** Download a list of keyboard shortcuts to learn faster ways to get the job done.

More Content

- **Photographs.** Download photographs and other graphics to use in your Office documents.

- **More Content.** Download new content developed after publication. For example, you can download a complete chapter on Office SharePoint Server 2007.

You can access these additional resources on the Web at *www.perspection.com*.

Working Together on Office SharePoint Documents

S

Introduction

Microsoft Windows SharePoint Services is a collection of products and services which provide the ability for people to engage in communication, document and file sharing, calendar events, sending alerts, tasks planning, and collaborative discussions in a single community solution.

Office SharePoint Server 2007 is a product that uses Windows SharePoint Services 3.0 or later technology to work effectively with Microsoft Office 2007 programs. You can create a slide library on a Office SharePoint site in PowerPoint 2007 (New!), use Office SharePoint list data to create reports in Access 2007, create a meeting workspace and synchronize calendar and contacts in Outlook 2007, design browser form templates in InfoPath 2007 (New!), and save worksheets on an Office SharePoint site in Excel 2007. In many of the Office 2007 programs, you can update properties for a server document in a Document Information Panel (New!), and participate in workflows (New!), which is the automated movement of documents or items through a sequence of actions or tasks, such as document approval.

Office 2007 programs use the Document Management task pane to access many Office SharePoint Server 2007 features. The Document Management task pane allows you to see the list of team members collaborating on the current project, find out who is online, send an e-mail message, and review tasks and other resources. You can also use the Document Management task pane to create document workspaces where you can collect, organize, modify, share, and discuss Office documents.

Before you can use Office SharePoint Server 2007, the software needs to be set up and configured on a Windows 2003 Server or later by your network administrator. You can view Office SharePoint Server sites using a Web browser or a mobile device (New!) while you're on the road.

What You'll Do

View and Navigate Office SharePoint Sites

Create a Document Workspace Site

Create a Document Library Site

Add and Upload Documents to a Site

Add Pages to a Site

Publish Slides to a Library

Saving a File to a Document Management Server

View Versions of Documents

Check Documents In and Out to Edit

Work with Shared Workspace

View Team Members

Create Lists

Create Events

Hold Web Discussions

Set Up Alerts

Customize Quick Launch or Top Link Bar

1

Additional content is available on the Web. You can download a chapter on SharePoint.

Getting Started with PowerPoint

1

Introduction

Whether you need to put together a quick presentation of sales figures for your management team or create a polished slide show for your company's stockholders, Microsoft Office PowerPoint 2007 can help you present your information efficiently and professionally.

PowerPoint is a **presentation graphics program**—software that helps you create a slide show presentation and supplements, such as handouts and speaker's notes. A slide show presentation is made up of a series of slides that can contain charts, diagrams, pictures, SmartArt graphs (**New!**), bulleted lists, eye-catching text, multimedia video and sound clips, and more. PowerPoint is set up with a tab-based Ribbon (**New!**) and dialog boxes that provide you with the tools you need when you need them to get tasks done. The customizable Quick Access Toolbar (**New!**) gives you easy access to commonly-used commands, such as Save, Undo, and Print.

PowerPoint provides a variety of professionally designed templates, themes (**New!**), and style galleries (**New!**) to help you create great-looking presentations. When it comes time to develop your presentation, PowerPoint offers a selection of views and panes—Normal view, Slide Sorter view, Notes Page view, and Slide Show view. Normal view is helpful for working on individual slides and notes, while Slide Sorter view helps you organize all of your slides and add transition elements. If you need to write extensive notes, Notes Page view provides the additional space you need. Slide Show view pulls it all together, allowing you to view your presentation on your computer monitor for fine tuning.

When you complete your presentation, you can save it in a more efficient PowerPoint XML format (**New!**) or as a PDF or XPS document (**New!**), send it through e-mail for review, package it on a CD for clients, or even collaborate and share it with co-workers using a SharePoint slide library (**New!**).

What You'll Do

Start PowerPoint

View the PowerPoint Window

Use the Ribbon and Status Bar

Choose Commands

Work with Toolbars

Choose Dialog Boxes Options

Choose the Best Method to Start a Presentation

Create a Presentation

Arrange Windows

Use Task Panes and Window Panes

Understand PowerPoint Views

Browse a Presentation

Get Help While You Work

Save a Presentation

Get PowerPoint Updates on the Web

Recover a Presentation

Diagnose and Repair Problems

Close a Presentation and Quit PowerPoint

Starting PowerPoint

The two quickest ways to start PowerPoint are to select it on the Start menu or double-click a shortcut icon on the desktop. By providing different ways to start a program, Office lets you work the way you like and start programs with a click of a button. When you start PowerPoint, a program window opens, displaying a blank presentation, where you can create a new presentation or open an existing one.

Start PowerPoint from the Start Menu

① Click the **Start** button on the taskbar.

② Point to **All Programs**.

③ Click **Microsoft Office**.

④ Click **Microsoft Office PowerPoint 2007**.

If Microsoft Office asks you to activate the program, follow the instructions to complete the process.

TIMESAVER *To activate Microsoft Office later, click the Office button, click PowerPoint Options, click Resources, and then click Activate.*

If a Privacy dialog box appears, select the options you want, and then click OK.

Did You Know?

You can create a program shortcut from the Start menu to the desktop. Click the Start menu, point to All Programs, click Microsoft Office, right-click Microsoft Office PowerPoint 2007, point to Send To, and then click Desktop (Create Shortcut).

You can start PowerPoint and open a presentation from Windows Explorer. Double-clicking any PowerPoint presentation icon in Windows Explorer opens that file and PowerPoint.

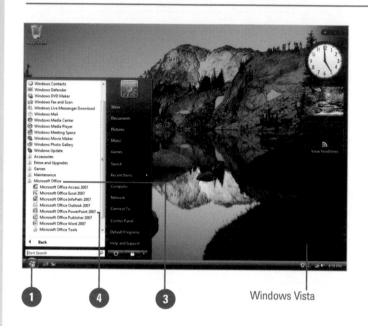

Windows Vista

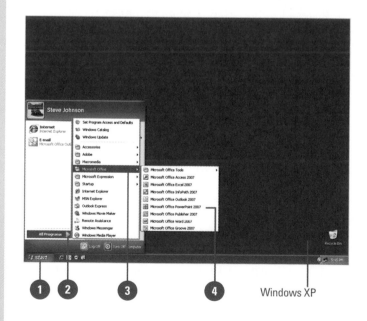

Windows XP

Viewing the PowerPoint Window

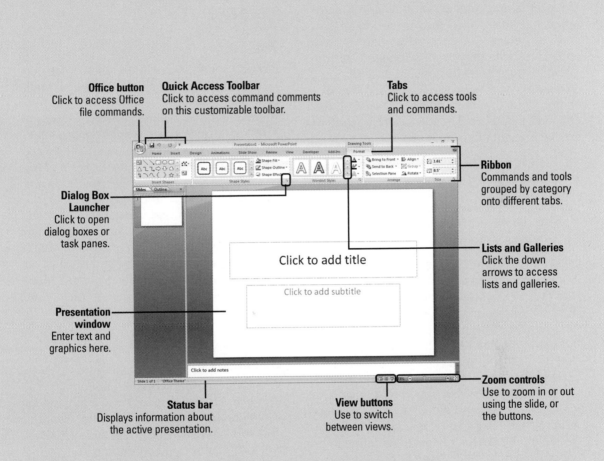

Office button
Click to access Office file commands.

Quick Access Toolbar
Click to access command comments on this customizable toolbar.

Tabs
Click to access tools and commands.

Ribbon
Commands and tools grouped by category onto different tabs.

Dialog Box Launcher
Click to open dialog boxes or task panes.

Lists and Galleries
Click the down arrows to access lists and galleries.

Presentation window
Enter text and graphics here.

Zoom controls
Use to zoom in or out using the slide, or the buttons.

Status bar
Displays information about the active presentation.

View buttons
Use to switch between views.

Using the Ribbon

The **Ribbon** (New!) is a new look for PowerPoint 2007. It replaces menus, toolbars, and most of the task panes found in PowerPoint 2003. The Ribbon is located at the top of the presentation window and is comprised of **tabs** (New!) that are organized by task or objects. The controls on each tab are organized into **groups**, or subtasks. The controls, or **command buttons**, in each group execute a command, or display a menu of commands or a drop-down gallery. Controls in each group provide a visual way to quickly make presentation changes.

> **TIMESAVER** *To minimize the Ribbon, double-click the name of the tab that is displayed, or click the Customize Quick Access Toolbar list arrow, and then click Minimize the Ribbon. Click a tab to auto display it (Ribbon remains minimized). Double-click a tab to maximize it.*

If you prefer using the keyboard instead of the mouse to access commands on the Ribbon, Microsoft Office provides easy to use shortcuts. Simply press and release the [Alt] or [F10] key to display **KeyTips** (New!) over each feature in the current view, and then continue to press the letter shown in the KeyTip until you press the one that you want to use. To cancel an action and hide the KeyTips, press and release the [Alt] or [F10] key again. If you prefer using the keyboard shortcuts found in previous versions of Microsoft Office, such as Ctrl+P (for Print), all the keyboard shortcuts

and keyboard accelerators work exactly the same in Microsoft Office 2007. Office 2007 includes a legacy mode that you can turn on to use familiar Office 2003 keyboard accelerators.

Tabs

PowerPoint provides three types of tabs on the Ribbon. The first type is called a **standard** tab—such as Home, Insert, Design, Animations, Slide Show, Review, View, and Add-Ins—that you see whenever you start PowerPoint. The second type is called a **contextual** tab—such as Picture Tools, Drawing, or Table—that appears only when they are needed based on the type of task you are doing. PowerPoint recognizes what you're doing and provides the right set of tabs and tools for you to use when you need them. The third type is called a **program** tab—such as Print Preview, Slide Master, Handout Master, or Notes Master—that replaces the standard set of tabs when you switch to certain views or modes.

Live Preview

When you point to a gallery option, such as WordArt, on the Ribbon, PowerPoint displays a **live preview** (New!) of the option change so that you can see exactly what your change will look like before committing to it.

Standard tabs   Contextual tab

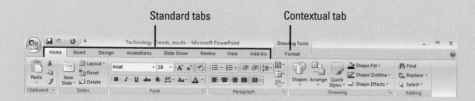

Choosing Commands ▶

The PowerPoint commands are organized in groups on the Ribbon, Office menu, Quick Access Toolbar, and Mini-Toolbar. The Office button opens to display file related menu commands, while the Quick Access Toolbar and Mini-Toolbar display frequently used buttons that you are already familiar with from PowerPoint 2003. In addition to the Office menu, you can also open a **shortcut menu** with a group of related commands by right-clicking a PowerPoint element.

Choose a Command from the Office Menu

① Click the **Office** button on the Ribbon.

② Click the command you want.

If the command is followed by an arrow, point to the arrow to see a list of related options, and then click the option you want.

TIMESAVER *You can use a shortcut key to choose a command. Press and hold down the first key and then press the second key. For example, press and hold the Ctrl key and then press S (or Ctrl+S) to select the Save command.*

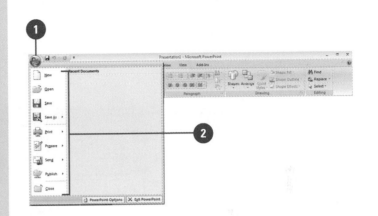

Choose a Command from a Shortcut Menu

① Right-click an object (a text or graphic element).

TIMESAVER *Press Shift+F10 to display the shortcut menu for a selected command.*

② Click a command on the shortcut menu. If the command is followed by an arrow, point to the command to see a list of related options, and then click the option you want.

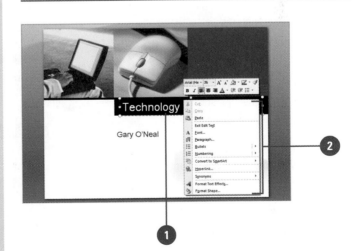

Working with Toolbars

PowerPoint includes its most common commands, such as Save and Undo, on the **Quick Access Toolbar** (**New!**). Click a toolbar button to choose a command. If you are not sure what a toolbar button does, point to it to display a ScreenTip. When PowerPoint starts, the Quick Access Toolbar appears at the top of the PowerPoint window, unless you've changed your settings. You can customize the toolbar by adding command buttons or groups to it. You can also move the toolbar below or above the Ribbon so it's right where you need it. In addition to the Quick Access Toolbar, PowerPoint also displays the Mini-Toolbar when you point to selected text. The **Mini-Toolbar** (**New!**) appears above the selected text and provides quick access to formatting tools.

Choose a Command Using a Toolbar or Ribbon

◆ **Get command help**. If you're not sure what a button does, point to it to display a ScreenTip. If the ScreenTip includes *Press F1 for more help*, continue to point to the item, and then press F1.

◆ **Choose a command**. Click the button, or button arrow, and then click a command or option.

Did You Know?

You can move the Quick Access Toolbar to another location. Click the Customize Quick Access Toolbar list arrow, and then click Show Below the Ribbon or Show Above the Ribbon.

You can turn off ScreenTips. Click the Office button, click PowerPoint Options, click Popular, click the ScreenTip Scheme list arrow, click Don't Show Enhanced ScreenTips or Don't Show ScreenTips, and then click OK.

You can reset the Quick Access Toolbar. In the PowerPoint Options dialog box, click Customize, click Reset, and then click OK.

You can minimize the Ribbon. Click the Customize Quick Access Toolbar list arrow, and then click Minimize the Ribbon. Click a tab to maximize it.

Quick Access Toolbar   Screen Tip

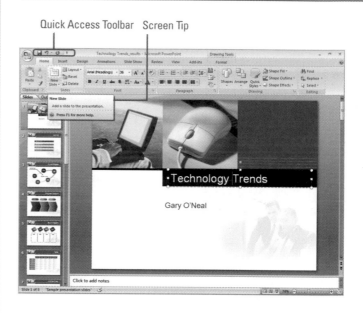

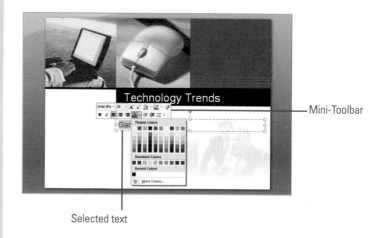

Mini-Toolbar

Selected text

Add or Remove Items from the Quick Access Toolbar

◆ **Add or remove a common button**. Click the Customize Quick Access Toolbar list arrow, and then click a button name (checked item appears on the toolbar).

◆ **Add a Ribbon button or group**. Right-click the button or group name on the Ribbon, and then click Add to Quick Access Toolbar.

◆ **Remove a button or group**. Right-click the button or group name on the Quick Access Toolbar, and then click Remove from Quick Access Toolbar.

Customize Quick Access Toolbar list arrow

Click to add or remove frequently used buttons

Click to add a button or group

Customize the Quick Access Toolbar

1. Click the **Customize Quick Access Toolbar** list arrow, and then click **More Commands**.

2. Click the **Choose commands from** list arrow, and then click **All Commands** or a specific Ribbon.

3. Click the **Customize Quick Access Toolbar** list arrow, and then click **For all documents (default)**.

   Select the current presentation if you only want the commands available in the presentation.

4. Click the command you want to add (left column) or remove (right column), and then click **Add** or **Remove**.

   TIMESAVER Click *<Separator>*, and then click Add to insert a separator line between buttons.

5. Click the **Move Up** and **Move Down** arrow buttons to arrange the order.

6. Click **OK**.

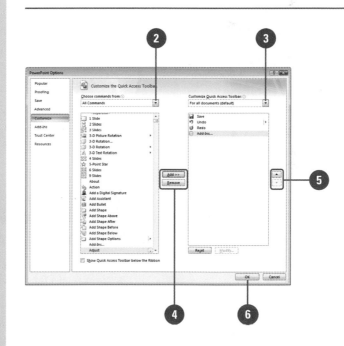

Choosing Dialog Box Options

A **dialog box** is a window that opens when you click a Dialog Box Launcher. **Dialog Box Launchers** (**New!**) are small icons that appear at the bottom corner of some groups. When you point to a Dialog Box Launcher, a ScreenTip with a thumbnail of the dialog box appears to show you which dialog box opens (**New!**). A dialog box allows you to supply more information before the program carries out the command you selected. After you enter information or make selections in a dialog box, click the OK button to complete the command. Click the Cancel button to close the dialog box without issuing the command. In many dialog boxes, you can also click an Apply button to apply your changes without closing the dialog box.

Choose Dialog Box Options

All dialog boxes contain the same types of options, including the following:

◆ **Tabs**. Click a tab to display its options. Each tab groups a related set of options.

◆ **Option buttons**. Click an option button to select it. You can usually select only one.

◆ **Up and down arrows**. Click the up or down arrow to increase or decrease the number, or type a number in the box.

◆ **Check box**. Click the box to turn on or off the option. A checked box means the option is selected; a cleared box means it's not.

◆ **List box**. Click the list arrow to display a list of options, and then click the option you want.

◆ **Text box**. Click in the box and type the requested information.

◆ **Button**. Click a button to perform a specific action or command. A button name followed by an ellipsis (...) opens another dialog box.

◆ **Preview box**. Many dialog boxes show an image that reflects the options you select.

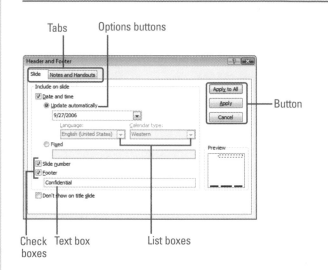

Tabs   Options buttons

Button

Check boxes   Text box   List boxes

For Your Information

Navigating a Dialog Box

Rather than clicking to move around a dialog box, you can press the Tab key to move from one box or button to the next. You can also use Shift+Tab to move backward, or Ctrl+Tab and Ctrl+Shift+Tab to move between dialog box tabs.

Using the Status Bar

The **Status bar** appears across the bottom of your screen and displays presentation information—slide number, Office theme name, and current slide display zoom percentage—and some PowerPoint controls, such as view shortcut buttons, zoom slider, and Fit To Window button. With the click of the mouse, you can quickly customize exactly what you see on the Status bar (**New!**). In addition to displaying information, the Status bar also allows you to check the on/off status of certain features (**New!**), including Signatures, Permissions, and Macro Playback.

Add or Remove Items from the Status Bar

◆ **Add Item**. Right-click the Status bar, and then click an unchecked item.

◆ **Remove Item**. Right-click the Status bar, and then click a checked item.

See Also

See "Adding a Digital Signature" on page 346 or "Simplifying Tasks with Macros" on page 410 for information on changing the status of items on the Status bar.

Right-click the Status bar   Status information

Choosing the Best Method to Start a Presentation

To begin working with PowerPoint, you can create a new presentation or you can open one that you've already worked on. You can use the New Presentation dialog box as your starting point. The option that you choose depends on how you want to start a presentation. If you have content ready and have a design in mind, choose the Blank Presentation option. If you have content ready but need help with a presentation look, choose the My Templates option or one of the many installed templates or Microsoft Office Online templates available to you through the Web. Microsoft Office Online provides easy access to an expanding online library of templates.

The New Presentation dialog box also includes a section called **Spotlight (New!)**, which features articles, tips, and links to Office Online templates, trainings, downloads, and more. If you like the Spotlight online content, you can turn on automatic updates by clicking the link on the orange bar at the bottom. If you have an existing presentation and want to make design and content changes to it for a new presentation without altering the original, choose the New from existing option. If you can't find the template you want, you can use the Search box at the top of the New Presentation dialog box to help you.

New Presentation Options

Click	To
Blank and recent (under Templates), and then click **Blank Presentation**	Create a new, blank presentation. When you click this option, a new presentation window appears with a title slide layout. At this point, you can add text to the title slide and then create new slides.
Installed Templates (under Templates)	Create a new presentation based on a design template installed along with the PowerPoint software, or downloaded and installed as a PowerPoint Template Pack from the Microsoft Web site.
Installed Themes (under Templates)	Create a new presentation based on a theme installed along with the PowerPoint software, or custom themes of your own design.
My Templates (under Templates)	Create a new presentation based on a design template, which is a presentation with predefined slide colors and styles. When you click this option, the New Presentation dialog box appears, where you can select one of your custom templates.
New from existing (under Templates)	Create a copy of an existing PowerPoint presentation in order to make design and content changes the new presentation, without changing the original presentation. After you click this option, the New From Existing Presentation dialog box appears, from which you can locate the presentation that you want to open.
Featured (under Microsoft Office Online), and then an Office Online template (in Spotlight)	Create a new presentation based on a design template installed from Microsoft Office Online Web site. Spotlight provides new and updated templates and content for you to use.
A template category (under Microsoft Office Online)	Create a new presentation based on a design template downloaded and installed from Microsoft Office Online Web site.

Creating a Blank Presentation

Microsoft
Certified
Application
Specialist

PP07S-1.1.1

If you are not sure how you want your presentation to look, you can start a new presentation from scratch. You can create a blank presentation when you first start PowerPoint or after you have already started PowerPoint. Either way, a blank presentation appears, ready for you to use. When you create a new presentation, PowerPoint names them Presentation1, Presentation2, etc. until you save and name them. The presentation name appears on the title bar and taskbar buttons.

Start a Blank Presentation

 Start PowerPoint.

A blank presentation appears when you first open PowerPoint.

See Also

See "Viewing and Applying a Theme" on page 90 for information on creating a consistent look for a blank presentation.

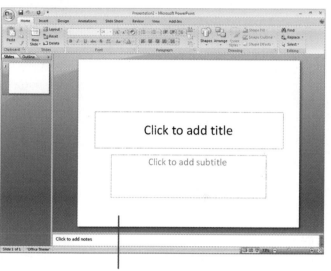

Blank presentation

Start a Blank Presentation Within PowerPoint

1 Click the **Office** button, and then click **New**.

TIMESAVER *To create a blank presentation without a dialog box, press Ctrl+N.*

The New Presentation dialog box appears, display the Blank and recent category.

2 Click **Blank Presentation**.

3 Click **Create**.

A new blank presentation appears in the PowerPoint window.

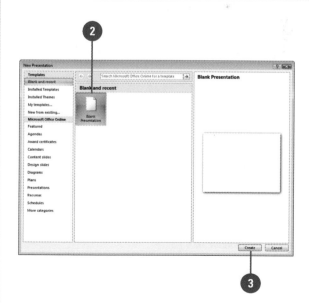

Creating a Presentation Using a Template

PowerPoint provides a collection of professionally designed templates that you can use to help you create presentations. Start with a template when you have a good idea of your content but want to take advantage of a template's professional look. A **template** is a PowerPoint presentation file (.potx) that provides you with a unified presentation design, which includes layouts, themes and slide masters, so you only need to add text and graphics. In the New Presentation dialog box, you can choose a template from those already installed with PowerPoint or from Microsoft Office Online, an online content library. You can choose a Microsoft Office Online template from one of the listed categories or from the Spotlight (**New!**) section, which highlights new PowerPoint content.

Create a Presentation with a Template

1. Click the **Office** button, and then click **New**.

2. Choose one of the following:

   ◆ Click the **Blank and recent** category to open recently used templates.

   ◆ Click the **Installed Templates** category, and then click a template.

   ◆ Click the **My Templates** category to open a dialog box.

   ◆ Click the **Featured** category, and then click a template from the Spotlight section.

   ◆ Click a Microsoft Office Online template category, and then click a template.

3. Click **Create** or **Download**.

4. If necessary, click the template you want, and then click **OK**.

Did You Know?

You can download template packs on the Web. Go to *www.microsoft.com*, click the Office link, and then search for PowerPoint Templates.

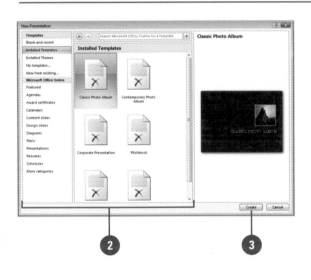

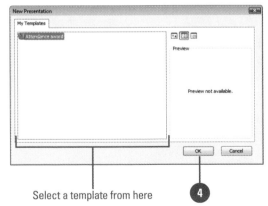

Select a template from here

Opening a Presentation

Microsoft
Certified
Application
Specialist

PP07S-1.1.3

You can open an existing presentation from within PowerPoint by using the Office button. On the Office menu, you can choose the Open command to locate and select the presentation you want or choose a recently used presentation from the Recent Documents list. The Recent Documents list allows you to pin documents (**New!**) to the list that you want to remain accessible regardless of recent use. The Pin icon on the Recent Documents list makes it easy to pin or unpin documents as needed. When you open a presentation from PowerPoint 97-2003, PowerPoint 2007 goes into compatibility mode (**New!**)—indicated on the title bar—where it disables new features that cannot be displayed or converted well by previous versions. The presentation stays in compatibility mode until you convert it to the PowerPoint 2007 file format.

Open a Presentation

1. Click the **Office** button, and then click **Open**, or click a recently used presentation.

2. If you want to open a specific file type, click the **Files of type** list arrow, and then click a file type.

3. If the file is located in another folder, click the **Look in** list arrow, and then navigate to the file.

4. Click the PowerPoint file you want, and then click **Open**, or click the **Open** button arrow, and then click one of the following options:

   ◆ **Open Read-Only** to open the selected file with protection.

   ◆ **Open as Copy** to open a copy of the selected file.

   ◆ **Open in Browser** to open the selected Web file in a browser.

   ◆ **Open and Repair** to open the damaged file.

Did You Know?

You can pin or unpin a recently used document to the Office menu. Click the Office button, and then click the Pin icon (right-side) to toggle between a grey pin (document is unpinned) and a green pin (document is pinned) on the Recent Documents list.

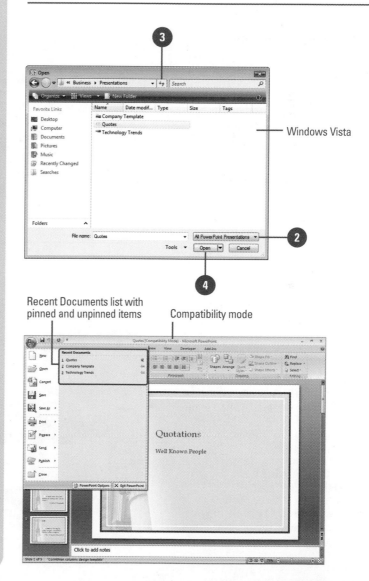

Windows Vista

Recent Documents list with pinned and unpinned items

Compatibility mode

Arranging Windows

PowerPoint presentations open inside a window, which contains a title bar and a work area. This is where you create and edit your presentations. Most often, you'll probably fill the entire screen with one window. But when you want to move or copy information between programs or documents, it's easier to display several windows at once. You can arrange two or more windows from one program or from different programs on the screen at the same time. However, you must make the window active to work in it. You can also click the document buttons on the taskbar to switch between open documents.

Resize and Move a Window

◆ **Maximize button**. Click to make a window fill the entire screen.

◆ **Restore Down button**. Click to reduce a maximized window to a reduced size.

◆ **Minimize button**. Click to shrink a window to a taskbar button. To restore the window to its previous size, click the taskbar button.

◆ **Close button**. Click to shut a window.

Maximize/Restore Down button

Minimize button

Close button

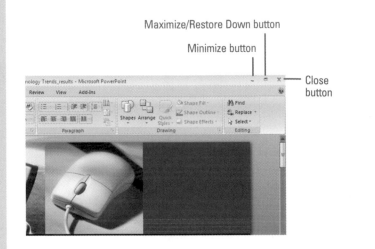

Arrange or Switch Between Windows

1 Open the presentations you want to arrange or switch between.

2 Click the **View** tab.

3 In the Window group, click:

◆ **Switch Windows**, and then click the presentation name you want.

◆ **Arrange All** to fit the windows on the screen.

◆ **Cascade Windows** to arrange windows diagonally.

◆ **New Window** to open a new window containing a view of the current presentation.

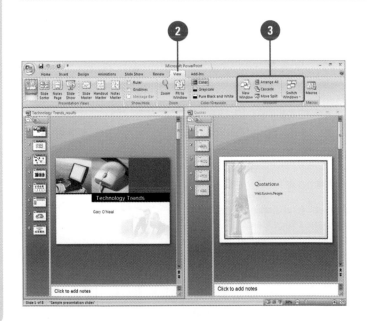

Using Task Panes and Window Panes

Task panes are separate windows that appear when you need them, such as Document Recovery, or when you click a Dialog Box Launcher icon (**New!**), such as Office Clipboard and Clip Art. A task pane displays various options that relate to the current task. **Window panes** are sections of a window, such as the Slides and Outline pane and Notes pane in Normal view. If you need a larger work area, you can use the Close button in the upper-right corner of the pane to close a task or window pane, or move a border edge (for task panes) or **splitter** (for window panes) (**New!**) to resize it.

Work with Task and Window Panes

◆ **Open a Task Pane**. It appears when you need it or when you click a Dialog Box Launcher icon.

◆ **Close a Task or Window Pane**. Click the Close button in upper-right corner of the pane.

◆ **Resize a Task Pane**. Point to the Task Pane border edge until the pointer changes to double arrows, then drag the edge to resize it.

◆ **Resize a Window Pane**. Point to the window pane border bar until the pointer changes to a double bar with arrows, then drag the edge to resize it.

IMPORTANT *To open the Slides and Outline pane after you close it, drag the border edge near the left edge of the PowerPoint window to the right.*

Did You Know?

You can resize window panes using the keyboard. Click the View tab, click the Move Split button (**New!**) in the Window group, use the arrow keys to move the splitters and then press Enter to return to the document.

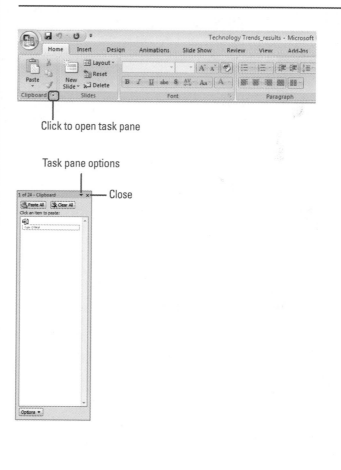

Click to open task pane

Task pane options

Close

Understanding PowerPoint Views

To help you during all phases of developing a presentation, PowerPoint provides three different views: Normal, Slide Sorter, and Slide Show. You can switch from one view to another by clicking a view button located on the Status bar or by using the buttons in the Presentation Views group on the View tab. In any view, you can use the Zoom feature on the Status bar to increase and decrease the page view size and display the slide to fit the screen.

pane. These panes provide an overview of your presentation and let you work on all of its parts. You can adjust the size of the panes by dragging the pane borders. You can use the Outline pane to develop and organize your presentation's content. Use the Slide pane to add text, graphics, movies, sounds, and hyperlinks to individual slides, and the Notes pane to add speaker notes or notes you want to share with your audience.

Normal view

Use the Normal view to work with the three underlying elements of a presentation—the outline, slide, and notes—each in its own

Outline pane

Use the Outline pane in Normal view to develop your presentation's content. Individual slides are numbered and a slide icon appears for each slide.

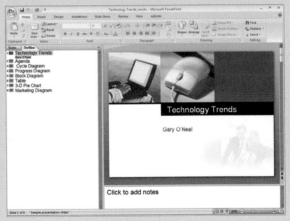

Slides pane

Use the Slides pane in Normal view to pre-view each slide. Click the slide you want to view. You can also move through your slides using the scroll bars or the Previous Slide and Next Slide buttons. When you drag the scroll box up or down on the vertical scroll bar, a label appears that indicates which slide will be displayed if you release the mouse button.

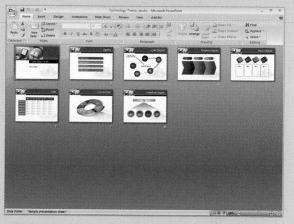

Slide Show view

Slide Show view presents your slides one at a time. Use this view when you're ready to rehearse or give your presentation. To move through the slides, click the screen, or press Enter to move through the show.

Slide Sorter view

Use the Slide Sorter view to organize your slides, add actions between slides—called slide transitions—and apply other effects to your slide show. The Animations tab helps you add slide transitions and control your presentation. When you add a slide transition, you see an icon that indicates an action will take place as one slide replaces another during a show. If you hide a slide, you see an icon that indicates the slide will not be shown during the presentation.

Browsing a Presentation

You might want to browse through a completed presentation to view the contents and design of each slide and to evaluate the types of slides in a presentation in several ways. When a slide doesn't fit the screen, you can change the presentation view size, or click the scroll arrows to scroll line by line or click above or below the scroll box to scroll window by window and move to another slide. To move immediately to a specific slide, you can drag the scroll box. In Slides pane, you can click the Next Slide and Previous Slide buttons, which are located at the bottom of the vertical scroll bar, to switch between slides in a presentation.

Browse Through a Presentation

◆ Click the **Up** scroll arrow or **Down** scroll arrow to scroll line by line.

When you scroll to the top or bottom of a slide, you automatically move to the previous or next page.

◆ Click above or below the **Scroll** box to scroll window by window.

◆ Drag the **Scroll** box to move immediately to a specific slide.

As you drag, a slide indicator box appears, telling you the slide number and title.

◆ Click the **Previous Slide** or **Next Slide** button.

Slide indicator

Up scroll arrow

Scroll box

Vertical scroll bar

Down scroll arrow

Previous Slide and Next Slide buttons

Did You Know?

You can use the keyboard to browse slides. Press the Page Up or Page Down key to switch between slides. If you use these keys, the slides in the Slides pane will change also.

Browse Through Slides or an Outline

1 In Normal view, click the **Outline** or **Slides** tab.

◆ Click the **Up** scroll arrow or **Down** scroll arrow to scroll line by line.

The slide doesn't change as you scroll.

◆ Click a slide icon or slide miniature to display the slide.

Change Presentation View Size

◆ Click the zoom percentage on the Status bar, click the option size you want, and then click **OK**.

◆ Click the **Zoom In** (+) or **Zoom Out** (-) buttons on the Status bar.

◆ Drag the **Zoom** slider on the Status bar.

◆ Click the **Fit To Window** button to resize the slide to the current window.

Zoom controls

Getting Help While You Work

At some time, everyone has a question or two about the program they are using. The PowerPoint Help Viewer provides the answers and resources you need, including feature help, articles, tips, templates, training, and downloads. By connecting to Microsoft Office Online, you not only have access to standard product help information, but you also have access to updated information over the Web without leaving the Help Viewer. The Web browser-like Help Viewer allows you to browse an extensive catalog of topics using a table of contents to locate information, or ask a question or enter phrases to search for specific information. When you use any of these help options, a list of possible answers is shown to you with the most likely answer or most frequently-used at the top of the list.

Using the Help Viewer to Get Answers

1. Click the **Help** button on the Ribbon (located in the upper-right corner).

   TIMESAVER *Press F1.*

2. Locate the Help topic you want.

   ◆ Click a Help category on the home page, and then click a topic (? icon).

   ◆ Click the **Table Of Contents** button on the toolbar, click a help category (book icon) and then click a topic (? icon).

3. Read the topic, and then click any links to get Help information.

4. Click the **Back**, **Forward**, **Stop**, **Refresh**, and **Home** buttons on the toolbar to move around in the Help Viewer.

5. If you want to print the topic, click the **Print** button on the toolbar.

6. To keep the Help Viewer window (not maximized) on top or behind, click to toggle the **Keep On Top** button (pin pushed in) and **Not On Top** button (pin not pushed in) on the toolbar.

7. When you're done, click the **Close** button.

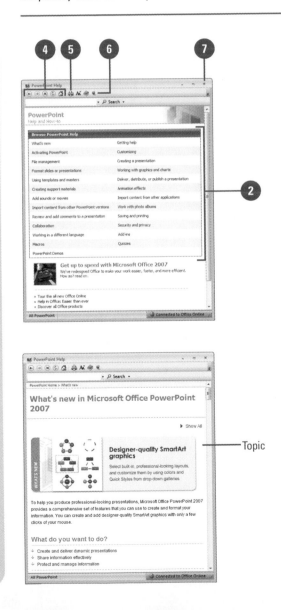

Topic

Search for Help

1. Click the **Help** button on the Ribbon.

2. Click the **Search button** list arrow below the toolbar, and then select the location and type of information you want.

3. Type one or more keywords in the Search For box, and then click the **Search** button.

4. Click a topic.

5. Read the topic, and then click any links to get information on related topics or definitions.

6. When you're done, click the **Close** button.

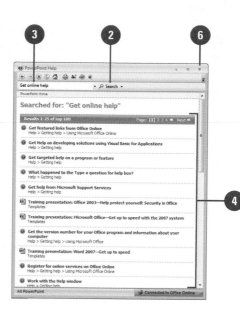

Check Help Connection Status

1. Click the **Help** button on the Ribbon.

2. Click the Connection Status at the bottom of the Help Viewer.

3. Click the connection option where you want to get help information:

   ◆ **Show content from Office Online** to get help from this computer and the internet (online).

   ◆ **Show content only from this computer** to get help from this computer only (offline).

   This setting is maintained for all Office 2007 program Help Viewers.

4. When you're done, click the **Close** button.

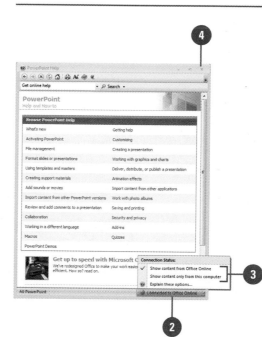

Saving a Presentation

PP07S-4.3.6

After you create a PowerPoint presentation, save it as a file on your computer so you can work with it later. When you save a presentation for the first time or if you want to save a copy of a file, use the Save As command. When you want to save an open presentation, use the Save button on the Quick Access Toolbar. When you save a presentation, PowerPoint 2007 saves PowerPoint 97-2003 files in their older format using compatibility mode (**New!**) and new PowerPoint 2007 files in an XML (Extensible Markup Language) based file format .pptx (**New!**). The XML format significantly reduces file sizes, provides enhanced file recovery, and allows for increased compatibility, sharing, reuse, and transportability. A PowerPoint 97-2003 presentation stays in compatibility mode—indicated on the title bar—until you convert it to the new PowerPoint 2007 file format. Compatibility mode disables new features that cannot be displayed or converted well by previous versions.

Save a Presentation for PowerPoint 2007

1. Click the **Office** button, point to **Save As**, and then click **PowerPoint Presentation**.

   TIMESAVER *Press Ctrl+S to save an existing presentation.*

2. Click a location on **Favorite Links** (Vista) or the **Places bar** (XP), or click the **Save in** list arrow, and then click the drive or folder where you want to save the file.

   TIMESAVER *Click the New Folder button in the Save As dialog box to save the file to a new folder.*

3. Type a presentation file name.

4. Click **Save**.

Did You Know?

You can access options from the Save dialog box. To change file related options in the Save dialog box, click Tools, and then click the command option you want, either Save, General, Web, or Compress Pictures.

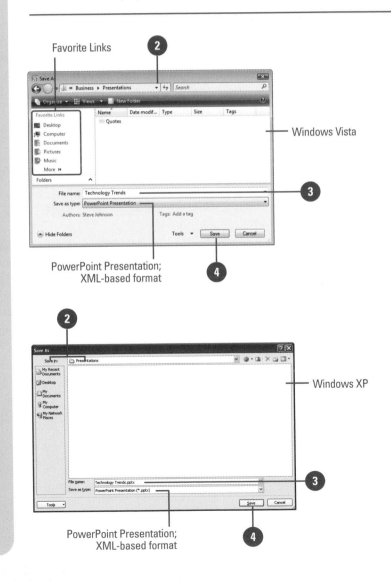

Favorite Links

Windows Vista

PowerPoint Presentation;
XML-based format

Windows XP

PowerPoint Presentation;
XML-based format

Convert a PowerPoint 97-2003 Presentation to PowerPoint 2007

1. Open the PowerPoint 97-2003 presentation in compatibility mode.

2. Click the **Office** button, and then click **Convert**.

3. Click **OK** to convert the file to new PowerPoint 2007 format.

   PowerPoint exits compatibility mode, which is only turned on when a previous version is in use.

> ### Did You Know?
>
> *You can display extensions in the Save and Open dialog boxes and Recent Documents list.* Changing the Windows option also changes PowerPoint. In the Folder Options dialog box on the View tab, clear the Hide extensions for known file types check box.

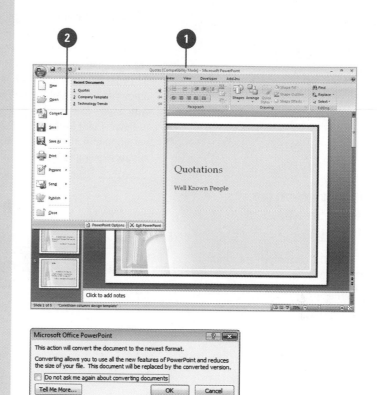

Set Save Options

1. Click the **Office** button, and then click **PowerPoint Options**.

2. In the left pane, click **Save**.

3. Set the save options you want:

   ◆ **Default Save Format.** Click Save files in this format list arrow, and then click the default format you want.

   ◆ **Default File Location.** Specify the complete path to the folder location where you want to save your presentation.

4. Click **OK**.

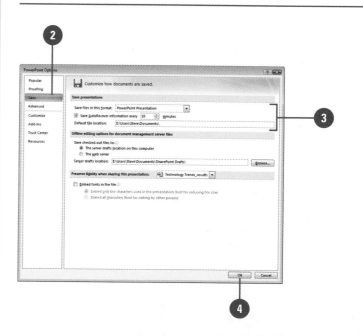

Saving a Presentation with Different Formats

PowerPoint 2007 is a versatile graphics presentation program that allows you to save your presentation in a variety of different formats—see the table on the following page for a complete list and description. For example, you might want to save your presentation as a Web page that you can view in a Web browser. Or you can save a presentation in an earlier version of PowerPoint (97-2003) in case the people you work with have not upgraded to PowerPoint 2007. If you save a presentation to PowerPoint 97-2003, some new features and formatting are converted to uneditable pictures or not retained. PowerPoint 2007 doesn't support saving to PowerPoint 95 and earlier formats.

Save a Presentation for PowerPoint 97-2003 or Other Format

1. Click the **Office** button, and then point to **Save As**, and then click **PowerPoint 97-2003 Presentation** or **Other Formats**.

2. Click the **Save in** list arrow, and then click the drive or folder where you want to save the file.

3. Type a presentation file name.

4. Click the **Save as type** list arrow, and then click the file format you want.

5. Click **Save**.

   IMPORTANT *Some new features and formatting are converted to uneditable pictures or not retained.*

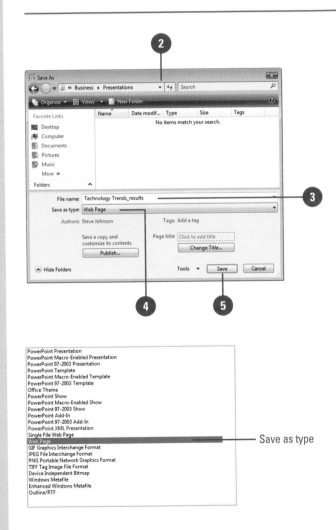

See Also

See "Creating a PDF Document" on page 291 or "Creating an XPS Document" on page 292 for information on saving presentations in other formats.

Save as type

PowerPoint 2007 Supported File Formats

Save As file type	Extension	Used to save
PowerPoint Presentation (**New!**)	.pptx	PowerPoint 2007 presentation
PowerPoint Macro-Enabled Presentation (**New!**)	.pptm	PowerPoint 2007 presentation that contains Visual Basic for Applications (VBA) code
PowerPoint 97-2003	.ppt	PowerPoint 97 to PowerPoint 2003 presentation
PDF Presentation (**New!**)	.pdf	Fixed-layout electronic file format that preserves document formatting developed by Adobe Systems
XPS Document Format (**New!**)	.xps	Fixed-layout electronic file format that preserves document formatting developed by Microsoft
PowerPoint Template (**New!**)	.potx	PowerPoint 2007 template
PowerPoint Macro-Enabled Template (**New!**)	.potm	PowerPoint 2007 template that includes preapproved macros
PowerPoint 97-2003 Template	.pot	PowerPoint 97 to PowerPoint 2003 template
Office Theme (**New!**)	.thmx	Style sheet that include theme definitions
PowerPoint Show (**New!**)	.pps; .ppsx	PowerPoint 2007 presentation that opens in Slide Show view
PowerPoint Macro-Enabled Show (**New!**)	.ppsm	PowerPoint 2007 show that includes preapproved macros
PowerPoint 97-2003 Show	.ppt	PowerPoint 97-2003 presentation that opens in Slide Show view
PowerPoint Add-In (**New!**)	.ppam	PowerPoint 2007 add-in that stores specialized functionality, such as VBA code
PowerPoint 97-2003 Add-in	.ppa	PowerPoint 97-2003 add-in that stores specialized functionality, such as VBA code
Single File Web Page	.mht; .mhtml	Web page as a single file with an .htm file
Web Page	.htm; .html	Web page as a folder with an .htm file
GIF, JPEG, PNG, TIFF, Device Independent Windows Metafile, Enhanced Windows Metafile	.gif, .jpg, .png, .tif, .wmf, .emf	Various graphics formats that open in other programs
Outline/RTF	.rtf	Presentation outline as a text-only document

Getting PowerPoint Updates on the Web

PowerPoint offers a quick and easy way to update with any new software downloads that improve the stability and security of the program. From the Resources area in the PowerPoint Options dialog box, simply click the Check for Updates button to connect to the Microsoft Update Web site to have your computer scanned for necessary updates. Then choose which Office updates you want to download and install.

Get PowerPoint Updates on the Web

1. Click the **Office** button, and then click **PowerPoint Options**.

2. Click **Resources**.

3. Click **Check for Updates** to open the Microsoft Update Web site.

4. Click one of the update buttons to find out if you need PowerPoint updates, and then choose the updates you want to download and install.

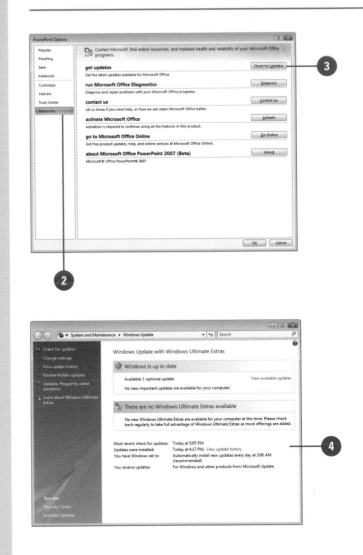

Did You Know?

You can contact Microsoft for help. You can get support over the phone, chat, or e-mail messages. To get online help, click the Office button, click PowerPoint Options, click Resources, and then click Contact Us. To get offline help, click the Office button, click PowerPoint Options, click Resources, click About, and then click Tech Support for contact information.

You can get better help information. At the bottom of a help topic, click Yes, No, or I don't know to give Microsoft feedback on the usefulness of a topic.

Recovering a Presentation

If PowerPoint encounters a problem and stops responding, the program tries to recover the file the next time you open PowerPoint. The recovered files appear in the Document Recovery task pane, which allows you to open the files, view what repairs were made, and compare the recovered versions. Each file appears in the task pane with a status indicator, either Original or Recovered, which shows what type of data recovery was performed. You can save one or all of the file versions. You can also use the AutoRecover feature to periodically save a temporary copy of your current file, which ensures proper recovery of the file.

Recover a Presentation

1. When the Document Recovery task pane appears, click the list arrow next to the name of each recovered file, and then perform one of the following:

   ◆ Click **Open** to view the file for review.

   ◆ Click **Save As** to save the file.

   ◆ Click **Delete** to close the file without saving.

   ◆ Click **Show Repairs** to find out how PowerPoint fixed the file.

2. When you're done, click the **Close** button.

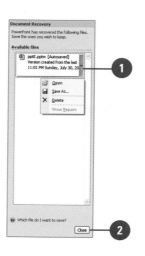

Use AutoRecover

1. Click the **Office** button, and then click **PowerPoint Options**.

2. Click **Save**.

3. Select the **Save AutoRecover information every x minutes** check box.

4. Enter the number of minutes, or click the **Up** and **Down** arrows to adjust the minutes.

5. Click **OK**.

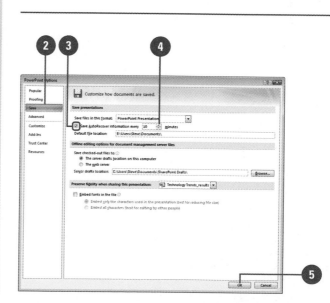

Diagnosing and Repairing Problems

At times you may determine that PowerPoint is not working as efficiently as it once did. This sometimes happens when you install new software or move files into new folders. Use the Diagnose command (**New!**) to improve performance by repairing problems, such as missing files from setup, corrupted file by malicious viruses, and registry settings. Note that this feature does not repair personal files, such as your presentations. If the Diagnose command does not fix the problem, you might have to reinstall PowerPoint. If you need to add or remove features, reinstall PowerPoint, or remove it entirely, you can use Office Setup's maintenance feature.

Diagnose and Repair Problems

1 Click the **Office** button, and then click **PowerPoint Options**.

2 In the left pane, click **Resources**.

3 Click **Diagnose**.

> **TIMESAVER** In Windows, click Start, point to All Programs, click Microsoft Office, click Microsoft Office Tools, and then click Microsoft Office Diagnostics.

The Microsoft Office Diagnostics dialog box appears.

4 Click **Continue**, and then click **Run Diagnostics**.

Office runs several diagnostics to determine and fix any problems. This might take 15 minutes or more. A diagnostic report appears in your browser:

◆ **Setup.** Checks for corrupt files and registry settings.

◆ **Disk.** Checks error logs.

◆ **Memory.** Checks integrity of computer RAM.

◆ **Update.** Checks for Office updates on the Web.

◆ **Compatibility.** Checks for conflicts with Outlook.

◆ **Check for known solutions.** Checks data on Office program crashes on your computer.

Perform Maintenance on Office Programs

1. Insert the PowerPoint or Office CD in your drive.

2. In Windows Explorer, double-click the Setup icon on the PowerPoint or Office CD.

3. Click one of the following maintenance buttons.

   ◆ **Add or Remove Features** to change which features are installed or remove specific features.

   ◆ **Repair** to reinstall or repair Microsoft Office 2007 to its original state.

   ◆ **Remove** to uninstall Microsoft Office 2007 from this computer.

4. Click **Continue**, and then follow the wizard instructions to complete the maintenance.

See Also

See "Working with Office Safe Modes" on page 358 for information on fixing problems with a Microsoft Office 2007 program.

Did You Know?

The Microsoft Office Application Recovery program is no longer available on the Start menu. Microsoft Office automatically detects programs that are not responding, and provides document recovery (**New!**).

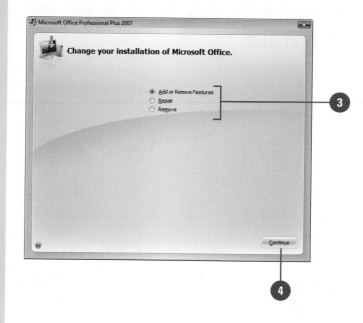

Add or Remove Features

Closing a Presentation and Quitting PowerPoint

After you finish working on a presentation, you can close it. Closing a file makes more computer memory available for other activities. Closing a presentation is different from quitting PowerPoint; after you close a presentation, PowerPoint is still running. When you're finished using PowerPoint, you can quit the program. To protect your files, always save your presentations and quit PowerPoint before turning off the computer.

Close a Presentation

1. Click the **Close** button on the presentation window, or click the **Office** button, and then click **Close**.

   TIMESAVER *Press Ctrl+W.*

   IMPORTANT *When you hide all windows in the taskbar, the Close button for the presentation window appears.*

2. If you have made changes to any open files since last saving them, a dialog box opens, asking if you want to save changes. Click **Yes** to save any changes, or click **No** to ignore your changes.

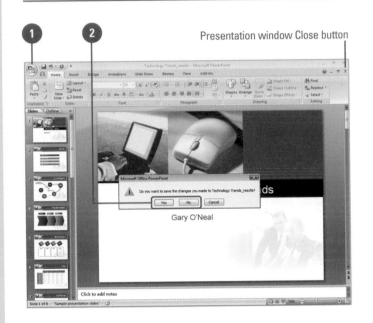

Presentation window Close button

Quit PowerPoint

1. Click the **Close** button on the PowerPoint window, or click the **Office** button, and then click **Exit PowerPoint**.

   TIMESAVER *Press Ctrl+Q.*

2. If you have made changes to any open files since last saving them, a dialog box opens asking if you want to save changes. Click **Yes** to save any changes, or click **No** to ignore your changes.

PowerPoint window Close button

Developing Presentation Content

Introduction

When creating a new presentation, there are things to con-sider as you develop your content. Microsoft Office PowerPoint can help you with this process. There are various elements to a presentation that make looking at your slides interesting: bulleted lists, clip art, charts and diagrams, organization charts and tables, and media clips or pictures. All of these items are considered graphic objects, and are separate from the text objects that you enter. Objects can be moved from one part of a presentation to another. You can also resize, move, and delete them.

As you develop your presentation, there are a few things to keep in mind—keep the text easy to read and straight to the point, make sure it isn't too wordy, and have a balance of text and graphics. Too much text can lose your audience while too many graphics can distract their focus.

PowerPoint offers many tools to help develop your text. Using the AutoCorrect feature, text is corrected as you type. A built-in Thesaurus is always a few keystrokes away, as is a research option that allows you to look for information is available in PowerPoint or has links to the Web.

Once you've begun to enter your text, you can adjust the spacing, change the alignment, set tabs, and change indents. You can also format your text by changing the font style or its attributes such as adding color to your text. If you decide to enter text in outline form, PowerPoint offers you the Outline pane to jot down your thoughts and notes. If bulleted or numbered lists are your preference, you can enter your ideas in this format. Should you need to rearrange your slides, you can do this in various PowerPoint views.

What You'll Do

Create New and Consistent Slides

Work with Objects

Develop and Modify Text

Set Editing Options

Correct and Resize Text While Typing

Insert Information the Smart Way

Insert and Develop an Outline

Move and Indent Text

Set Tabs

Change Text Alignment and Spacing

Change Character Spacing and Direction

Format Text

Modify a Bulleted List

AutoFormat Text While Typing

Apply a Format Style

Insert Symbols

Create a Text Box and Columns

Find and Replace Text

Rearrange Slides

Use Slides from Other Presentations

Creating New and Consistent Slides

Microsoft Certified Application Specialist

PP07S-1.5

Creating consistent looking slides makes it easier for your audience to follow and understand your presentation. PowerPoint provides a gallery of slide layouts (**New!**) to help you position and format slides in a consistent manner. A slide layout contains **placeholders**, such as text, chart, table, or SmartArt graphic, where you can enter text or insert elements. When you create a new slide, you can apply a standard layout or a custom layout of your own design. You can also apply a layout to an existing slide at any time. When you change a slide's layout, PowerPoint keeps the existing information and applies the new look.

Insert a New Slide

1. Click the **Home** tab.

2. Click the **New Slide** button arrow.

   TIMESAVER *To insert a slide quickly without using the gallery, click the Add Slide button (icon).*

3. In the Slide Layout gallery, click the slide layout you want to use.

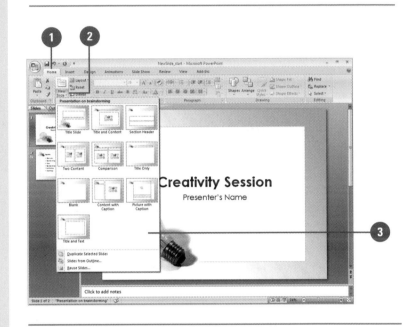

Apply an Layout to an Existing Slide

1. In Normal view, display the slide you want to change.

2. Click the **Home** tab.

3. Click the **Layout** button, and then click the slide layout you want.

See Also

See "Using Slides from Other Presentations" on page 72 for information on adding slides from other presentations.

Slide layouts

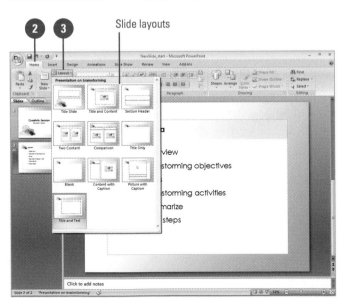

Enter Information in a Placeholder

◆ For text placeholders, click the placeholder, and then type the text.

◆ For other objects, click the icon in the placeholder, and then work with the accessory that PowerPoint starts.

AutoLayout Placeholder

A placeholder is a border that defines the size and location of an object.

Slide Layout Placeholders

Placeholder	Description
Title	Enter title text
Bulleted	Enter bulleted list
Table	Inserts a table
Chart	Inserts a chart
Clip Art	Inserts a picture from the Clip Organizer
Picture	Inserts a picture from a file
SmartArt (**New!**)	Inserts a diagram, chart, or other graphics
Movie	Inserts a movie or video clip

Working with Objects

Microsoft Certified Application Specialist

PP07S-2.1.2

Once you create a slide, you can modify any of its objects, even those added by a slide layout. To manipulate objects, use Normal view. To perform any action on an object, you first need to select it. When you select an object, such as text or graphic, the object is surrounded by a solid-lined rectangle, called a **selection box**, with sizing handles (small white circles at the corners and small white squares on the sides) around it (**New!**). You can resize, move, delete, and format selected objects.

Select and Deselect an Object

◆ To select an object, move the pointer (which changes to a four-headed arrow) over the object or edge, and then click to select.

◆ To select multiple objects, press and hold Shift as you click each object or drag to enclose the objects you want to select in the selection box. Press Ctrl+A to select all objects on a slide.

◆ To deselect an object, click outside its border.

◆ To deselect one of a group of objects, press and hold Shift, and then click the object.

Selection box   Four-headed arrow

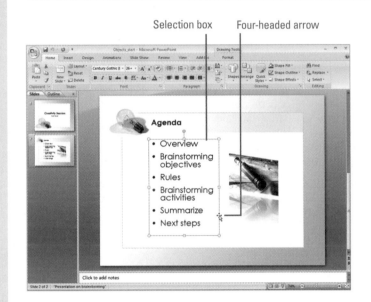

Resize an Object

1. Move the pointer over a sizing handle.

2. Drag the sizing handle until the object is the size you want.

> **TIMESAVER** *Use the Shift and Ctrl keys while you drag. The Shift key constrains an edge; the Ctrl key maintains a proportional edge; and the Shift and Ctrl keys together maintains a proportional object.*

Sizing handle   2

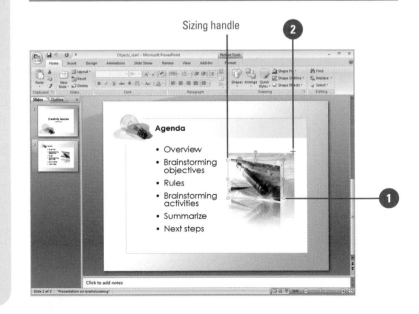

Move an Object

- ◆ **Using the mouse**. Move the pointer (which changes to a four-headed arrow) over the object, and then drag it to the new location. To move unfilled objects, drag the border. You can move an object in a straight line by pressing Shift as you drag the object.

- ◆ **Using the keyboard**. Click the object, and then press the arrow keys to move the object in the direction you want.

Did You Know?

You can use keyboard shortcuts to cut, copy, and paste objects. To cut an object from a slide, select the object and then press Ctrl+X. To copy an object, select the object, and then press Ctrl+C. To paste an object on a slide, press Ctrl+V.

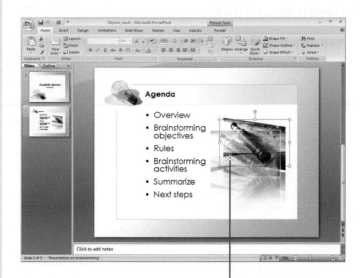

Use the four-headed arrow to drag the object to a new location

Delete an Object

1. Click the object you want to delete.

2. Press Delete.

Did You Know?

You can use the Tab key to select hard-to-click objects. If you are having trouble selecting an object that is close to other objects, click a different object and then press Tab until you select the object you want. See "Selecting Objects Using the Selection Pane" on page 142 for more information on selecting hard-to-click objects.

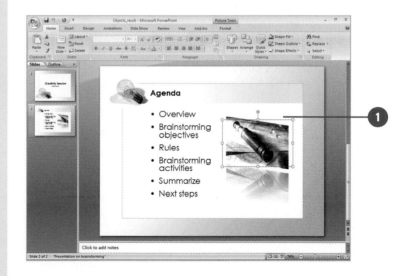

Developing Text

Your presentation's text lays the foundation for the presentation. Keep these basic presentation rules in mind when developing your text.

- ◆ Keep it simple.

- ◆ If you plan to present your slides to a large group, think about the people at the back of the room and what they can see.

- ◆ Keep the text to a minimum with no more than five bullets per slide and no more than five words per bullet.

- ◆ If you find a graphic that illustrates your point in a memorable way, use it instead of a lot of text.

PowerPoint provides several views that can help you organize your text. You can work with text and other objects one slide at a time in Normal view or, by clicking the Outline tab, you can work with all the presentation text on all slides at once.

PowerPoint also offers many text formatting features traditionally associated with word processing software. You can apply fonts and text attributes to create the look you want. You can set tabs, indents, and alignment. Finally, you can edit and correct your text using several handy tools, including style, grammar, and spelling checkers.

PowerPoint includes three types of text objects.

- ◆ **Title text objects**. Presized rectangular boxes that appear at the top of each slide—used for slide titles and, if appropriate, subtitles

- ◆ **Bulleted list objects**. Boxes that accommodate bulleted or numbered lists.

- ◆ **Text box objects**. Boxes that contain non-title text that you don't want to format in bulleted or numbered lists—often used for captions.

The first slide in a presentation typically contains title and text and a subtitle. Other slides often start with a title and then list major points in a bulleted list. Use text boxes only occasionally—when you need to include annotations or minor points that don't belong in a list.

When to Enter Text on a Slide

Use the slide pane of Normal view to enter text when you are focusing on the text or objects of one slide at a time.

Title text object

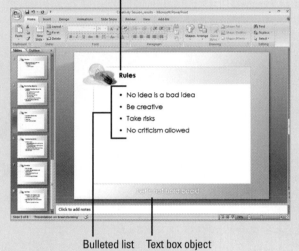

Bulleted list   Text box object

When to Enter Text in an Outline

If you are concentrating on developing presentation content, but not on how the text looks or interacts with other objects on the slide, use the Outline tab in Normal view. This view lets you see the titles, subtitles, and bulleted text on all your slides at a single glance.

The outline tab in Normal view is particularly useful for reorganizing the content of your presentation and ensuring that topics flow well from one to the next. You can easily move presentation topics up and down the outline.

Title text in the Outline pane appears next to the slide number and slide icon

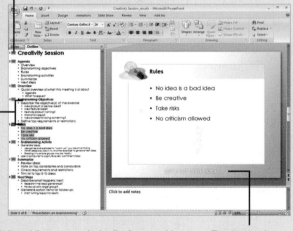

Bulleted lists appear in the list format with the different levels indented.

Text boxes do not appear in the Outline pane.

Entering Text

Microsoft Certified Application Specialist

PP07S-2.2.5

In Normal view, you can type text directly into the text placeholders. A **text placeholder** is an empty text box. If you type more text than fits in the placeholder, the text is automatically resized to fit on the slide. You can also manually increase or decrease the line spacing or font size of the text. The insertion point (the blinking vertical line) indicates where text will appear when you type. To place the insertion point into your text, move the pointer over the text. The pointer changes to an I-beam to indicate that you can click and then type. When a selection box of dashed lines appears, your changes affect only the selected text. When a solid-lined selection box appears, changes apply to the entire text object.

Enter Text into a Placeholder

1. In Normal view, click the text placeholder if it isn't already selected.

2. Type the text you want to enter.

3. Click outside the text object to deselect it.

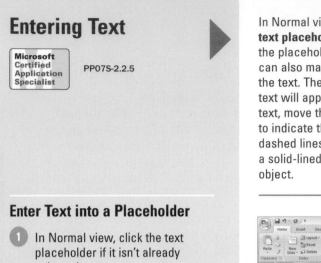

Place-holder

Insert Text

1. Click to place the insertion point where you want to insert the text.

2. Type the text.

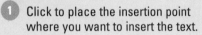

Enter Text in a Bulleted or Numbered List

1. In Normal view, click the bulleted text placeholder.

2. To switch to a numbered list, click the **Home** tab, if necessary, and then click the **Numbering** button.

3. Type the first item.

4. Press Enter.

   ◆ To increase the list level, press Tab or click the **Increase List Level** button on the Home tab.

   ◆ To decrease the list level, press Shift+Tab, or click the **Decrease List Level** button on the Home tab.

5. Type the next item.

6. Repeat steps 4 and 5 until you complete the list.

See Also

See "Moving and Indenting Text" on page 50 or "Modifying a Bulleted and Numbered List" on page 60 for information on changing text in a bulleted list.

Editing Text

Microsoft
Certified
Application
Specialist

PP07S-2.2.1

If you are familiar with word processing programs, you probably already know how to perform most text editing tasks in PowerPoint. You can move, copy, or delete existing text; replace it with new text; and undo any changes you just made. Some of the editing methods require that you select the text first. When you select text, the text is surrounded by a rectangle of gray dashed lines, indicating you can now edit the text.

Select and Modify Text

1. Position the mouse pointer to the left of the text you want to highlight.

2. Drag the pointer over the text—just a few words, a few lines, or entire paragraphs, and then release the mouse button.

3. To select discontinuous text, press Ctrl, and then drag the pointer over text (**New!**).

4. Modify the text the way you want.

   ◆ To delete text, press Delete.

   ◆ To replace text, type your new text.

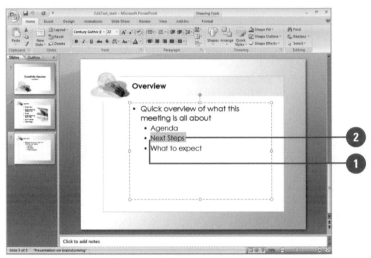

Move or Copy Text

1. Select the text you want to move or copy.

2. Move or copy the text the way you want.

   ◆ To move text short distances in the Outline tab or on a slide, drag the text to the new location. To copy text, press and hold the Ctrl key as you drag the text.

   ◆ To move or copy text between slides, click the **Cut** or **Copy** button on the Home tab, click where you want to insert the text, and then click the **Paste** button.

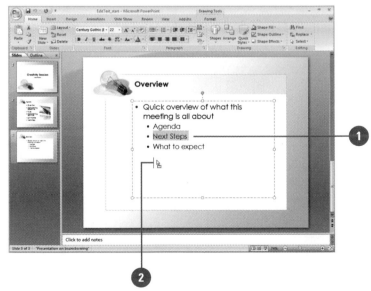

Setting Editing Options

Microsoft Certified Application Specialist   PP07S-2.2.1

PowerPoint provides advanced options that make editing text and working with objects easier. For example, PowerPoint can help you automatically select an entire word and allow text to be dragged and dropped. When you cut, copy, and paste text and objects, PowerPoint provides options that automatically adjust word spacing when you paste text with Smart Cut and Paste and Show Paste Options buttons when they are needed. When you use the Cut or Copy and Paste commands to move a slide to a new location, Paste Options button appears, allowing you to control how your slide appears after you paste it.

Set Editing Options

1. Click the **Office** button, and then click **PowerPoint Options**.

2. Click **Advanced**.

3. Select or deselect the check box options you want turned on or off:

   ◆ **When selecting, automatically select entire word** (default on). Select to have PowerPoint select the entire word when you click a word.

   ◆ **Allow text to be dragged and dropped** (default on). Select to move or copy text by dragging the text.

   ◆ **Maximum number of undos** (default 20). Enter the number of recent changes you want PowerPoint to track.

   ◆ **Use smart cut and paste** (default on). Select to have PowerPoint adjust the spacing of words and objects.

   ◆ **Show Paste Options buttons** (default on). Select to show the Paste Options button alongside text that you paste.

4. Click **OK**.

Correcting Text While Typing

With AutoCorrect, PowerPoint corrects common capitalization and spelling errors as you type. For example, if you accidentally type two capital letters or forget to capitalize the first letter of a sentence or table cell, AutoCorrect will fix it for you. You can customize AutoCorrect to recognize or ignore routine misspellings make or to ignore specific text that you do not want AutoCorrect to change. When you point to a word that AutoCorrect changed, a small blue box appears under the first letter. When you point to the small blue box, the AutoCorrect Options button appears. The AutoCorrect Options button gives you control over whether you want the text to be corrected. You can change text back to its original spelling, or you can stop AutoCorrect from automatically correcting text. You can also display the AutoCorrect dialog box and change AutoCorrect settings.

Add an Entry to AutoCorrect

1. Click the **Office** button, and then click **PowerPoint Options**.

2. In the left pane, click **Proofing**, and then click **AutoCorrect Options**.

3. Click the **AutoCorrect** tab.

4. Select the check boxes of the AutoCorrect features you want to enable.

5. Type the abbreviation or misspelling you want to add to the list of AutoCorrect entries in the Replace box.

6. Type the replacement text for your AutoCorrect entry in the With box.

7. Click **OK**.

Did You Know?

You can use AutoCorrect to recognize abbreviations or codes. Use AutoCorrect to recognize abbreviations or codes that you create to automate typing certain text. For example, you can customize AutoCorrect to type your full name when you type in only your initials.

Correcting Text as You Type

1. If you misspell a word that PowerPoint recognizes, it will correct it and the AutoCorrect button will appear.

2. Point to the small blue box under the corrected word, and then click the **AutoCorrect Options** button list arrow to view your options.

3. Click an option, or click a blank area of the slide to deselect the AutoCorrect Options menu.

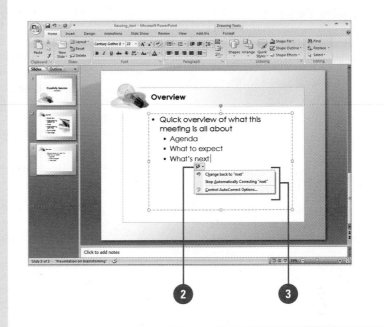

Undo an Action

- To undo an action, click the **Undo** button on the Quick Access toolbar; click it repeatedly to undo previous actions.

- To undo multiple actions, click the **Undo** button arrow on the Quick Access toolbar to view a list of the most recent changes, and then click the actions you want to undo.

Click to undo the previous action   Select multiple actions to undo

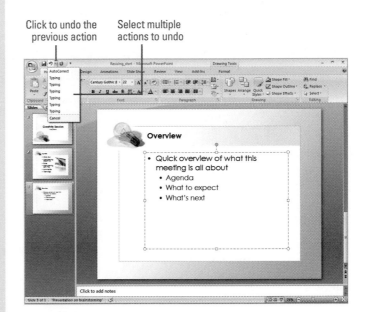

Did You Know?

You can change the number of undos. Click the Office button, click PowerPoint Options, click Advanced, specify the maximum number of undos, and then click OK.

You can redo one or more actions you just undid. Click the Redo button on the Quick Access toolbar to redo one action. Click the Redo button arrow on the Quick Access toolbar, and then click the actions you want to redo.

Resizing Text While Typing

If you type text in a placeholder, PowerPoint uses AutoFit to resize the text, if necessary, to fit into the placeholder. The AutoFit Text feature changes the line spacing—or paragraph spacing—between lines of text and then changes the font size to make the text fit. The AutoFit Options button, which appears near your text the first time that it is resized, gives you control over whether you want the text to be resized. The AutoFit Options button displays a menu with options for controlling how the option works. You can also display the AutoCorrect dialog box and change the AutoFit settings so that text doesn't resize automatically.

Resize Text as You Type

1. If the AutoFit Options box appears while you type, click the **AutoFit Options** button to select an option, or continue typing and PowerPoint will automatically adjust your text to fit.

2. If you click the AutoFit Options button, click the option you want to fit the text on the slide.

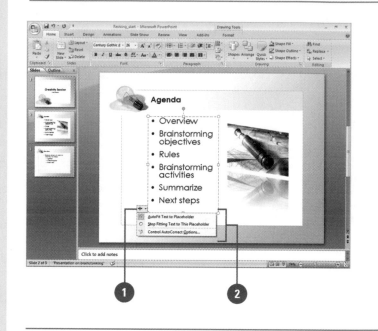

Turn Off AutoFit

1. Click the **Office** button, and then click **PowerPoint Options**.

2. In the left pane, click **Proofing**, and then click **AutoCorrect Options**.

3. Click the **AutoFormat As You Type** tab.

4. Clear the **AutoFit Title Text To Placeholder** and **AutoFit Body Text To Placeholder** check boxes.

5. Click **OK**.

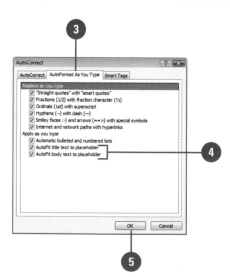

Change AutoFit Options for a Specific Object

1. Right-click the object with text you want to change, and then click **Format Shape**.

2. In the left pane, click **Text Box**.

3. Click the Autofit option you want.

   ◆ **Do not AutoFit.** To turn off AutoFit for the selected object.

   ◆ **Shrink text on overflow.** To resize text to fit in the selected object (default).

   ◆ **Resize shape to fit text.** To change the size of the shape to fit the text.

4. Click **Close**.

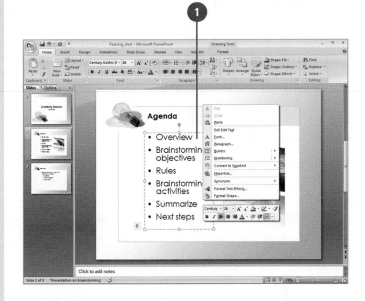

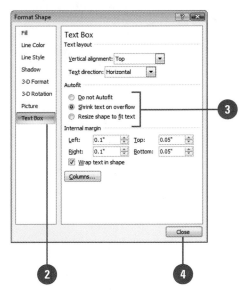

Inserting Information the Smart Way

Smart Tags help integrate actions typically performed in other programs directly in PowerPoint. For example, you can insert a financial symbol to get a stock quote, add a person's name and address in a presentation to the contacts list in Microsoft Outlook, or copy and paste information with added control. PowerPoint analyzes the data you type and recognizes certain types that it marks with Smart Tags. The types of actions you can take depend on the type of data with the Smart Tag.

Change Smart Tag Options

1. Click the **Office** button, and then click **PowerPoint Options**.

2. In the left pane, click **Proofing**, and then click **AutoCorrect Options**.

3. Click the **Smart Tags** tab.

4. Select the **Label text with smart tags** check box.

5. Select the check boxes with the Smart Tags you want.

6. To check the presentation for new Smart Tags, click **Check Presentation**.

7. To add more Smart Tags, click **More Smart Tags**, and then follow the online instructions.

8. Click **OK**.

9. Click **OK** again.

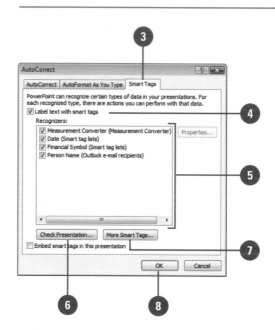

Did You Know?

You can save a smart tag in a presentation. Smart tags are not automatically saved when you close your presentation. To save smart tags, click the Office button click PowerPoint Options, click Proofing, click AutoCorrect Options, click the Smart Tags tab, select the Embed Smart Tags In This Presentation check box, click OK, and then click OK.

Access Information Using a Smart Tag

1. Click a text box where you want to insert information using a smart tag.

2. Type the information needed for the smart tag, such as the date, a recognized financial symbol in capital letters, or a person's name from you contacts list, and then press Spacebar.

3. Point to the text with the purple dotted line underneath to display the Smart Tag button.

   The purple dotted line indicates a smart tag is available for the text.

4. Click the **Smart Tag** button, and then click the list arrow next to the button.

5. Click the smart tag option you want; options vary depending on the smart tag.

Did You Know?

You can remove a smart tag from text. Point to the text with the smart tag, click the Smart Tag button, and then click Remove This Smart Tag.

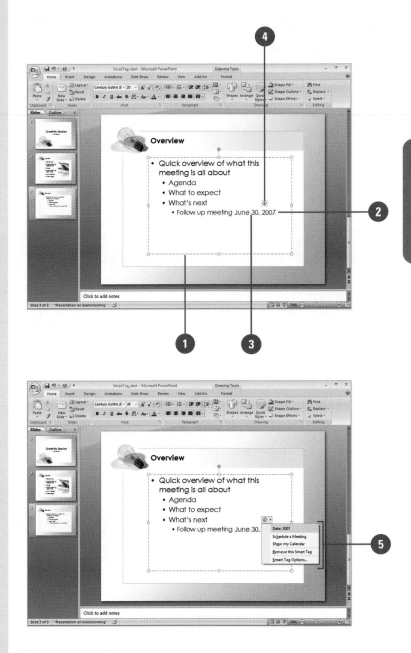

Inserting and Developing an Outline

Microsoft
Certified
Application
Specialist

PP07S-1.1.4

Outlining your content is a great way to create a presentation. You can outline and organize your thoughts right in PowerPoint or insert an outline you created in another program, such as Microsoft Word. If you prefer to develop your own outline, you can create a blank presentation, and then type your outline in the Outline pane of Normal view. As you develop an outline, you can add new slides and duplicate existing slides in your presentation. If you already have an outline, make sure the document containing the outline is set up using outline heading styles. When you insert the outline in PowerPoint, it creates slide titles, subtitles, and bulleted lists based on those styles.

Enter Text in the Outline Pane

1. In the Outline pane of Normal view, click to place the insertion point where you want the text to appear.

2. Type the title text you want, pressing Enter after each line.

   To indent right a level for bullet text, press Tab before you type. Press Shift+Tab to indent left a level.

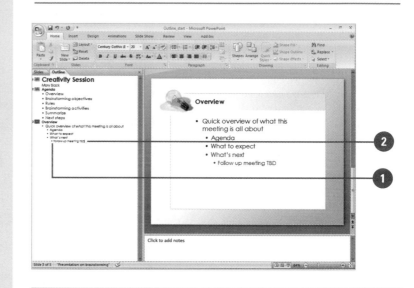

Add a Slide in the Outline Pane

1. In the Outline pane of Normal view, click at the end of the slide text where you want to insert a new slide.

2. Press Ctrl+Shift, or click the **Home** tab, click the **New Slide** button arrow, and then click a layout.

Did You Know?

You can delete a slide. In the Outline or Slides pane or in Slide Sorter view, select the slide you want to delete. Press Delete, or click the Delete button in the Slides group on the Home tab.

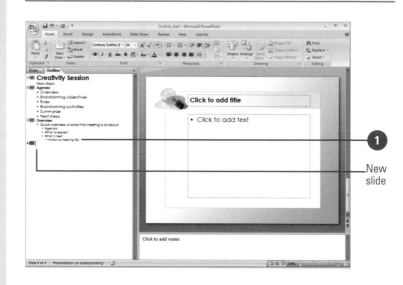

New slide

Duplicate a Slide

1. In the Outline pane of Normal view, click the slide you want to duplicate.

   TIMESAVER *To select slides in a sequence, click the first slide, hold down the Shift key, and then click the last slide. To select multiple slides, use the Ctrl key.*

2. Click the **Home** tab.

3. Click the **New Slide** button arrow.

4. Click **Duplicate Selected Slides**.

   The new slide appears directly after the slide duplicated.

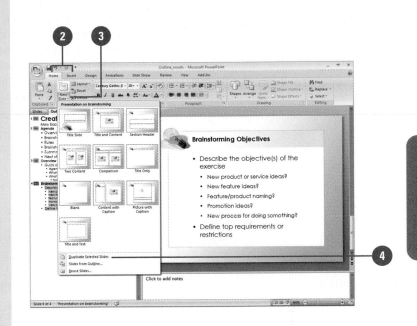

Insert an Outline from Another Program

1. In the Outline pane of Normal view, click the slide after which you want to insert an outline.

2. Click the **Home** tab.

3. Click the **New Slide** button arrow, and then click **Slides from Outline**.

4. Locate and select the file containing the outline you want to insert.

5. Click **Insert**.

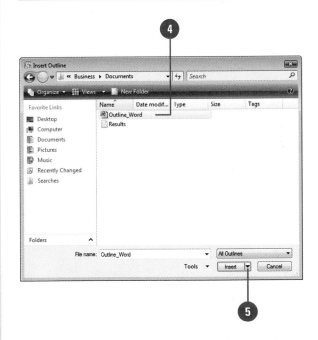

Did You Know?

You can open an outline from another program in PowerPoint. Click the Office button, click Open, click the Files Of Type list arrow, click All Outlines, and then double-click the outline file you want to open.

Moving and Indenting Text

PP07S-2.2.5, PP07S-2.2.6

Body text on a slide typically contains bulleted text, which you can indent to create levels. You can indent paragraphs of body text up to five levels using the Increase List Level and Decrease List Level buttons. In an outline, these tools let you demote text from a title, for example, to bulleted text. You can view and change the locations of the indent markers within an object with text using the ruler. In PowerPoint, pressing Enter within an object with text creates a paragraph. You can set different indent markers for each paragraph in an object (**New!**).

Change the Indent Level

1. In Normal view (Outline pane or slide), click the paragraph text or select the lines of text you want to indent.

2. Click the **Home** tab.

3. Click the indent level option you want:

   ◆ Click the **Increase List Level** button to move the line up one level (to the left).

   ◆ Click the **Decrease List Level** button to move the line down one level (to the right).

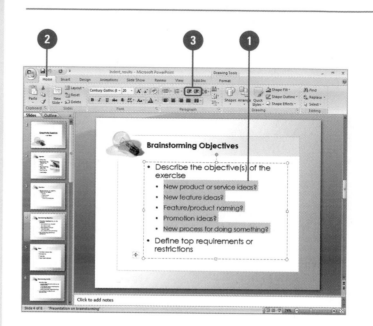

Display or Hide the Ruler

1. In Normal view, click the **View** tab.

2. Select the **Ruler** check box to display it, or clear the **Ruler** check box to hide it.

Did You Know?

You can use the Ruler with shape text. When you select a text object and then view the ruler, the ruler runs the length of just that text object, and the origin (zero point) of the ruler is at the box borders, starting with the upper left.

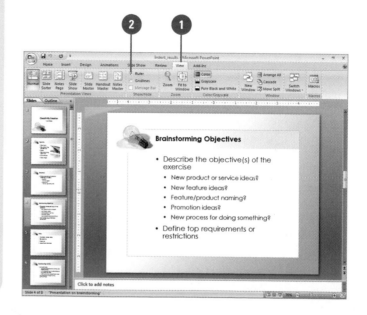

Change the Indent

1. Display the ruler.

2. Select the text for which you want to change the indentation.

3. Change the indent level the way you want.

   - To change the indent for the first line of a paragraph, drag the first-line indent marker.

   - To change the indent for the rest of the paragraph, drag the left indent marker.

   - To change the distance between the indents and the left margin, but maintain the relative distance between the first-line and left indent markers, drag the rectangle below the left indent marker.

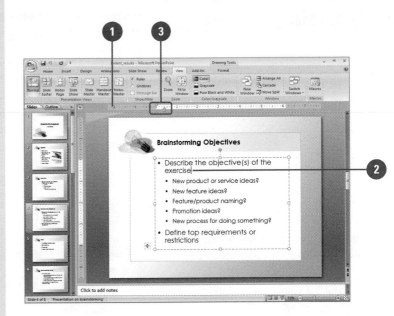

Did You Know?

You can use the mouse to increase or decrease list level text. Move the mouse pointer over the bullet you want to increase or decrease, and then when it changes to a four-headed arrow, drag the text to the left to increase the level or to the right to decrease the level.

You can show or hide formatting in Outline pane. In Outline pane, right-click a slide icon, and then click Show Text Formatting. Turning off formatting is useful for viewing more slides.

Setting Tabs

PowerPoint includes default tab stops at every inch; when you press the Tab key, the text moves to the next tab stop. You can control the location of the tab stops using the ruler. When you set a tab, tab markers appear on the ruler. Tabs apply to an entire paragraph, not a single line within that paragraph. You can also clear a tab by removing it from the ruler.

Set a Tab

1. Click the paragraph or select the paragraphs whose tabs you want to modify. You can also select a text object to change the tabs for all paragraphs in that object.

2. If necessary, click the **View** tab, and then select the **Ruler** check box to display the ruler.

3. Click the **Tab** button at the left of the horizontal ruler until you see the type of tab you want.

4. Click the ruler where you want to set the tab.

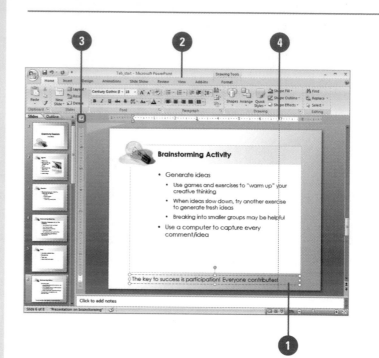

Did You Know?

You can use the Tabs dialog box to make multiple changes at one time. On the Home tab, click the Paragraph Dialog Box Launcher, click Tabs, select the tab stop you want to change, click Clear or make a change and click Set, and then click OK.

You must use caution when you change a default tab. When you drag a default tab marker to a new location, the spaces between all the tab markers change proportionally.

Tab Button Alignments

Tab Button	Aligns Text with
∟	Left edge of text
⊥	Center of text
⌐	Right edge of text
⊥·	Decimal points in text

Change the Distance Between Default Tab Stops

1. Select the text object in which you want to change the default tab stops.

2. If necessary, click the **View** tab, and then select the **Ruler** check box to display the ruler.

3. Drag any default tab stop marker to a new position.

Clear a Tab

1. Select the text object in which you want to clear tab stops.

2. If necessary, click the **View** tab, and then select the **Ruler** check box to display the ruler.

3. Drag the tab marker off the ruler.

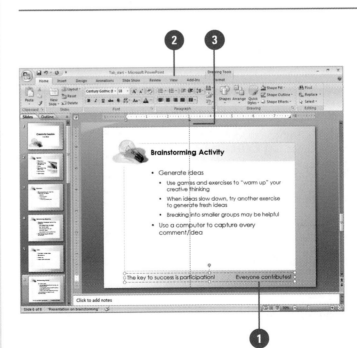

Changing Text Alignment and Spacing

PowerPoint enables you to control the way text lines up on the slide. You can align text horizontally to the left or right, to the center, or to both left and right (justify) in a text object. You can also align text vertically to the top, middle, or bottom within a text object (**New!**). In addition to vertical text alignment in a text object, you can also adjust the vertical space between selected lines and the space before and after paragraphs. You set specific line spacing settings before and after paragraphs in points. A **point** is equal to about 1/72 of an inch (or .0138 inches) and is used to measure the height of characters. Points are typically used in graphics and desktop publishing programs.

Adjust Line Spacing Quickly

1. Select the text box.

2. Click the **Home** tab.

3. Click the **Line Spacing** button, and then click **1.0 - 3.0**.

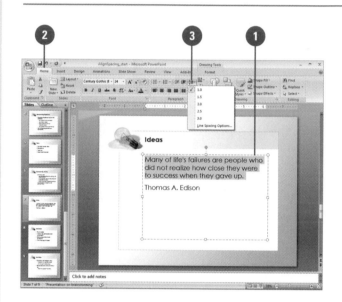

Adjust Line Spacing Exactly

1. Select the text box.

2. Click the **Home** tab.

3. Click the **Line Spacing** button, and then click **Line Spacing Options**.

4. Click the **Before Spacing** or **After Spacing** up or down arrows to specify a setting.

5. Click the **Line Spacing** list arrow, and then select a setting.

   If you select Exactly or Multiple, specify at what spacing you want.

6. Click **OK**.

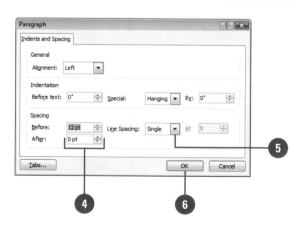

Change Text Alignment
Horizontally

1. Select the text box.
2. Click the **Home** tab.
3. Click an alignment button:

   ◆ **Align Left** to align text evenly along the left edge and is useful for paragraph text.

   ◆ **Center** to align text in the middle and is useful for titles and headings.

   ◆ **Align Right** to align text evenly along the right edge and is useful for text labels.

   ◆ **Justify** to align both left and right and is useful for column text.

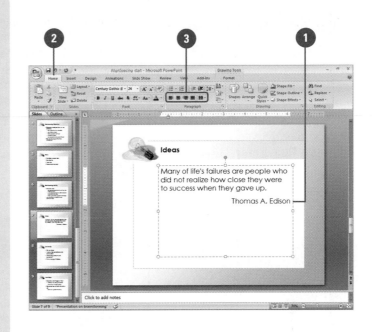

Change Text Alignment
Vertically

1. Select the text box.
2. Click the **Home** tab.
3. Click the **Alight Text** button, and then click one of the following:

   ◆ **Top**, **Middle**, or **Bottom** to quickly align text within a text box.

   ◆ **More Options** to select from additional alignment options, including Top Centered, Middle Centered, and Bottom Centered.

4. If you selected More Options, click the **Vertical Alignment** list arrow, and then select an align option.

5. If you selected More Options, click **Close**.

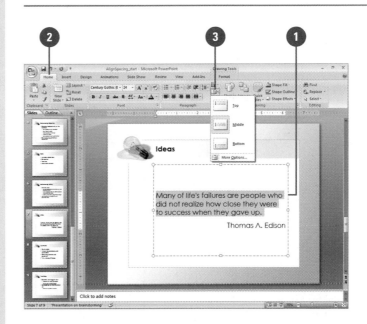

Changing Character Spacing

Kerning (New!) is the amount of space between each individual character that you type. Sometimes the space between two characters is larger than others, which makes the word look uneven. Kerning works only with TrueType or Adobe Type Manager fonts. You can expand or condense the character spacing to create a special effect for a title, or realign the position of characters to the bottom edge of the text—this is helpful for positioning the copyright or trademark symbols.

Quickly Change Character Spacing

1. Select the text you want to format.

2. Click the **Home** tab.

3. Click the **Character Spacing** button, and then click **Very Tight**, **Tight**, **Normal**, **Loose**, or **Very Loose**.

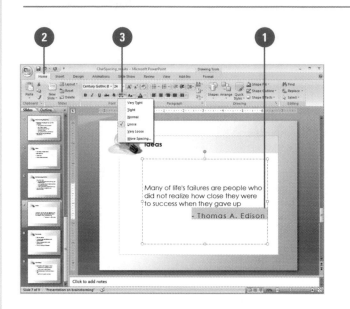

Exactly Change Character Spacing

1. Select the text you want to format.

2. Click the **Home** tab.

3. Click the **Character Spacing** button, and then click **More Spacing**.

4. Click the **Spacing** list arrow, and then select **Normal**, **Expanded**, or **Condensed**.

5. If you want, click the **By** up and down arrows to set the spacing distance (in points).

6. To apply conditional kerning, select the **Kerning for fonts** check box, and then specify a font point size.

7. Click **OK**.

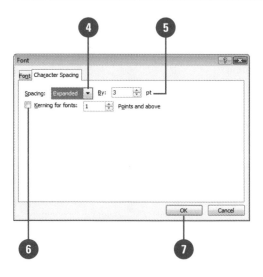

Changing Character Direction

Sometimes changing the direction of text on a slide creates a unique or special effect that causes the audience to remember it. In PowerPoint, you can rotate all text in an object 90 and 270 degrees or stack letters on top of one another (**New!**) to create the look you want. For a more exact rotation, which you cannot achieve in 90 or 270 degree increments, you can drag the green rotate lever at the top of an object to rotate it to any position. This is useful when you want to change the orientation of an object, such as the direction of an arrow.

Quickly Change Character Direction

1. Select the text you want to format.

2. Click the **Home** tab.

3. Click the **Character Direction** button, and then click one of the following:

   ◆ **Horizontal** to align text normally across the slide from left to right.

   ◆ **Rotate all text 90°** to align text vertically down the slide from top to bottom.

   ◆ **Rotate all text 270°** to align text vertically down the slide from bottom to top.

   ◆ **Stacked** to align text vertically down the slide one letter on top of another.

   ◆ **More Options** to select additional options, such as alignment, direction or resize shape to fit text.

4. If necessary, resize text box.

See Also

See "Rotating and Flipping a Shape" on page 144 for information on rotating an object using the green rotate lever.

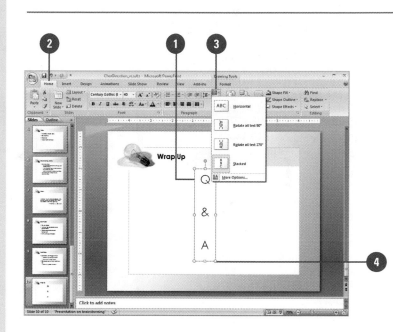

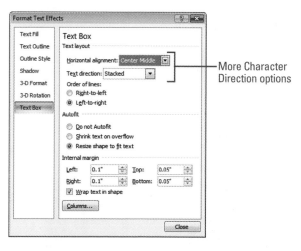

More Character Direction options

Formatting Text

Microsoft
Certified
Application
Specialist

PP07S-2.1.3, PP07S-2.2.3,
PP07S-2.2.6

Although PowerPoint's layouts and themes provide preformatted styles for text, you can change the formatting or add extra emphasis to a word or text object. You can format a single letter, a word, a phrase, or all the text in a text object. The basic formats you apply to text are available on the Home tab in the Font group or in the Font dialog box. Some of the formats (**New!**) include strikethrough or double strike-through, all caps or small caps, and double or color underline. If you no longer like your text formatting, you can quickly remove it (**New!**).

Change the Font Using the Ribbon

1. Select the text or text object whose font you want to change.

2. Click the **Home** tab, click the **Font** list arrow, and then point for a live preview (**New!**), or click the font you want, either a theme font (**New!**) or any available fonts.

3. Click one to change the font size:

   ◆ Click the **Font Size** list arrow on the Home tab, and then click the font size you want.

   ◆ Click the **Increase Font Size** button (**New!**) or **Decrease Font Size** button (**New!**) on the Home tab.

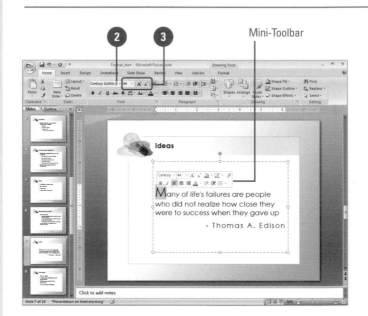

Format or Unformat Text Using the Ribbon

1. Select the text you want to format, or click the selection box of a text object to format all the text in the box.

2. Click one or more of the formatting buttons on the Home tab in the Font group: **Bold**, **Italic**, **Underline**, **Shadow**, **Strikethrough** (**New!**), or **Font Color**.

3. To clear all formatting and return to default text style, click the **Clear All Formatting** button (**New!**) on the Home tab.

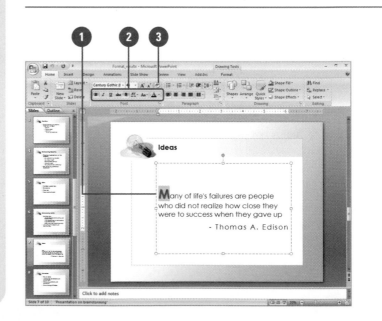

Format the Text Font

1. Select the text you want to format, or click the selection box of a text object to format all the text in the box.

2. Click the **Home** tab.

3. Click the **Font Dialog Box Launcher**.

4. Make any changes you want to the Font, Font Style, and Size.

5. Select or clear the effects you want or don't want: **Strikethrough** (**New!**), **Double Strikethrough** (**New!**), **Superscript**, **Subscript**, **Small Caps** (**New!**), **All Caps** (**New!**), and **Equalize Character Height** (**New!**).

6. If you want, click **Font Color**, and then click a color.

7. If you want, click **Underline Style list arrow**, and then click a style (**New!**). If you want to add an underline style, click **Underline Color**, and then click a color (**New!**).

8. Click **OK**.

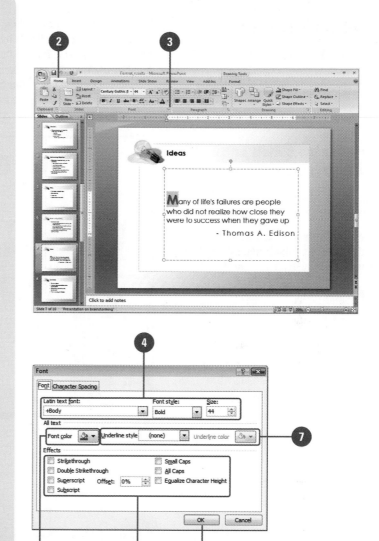

Did You Know?

You can replace fonts for an entire presentation. Click the Replace Fonts button on the Quick Access Toolbar. If necessary, use PowerPoint Options to add the button to the toolbar. Click the Replace list arrow, select the font in which you want to replace, click the With list arrow, and the select the font in which you want to replace it with, and then click Replace.

For Your Information

Quick Formatting with the Mini-Toolbar

When you point to selected text, PowerPoint displays the Mini-toolbar above it. The Mini-toolbar (**New!**) provides easy access to common formatting toolbar buttons, such as font, font size, increase and decrease font size, format painter, bold, italic, left align, center, right align, font color, increase and decrease list level, and bullets. If you don't want to display the Mini-Toolbar, you can use PowerPoint Options to turn it off.

Modifying a Bulleted and Numbered List

Microsoft Certified Application Specialist

PP07S-2.2.5

When you create a new slide, you can choose the bulleted list slide layout to include a bulleted list placeholder. You can customize the appearance of your bulleted list in several ways, including symbols or numbering. You also have control over the appearance of your bullets, including size and color. You can change the bullets to numbers or pictures. You can also adjust the distance between a bullet and its text using the PowerPoint ruler.

Add and Remove Bullets or Numbering from Text

1. Select the text in the paragraphs in which you want to add a bullet.

2. Click the **Bullets** or **Numbering** button arrow on the Home tab, and then select the style you want.

   TIMESAVER *Click the Bullets or Numbering button (not the arrow) on the Home tab to turn it on with the default setting.*

3. To remove the bullet or numbering, select the text, and then click the **Bullets** or **Numbering** button on the Home tab.

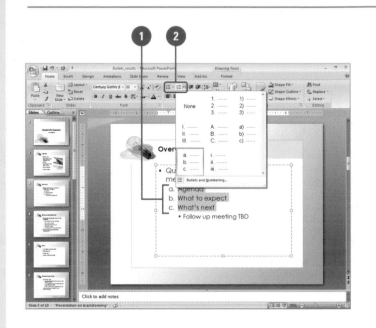

Change the Distance Between Bullets and Text

1. Select the text you want to indent.

2. If the ruler isn't visible, click the **View** tab, and then select the Ruler check box.

3. Drag the indent markers on the ruler.

   ◆ **First-line Indent.** The top upside down triangle marker indents the first line.

   ◆ **Hanging Indent.** The middle triangle marker indent second line and later.

   ◆ **Left Indent.** The bottom square marker indent entire line.

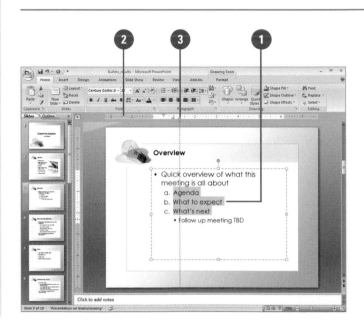

Change the Bullet or Number Character

1. Select the text or text object whose bullet character you want to change.

2. Click the **Bullets** or **Numbering** button arrow on the Home tab, and then click **Bullets and Numbering**.

3. Click the **Bulleted** or **Numbered** tab.

4. Click one of the predefined styles or do one of the following:

   ◆ Click **Customize**, and then click the character you want to use for your bullet character.

   ◆ Click **Picture**, and then click the picture you want to use for your bullet character.

5. To change the bullet or number's color, click the **Color** arrow, and then select the color you want.

6. To change the bullet or number's size, enter a percentage in the Size box.

7. Click **OK**.

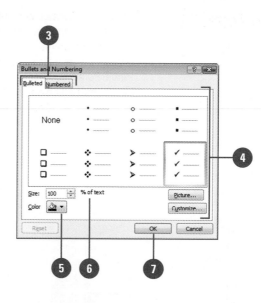

Did You Know?

You can select bulleted or numbered text. Position the mouse pointer over the bullet or number next to the text you want to select; when the pointer changes to the four-headed arrow, click the bullet.

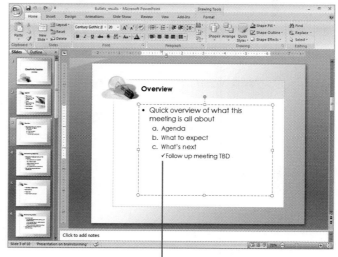

Bullet change

AutoFormatting Text While Typing

PowerPoint recognizes ordinals, fractions, em-dashes and en-dashes, formatted AutoCorrect entries and smart quotes followed by a number, and formats them as you type. For example, if you type 1/2, PowerPoint replaces it with ½. You can also automatically number a list. PowerPoint recognizes your intent; when you enter a number followed by a period and a space, PowerPoint will format the entry and the subsequent entries as a numbered list. If you insert a new line in the middle of the numbered list, PowerPoint automatically adjusts the numbers.

AutoFormat Text as You Type

1 In Normal view, click to place the insertion point in the text where you want to type.

2 Type text you can AutoFormat, such as 1/2, and then press the Spacebar or Enter.

PowerPoint recognizes this as a fraction and changes it to ½.

You can also type and replace any of the following:

◆ Straight quotes with "smart quotes"

◆ Ordinals (1st) with superscript.

◆ Hyphens (--) with dash (—).

◆ Smiley faces :-) and arrows (==>) with special symbols.

◆ Internet and network paths with hyperlinks.

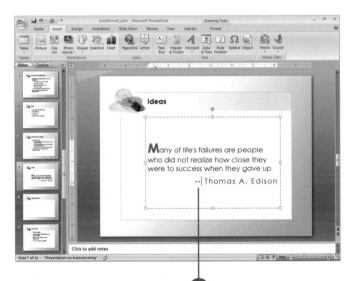

2 Changes to dash (–)

Did You Know?

You can use the AutoCorrect Options button to undo automatic numbering or fractions. Click the AutoCorrect Options button that appears when you AutoCorrect makes a change, and then click the Undo Automatic *x* command. If you want to stop AutoCorrect from making a change, click Stop Automatically *x* command.

AutoNumber a List as You Type

1. In Normal view, click to place the insertion point in the text at the beginning of a blank line where you want to begin a numbered list.

2. Type 1., press the Spacebar, type text, and then press Enter.

   PowerPoint recognizes this as a numbered list and displays the next number in the list in gray.

3. Type text, and continue until you complete the list.

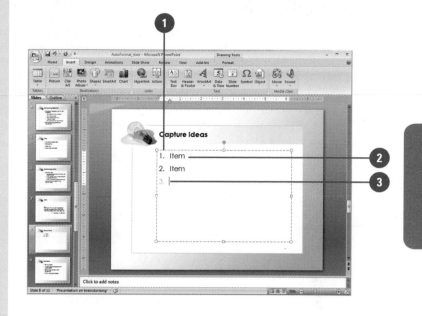

Change AutoFormat Options

1. Click the **Office** button, and then click **PowerPoint Options**.

2. Click **Proofing**, and then click **AutoCorrect Options**.

3. Click the **AutoFormat As You Type** tab.

4. Select or clear any of the following check boxes:

   - Straight quotes with "smart quotes".

   - Fractions (1/2) with fraction character (½).

   - Ordinals (1st) with superscript.

   - Hyphens (--) with dash (—).

   - Smiley faces :-) and arrows (==>) with special symbols.

   - Internet and network paths with hyperlinks.

5. Click **OK**.

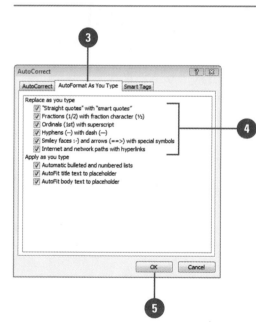

Applying a Format Style

Microsoft
Certified
Application
Specialist

PP07S-2.1.3, PP07S-2.2.4

The Format Painter lets you "pick up" the style of one section of text or object and apply, or "paint," it to another. The Format Painter is useful for quickly applying formatting styles to one or more text or shape objects. To apply a text or shape style to more than one item, double-click the Format Painter button on the Home tab instead of a single-click. The double-click keeps the Format Painter active until you want to press Esc to disable it, so you can apply formatting styles to any text or object you want in your presentation.

Apply a Format Style Using the Format Painter

1. Select the word or object whose format you want to pick up.

2. Click the **Home** tab.

3. Click the **Format Painter** button.

   If you want to apply the format to more than one item, double-click the Format Painter button.

4. Drag to select the text or click the object to which you want to apply the format.

5. If you double-clicked the Format Painter button, drag to select the text or click the object to which you want to apply the format, and then press Esc when you're done.

See Also

See Chapter 4, "Drawing and Modifying Shapes," on page 105 for information on formatting text boxes by applying Quick Styles, fills, outline borders, and effects.

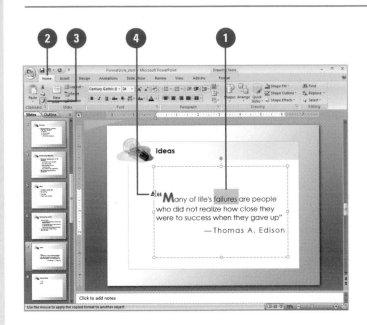

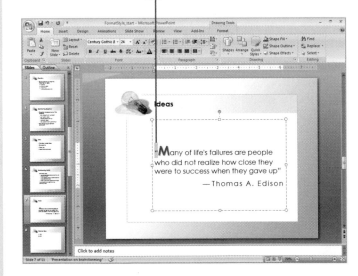

Apply new Format

Inserting Symbols

PowerPoint comes with a host of symbols for every need. Insert just the right one to keep from compromising a presentation's professional appearance with a hand-drawn arrow («) or missing mathematical symbol (å). In the Symbol dialog box, you use the Recently used symbols list to quickly insert a symbol that you want to insert again. If you don't see the symbol you want, use the Font list to look at the available symbols for other fonts installed on your computer.

Insert Symbols and Special Characters

1. Click the document where you want to insert a symbol or character.

2. Click the **Insert** tab, and then click the **Symbol** button.

3. To see other symbols, click the **Font** list arrow, and then click a new font.

4. Click a symbol or character.

   You can use the Recently used symbols list to use a symbol you've already used.

5. Click **Insert**.

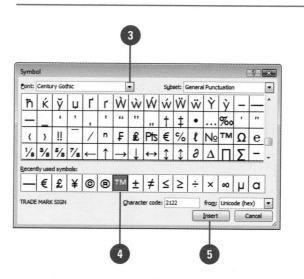

Did You Know?

You can insert a symbol using a character code. When the From box displays ASCII (decimal), you can use the number shown in the Character Code box to insert a character or symbol. Place your insertion point where you want the character on the slide, make sure Num Lock is on, hold down the Alt key, and then use the numeric keypad to type 0 (zero) followed by the character code. Then release the Alt key. The code applies to the current code page only, so some characters may not be available this way.

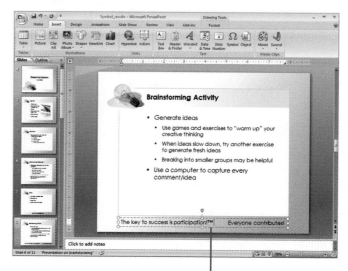

Trademark symbol

Creating a Text Box

Microsoft Certified Application Specialist

PP07S-2.1.1, PP07S-2.1.5

Usually you use the title, subtitle, and bulleted list placeholders to place text on a slide. However, when you want to add text outside one of the standard placeholders, such as for an annotation to a slide or shape text, you can create a text box. Text boxes appear in all views and panes. In Outline pane, PowerPoint labels slides with multiple text boxes in numbered order (**New!**). Your text box doesn't have to be rectangular—you can also use one of PowerPoint's shapes, a collection of shapes that range from rectangles and circles to arrows and stars. When you place text in a shape, the text becomes part of object. You can format and change the object using Font options, as well as Shape and WordArt styles. You can also adjust the text margins with a text box or a shape to create the look you want.

Create a Text Box

1. In Normal view, click the **Insert** tab.

2. Click the **Text Box** button.

3. Perform one of the following:

   ◆ To add text that wraps, drag to create a box, and then start typing.

   ◆ To add text that doesn't wrap, click and then start typing.

4. To delete a text box, select it, and the press Delete.

5. Click outside the selection box to deselect the text box.

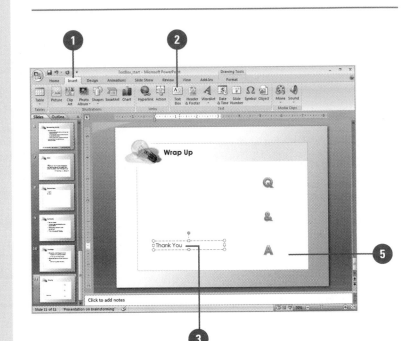

Did You Know?

You can use the sizing handles to adjust text boxes. If you create a text box without word wrapping and then find that the text spills over the edge of your slide, use the sizing handles to resize the text box so it fits on your slide. The text then wraps to the size of the box.

You can edit a text box. Click the text box, and then select the text you want to edit. Edit the text, and then click outside the text box to deselect it.

Add Text to a Shape

1. Click the **Home** or **Insert** tab.

2. Click the **Shapes** button to display a complete list of shapes.

3. Click the shape you want.

4. Drag to draw the shape on your slide.

5. Type your text.

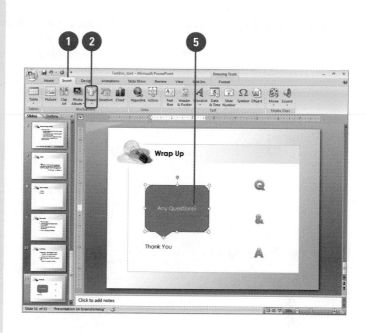

Wrap and Adjust Text Margins

1. Select an object with text.

2. Click the **Home** tab.

3. Click the **Drawing Dialog Box Launcher**.

4. In the left pane, click **Text Box**.

5. Select the **Wrap text in shape** check box.

6. Use the Internal margin **up** and **down** arrows to change the left, right, top, and bottom slides of the shape.

7. Click **Close**.

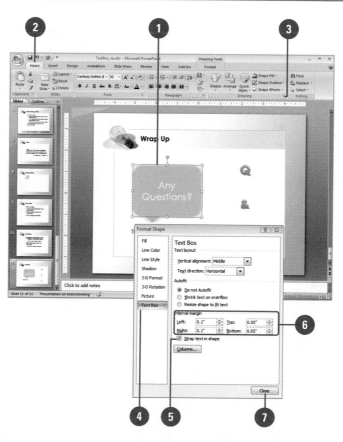

Creating Text Columns

Microsoft Certified Application Specialist

PP07S-2.1.6

Like Microsoft Word, PowerPoint can now create text columns (**New!**) within a text box. You can quickly transform a long list of text into a two, three, or more columns. After you create text columns, you can change the spacing between them to create the exact look you want. If you want to return columns back to a single column, simply change a text box to one column.

Create Text Columns

1. Select the text box.

2. Click the **Home** tab.

3. Click the **Columns** button, and then click one of the following:

   ◆ **One**, **Two**, or **Three** to quickly create text columns.

   ◆ **More Columns** to create larger text columns and change columns spacing.

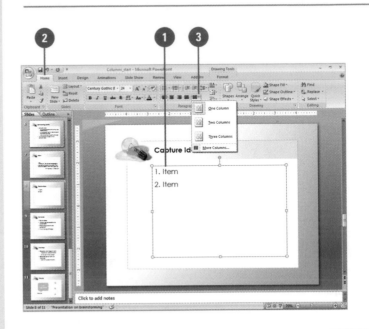

Adjust Column Spacing

1. Select the text box with the columns.

2. Click the **Home** tab.

3. Click the **Columns** button, and then click **More Columns**.

4. Click the Spacing **up** and **down** arrows, or enter a specific size.

5. Click **OK**.

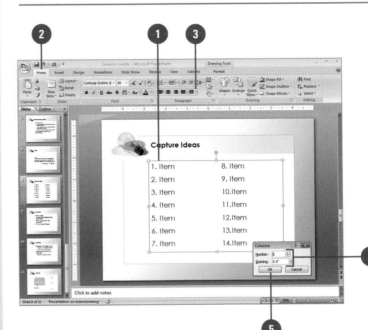

Finding and Replacing Text

The Find and Replace commands on the Home tab allow you to locate and change specific text in a presentation. Find helps you locate each occurrence of a specific word or set of characters, while Replace locates every occurrence of a specific word or set of characters and replaces it with a different one. You can change every occurrence of specific text all at once, or you can individually accept or reject each change.

Find and Replace Text

1. Click the **Home** tab.

2. Click the **Replace** button.

3. Click the **Find What** box, and then type the text you want to replace.

4. Click in the **Replace With** box, and then type the replacement text.

5. Click one of the following buttons.

   ◆ **Match Case.** Select to find text with the same upper and lower case.

   ◆ **Find whole words only.** Select to find entire text as a word.

6. Click one of the following buttons.

   ◆ **Find Next.** Click to find the next occurrence of the text.

   ◆ **Replace.** Click to find and replace this occurrence of the text.

   ◆ **Replace All.** Click to find and replace all occurrences of the text.

7. Click **OK** when you reach the end of the presentation, and then click **Close.**

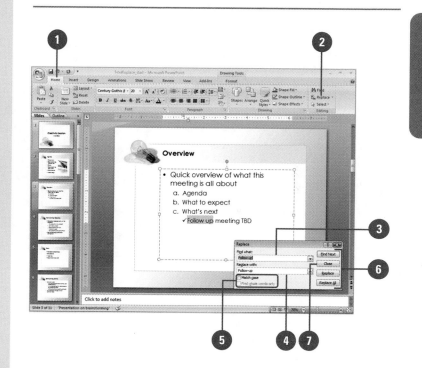

Rearranging Slides

Microsoft Certified Application Specialist   PP07S-1.5

You can instantly rearrange slides in Outline or Slides pane in Normal view or in Slide Sorter view. You can use the drag-and-drop method or the Cut and Paste buttons to move slides to a new location. In the Outline pane, you can also collapse the outline to its major points (titles) so you can more easily see its structure and rearrange slides, and then expand it back.

Rearrange a Slide in Slide Pane or Slide Sorter View

1. Click **Slides** pane in Normal view or click the **Slide Sorter View** button.

2. Select the slide(s) you want to move.

3. Drag the selected slide to a new location.

   A vertical bar appears where the slide(s) will be moved when you release the mouse button.

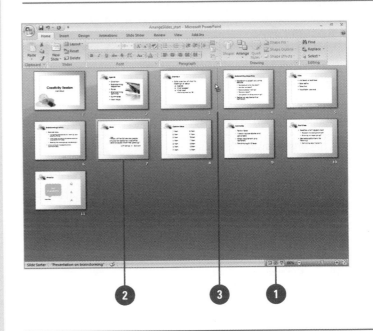

Move a Slide Using Cut and Paste

1. In the Outline or Slides pane or in Slide Sorter view, select the slide(s) you want to move.

2. Click the **Cut** button on the Home tab.

   The Clipboard task pane might open, displaying items you have cut or copied.

3. Click the new location.

4. Click the **Paste** button on the Home tab.

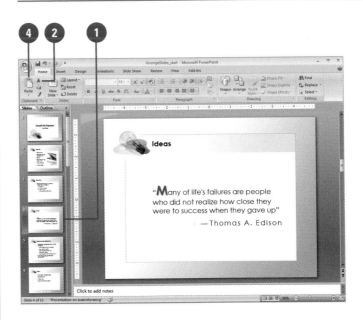

Rearrange a Slide in the Outline Pane

1. In the Outline pane in Normal view, select the slide(s) icons you want to move.

   TIMESAVER *To select slides in a sequence, click the first slide, hold down the Shift key, and then click the last slide. To select multiple slides, use the Ctrl key.*

2. Drag the selected slide up or down to move it in Outline pane to a new location.

   A vertical bar appears where the slide(s) will be moved when you release the mouse button.

Collapse and Expand Slides in the Outline Pane

1. In the Outline pane in Normal view, select the slide text you want to work with, and then:

   ◆ To collapse selected or all slides, right-click the slides, point to **Collapse**, and then click **Collapse**, or **Collapse All**.

   A horizontal line appears below a collapsed slide in Outline view.

   ◆ To expand selected or all slides, right-click the slides, point to **Expand**, and then click **Expand**, or **Expand All**.

   TIMESAVER *Double-click a slide icon in the Outline pane to collapse or expand it.*

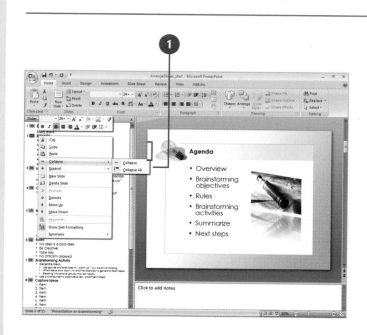

Using Slides from Other Presentations

Microsoft Certified Application Specialist

PP07S-1.5, PP07S-2.3.1

Insert Slides from Another Presentation

1. Click the **Home** tab.

2. Click the **New Slide** button arrow, and then click **Reuse Slides**.

3. If the presentation you want is not available, click **Browse**, click **Browse File**, locate and select the file you want, and then click **Open**.

4. Select the slides you want to insert.

   ◆ To display a larger preview, point to the slide.

   ◆ To insert a slide, click the slide.

   ◆ To insert all slides, right-click a slide, and then click **Insert All Slides**.

   ◆ To insert only the theme for all slides, right-click a slide, and then click **Apply Theme to All Slides**.

   ◆ To insert only the theme for the selected slides, right-click a slide, and then click **Apply Theme to Selected Slides**.

5. When you're done, click the **Close** button on the task pane.

See Also

See "Publishing Slides to a Library" on page 388 for information on using Office SharePoint 2007. For additional online SharePoint information, visit www.perspection.com.

To insert slides from other presentations, you can open the presentation and copy and paste the slides you want, or you can use the Reuse Slides task pane (**New!**). With the Reuse Slides task pane, you don't have to open the presentation first; instead, you can view a miniature of each slide in a presentation and then insert only the ones you select. If you only want to reuse the theme from another presentation, the Reuse Slides task pane can do that too (**New!**).

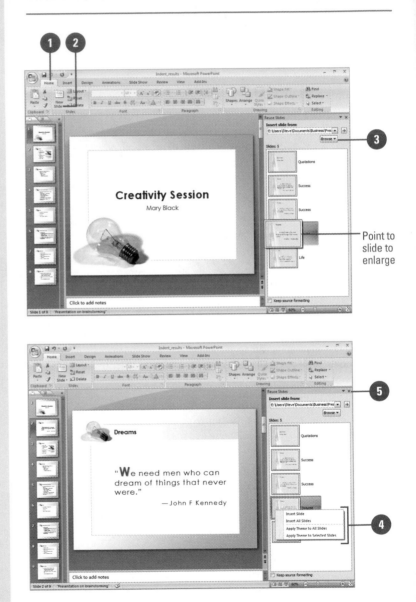

Point to slide to enlarge

Designing a Look

Introduction

As you develop your presentation, an important element needs to be considered: the look of your slides. The design of your presentation is just as important as the information that it contains. A poorly designed presentation without the eye-catching design elements will lose your audience, and then what your presentation has to say won't really matter.

Microsoft Office PowerPoint 2007 comes with professionally designed templates to help you create a consistent presentation look. A template is a presentation file that consists of one or more slide masters. A **slide master** is the part of a template that contains all of the properties of your PowerPoint presentation—slide layouts, themes, effects, animation, backgrounds, text font style and color, date and time, and graphic placement. Each slide master contains one or more slide layouts, which defines the positioning and formatting of content on a slide. Layouts contain placeholders, which hold and format future text and other slide content, such as slide numbers, date, time, and headers and footers.

Besides the text and graphics that you place on your slides, another important part of a presentation is the use of color. Not everyone has an eye for color, and pulling it all together can be daunting, so PowerPoint provides you with professionally designed color themes, which you can apply to any slide master. A **theme** is a set of unified design elements that provides a consistent look for a presentation by using color themes, fonts, and effects, such as shadows, shading, and animations.

Once you've set up your masters and themes to be exactly the way you want them, you can save it as a design template. Company specific styles, logos, colors themes and other elements, can now become a new template to be used with other presentations in the future.

What You'll Do

Make Your Presentation Look Consistent

View Masters

Control Slide Appearance with Masters

Control a Slide Layout with Masters

Modify Placeholders

Control a Slide Background with Masters

Add a Header and Footer

Insert Slide Numbers

Insert the Date and Time

View and Applying a Theme

Understand and Create Color Themes

Choose Theme Effects and Font

Create a Custom Theme

Add Colors to a Presentation

Add and Modify a Background Style

Save a Template

Making Your Presentation Look Consistent

PP07S-1.2.1

Each PowerPoint presentation comes with a set of **masters**: slide, notes, and handout. A master controls the properties of each corresponding slide or page in a presentation. For example, when you make a change on a slide master, the change affects every slide. If you place your company logo, other artwork, the date and time, or slide number on the slide master, the element will appear on every slide.

Each master contains placeholders and a theme (**New!**) to help you create a consistent looking presentation. A placeholder provides a consistent place on a slide or page to store text and information. A theme provides a consistent look, which incorporates a color theme, effects, fonts, and slide background style. Placeholders appear on the layouts associated with the master. The notes and handout masters use one layout while the slide master uses multiple layouts. Each master includes a different set of placeholders, which you can show or hide at any time. For example, the slide master includes master title and text placeholders, which control the text format for every slide in a presentation,

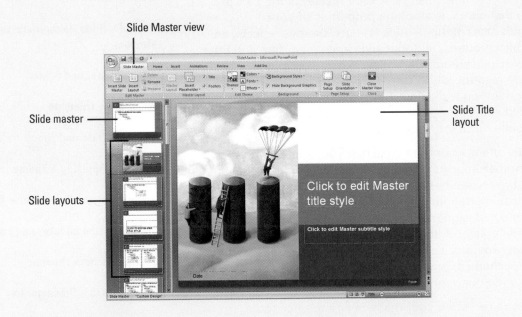

Slide Master view

Slide master

Slide layouts

Slide Title layout

while the handout master includes header, footer, date, page number, and body placeholders. You can modify and arrange placeholders on all of the master views to include the information and design you want.

You can also view and make changes to a master—either slide, notes, or handout—in one of the master views, which you can access using the View tab. When you view a master, the Ribbon adds a Program tab that correspond to the master (**New!**). For example, when you switch to Slide Master view, the Slide Master tab appears. The Ribbon on each master view also includes a Close Master View button, which returns you to the view you were in before you opened the master.

The Ribbon for each master view also includes commands specific to the type of master. For example, the Slide Master tab contains several buttons to insert, delete, rename, duplicate, and preserve slide masters. You can insert one or more slide masters into a presentation, which is useful for creating separate sections within the same presentation. When you preserve a slide master, you protect it from being deleted. As you work with slide masters in Slide Master view, you can create custom slide layouts and insert placeholders.

Edit master slides

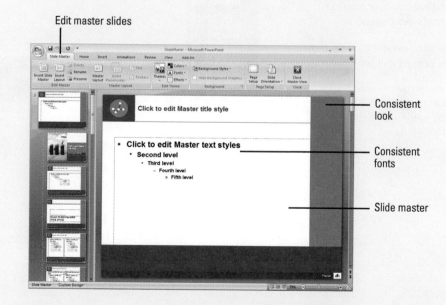

Consistent look

Consistent fonts

Slide master

Viewing Masters

If you want to change the appearance of each instance of a slide element, like all the title fonts or all the bullet characters, you don't have to change every slide individually. Instead, you can change them all at once using a slide master. PowerPoint updates the existing slides, and then applies your settings to any slides you add. Each PowerPoint presentation contains three masters: slide, notes, and handout. Which master you open depends on what part of your presentation you want to change. The slide master controls all the presentation slides, while the **notes master** and **handout master** controls the appearance of all speaker notes pages, and handout pages, respectively.

View the Slide Master

1 Click the **View** tab.

2 Click the **Slide Master** button.

The slide master appears in the left pane as a larger slide miniature with a number next to it and the slides layouts associated with it appear below it.

TIMESAVER *You can view the slide master quickly. Press and hold the Shift key, and then click the Normal view button.*

3 Click the slide master or slide layout to display it in the slide master view.

Use the scroll bar in the left pane to display additional slide masters and slide layouts.

4 Click the **Close Master View** button on the Ribbon.

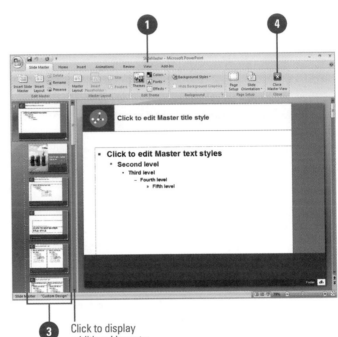

Click to display additional layouts and slide masters

View the Notes Master

① Click the **View** tab.

② Click the **Notes Master** button.

The Notes Master controls the look of your notes pages.

③ Click the **Close Master View** button on the Ribbon.

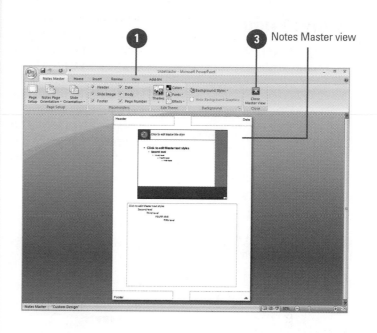

View the Handout Master

① Click the **View** tab.

② Click the **Handout Master** button.

TIMESAVER *You can view the handout master quickly. Press and hold the Shift key, and then click the Slide Sorter view button.*

The Handout Master controls the look of your handouts.

③ Click the **Slides-per-page** button, and then use one of the following:

◆ Click the number of slides you want on your handout pages: **1**, **2**, **3**, **4**, **6**, or **9**.

◆ Click **Show Slide Outline** to show the slide outline, click the Slides-per-page button.

The item you select in steps 2 or 3

④ Click the **Close Master View** button on the Ribbon.

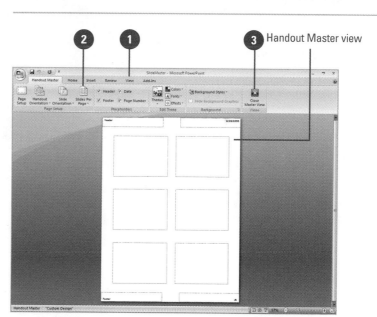

Controlling Slide Appearance with Masters

If you want an object, such as a company logo or clip art, to appear on every slide in your presentation, place it on the **Slide Master**. All of the characteristics of the Slide Master (background color, text color, font, and font size) appear on every slide. However, if you want an object to appear on a certain slide type, place it on a slide layout (**New!**) in Slide Master view. The Slide Master tab contains several buttons to insert, delete, rename, duplicate, and preserve masters. You can create unique slides that don't follow the format of the masters. When you preserve a master, you protect (lock) it from being deleted. You can also arrange the placeholders the way you want them.

Include an Object on Every Slide or Only Specific Slides

1. Click the **View** tab, and then click the **Slide Master** button.

2. Add the objects you want to a slide master or slide layout, and then modify its size and placement.

   ♦ **Slide master.** Includes object on every slide.

   Slide master is the top slide miniature in the left column.

   ♦ **Slide layout.** Includes object only on the specific layout.

3. Click the **Close Master View** button on the Ribbon.

Did You Know?

You can delete a slide master. Click the View tab, click the Slide Master button, select the slide master you want to delete in the left pane, click the Delete button in the Edit Master group, and then click the Close Master View button.

You can rename a slide master. Click the View tab, click the Slide Master button, select the slide master you want to rename, click the Rename button in the Edit Master group, type a new name, click Rename, and then click the Close Master View button.

Slide master

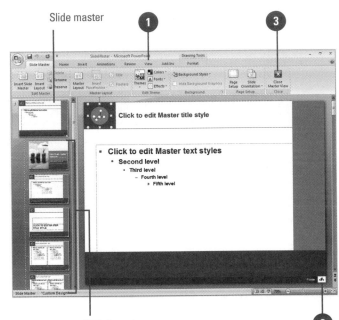

Slide layouts

Insert a New Slide Master

① Click the **View** tab, and then click the **Slide Master** button.

② Click the **Insert Slide Master** button.

The new slide master appears at the bottom of the left pane with a push pin indicating the new master is preserved.

③ Click the **Close Master View** button on the Ribbon.

The new slide master and associated layouts appears in the Add Slide and Layout galleries at the bottom (scroll down if necessary).

New slide master and layouts

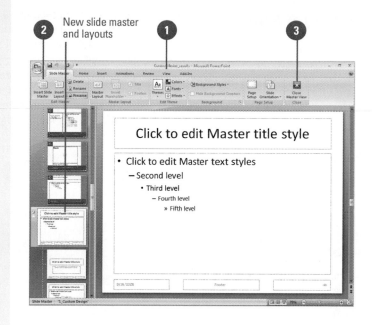

Preserve or Not Preserve a Slide Master

① Click the **View** tab, and then click the **Slide Master** button.

② Click the master that you want to preserve or not preserve.

A push pin appears under the slide master number to indicate the master is currently preserved.

③ Use the **Preserve** button to toggle it on (highlighted) and off (not highlighted).

◆ **Preserve.** Click the Preserve button to lock the master (highlighted).

◆ **Not preserve.** Click the Preserve button to unlock the master (not highlighted), and then click Yes or No to delete the master (if not used).

④ Click the **Close Master View** button on the Ribbon.

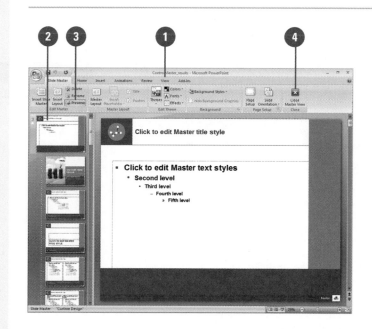

Controlling a Slide Layout with Masters

PP07S-1.3

Each slide master includes a standard set of slide layouts (**New!**). If the standard layouts don't meet your specific needs, you can modify one to create a new custom slide layout, or insert and create a new custom slide layout from scratch. You can use the Ribbon in Slide Master view to help you create a custom slide layout. In the Master Layout group, you can show and hide available placeholders or insert different types of placeholders (**New!**), such as Content, Text, Picture, Chart, Table, Diagram, Media, and Clip Art.

Insert a New Slide Layout

1. Click the **View** tab, and then click the **Slide Master** button.

2. Select the slide master in the left pane in which you want to associate a new layout.

3. Click the **Insert Slide Layout** button.

   The new slide layout appears at the end of the current slide layouts for the slide master.

4. Click the **Close Master View** button on the Ribbon.

See Also

See "Modifying Placeholders" on page 82 for information on showing, hiding, and formatting placeholders.

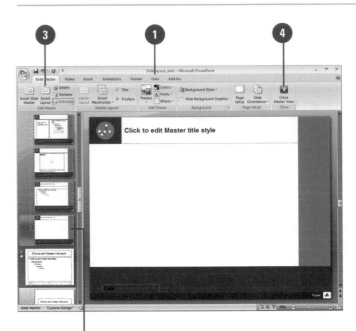

New slide layout

Create a New Slide Layout from an Existing One

1. Click the **View** tab, and then click the **Slide Master** button.

2. Right-click the slide layout you want to use, and then click **Duplicate Layout**.

   The duplicate layout appears below the original one.

3. Click the **Rename** button.

4. Type a new layout name.

5. Click **Rename**.

6. Click the **Close Master View** button on the Ribbon.

Insert a Placeholder

1. Click the **View** tab, and then click the **Slide Master** button.

2. Select the slide layout to which you want to insert a placeholder.

3. Click the **Insert Placeholder** button arrow, and then click the placeholder you want to insert.

   TIMESAVER *Click the Insert Placeholder button to insert a placeholder used to hold any kind of content.*

4. On the slide, drag to create a placeholder the size you want on the slide layout.

5. Click the **Close Master View** button on the Ribbon.

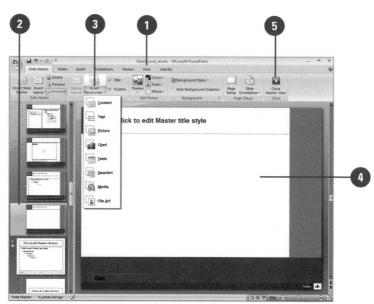

Modifying Placeholders

Microsoft Certified Application Specialist

PP07S-1.3, PP07S-2.2.4, PP07S-4.4.1

Each PowerPoint master comes with a different set of standard place-holders. The slide master comes with Title and Footer placeholder, while the handouts master comes with Header, Footer, Date, and Page Number placeholders. If a master doesn't contain the information you need, you can modify it by showing or hiding placeholders. After you display the placeholders you want, you can insert content—such as header or footer text—and format it like any other text box with the look you want. For example, you can format placeholder text using WordArt styles and Font and Paragraphs tools on the Home tab.

Show or Hide a Placeholder

1. Click the **View** tab, and then click the master view (**Slide Master**, **Handout Master**, or **Notes Master**) button with the master you want to change.

2. If you're in Slide Master view, select the slide master or slide layout you want to change.

3. Select or clear the check box for the placeholder you want to show or hide.

   ◆ **Slide Master.** Select or clear the Title or Footers check boxes.

   ◆ **Handout Master.** Select or clear the Header, Footer, Date, or Page Number check boxes.

   ◆ **Notes Master.** Select or clear the Header, Slide Image, Footer, Date, Body, or Page Number check boxes.

4. Click the **Close Master View** button on the Ribbon.

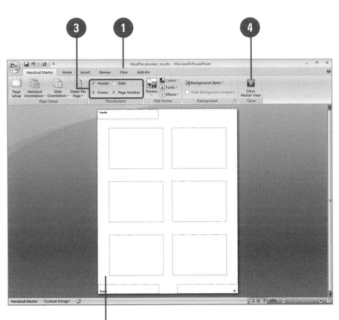

Handout Master view

See Also

See "Controlling a Slide Layout with Masters" on page 80 for information on inserting placeholders on a slide master or slide layout.

Modify and Format Placeholders

① Click the **View** tab, and then click the master view (**Slide Master**, **Handout Master**, or **Notes Master**) button with the master you want to change.

② If you're in Slide Master view, select the slide master or slide layout you want to change.

③ Select the placeholder you want to change.

④ To add information to a placeholder, such as a header or footer, click the text box to insert the I-beam, and then type the text you want.

⑤ To format the placeholder, click the **Home** and **Format** (under Drawing Tools) tabs, and then use the formatting tools on the Ribbon.

◆ Use the WordArt Styles to apply Quick Styles from the Style gallery.

◆ Use tools in the Font and Paragraph groups to modify the placeholder.

⑥ To delete the placeholder, press the Delete key.

⑦ Click the **Close Master View** button on the Ribbon.

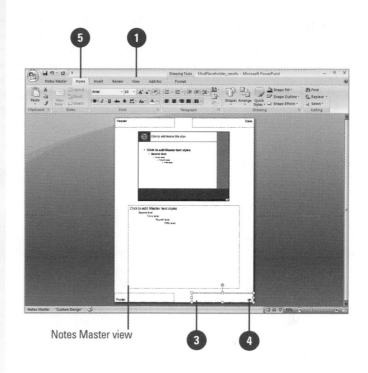

Notes Master view

Did You Know?

You can change the slide master layout. If you delete an item from the slide master, you can reshow it again. Select the slide master in Slide Master view, click the Slide Layout button, select the placeholder check boxes you want, and then click OK.

Controlling a Slide Background with Masters

PP07S-1.3

You may want to place an object onto most slides, but not every slide. Placing the object on the slide master saves you time. Use the Insert tab to help you insert objects. Once an object is placed on the slide master, you can hide the object in any slide you want. You can even choose to hide the object on every slide or only on specific ones. If you select the slide master in Slide Master view, you can hide background graphics on all slides. If you select a slide layout, you can hide them on the selected layout.

Hide Master Background Objects on a Slide

1. Click the **View** tab, click the **Slide Master** button, and then select the slide master (for all slides) or slide layout (for specific slides) you want to hide background objects.

2. Select the **Hide Background Graphics** check box.

   ◆ To hide a background object on a single slide, display the slide in Normal view, click the Design tab, and then select the Hide Background Graphics check box.

3. Click the **Close Master View** button on the Ribbon.

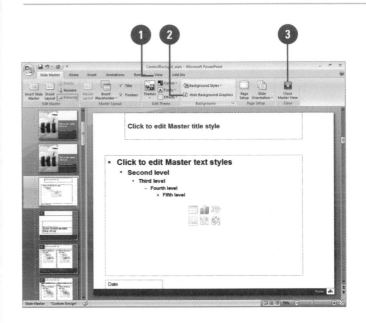

Add Background Graphics

1. Click the **View** tab, and then click the master view (**Slide Master**, **Handout Master**, or **Notes Master** button with the master you want to change.

2. Click the **Insert** tab, click the **Insert Picture** button, locate and select the picture you want, and then click **Insert**.

3. Click the **Close Master View** button on the Ribbon.

Inserted graphic

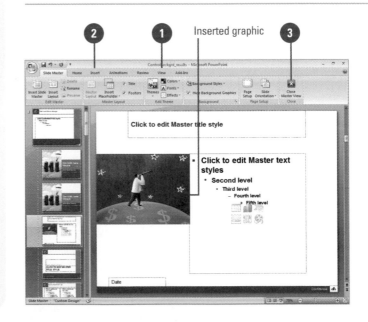

Adding a Header and Footer

Microsoft Certified Application Specialist PP07S-1.3, PP07S-4.4.1

Headers and footers appear on every slide. You can choose to not have them appear on the title slide. They often include information such as the presentation title, slide number, date, and name of the presenter. Use the masters to place header and footer information on your slides, handouts, or notes pages. Make sure your header and footer don't make your presentation look cluttered. The default font size is usually small enough to minimize distraction, but you can experiment by changing their font size and placement to make sure.

Add a Header and Footer

1. Click the **Insert** tab, and then click the **Header & Footer** button.

2. Click the **Slide** or **Notes and Handouts** tab.

3. Enter or select the information you want to include on your slide or your notes and handouts.

4. To not include a header and footer on the title slide, select the **Don't show on title slide** check box.

5. Click **Apply** to apply your selections to the current slide (if available), or click **Apply to All** to apply the selections to all slides.

Change the Look of a Header or Footer

1. Click the **View** tab, and then click the master view (**Slide Master**, **Handout Master**, or **Notes Master** button with the master you want to change.

2. Make the necessary changes to the header and footer like any other text box. You can move or resize them or change their text attributes using the Home tab.

3. Click the **Close Master View** button on the Ribbon.

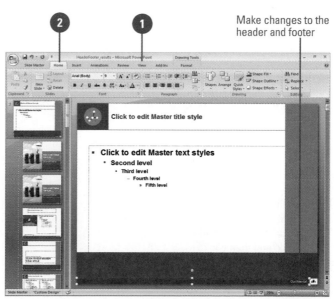

Make changes to the header and footer

Inserting Slide Numbers

Microsoft Certified Application Specialist

PP07S-1.3, PP07S-4.4.1

You can insert slide numbers into the text of your presentation. When you insert slide numbers, PowerPoint keeps track of your slide numbers for you. You can insert slide numbers on every slide or only on a specific slide. To insert a slide number on every page, you place it in a placeholder on the slide master. In the Slide Master view, PowerPoint inserts a code <#> for the slide number. When you view slides in other views, the slide number is shown. To insert a slide number only on a specific page, you insert it in a text box on the slide you want. You can even start numbering with a page number other than one. This is useful when your slides are a part of a larger presentation.

Insert Slide Numbering on Slides, Notes, and Handouts

1. Click the **View** tab, and then click the **Slide Master** button.

2. Select the slide master or slide layout in the left pane in which you want to insert a slide number.

   If the slide already contains a placeholder with the <#> symbol, which indicates slide numbering, you don't need to continue.

3. Click to place the insertion point in the text object where you want to insert the current slide number.

4. Click the **Insert** tab.

5. Click the **Insert Slide Number** button.

   The <#> symbol appears in the text.

6. Click the **Slide Master** tab, and then click **Close Master View** button on the Ribbon.

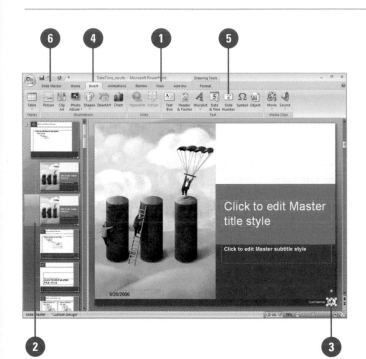

Did You Know?

Insert slide numbers on slides, notes, and handout using the default placeholder. Click the Insert tab, click the Slide or Notes and Handouts tab, click Date & Time button, select the Slide number check box, and then click Apply or Apply to All.

Insert Slide Numbering on a Specific Slide

1. Click to place the insertion point in the text object where you want to insert the current slide number.

2. Click the **Insert** tab.

3. Click the **Insert Slide Number** button.

   The current slide number is inserted into the text box.

   TROUBLE? *If you don't place the insertion point, the Header and Footer dialog opens.*

Start Numbering with a Different Number

1. Insert the slide number if you need one on the slide or slide master.

2. Click the **View** tab, and then click the master view (**Slide Master**, **Handout Master**, or **Notes Master**) button with the master you want to change.

3. Click the **Page Setup** button.

4. Click the **Number Slides From** up or down arrow to set the number you want.

5. Click **OK**.

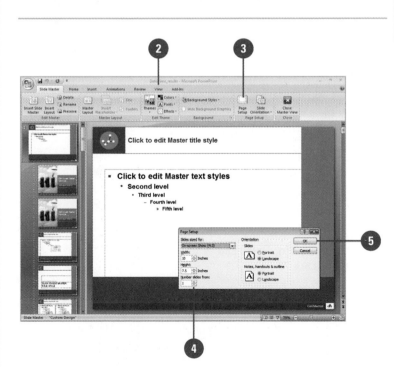

Inserting the Date and Time

You can insert the date and time into your presentation. For example, you might want today's date to appear in a stock market quote. You can insert the date and time on every slide, notes page or handout, or only on a specific slide. To insert the date and time on every page, you place it in a placeholder on the slide master. To insert the date and time only on a specific page, you insert it in a text box on the slide you want. You can set the date and time to automatically update to your computer's clock or stay fixed until you change it.

Insert the Date and Time on a Specific Slide

1. Click to place the insertion point in the text object where you want to insert the date and time.

2. Click the **Insert** tab.

3. Click the **Date & Time** button.

4. Click the date or time format you want.

5. To have the date and time automatically update, select the **Update automatically** check box.

6. To change the default date and time format, click **Default**, and then click **Yes** to confirm.

7. Click **OK**.

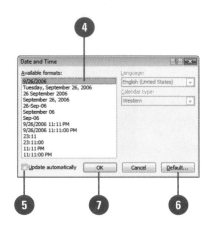

Insert the Date and Time on Slides, Notes, and Handouts

1. Click the **Insert** tab.

2. Click the **Date & Time** button.

3. Click the **Slide** or **Notes and Handouts** tab.

4. Click the **Date and time** check box.

5. Click the **Update automatically** or **Fixed** option, and then specify or select the format you want.

6. Click **Apply** to apply your selections to the current slide, or click **Apply to All** to apply the selections to all slides.

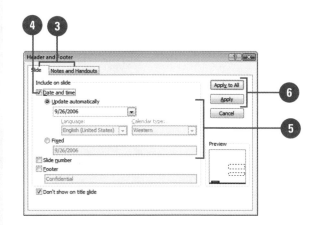

Understanding Color Themes

Every presentation has at least one color theme. A presentation with more than one set of slide masters can have more than one color theme. A color theme helps you create professional-looking presentations that use an appropriate balance of color for your presentation content. You can use a default color theme (**New!**) or create a custom one.

Color themes in PowerPoint are made up of a palette of twelve colors (**New!**). These colors appear on color palettes when you click the Shape Fill and Outline Color or Font Color button arrow on the Home and Format tabs.

These twelve colors correspond to the following elements in a presentation:

Four Text and Background. The two background colors (light and dark combinations) are the canvas, or drawing area, color of the slide. The two text colors (light and dark combinations) are for typing text and drawing lines, and contrast with the background colors.

Six Accent. These colors are designed to work as a complementary color palette for objects, such as shadows and fills. These colors contrast with both the background and text colors.

One hyperlink. This color is designed to work as a complementary color for objects and hyperlinks.

One followed hyperlink. This color is designed to work as a complementary color for objects and visited hyperlinks.

The first four colors in the Theme Colors list represent the presentation text and background colors (light and dark for each). The remaining colors represent the six accent and two hyperlink colors for the theme. When you apply another theme or change any of these colors to create a new theme, the colors shown in the Theme Colors dialog box and color palettes change to match the current colors.

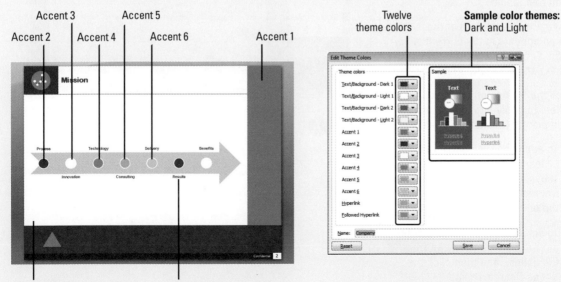

Accent 3
Accent 5
Accent 2
Accent 4
Accent 6
Accent 1

Text/Background - Light 1
Text/Background - Dark 1

Twelve theme colors
Sample color themes: Dark and Light

Viewing and Applying a Theme

**Microsoft
Certified
Application
Specialist**

PP07S-1.2.1

A presentation theme (**New!**) consists of theme colors, fonts, and effects. You can quickly format an entire presentation with a professional look by applying a theme. To quickly see if you like a theme, point to one on the Design tab to display a ScreenTip with name and information about it, and a live preview (**New!**) of it in the current slide. If you like it, you can apply it. When you apply a theme, the background, text, graphics, charts, and tables all change to reflect the theme. You can apply a theme to a matching slide, selected slides or all slides in a presentation. You can choose from one or more standard themes. When you add new content, the slide elements change to match the theme ensuring all of your material will look consistent. You can even use the same theme in other Microsoft Office 2007 programs, such as Word and Excel, so all your work matches. Can't find a theme you like? Search Microsoft Office Online.

View and Apply a Theme

① Select the slide with the slide master you want to change.

② Click the **Design** tab.

③ Click the scroll up or down arrow, or click the **More** list arrow in the Themes gallery to see additional themes.

The current theme appears highlighted in the gallery.

④ Point to a theme.

A live preview (**New!**) of the theme appears in the current slide, and a ScreenTip with the theme name and how many slides use it.

⑤ Click the theme you want from the gallery to apply it to the selected slide master (and all its slides).

◆ To apply the theme to matching slides, all slides, or selected slides, right-click the theme from the gallery, and then click the option you want.

◆ To set a theme as default, right-click the theme you want from the gallery, and then click the Set as Default Theme.

Click arrow on Theme gallery to display a menu to display the Themes you want in the gallery.

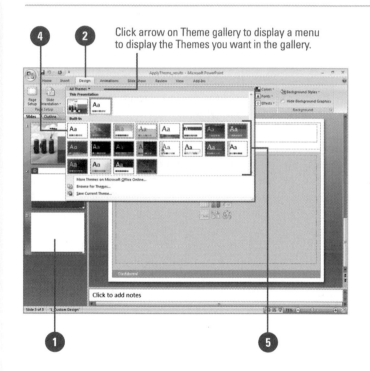

Apply the Theme of One Slide to Another

① Click the **Normal View** or Slide **Sorter View** button.

② Click the **Home** tab.

③ Click the slide with the color theme you want to apply.

④ Click the **Format Painter** button on the Home tab to apply the color theme to one slide, or double-click the button to apply the color theme to multiple slides.

⑤ Click the slides to which you want to apply the color theme. The slides can be in the current presentation or in another open presentation.

⑥ If you are applying the theme to more than one slide, press Esc to cancel the Format Painter. If you are applying the theme to only one slide, the Format Painter is canceled automatically.

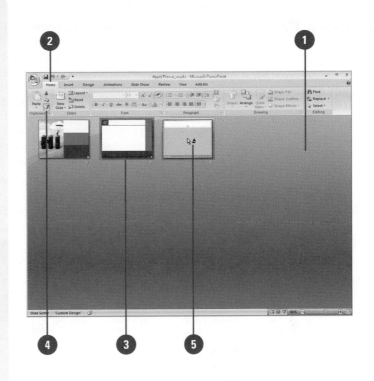

Did You Know?

You can search for themes at Microsoft Office Online. Select the slide with the slide master you want to change, click the Design tab, click the More list arrow in the Themes gallery, and then click Search Office Online. Follow Microsoft Office Online Web site instructions to download and use online themes.

You can create a new presentation based on a theme. Click the Office button, click New, click Installed Themes in the left pane, click the theme you want, and then click Create.

Creating a Color Theme

You may like a certain color theme except for one or two colors. You can change an existing color theme (**New!**) and apply your changes to the entire presentation or to just a few slides. You can add other custom colors to your theme by using RGB (Red, Green, and Blue) or HSL (Hues, Saturation, and Luminosity) color modes. The RGB color mode is probably the most widely used of all the color modes. You can accomplish this by using sliders, dragging on a color-space, or entering a numeric value that corresponds to a specific color. Once you create this new color theme, you can add it to your collection of color themes so that you can make it available to any slide in the presentation.

Change a Color in a Standard Color Theme

1. Click the **Design** tab.

2. Click the **Theme Colors** button, and then click **Create New Theme Colors**.

3. Click the Theme Colors buttons (Text/Background, Accent, or Hyperlink, etc.) for the colors you want to change.

4. Click a new color, or click **More Colors** to select a color from the **Standard** or **Custom** tab, and then click **OK**.

   ◆ To select a custom color, drag across the palette until the pointer is over the color you want, or choose a Color Model, and then enter the Hue, Sat, Lum, or Red, Green, and Blue values.

5. If you don't like your color choices, click the **Reset** button to return all color changes to their original colors.

6. Type a new name for the color theme.

7. Click **Save**.

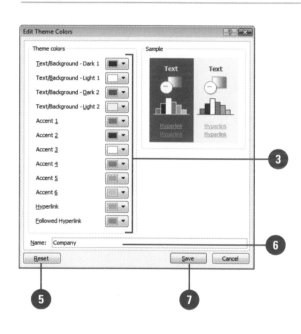

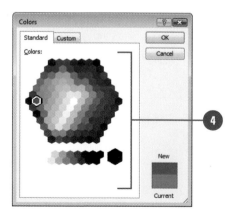

Select Custom Colors

1 Select a text box.

2 Click the **Font Color** button on the Home tab, and then click **More Colors**.

> This is one method. You can also use other color menus to access the Colors dialog box.

3 Click the **Custom** tab.

4 Click the **Color Mode** list arrow, and then click **RGB** or **HSL**.

5 Select a custom color using one of the following methods:

- ◆ If you know the color values, enter them, either Hue, Sat, Lum, or Red, Green, and Blue.

- ◆ Drag across the palette until the pointer is over the color you want.. Drag the black arrow to adjust the amount of black and white in the color.

> The new color appears above the current color at the bottom right.

6 Click **OK**.

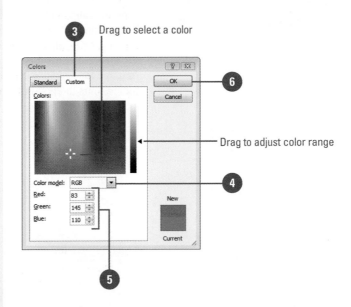
Drag to select a color

Drag to adjust color range

Did You Know?

You can edit a custom color theme. On the Design tab, click the Theme Colors button, right-click the theme color you want to edit, click Edit, make changes, and then click Save.

You can delete a custom color theme. On the Design tab, click the Theme Colors button, right-click the theme color you want to edit, click Edit, click Delete, and then click Yes.

The Properties of Color

Characteristic	Description
Hue	The color itself; every color is identified by a number, determined by the number of colors available on your monitor.
Saturation	The intensity of the color. The higher the number, the more vivid the color.
Luminosity	The brightness of the color, or how close the color is to black or white. The larger the number, the lighter the color.
Red, Green, Blue	Primary colors of the visible light spectrum. RGB generates color using three 8-bit channels: 1 red, 1 green, and 1 blue. RGB is an additive color system, which means that color is added to a black background. The additive process mixes various amounts of red, green and blue light to produce other colors.

Choosing Theme Fonts

A presentation theme consists of theme colors, fonts, and effects. Theme fonts (**New!**) include heading and body text fonts. Each presentation uses a set of theme fonts. When you click the Theme Fonts button on the Design tab, the name of the current heading and body text font appear highlighted in the gallery menu. You can apply a set of theme fonts to another theme or create your own set of theme fonts.

View and Apply Theme Fonts

① Select the slide with the slide master you want to change.

② Click the **Design** tab.

③ Click the **Theme Fonts** button.

The current theme fonts appear highlighted in the menu.

TIMESAVER *Point to the Fonts button to display a ScreenTip with the current theme fonts.*

④ Click the theme fonts you want from the gallery menu.

◆ To apply the theme fonts to matching slides or all slides, right-click the theme fonts name on the menu, and then click the option you want.

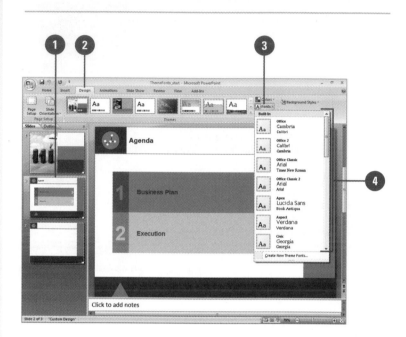

Create Theme Fonts

① Click the **Design** tab.

② Click the **Theme Fonts** button, and then click **Create New Theme Fonts**.

③ Click the **Heading font** list arrow, and then select a font.

④ Click the **Body font** list arrow, and then select a font.

⑤ Type a name for the custom theme fonts.

⑥ Click **Save**.

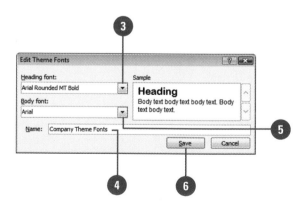

Choosing Theme Effects

A presentation theme consists of theme colors, fonts, and effects. Theme effects (**New!**) are sets of lines, fills, and special effects styles for shapes, graphics, charts, SmartArt, and other design elements. By combining the lines, fills, and special effects styles with different formatting levels (subtle, moderate, and intense), PowerPoint provides a variety of visual theme effects. Each presentation uses a set of theme effects. Some are more basic while others are more elaborate. When you click the Theme Effects button on the Design tab, the name of the current theme effects appears highlighted in the gallery menu. While you can apply a set of theme effects to another theme, you cannot create your own set of theme effects at this time.

View and Apply Theme Effects

1. Select the slide with the slide master you want to change.

2. Click the **Design** tab.

3. Click the **Theme Effects** button.

   The current theme effects appear highlighted in the menu.

   TIMESAVER *Point to the Effects button to display a ScreenTip with the current theme effects name.*

4. Click the theme effects you want from the menu.

   ◆ To apply the theme effects to matching slides or all slides, right-click the theme effects name on the menu, and then click the option you want.

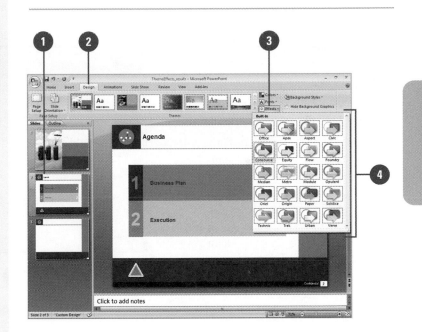

Did You Know?

You can delete a custom theme effects or fonts. On the Design tab, click the Theme Effects or Theme Fonts button, right-click the theme you want to edit, click Edit, click Delete, and then click Yes.

Creating a Custom Theme

If you have special needs for specific colors, fonts, and effects, such as a company sales or marketing presentation, you can create your own theme by customizing theme colors, theme fonts, and theme effects, and saving them as a theme file (.thmx) (**New!**), which you can reuse. You can apply the saved theme to other presentations and slides. When you save a custom theme, the file is automatically saved in the Document Themes folder and added to the list of custom themes used by PowerPoint 2007 and other Office 2007 programs. When you no longer need a custom theme, you can delete it.

Create a Custom Theme

1. Click the **Design** tab, and then create a theme by customizing theme colors, theme fonts, and theme effects.

2. Click the **More** list arrow in the Themes gallery, and then click **Save Current Theme**.

3. Type a name for the theme file.

4. Click **Save**.

Custom theme

Choose a Custom Theme

1. Click the **Design** tab.

2. Click the scroll up or down arrow, or click the **More** list arrow in the Themes gallery to see additional themes.

3. To display only the custom themes on the gallery, click the title bar for the gallery, and then click **Custom**.

4. Point to gallery to want to display the theme name, and then click the one you want.

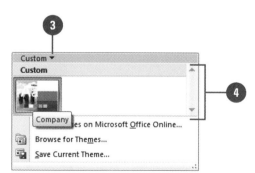

Apply a Custom Theme From a File

1. Select the slide with the slide master you want to change.

2. Click the **Design** tab.

3. Click the **More** list arrow in the Themes gallery, and then click **Browse for Themes**.

4. If you want to open a specific file type, click the **Files of type** list arrow, and then click a file type.

   ◆ Office Themes and Themed Documents.

   ◆ Office Themes.

   ◆ Office Themes and PowerPoint Templates.

5. Click one of the icons on the **Places bar** for quick access to an often-used folder.

6. If the file is located in another folder, click the **Look in** list arrow, and then navigate to the file.

7. Click the theme file you want.

8. Click **Apply**.

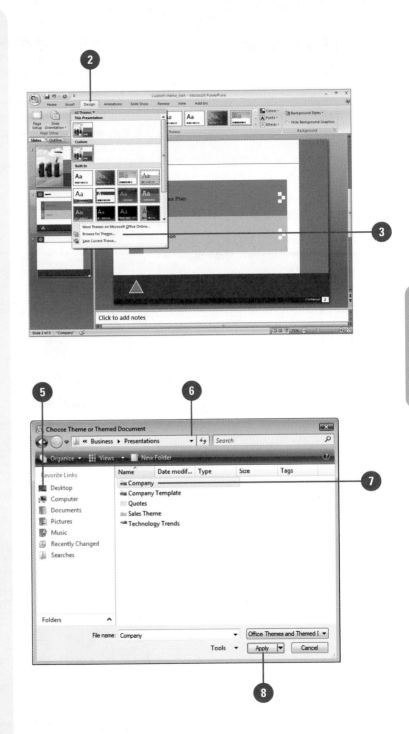

See Also

See "Viewing and Applying a Theme" on page 90 for information on applying a theme from the Themes gallery.

Did You Know?

You can remove a custom theme from the gallery menu. Simply move the theme file from the Document Themes folder into another folder.

Adding Colors to a Presentation

In addition to the twelve color theme colors (**New!**), PowerPoint allows you to add more colors to your presentation. These additional colors are available on each color button palette on the Ribbon or in a dialog box, such as the Font Color button. These colors are useful when you want to change the color of an object to a specific color, but the presentation color theme does not have that color. Colors that you add to a presentation appear in all color palettes and remain in the palette even if the color theme changes. PowerPoint "remembers" up to ten colors that you've added. If you add an eleventh, it appears first on the palette, replacing the oldest.

Add a Color to the Menus

1. Click the object whose color you want to change, and then click the **Format** tab under Drawing Tools.

2. Click the **Shape Fill Color**, **Shape Outline Color**, or **Font Color** button arrow on the Home or Format tabs to change an object's color.

3. Click **More Fill Colors**, **More Outline Colors**, or **More Colors**, and then select a color from the **Standard** or **Custom** tab.

   ◆ To select a custom color, drag across the palette until the pointer is over the color you want, or choose a Color Model, and then enter the Hue, Sat, Lum, or Red, Green, and Blue values.

4. Click **OK**.

   The current selection is changed to the new color, plus the new color is added to the Recent Colors section of the menu and is now available to use throughout the presentation.

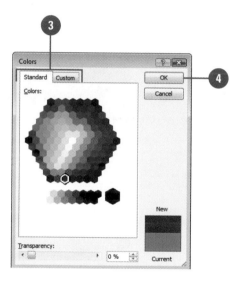

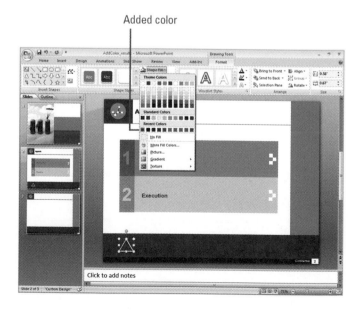

Added color

Adding a Background Style

Microsoft Certified Application Specialist

PP07S-1.2.2

In PowerPoint, you can add a background style to your presentation. A **background style** is a background fill made up of different combinations of theme colors (**New!**). When you change a presentation theme, the background styles change to reflect the new theme colors and backgrounds. To quickly see if you like a background style, you can point to one in the Background Styles gallery to display a live preview of it with the current slide. If you like it, you can apply it.

Add a Background Style

1. Click the **Design** tab to change the background of the selected slide, or click the **View** tab, and then click the **Slide Master View** tab to change the background of the selected slide master or slide layout.

2. Click the **Background Styles** button.

   The current style appears highlighted in the gallery.

3. Point to a style.

   A live preview (**New!**) of the style appears in the current slide, and a ScreenTip with the style name.

4. Click the style you want from the gallery to apply it to the selected slide, slide master (and all its slides), or slide layout.

   ◆ To apply the style to matching slides, all slides, selected slides, or slide master, right-click the style from the gallery, and then click the option you want.

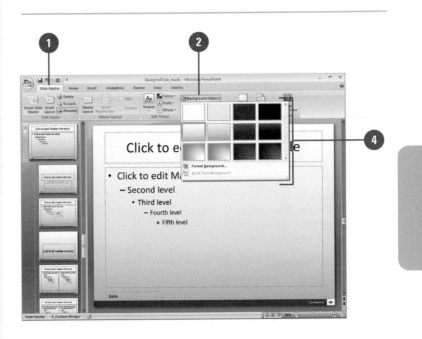

> ### Did You Know?
>
> ***You can reset the slide background.***
> Click the Design tab, click the Background Styles button, and then click Reset Slide Background.

Modifying a Background Style

PP07S-1.2.2

In PowerPoint, you can create a background style by adding a solid, a gradient, a texture, a pattern, or even a picture. A gradient background is a visual effect in which a solid color gradually changes from light to dark or dark to light. PowerPoint offers one-color and two-color gradient backgrounds with six styles: horizontal, vertical, diagonal up, diagonal down, from corner, and from title. For a one-color gradient background, the shading color can be adjusted lighter or darker, depending on your needs. You can also choose one of 24 professionally designed backgrounds in which the color gradient changes direction according to the shading style selected. In addition to a shaded background, you can also have a background with a texture, a pattern, or a picture. PowerPoint has several different textures, patterns, and pictures that you can apply to a presentation.

Create a Picture or Texture Background Style

1. Click the **Design** tab to change the selected slide background, or click the **View** tab, and then click the **Slide Master View** tab to change the selected slide master or slide layout background.

2. Click the **Background Styles** button, and then click **Format Background**.

3. Click the **Picture or texture fill** option to display the available fill effects.

4. Click the **Texture** button, and select a texture, or click **File**, **Clipboard**, or **ClipArt**, and select a picture.

5. To tile the background, select the **Tile picture as texture** check box, and then specify the offset x and y, scale x and y, alignment, and mirror type you want. If you clear the check box, specify the stretch background options you want.

6. Drag the **Transparency** slider to specify a percentage.

7. Click **Apply to All** to apply the fill effect to all slides, or click **Close** to apply only to the selected slide or slide master.

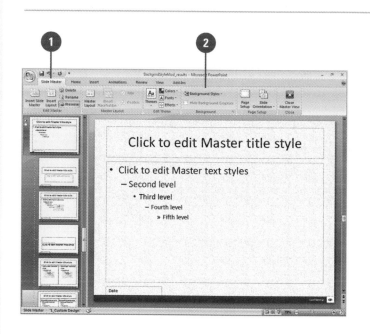

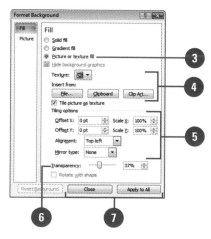

Create a Gradient Background Style

1. Click the **Design** tab to change the selected slide background, or click the **View** tab, and then click the **Slide Master View** tab to change the selected slide master or slide layout background.

2. Click the **Background Styles** button, and then click **Format Background**.

3. Click the **Gradient fill** option to display the available fill effects.

4. Click the **Preset Colors** button, and then select a color style.

5. Click the **Type** list arrow, and then click a type: Linear, Radial, Rectangle, or Path.

6. Click the **Direction** list arrow, select a direction, and then specify an angle.

7. Add or remove gradient stops, select a color, and then drag the **Stop position** slider to specify a percentage.

8. Drag the **Transparency** slider to specify a percentage.

9. Select or clear the **Rotate with shape** check boxes as desired.

10. Click **Apply to All** to apply the fill effect to all slides, or click **Close** to apply only to the selected slide or slide master.

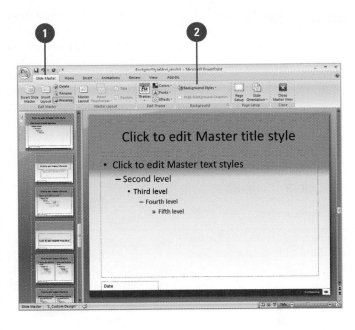

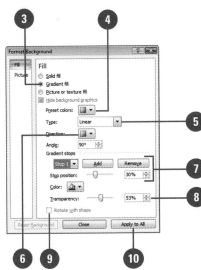

Did You Know?

You can create a solid fill background style. Click the Design tab, click the Background Styles button, click Background, click the Solid fill options, select a color, specify a color transparency, and then click Apply to All.

Saving a Template

A template file (.potx) saves all the customizations you made to slide masters, slide layouts, and themes to reuse in other presentations. You can save any presentation as a template file and use it to form the basis of your next presentation, which is useful for standard company presentations. Although you can store your template anywhere you want, you may find it handy to store it in the Templates folder that PowerPoint and Microsoft Office uses to store its templates. If you store your design templates in the Templates folder, those templates appear as options when you choose the New command on the Office menu, and then click My Templates.

Create a Custom Template

1. Open any presentation.

2. If you want, create and customize one or more slide masters or slide layouts.

3. Format the placeholders on the slide masters and slide layouts.

4. Place objects or insert pictures on the slide masters and slide layouts.

5. Add the footer and header information you want to include.

6. Click the **Office** button, and then click **Save As**.

7. Enter a name for your template.

8. Click the **Save as type** list arrow, and then click **PowerPoint Template**.

   Microsoft Office templates are typically stored in the following location:

   Windows Vista. C:/Users /*your name*/AppData/Roaming /Microsoft/Templates

   Windows XP. C:/Documents and Settings/*your name*/Application Data/Microsoft/Templates

9. Click **Save**.

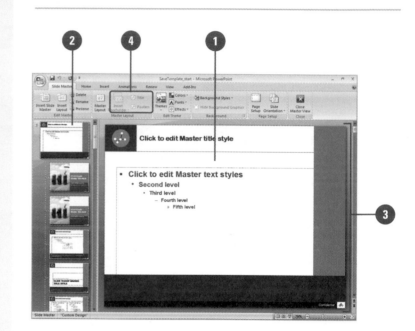

Change an Existing Design Template

1. Click the **Office** menu, and then click **Open**.

2. Click the **Files of type** list arrow, and then click PowerPoint Template.

3. If necessary, click the **Look in** list arrow, and then select the folder containing the template you want to open.

   Microsoft Office templates are typically stored in the following location:

   Windows Vista. C:/Users/ *your name*/AppData/Roaming /Microsoft/Templates

   Windows XP. C:/Documents and Settings/*your name*/Application Data/Microsoft/Templates

4. Click the template you want to change.

5. Click **Open**.

6. Make your changes to the template.

7. Click the **Office** button, and then click **Save As**.

8. Click the **Save as type** list arrow, and then click **PowerPoint Template**.

9. Click **Save**.

10. Click **Yes** to replace the existing file.

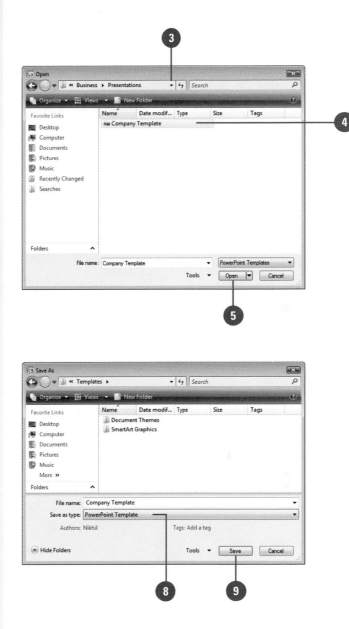

Drawing and Modifying Shapes

Introduction

When you want to add objects to your presentations, you can use Microsoft Office PowerPoint 2007 as a drawing package. PowerPoint offers a wide range of predesigned shapes, line options or freeform tools that allow you to draw, size, and format your own shapes and forms.

You can add three types of drawing objects to your PowerPoint presentations—shapes, lines, and freeforms. **Shapes** are preset objects, such as stars, circles, or ovals. **Lines** are simply the straight or curved lines (arcs) that can connect two points or are used as arrows. **Freeforms** are irregular curves or polygons that you can create as a free-hand drawing.

Once you create a drawing object, you can move, resize, nudge, copy or delete it on your slides. You can also change its style, by adding color, creating a fill pattern, rotating it, applying a shadow, or 3-D effect. Take a simple shape and by the time you are done adding various effects, it could become an attractive piece of graphic art for your presentation. If you'd like to use it later, you can save it to the Clip Organizer.

Object placement on your slides is a key factor to all of your hard work. Multiple objects should be grouped if they are to be considered one larger object. Grouping helps you make changes later on, or copy your objects to another slide. PowerPoint has the ability to line up your objects with precision—rulers and guides are part of the alignment process to help you. By grouping and aligning, you are assured that your drawing objects will be accurately placed.

What You'll Do

Draw, Resize and Insert Multiple Shapes

Add Text to a Shape

Draw Lines and Arrows

Create, Edit and Modify Freeforms

Copy and Move an Object

Add a Quick Style to a Shape and Shape Text

Apply Fill Colors and Shape Effects

Apply Picture, Texture and Gradient Fills

Create Shadows

Add 3-D Effects and Rotation Effects to a Shape

Distribute Objects and Align to Grids and Guides

Connect Shapes

Select Objects using the Selection Pane

Change Stacking Order

Rotate and Flip, Group and Ungroup a Shape

Insert AutoShapes from the Clip Gallery

Add a Shape to the Clip Organizer

Drawing and Resizing Shapes

Microsoft Certified Application Specialist

PP07S-3.3.2

PowerPoint supplies ready-made shapes, ranging from hearts to lightning bolts to stars. The ready-made shapes are available directly on the Shapes gallery on the Insert and Format tabs. Once you have placed a shape on a slide, you can resize it using the sizing handles. Many shapes have an **adjustment handle**, a small yellow or pink diamond located near a resize handle that you can drag to alter the shape. For precision when resizing, use the Size Dialog Box Launcher (**New!**) to specify the new size of the shape.

Draw a Shape

1. Click the **Home** or **Insert** tab.

2. Click the **Shapes** button.

3. Click the shape you want to draw.

4. Drag the pointer on the slide where you want to place the shape until the drawing object is the shape and size that you want.

   The shape you draw uses the line and fill color defined by the presentation's theme.

   TIMESAVER *To draw a proportional shape, hold down Shift as you drag the pointer.*

Did You Know?

You can quickly delete a shape. Click the shape to select it, and then press Delete.

You can draw a perfect circle or square. To draw a perfect circle or square, click the Oval or Rectangle button on the Shapes gallery, and then press and hold Shift as you drag.

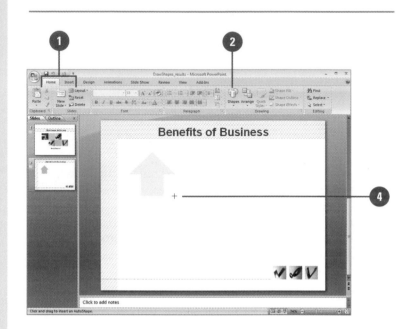

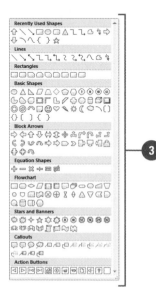

3 Shapes

Resize a Shape

1. Click the object you want to resize.

2. Drag one of the sizing handles.

   ◆ To resize the object in the vertical or horizontal direction, drag a sizing handle on the side of the selection box.

   ◆ To resize the object in both the vertical and horizontal directions, drag a sizing handle on the corner of the selection box.

   ◆ To resize the object with precise measurements, click the **Format** tab under Drawing Tools, and then specify exact height and width settings in the Size group.

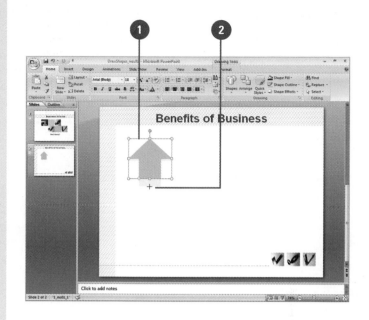

Adjust a Shape

1. Click the shape you want to adjust.

2. Click one of the adjustment handles (small yellow diamonds), and then drag the handle to alter the form of the shape.

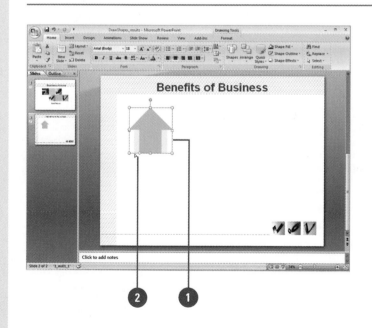

Did You Know?

You can replace a shape. Replace one shape with another, while retaining the size, color, and orientation of the shape. Click the shape you want to replace, click the Format tab, click the Edit Shape button, point to Change Shape, and then click the new shape you want.

Inserting Multiple Shapes

PP07S-3.3.2

If you need to draw the same shape several times on one or more slides in your presentation, you can use PowerPoint's Lock Drawing Mode to draw as many of the same shapes as you want without having to reselect it from the Shapes gallery. This can be a timesaver and save you extra mouse clicks. PowerPoint stays in Lock Drawing Mode until you press Esc. If a shape doesn't look the way you want, you can change the shape instead of redrawing it.

Insert Multiple Shapes

1. Click the **Home** or **Insert** tab.

2. Click the **Shapes** button.

3. Right-click the shape you want to add, and then click **Lock Drawing Mode**.

4. Drag the pointer on the slide where you want to place the shape until the drawing object is the shape and size that you want. Continue to draw shapes as you want in your presentation.

5. When you're done, press Esc.

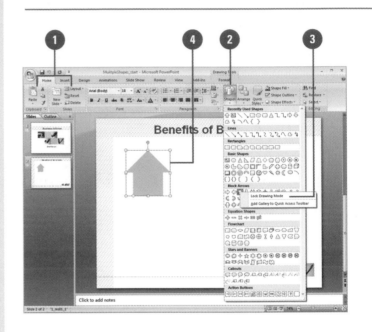

Change a Shape to Another Shape

1. Select the shape you want to modify.

2. Click the **Format tab** under Drawing Tools.

3. Click the **Edit Shape** button, point to **Change Shape**.

4. Click the shape you want to use from the Shapes gallery.

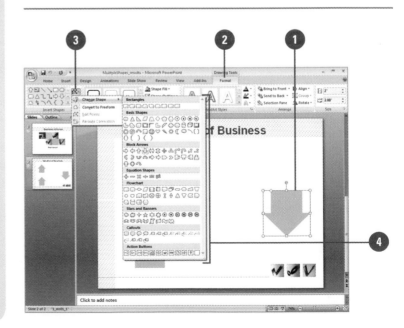

Adding Text to a Shape

PP07S-3.3.4

You can add text to a shape in the same way you add text to a text box. Simply, select the shape object, and then start typing. After you add text to a shape, you can select and change it to bullets or numbering. The text you add becomes part of the shape. If you rotate or flip the shape, the text rotates or flips too. You can use tools, such as an alignment button or Font Style, on the Mini-toolbar and Home tab to format the text in a shape like the text in a text box.

Add Text to a Shape

1. Click the shape in which you want to add text.

2. Type the text you want.

3. To edit the text in a shape, click the text to place the insertion point, and then edit the text.

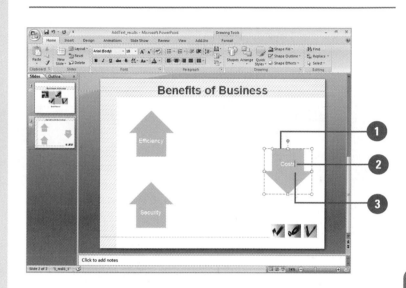

Add a Bulleted or Numbered List to a Shape

1. Click the text in the shape in which you want to add bullets or numbering to.

2. Click the **Home** tab.

3. Click the **Bullets** or **Numbering** button arrow, and then select the style you want.

   ◆ To select additional bullets and numbering options, click the **Bullets and Numbering** button arrow on the Mini-toolbar, and then click **Bullets and Numbering**.

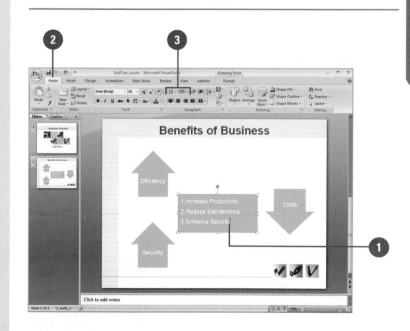

Drawing Lines and Arrows

The most basic drawing objects you can create on your slides are lines and arrows. Use the Line shape to create line segments or the Arrow shape to create arrows that emphasize key features of your presentation. You can quickly add multiple formatting to a line or arrow using Shape Quick Styles (**New!**) or change individual formatting—solid, dashed, or a combination—using the Shape Outline button. The Shape Outline button lets you change the type of line or arrow you want to create. You can add arrowheads to any lines on your slide.

Draw a Straight Line or Arrow

1. Click the **Home** or **Insert** tab.

2. Click the **Shapes** button, and then click a Line or Arrow shape in the Shapes gallery.

3. Drag the pointer to draw a line. The endpoints of the line or arrow are where you start and finish dragging.

4. Release the mouse button when the line or arrow is the correct length. Sizing handles appear at both ends of the line. Use these handles to resize your line or move an endpoint.

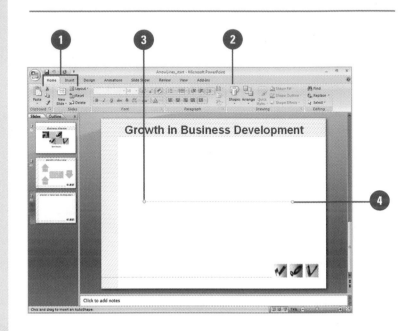

Add a Quick Style to a Line

1. Click the shape you want to apply a new or different Quick Style.

2. Click the **Home** tab.

3. Click the **Quick Styles** button.

4. Point to a style.

   A live preview (**New!**) of the style appears in the current shape.

5. Click the style you want from the gallery to apply it to the selected line.

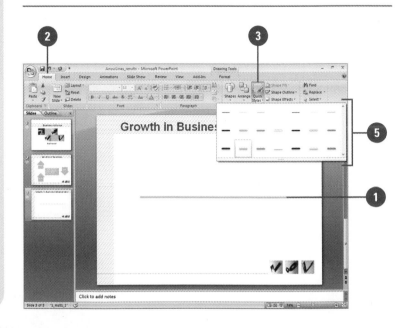

Edit a Line or Arrow

1. Click the line or arrow you want to edit.

2. Click the **Home** or **Format** tab under Drawing Tools.

3. Click the **Shape Outline** button to select a line or arrow style or thickness.

4. Click a color, or point to **Weight**, **Dashes**, or **Arrows**, and then select a style.

5. Drag a sizing handle to change the size or angle of the line or arrow.

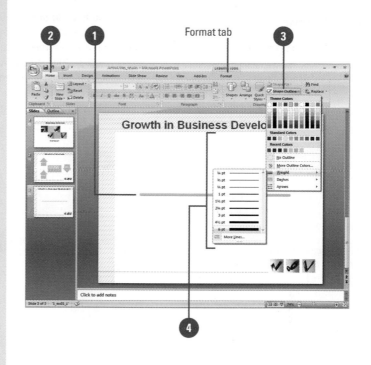

Format tab

Modify a Line or Arrow

1. Click the line or arrow you want to edit.

2. Click the **Home** or **Format** tab under Drawing Tools.

3. Click the **Shape Outline** button, point to **Weight**, **Dashes**, or **Arrows**, and then click **More Lines** or **More Arrows**.

4. For a line and arrow, select a width, compound type (double or triple lines), dash type, cap type—end of line style (square, round, or flat end), or join type—style used to connect two lines together (round, bevel, or miter).

5. For an arrow, select a begin type, end type, begin size, and end size.

6. Click **Close**.

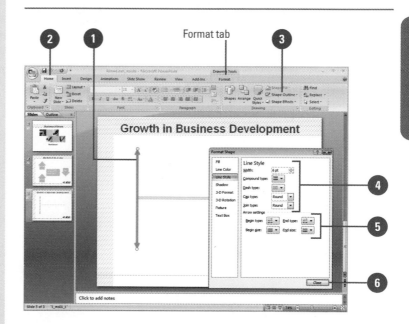

Format tab

Creating and Editing Freeforms

When you need to create a customized shape, use the PowerPoint freeform tools. Choose a freeform tool from the Lines category in the list of shapes. Freeforms are like the drawings you make with a pen and paper, except that you use a mouse for your pen and a slide for your paper. A freeform shape can either be an open curve or a closed curve. You can edit a freeform by using the Edit Points command to alter the vertices that create the shape.

Draw a Freeform Polygon

1. Click the **Home** or **Insert** tab.

2. Click the **Shapes** button and then **Freeform** in the Shapes gallery under Lines.

3. Click the slide where you want to place the first vertex of the polygon.

4. Move the pointer, and then click to place the second point of the polygon. A line joins the two points.

   ◆ To draw a line with curves, drag a line instead of clicking in steps 3 and 4.

5. Continue moving the mouse pointer and clicking to create additional sides of your polygon.

6. Finish the polygon. For a closed polygon, click near the starting point. For an open polygon, double-click the last point in the polygon.

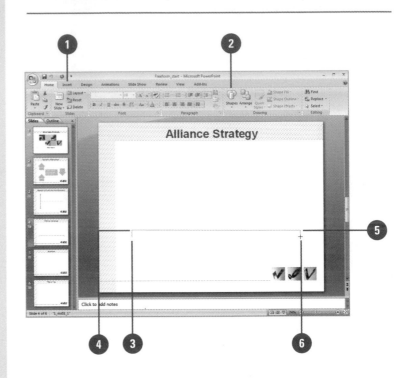

Did You Know?

You can convert a shape to a freeform. Select the shape, click the Edit Shape button, and then click Convert to Freeform.

You can switch between a closed curve and an open curve. Right-click the freeform drawing, and then click Close Path or Open Path.

Draw a Curve

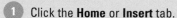

1. Click the **Home** or **Insert** tab.

2. Click the **Shapes** button and then **Curve** in the Shapes gallery.

3. Click the slide where you want to place the curve's starting point.

4. Click where you want your curve to bend. Repeat this step as often as you need to create bends.

5. Finish the curve. For a closed curve, click near the starting point. For an open curve, double-click the last point in the curve.

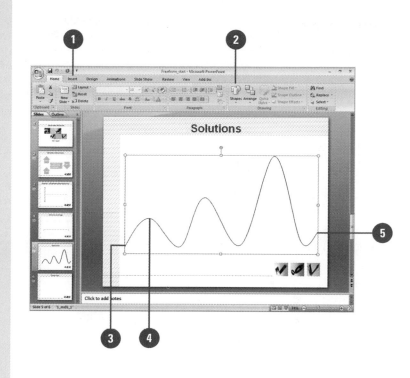

Scribble

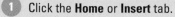

1. Click the **Home** or **Insert** tab.

2. Click the **Shapes** button and then **Scribble** in the Shapes gallery.

3. Drag the pointer across the screen to draw freehand.

Did You Know?

You can format freeforms and curves. Enhance freeforms and curves just as you can enhance other shapes. For example, you can add color or a pattern, change the line style, flip or rotate them, and add shadow or 3-D effects.

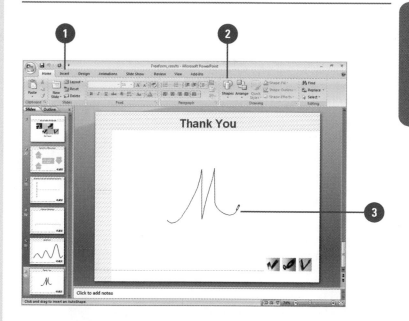

Modifying a Freeform

Microsoft
Certified
Application
Specialist

PP07S-3.3.2

Each **vertex** indicated by a black dot (a corner in an irregular polygon and a bend in a curve) has two attributes: its position, and the angle at which the curve enters and leaves it. You can move the position of each vertex and control the corner or bend angles. You can also add or delete vertices as you like. When you delete a vertex, PowerPoint recalculates the freeform and smooths it among the remaining points. Similarly, if you add a new vertex, PowerPoint adds a corner or bend in your freeform.

Move a Vertex in a Freeform

1. Click the freeform object you want to edit.

2. Click the **Format** tab under Drawing Tools.

3. Click the **Edit Shape** button, and then click **Edit Points**.

4. Drag one of the freeform vertices to a new location.

5. Click outside the freeform to set the new shape.

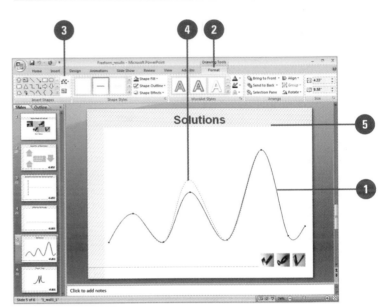

Insert a Freeform Vertex

1. Click the freeform object in which you want to insert a vertex.

2. Click the **Format** tab under Drawing Tools.

3. Click the **Edit Shape** button, and then click **Edit Points**.

4. Position the pointer on the curve or polygon border (not on a vertex), and then drag in the direction you want the new vertex.

5. Click outside the freeform to set the new shape.

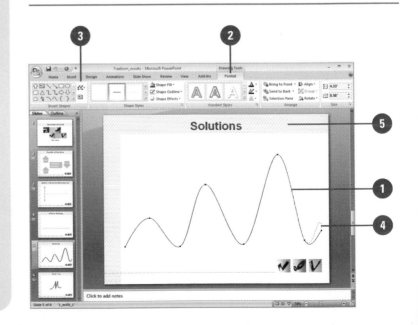

Delete a Freeform Vertex

① Click the freeform object you want to edit.

② Click the **Format** tab under Drawing Tools.

③ Click the **Edit Shape** button, and then click **Edit Points**.

④ Right-click the vertex and then click **Delete**.

⑤ Click outside the freeform to set the new shape.

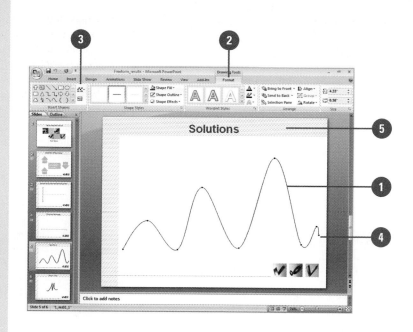

Modify a Vertex Angle

① Click the freeform object.

② Click the **Format** tab under Drawing Tools.

③ Click the **Edit Shape** button, and then click **Edit Points**.

④ Right-click a vertex and click **Auto Point (New!)**, **Smooth Point**, **Straight Point**, or **Corner Point**. Angle handles appear.

⑤ Drag one or both of the angle handles to modify the shape of the line segments going into and out of the vertex.

⑥ Click outside the freeform to set the new shape.

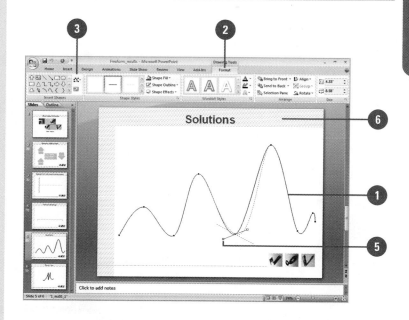

Copying and Moving Objects

Microsoft
Certified
Application
Specialist

PP07S-2.3.2

After you create a drawing object, you can copy or move it. You can quickly move objects using the mouse, or if you want precise control over the object's new position, use PowerPoint's Size and Position dialog box to specify the location of the drawing object. You can copy a selected object or multiple objects to the Office Clipboard and then paste the objects in other parts of the presentation. When you copy multiple items, the Office Clipboard task pane appears and shows all of the items stored there. You can paste these items of information into PowerPoint, either individually or all at once. You can also copy an object to another location in a single movement by using the Ctrl key.

Copy or Move an Object in One Step

1. Hold down the Ctrl key, and then drag the object to copy it, or simply drag the object to move it.

   Make sure you aren't dragging a sizing handle or adjustment handle. If you are working with a freeform and you are in Edit Points mode, drag the interior of the object, not the border, or you will end up resizing or reshaping the object, not moving it.

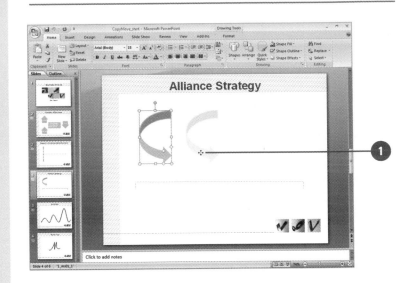

Copy or Move an Object

1. Select the object.

2. Click the **Home** tab.

3. Click the **Copy** button (to copy) or click the **Cut** button (to move).

4. Display the slide on which you want to paste the object.

5. Click the **Paste** button.

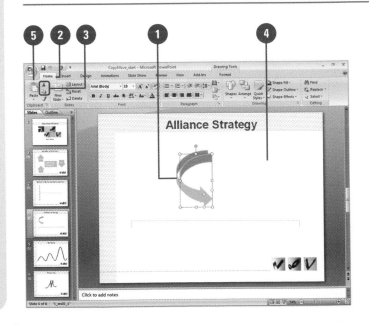

Move an Object with Precision

1. Select the object.

2. Click the **Format** tab under Drawing Tools.

3. Click the **Size Dialog Box Launcher**.

4. Click the **Position** tab to move the object and change settings as necessary.

5. Click **Close**.

> ### Did You Know?
>
> ***You can use the keyboard to nudge a drawing object.*** Click the object you want to nudge, and then press the Up, Down, Left or Right arrow key.

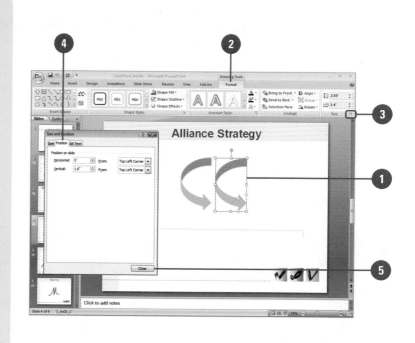

Copy Multiple Objects Using the Office Clipboard Task Pane

1. Select the multiple objects you want to copy.

2. Click the **Home** tab.

3. Click the **Copy** button.

4. Click the **Clipboard Dialog Box Launcher**.

5. Display the slide on which you want to paste the object(s).

6. In the Clipboard task pane, click an item to paste it on the slide.

> ### Did You Know?
>
> ***You can change the Office Clipboard options.*** To change the way the Office Clipboard works, click the Options button on the Office Clipboard task pane and turn on or off your preferences.

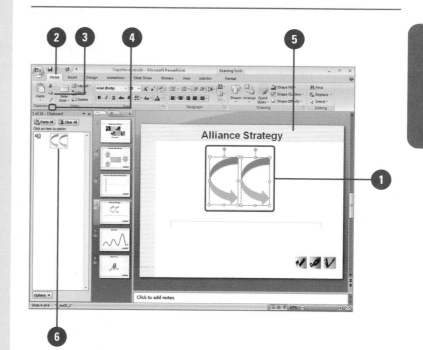

Adding a Quick Style to a Shape

Microsoft Certified Application Specialist

PP07S-2.1.3, PP07S-2.2.2

Instead of changing individual attributes of a shape—such as shape fill, shape outline, and shape effects—you can quickly add them all at once with the Shape Quick Style gallery. The Shape Quick Style gallery (**New!**) provides a variety of different formatting combinations. To quickly see if you like a Shape Quick Style, point to a thumbnail in the gallery to display a live preview (**New!**) of it in the selected shape. If you like it, you can apply it.

Add a Quick Style to a Shape

1. Click the shape you want to apply a new or different Quick Style.

2. Click the **Format** tab under Drawing Tools.

3. Click the scroll up or down arrow, or click the **More** list arrow in the Shapes Styles group to see additional styles.

   The current style appears highlighted in the gallery.

4. Point to a style.

   A live preview (**New!**) of the style appears in the current shape.

5. Click the style you want from the gallery to apply it to the selected shape.

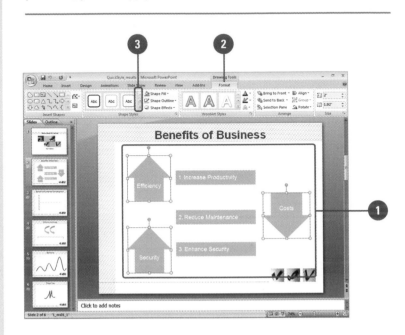

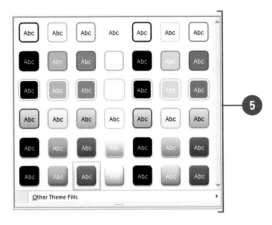

Adding a Quick Style to Shape Text

Microsoft Certified Application Specialist

PP07S-2.1.3, PP07S-2.2.2

Instead of changing individual attributes of text in a shape, such as text fill, text outline, and text effects, you can quickly add them all at once with the WordArt Quick Style gallery. The WordArt Quick Style gallery (**New!**) provides a variety of different formatting combinations. To quickly see if you like a WordArt Quick Style, point to a thumbnail in the gallery to display a live preview (**New!**) of it in the selected shape. If you like it, you can apply it.

Add a Quick Style to Shape Text

1. Click the shapes with the text you want to apply a new or different Quick Style.

2. Click the **Format** tab under Drawing Tools.

3. Click the scroll up or down arrow, or click the **More** list arrow in the WordArt Styles group to see additional styles.

   The current style appears highlighted in the gallery.

4. Point to a style.

   A live preview (**New!**) of the style appears in the current shape text.

5. Click the style you want from the gallery to apply it to the selected shape.

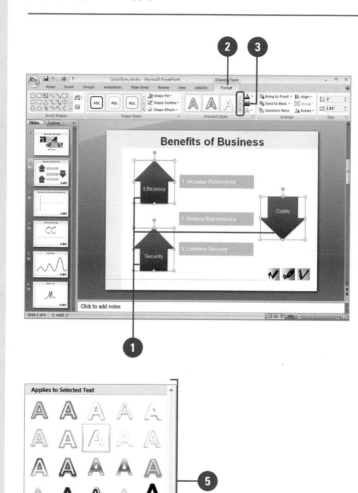

Applying Color Fills

Microsoft
Certified
Application
Specialist

PP07S-2.1.3, PP07S-3.4.1

When you create a closed drawing object such as a square, it applies the Shape Fill color to the inside of the shape, and the Shape Outline color to the edge of the shape. A line drawing object uses the Shape Outline color. You can set the Shape Fill to be a solid, gradient, texture or picture, and the Shape Outline can be a solid or gradient (**New!**). If you want to make multiple changes to a shape at the same time, the Format Shape dialog box allows you to do everything in one place. If the solid color appears too dark, you can make the color fill more transparent. If you no longer want to apply a shape fill to an object, you can remove it.

Apply a Color Fill to a Shape

1. Click the drawing object whose fill color you want to change.

2. Click the **Format** tab under Drawing Tools.

3. Click the **Shape Fill** button.

4. Select the fill color option you want.

5. To remove a color fill, click the **Shape Fill** button, and then click **No Fill**.

Did You Know?

You can set the color and line style for an object as the default. Right-click the object, and then click Set as Default Shape. Any new objects you create will use the same styles.

You can use the presentation background as the fill for a shape. Right-click the object, click Format Shape, click Fill in the left pane, click the Background option, and then click Close.

You can undo changes made in the Format Shape dialog box. Since changes made in the Shape Format dialog box are instantly applied to the shape, it is not possible to Cancel the dialog box. To remove changes, you can click the Undo button on the Quick Access Toolbar.

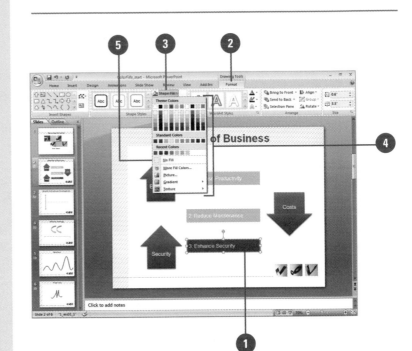

Apply a Shape Color Fill with a Transparency

1. Right-click the drawing object you want to modify, and then click **Format Shape**.

2. In the left pane, click **Fill**.

3. Click the **Solid Fill** option.

4. Click the **Color** button, and then select the fill color you want.

5. Drag the **Transparency** slider or enter a number from 0 (fully opaque) to 100 (fully transparent).

   All your changes are instantly applied to the shape.

6. Click **Close**.

   TROUBLE? *To cancel changes, click the Undo button on the Quick Access Toolbar.*

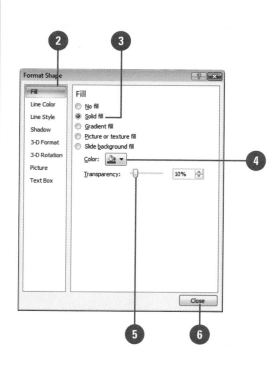

Apply a Color Outline to a Shape

1. Click the drawing object whose fill color you want to change.

2. Click the **Format** tab under Drawing Tools.

3. Click the **Shape Outline** button.

4. Select the outline color you want.

5. To remove an outline color, click the **Shape Outline** button, and then click **No Outline**.

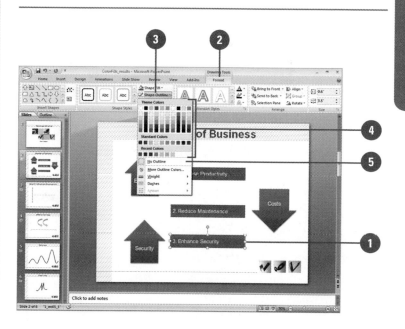

Applying Picture Fills

Microsoft
Certified
Application
Specialist

PP07S-2.1.3, PP07S-3.4.1

Applying a shape fill to a drawing object can add emphasis or create a point of interest in your presentation. You can insert a picture or clip art into a shape. You can insert a picture from a file or clip art from the Clip Art task pane, or paste one in from the Office Clipboard. Stretch a picture to fit across the selected shape or repeatedly tile the same picture horizontally and vertically to fill the shape. When you stretch a picture, you can also set offsets, which determine how much to scale a picture to fit a shape relative to the edges. A positive offset number moves the picture edge toward the center of the shape, while a negative offset number moves the picture edge away from the shape. If the picture appears too dark, you can make the picture more transparent.

Apply a Picture Fill to a Shape

1. Click the drawing object whose fill you want to change.

2. Click the **Format** tab under Drawing Tools.

3. Click the **Shape Fill** button, and then click **Picture**.

4. Locate and select a picture file you want.

5. Click **Insert**.

Did You Know?

You can undo changes made in the Format Shape dialog box. Since changes made in the Shape dialog box are instantly applied to the shape, it is not possible to Cancel the dialog box. To remove changes, you can click the Undo button on the Quick Access Toolbar.

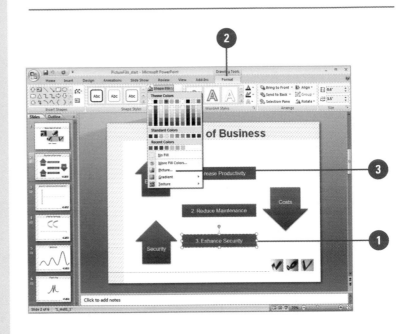

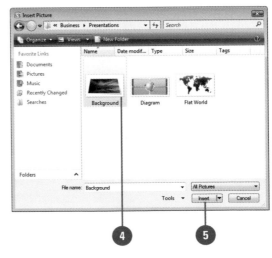

Apply a Custom Picture Fill

1. Right-click the drawing object you want to modify, and then click **Format Shape**.

2. In the left pane, click **Fill**.

3. Click the **Picture or texture fill** option.

4. Click one of the following buttons:

   ◆ **File** to insert a picture from a file.

   ◆ **Clipboard** to paste a picture from the Office Clipboard or another program. Copy the picture to the clipboard before you click this button.

   ◆ **Clip Art** to open the Clip Art task pane and insert a clip. In the Clip Art task pane, find the clip you want, and then click the clip to insert it. Select the Include from Office Online check box to search for online clip art.

5. Clear the **Tile picture as texture** check box.

6. Specify a stretch option percentage for the picture from the **Left**, **Right**, **Top**, and **Bottom** of the picture.

   Positive numbers move the picture edge toward the center and negative numbers move the edge away from the shape.

7. Drag the **Transparency** slider or enter a number from 0 (fully opaque) to 100 (fully transparent).

8. Select the **Rotate with shape** check box to rotate the picture with the shape's rotation.

9. Click **Close**.

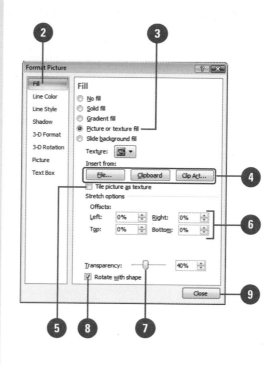

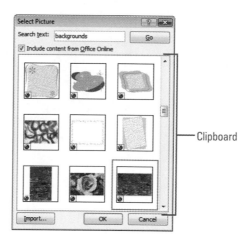

Clipboard

Applying Texture Fills

You can quickly apply a texture fill to a shape by using the Texture gallery or using the Format Shape dialog box to select custom options. Stretch a texture to fit across the selected shape or repeatedly tile the texture horizontally and vertically to fill the shape. If you tile a texture, you can also set offset, scale, alignment, and mirror options to determine the appearance of the texture in the selected shape. The offset x and y options determine how much to scale a texture to fit a shape relative to the edges, while scale x and y options determine horizontal and vertical scaling. If you want to play with the tile look, you can change the mirror type to determine whether the alternating tiles display a mirror or flip image with every other tile. If the texture doesn't provide enough contrast in the shape, you can make the texture more transparent.

Apply a Texture Fill to a Shape

1. Click the drawing object whose fill you want to change.

2. Click the **Format** tab under Drawing Tools.

3. Click the **Shape Fill** button.

4. Point to **Texture**, and then select a texture from the gallery.

Did You Know?

You can undo changes made in the Format Shape dialog box. Since changes made in the Shape dialog box are instantly applied to the shape, it is not possible to Cancel the dialog box. To remove changes, you can click the Undo button on the Quick Access Toolbar.

Apply a Custom Texture Fill

1 Right-click the drawing object you want to modify, and then click **Format Shape** or **Format Picture**.

2 In the left pane, click **Fill**.

3 Click the **Picture or texture fill** option.

4 Click the **Texture** button arrow, and then select a texture.

5 Select the **Tile picture as texture** check box.

6 Specify the following tiling options:

◆ **Offset x and y.** For offset x, enter a negative number to shift left and a positive number to shift right. For offset y, enter a negative number to shift up and a positive number to shift down.

◆ **Scale x and y.** For scale x, enter a percentage for horizontal scaling. For scale y, enter a percentage for vertical scaling.

◆ **Alignment.** Select an anchor position where the picture begins to tile.

◆ **Mirror type.** Specify an option to alternate the horizontal or vertical tile to display a mirror or flip image with every other tile.

7 Drag the **Transparency** slider or enter a number from 0 (fully opaque) to 100 (fully transparent).

8 Select the **Rotate with shape** check box to rotate the texture with the shape's rotation.

All your changes are instantly applied to the shape.

9 Click **Close**.

Applying Gradient Fills

Gradients are made up of two or more colors that gradually fade into each other. They can be used to give depth to a shape or create realistic shadows. Apply a gradient fill to a shape—now including lines (**New!**)—by using a gallery or presets for quick results, or by using the Format Shape dialog box for custom results. Four gradient modes are available: linear (parallel bands), radial (radiate from center), rectangle (radiate from corners), and path (radiate along path). A gradient is made up of several gradient stops, which are used to create non-linear gradients. If you want to create a gradient that starts blue and goes to green, add two gradient stops, one for each color. Gradient stops consist of a position, a color, and a transparency percentage.

Apply a Gradient Fill to a Shape

1. Click the drawing object whose fill you want to change.

2. Click the **Format** tab under Drawing Tools.

3. Click the **Shape Fill** button.

4. Point to **Gradient**, and then select a gradient from the gallery.

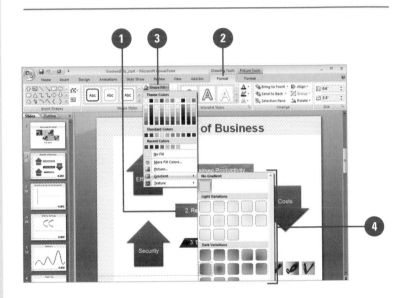

Apply a Gradient Fill with Presets

1. Right-click the drawing object you want to modify, and then click **Format Shape**.

2. In the left pane, click **Fill**.

3. Click the **Gradient fill** option.

4. Click the **Preset colors** button arrow, and then select the built-in gradient fill you want.

   All your changes are instantly applied to the shape.

5. Click **Close**.

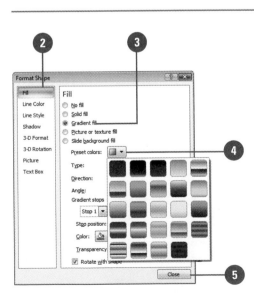

Apply a Custom Gradient Fill

1. Right-click the drawing object you want to modify, and then click **Format Shape**.

2. In the left pane, click **Fill**.

3. Click the **Gradient fill** option.

4. Click the **Preset colors** button arrow, and then select the built-in gradient fill you want.

5. Click the **Type** list arrow, and then select a gradient direction.

6. Click the **Direction** list arrow, and then select a shading progression. The options available depend on the gradient type.

7. If you selected the Linear type, specify the angle (in degrees) the gradient is rotated in the shape.

8. Specify the following tiling options:

   ◆ **Add.** Click Add, and then set the Stop position, Color, and Transparency you want.

   ◆ **Remove.** Click the Stop number list arrow, select a gradient stop, and then click Remove.

   ◆ **Stop position.** Specify a location for the color and transparency change in the gradient fill.

   ◆ **Color.** Click the Color button, and then select a color for the gradient stop.

   ◆ **Transparency.** Drag the Transparency slider or enter a number from 0 (fully opaque) to 100 (fully transparent) for the selected stop position.

9. Select the **Rotate with shape** check box to rotate the gradient with the shape's rotation.

   All your changes are instantly applied to the shape.

10. Click **Close**.

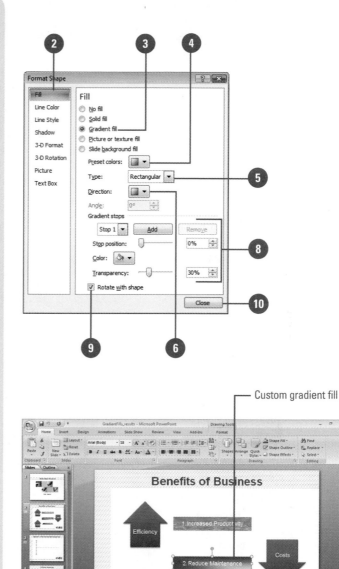

Custom gradient fill

Applying Shape Effects

Microsoft Certified Application Specialist

PP07S-2.1.3, PP07S-3.4.2

You can change the look of a shape by applying effects (**New!**), like shadows, reflections, glow, soft edges, bevels, and 3-D rotations. Apply effects to a shape by using the Shape Effects gallery for quick results, or by using the Format Shape dialog box for custom results. From the Shape Effects gallery you can apply a built-in combination of 3-D effects or individual effects to a shape. To quickly see if you like a shape effect, point to a thumbnail in the Shape Effects gallery to display a live preview (**New!**) of it in the selected shape. If you like it, you can apply it. If you no longer want to apply a shape effect to an object, you can remove it. Simply select the shape, point to the effect type in the Shape Effects gallery, and then select the No effect type option.

Add a Preset Effect to a Shape

1. Click the shape you want to apply a new or different shape effect.

2. Click the **Format** tab under Drawing Tools.

3. Click the **Shape Effects** button, and then point to **Preset**.

   The current effect appears highlighted in the gallery.

4. Point to an effect.

   A live preview (**New!**) of the style appears in the current shape.

5. Click the effect you want from the gallery to apply it to the selected shape.

6. To remove the preset effect, click the **Shape Effects** button, point to **Preset**, and then click **No Preset**.

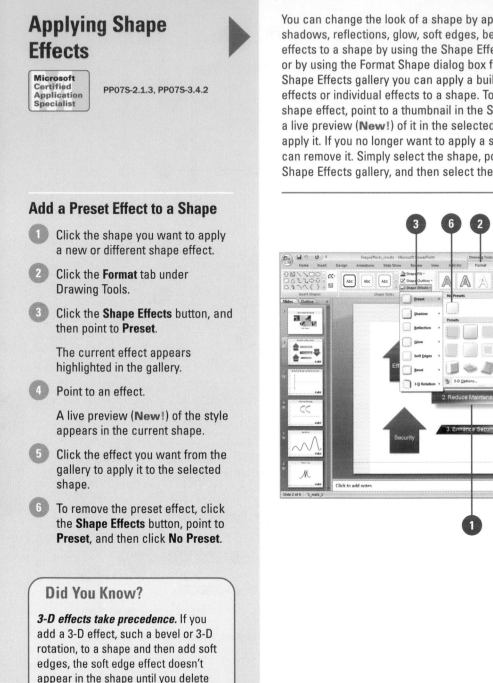

Did You Know?

3-D effects take precedence. If you add a 3-D effect, such a bevel or 3-D rotation, to a shape and then add soft edges, the soft edge effect doesn't appear in the shape until you delete the 3-D effect.

Add Individual Effects to a Shape

1. Click the shape you want to apply a new or different shape effect.

2. Click the **Format** tab under Drawing Tools.

3. Click the **Shape Effects** button, and then point to one of the following:

   ◆ **Shadow** to select No Shadow, one of the shadow types (Outer, Inner, or Perspective), or More Shadows.

   ◆ **Reflection** to select No Reflection or one of the Reflection Variations.

   ◆ **Glow** to select No Glow, one of the Glow Variations, or More Glow Colors.

   ◆ **Soft Edges** to select No Soft Edges, or a point size to determine the soft edge amount.

   ◆ **Bevel** to select No Bevel, one of the bevel variations, or More 3-D Settings.

   ◆ **3-D Rotation** to select No Rotation, one of the rotation types (Parallel, Perspective, or Oblique), or More 3-D Settings.

   When you point to an effect, a live preview (**New!**) of the style appears in the current shape.

4. Click the effect you want from the gallery to apply it to the selected shape.

Shadow

Glow

Bevel

Reflection

Soft edges

3-D Rotation

Creating Shadows

You can give objects on your slides the illusion of depth by adding shadows. PowerPoint provides several preset shadowing options, or you can create your own by specifying color, transparency, size, blur, angle, and distance (**New!**). You can change all these shadow options at the same time in the Format Shape dialog box. Instead of starting from scratch, you can select a preset shadow in the Format Shape dialog box, and then customize it.

Add a Preset Shadow to a Shape

1. Click the shape you want to apply a new or different shape effect.

2. Click the **Format** tab under Drawing Tools.

3. Click the **Shape Effects** button, and then point to **Shadow**.

   The current effect appears highlighted in the gallery.

4. Point to an effect.

   A live preview (**New!**) of the style appears in the current shape.

5. Click the effect you want from the gallery to apply it to the selected shape.

6. To remove the shadow, click the **Shape Effects** button, point to **Shadow**, and then click **No Shadow**.

Add a Custom Shadow to a Shape

1 Click the shape you want to apply a new or different shape effect.

2 Click the **Format** tab under Drawing Tools.

3 Click the **Shape Effects** button, point to **Shadow**, and then click **More Shadows**.

4 To customize a preset shadow, click the **Presets** button, and then select a starting shadow.

5 Specify the following custom options:

◆ **Color.** Select the color of the shadow.

◆ **Transparency.** Drag the slider or enter a number from 0 (fully opaque) to 100 (fully transparent).

◆ **Size.** Drag the slider or enter a number from 1 to 200 to set the shadow size relative to the original shape.

◆ **Blur.** Drag the slider or enter a number from 0 (no blur) to 25 (full blur) points to set the radius of the blur.

◆ **Angle.** Drag the slider or enter a number from 0 to 359 degrees to set the angle the shadow is drawn.

◆ **Distance.** Drag the slider or enter a number from 0 (no blur) to 25 (full blur) points to set the distance the shadow is drawn.

All your changes are instantly applied to the shape.

6 Click **Close**.

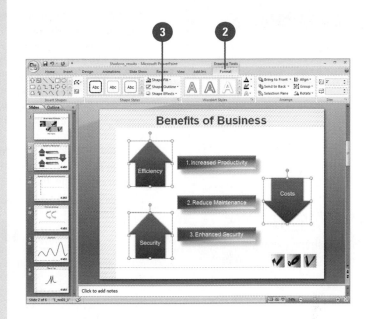

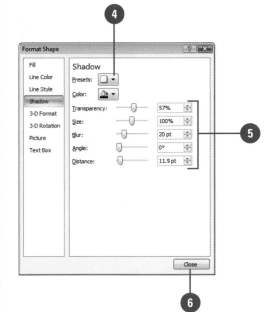

Adding 3-D Effects to a Shape

You can add the illusion of depth to your slides by adding a 3-D effect to a shape. Create a 3-D effect by using one of the preset 3-D styles, or use the 3-D format tools to customize your own 3-D style (**New!**). The settings you can control with the customization tools include the bevel (a 3-D top or bottom edge effect), the shape depth (distance of shape from its surface), the contour (raised border), the surface material and lighting. You can apply interesting surfaces—matte, plastic, metal, wire frame, soft or dark edges, flat, translucent, and clear (**New!**)—to a 3-D shape. In addition, you can change the type of lighting—neutral, warm, cool, flat, glow, and bright room (**New!**)—applied to a 3-D shape. Each lighting type defines one or more lights that illuminate a 3-D scene, not just for the shape. Each light contains a position, intensity, and color.

Add a 3-D Effect to a Shape

1. Click the shape you want to apply a new or different shape effect.

2. Click the **Format** tab under Drawing Tools.

3. Click the **Shape Effects** button, and then point to **Preset** or **Bevel**.

    The current effect appears highlighted in the gallery.

4. Point to an effect.

    A live preview (**New!**) of the style appears in the current shape.

5. Click the effect you want from the gallery to apply it to the selected shape.

6. To remove the 3-D effect, click the **Shape Effects** button, point to **Preset** or **Bevel**, and then click **No Preset** or **No Bevel**.

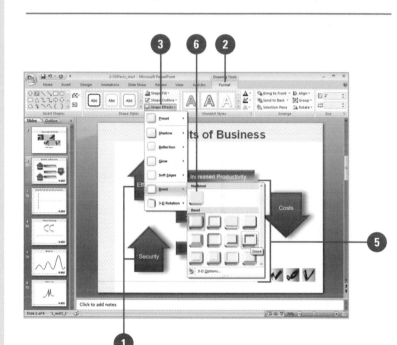

Add a Custom 3-D Effect to a Shape

1. Click the shape you want to apply a new or different shape effect.

2. Click the **Format** tab under Drawing Tools.

3. Click the **Shape Effects** button, point to **Preset** or **Bevel**, and then click **3-D Options**.

4. Specify the following custom options:

   ◆ **Bevel.** Click Top or Bottom to apply a raised edge to the top or bottom of a shape. The corresponding width and height numbers appear.

   ◆ **Depth.** Click the Color button to select a depth color, and then enter a depth number.

   ◆ **Contour.** Click the Color button to select a contour color, and then enter a size.

   ◆ **Surface.** Click Material to select a surface, and then click Lighting to specify the way light illuminates the 3-D shape.

   To rotate all of the lights around the front face of a shape, enter an angle.

   All your changes are instantly applied to the shape.

5. To remove 3-D formatting and restore default setting, click **Reset**.

6. Click **Close**.

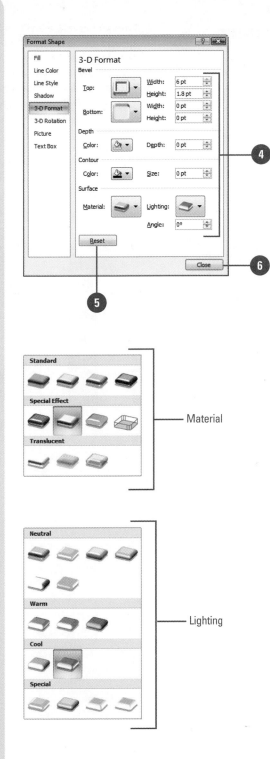

Material

Lighting

Adding 3-D Rotation Effects to a Shape

After you create a 3-D or even a 2-D shape, you can use 3-D rotation options to change the orientation and perspective of the shape. You can also create a 3-D rotation effect using one of the preset 3-D rotation styles, or you can use the 3-D rotation tools to create your own 3-D effect (**New!**). The settings control with the customization tools include the 3-D rotation (x, y, and z axis), text rotation, and object position (distance from ground).

Add a 3-D Rotation Effect to a Shape

1 Click the shape you want to apply a new or different shape effect.

2 Click the **Format** tab under Drawing Tools.

3 Click the **Shape Effects** button, and then point to **3-D Rotation**.

The current effect appears highlighted in the gallery.

4 Point to an effect.

A live preview (**New!**) of the style appears in the current shape.

5 Click the effect you want from the gallery to apply it to the selected shape.

6 To remove the 3-D rotation effect, click the **Shape Effects** button, point to **3-D Rotation**, and then click **No Rotation**.

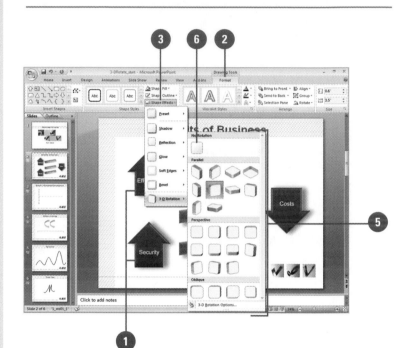

Add a Custom 3-D Rotation Effect to a Shape

1. Click the shape you want to apply a new or different shape effect.

2. Click the **Format** tab under Drawing Tools.

3. Click the **Shape Effects** button, point to **3-D Rotation**, and then click **3-D Options**.

4. Specify the following custom options:

   ◆ **Rotation x and y.** Change the orientation of the x (horizontal axis) and y (vertical axis). Use the arrow buttons to nudge the position left, right, up, and down.

   ◆ **Rotation z.** Change the position higher or lower than the shape. Use the arrow buttons to nudge the position clockwise or counter-clockwise.

   ◆ **Rotation perspective.** Change the field of view. Enter a number from 0 (parallel camera) to 120 (wide-angle camera). Use the arrow buttons to narrow or widen the view.

   ◆ **Text.** Select the Keep text flat check box to prevent text in a shape from rotating (always stays on top).

   ◆ **Object position.** Enter a distance from ground number to move the shape backward or forward in 3-D space.

   All your changes are instantly applied to the shape.

5. To remove 3-D formatting and restore default setting, click **Reset**.

6. Click **Close**.

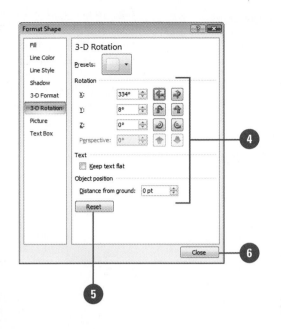

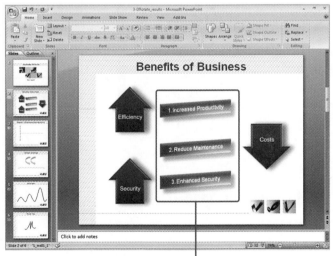

Custom 3-D rotation effect

Aligning Objects to Grids and Guides

Microsoft Certified Application Specialist

PP07S-3.5.4

Turn On or Turn Off the Visible Grid or Guides

1. Click the **Home** tab.

2. Click the **Arrange** button, point to **Align**, and then click **Grid Settings**.

   TIMESAVER *To quickly open the dialog box, right-click a blank slide area, and then click Grid and Guides.*

3. Select or clear the **Display grid on screen** check box.

4. Select or clear the **Display drawing guides on screen** check box.

6. Click **OK**.

Set Objects to Snap into Place

1. Click the **Home** tab.

2. Click the **Arrange** button, point to **Align**, and then click **Grid Settings**.

   TIMESAVER *To quickly open the Grid and Guides dialog box, right-click a blank area of the slide, and then click Grid and Guides.*

3. Select the **Snap objects to grid** check box or select the **Snap objects to other objects** check box.

4. Click **OK**.

PowerPoint guides can align an individual object or a group of objects to a vertical or horizontal guide. Turning on the visible grid or visible guides option makes it easier to create, modify, and align a shape. Within the Grid and Guides dialog box, you can select from a variety of options, such as snapping objects to the grid or to other objects and displaying drawing guides on-screen. To align several objects to a guide, you first turn the guides on. Then you adjust the guides and drag the objects to align them to the guide.

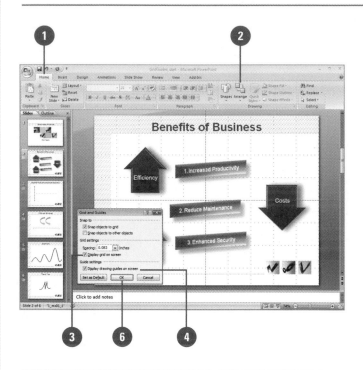

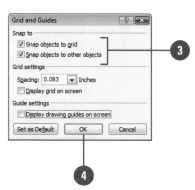

Add, Move, or Remove a Guide

◆ To move a guide, drag it.

◆ To add a new guide, press and hold the Ctrl key, and then drag the line to the new location. You can place a guide anywhere on the slide.

◆ To remove a guide, drag the guide off the slide. You cannot remove the original guides, they must be turned off.

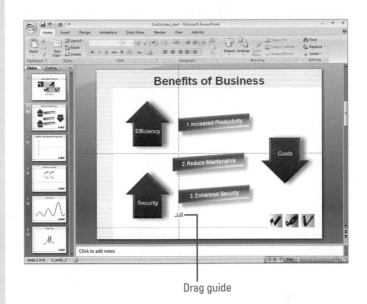

Drag guide

Align an Object to a Guide

1 If necessary, display guides on the screen (horizontal and vertical).

2 Drag the object's center or edge near the guide. PowerPoint aligns the center or edge to the guide.

Did You Know?

You can use the keyboard to override grid settings. To temporarily override settings for the grids and guides, press and hold the Alt key as you drag an object.

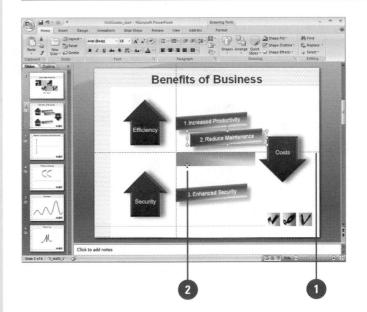

Aligning and
Distributing Objects

Microsoft
Certified
Application
Specialist   PP07S-3.5.3

In addition to using grids and guides to align objects to a specific point, you can align a group of objects to each other. The Align commands make it easy to align two or more objects relative to each other vertically to the left, center, or right, or horizontally from the top, middle, or bottom. To align several objects to each other evenly across the slide, either horizontally or vertically, you select them and then choose a distribution option. Before you select an align command, specify how you want PowerPoint to align the objects. You can align the objects in relation to the slide or to the selected objects.

Distribute Objects

① Select the objects you want to distribute.

② Click the **Home** tab.

③ Click the **Arrange** button, and then point to **Align**.

④ On the Align submenu, click the alignment method you want.

◆ Click **Align to Slide** if you want the objects to align relative to the slide.

◆ Click **Align Selected Objects** if you want the objects to align relative to each other.

⑤ On the Align submenu, click the distribution command you want.

◆ Click **Distribute Horizontally** to evenly distribute the objects horizontally.

◆ Click **Distribute Vertically** to evenly distribute the objects vertically.

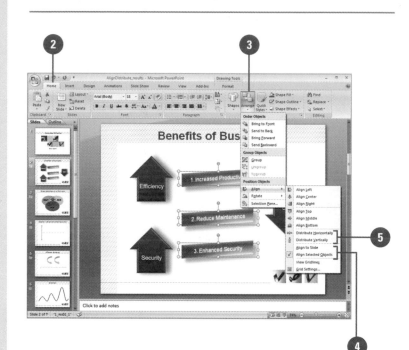

Align Objects with Other Objects

1. Select the objects you want to align.

2. Click the **Home** tab.

3. Click the **Arrange** button, and then point to **Align**.

4. On the Align submenu, click the alignment method you want.

   ◆ Click **Align to Slide** if you want the objects to align relative to the slide.

   ◆ Click **Align Selected Objects** if you want the objects to align relative to each other.

5. On the Align submenu, click the alignment command you want.

   ◆ Click **Align Left** to line up the objects with the left edge of the selection or slide.

   ◆ Click **Align Center** to line up the objects with the center of the selection or slide.

   ◆ Click **Align Right** to line up the objects with the right edge of the selection or slide.

   ◆ Click **Align Top** to line up the objects with the top edge of the selection or slide.

   ◆ Click **Align Middle** to line up the objects vertically with the middle of the selection or slide.

   ◆ Click **Align Bottom** to line up the objects with the bottom of the selection or slide.

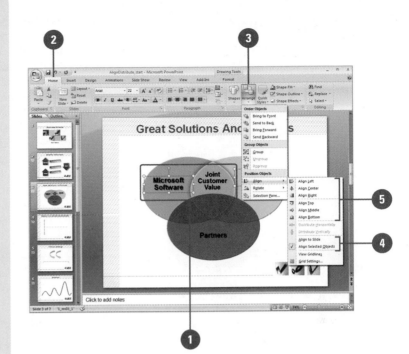

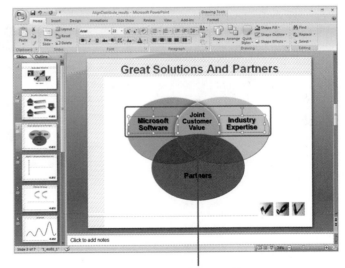

Arrange objects

Connecting Shapes

PowerPoint makes it easy to draw and modify flow charts and diagrams. Flow charts and diagrams consist of shapes connected together to indicate a sequence of events. With PowerPoint, you can join two objects with a connecting line. There are three types of connector lines: straight, elbow, and curved. Once two objects are joined, the connecting line moves when you move either object. The connecting line touches special connection points on the objects. When you position the pointer over an object, small red handles, known as connection sites, appear, and the pointer changes to a small box, called the connection pointer. You can drag a connection end point to another connection point to change the line or drag the adjustment handle (yellow diamond) to change the shape of the connection line. After you're done connecting shapes, you can format connector lines in the same way you format others lines in PowerPoint, including the use of Shape Quick Styles (**New!**).

Connect Two Objects

 Click the **Home** or **Insert** tab.

 Click the **Shapes** button, and then click a connector (located in the Lines category) in the Shapes gallery.

◆ To draw multiple connector lines, right-click the connector in the Shapes gallery, and then click Lock Drawing Mode.

TIMESAVER *In the Shapes gallery, point to shapes in the Lines category to display ScreenTips to locate a connector.*

 Position the pointer over an object handle (turns red).

 Drag the connector to the object handle (turns red) on another object.

TIMESAVER *To constrain the line at 15-degree angles from its starting point, hold down Shift while you drag.*

An attached connector point appears as red circles, while an unattached connector point appears as light blue (almost transparent).

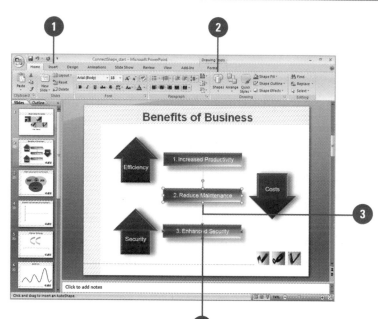

Drag to connect shapes

Change a Connector Line

① Click on the connector line you want to modify to select it.

② Use any of the following methods to change a connector line:

◆ Drag the adjustment handle (yellow diamond) to change the shape of the connector line.

◆ Drag a connection point (red circle) to another object handle to change a connection site, or right-click a connector line, and then click **Reroute Connectors**.

◆ Right-click a connector line, point to **Connector Types**, and then click the connector type to which you want change.

◆ Press Delete to remove it.

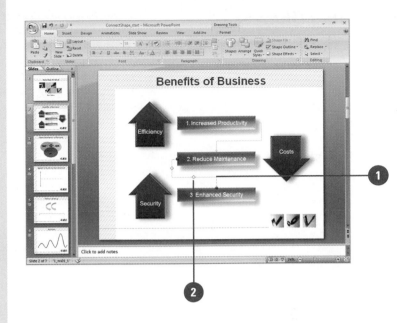

Format a Connector Line

① Click on the connector line you want to modify to select it.

To select more than one line, hold down Shift, and then click all the connector lines you want to modify.

② Click the **Format** tab under Drawing Tools.

③ Use any of the following formatting options:

◆ Click the **More** list arrow in the Shapes Styles group, point to a Quick Style, and then click the one you want.

◆ Click the **Shape Outline** button, and then select the options you want, such as color, weight, dashes, and arrows.

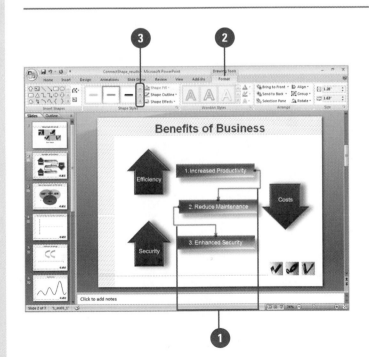

Selecting Objects Using the Selection Pane

Sometimes it's hard to select an object when it is behind another one. With the Selection task pane (**New!**), you can now select individual objects and change their order and visibility. When you open the Selection task pane, PowerPoint lists each shape on the current slide by name (in terms of object type). You can click a shape title to select a "hard-to-select" object on the slide, use the Re-order buttons to change the stacking order on the slide, or click the eye icon next to a shape title to show or hide "hard-to-see" individual objects.

Select Objects Using the Selection Pane

1. Display the slides with the objects you want to select.

2. Click the **Format** tab under Drawing or Picture Tools.

3. Click the **Selection Pane** button.

   Titles for all the shapes on the current slide appear in the task pane.

4. To select an object, click the title in the task pane.

5. To change the order of the objects, select an object, and then click the **Bring Forward** or **Send Back** buttons in the task pane.

6. To show or hide individual objects, click the eye icon in the task pane.

7. When you're done, click the **Close** button on the task pane.

Changing Stacking Order

Multiple objects on a slide appear in a stacking order, like layers of transparencies. Stacking is the placement of objects one on top of another. In other words, the first object that you draw is on the bottom and the last object that you draw is on top. You can change the order of this stack of objects by using Bring to Front, Send to Back, Bring Forward, and Send Backward commands on the Format tab under Drawing or Picture Tools.

Arrange a Stack of Objects

1. Select the object or objects you want to arrange.

2. Click the **Format** tab under Drawing or Picture Tools.

3. Click the stacking option you want.

   ◆ Click the **Bring to Front** button arrow, and then click **Bring to Front** or **Bring Forward** to move a drawing to the top of the stack or up one location in the stack.

   ◆ Click the **Send to Back** button arrow, and then click **Send to Back** or **Send Backward** to move a drawing to the bottom of the stack or back one location in the stack.

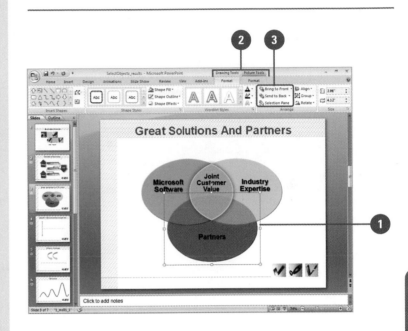

Did You Know?

You can view a hidden object in a stack. Press the Tab key or Shift+Tab to cycle forward or backward through the objects until you select the object you want.

Rotating and Flipping a Shape

Microsoft
Certified
Application
Specialist

PP07S-3.5.1

After you create an object, you can change its orientation on the slide by rotating or flipping it. Rotating turns an object 90 degrees to the right or left; flipping turns an object 180 degrees horizontally or vertically. For a more freeform rotation, which you cannot achieve in 90 or 180 degree increments, drag the green rotate lever at the top of an object. You can also rotate and flip any type of picture—including bitmaps—in a presentation. This is useful when you want to change the orientation of an object or image, such as changing the direction of an arrow.

Rotate an Object to any Angle

1. Click the object you want to rotate.

2. Position the pointer (which changes to the Free Rotate pointer) over the green rotate lever at the top of the object, and then drag to rotate the object.

3. Click outside the object to set the rotation.

Rotate or Flip an Object Using Preset Increments

1. Click the object you want to rotate or flip.

2. Click the **Format** tab under Drawing or Picture Tools.

3. Click the **Rotate** button, and then click the option you want.

   ◆ **Rotate.** Click Rotate Right 90° or Rotate Left 90°.

   ◆ **Flip.** Click Flip Vertical or Flip Horizontal.

Precisely Rotate an Object

1. Click the object you want to rotate.

2. Click the **Format** tab under Drawing or Picture Tools.

3. Click the **Rotate** button, and then click **More Rotation Options**.

4. Enter the angle of rotation, or click the up or down arrows.

5. Click **Close**.

Did You Know?

You can constrain the rotation to 15-degree increments. Press and hold Shift when you rotate the object.

You cannot rotate or flip some imported objects. Not all imported objects can be rotated or flipped. By ungrouping the imported object and then regrouping its components, you might be able to rotate or flip it.

Grouping and Ungrouping Shapes

Microsoft Certified Application Specialist

PP07S-3.5.3

Objects can be grouped, ungrouped, and regrouped to make editing and moving them easier. Rather than moving several objects one at a time, you can group the objects and move them all together. Grouped objects appear as one object, but each object in the group maintains its individual attributes. You can change an individual object within a group without ungrouping. This is useful when you need to make only a small change to a group, such as changing the color of a single shape in the group. You can also format specific shapes, drawings, or pictures within a group without ungrouping. Simply select the object within the group, change the object or edit text within the object, and then deselect the object. However, if you need to move an object in a group, you need to first ungroup the objects, move it, and then group the objects together again. After you ungroup a set of objects, PowerPoint remembers each object in the group and regroups those objects in one step when you use the Regroup command. Before you regroup a set of objects, make sure that at least one of the grouped objects is selected.

Group Objects Together

1. Select the objects you want to group together.

2. Click the **Format** tab under Drawing or Picture Tools.

3. Click the **Group** button, and then click **Group**.

Did You Know?

You can use the Tab key to select objects in order. Move between the drawing objects on your slide (even those hidden behind other objects) by pressing the Tab key.

You can use the shortcut menu to select Group related commands. Right-click the objects you want to group, point to Group, and then make your selections.

You can no longer ungroup tables. Due to the increased table size and theme functionality, tables can no longer be ungrouped.

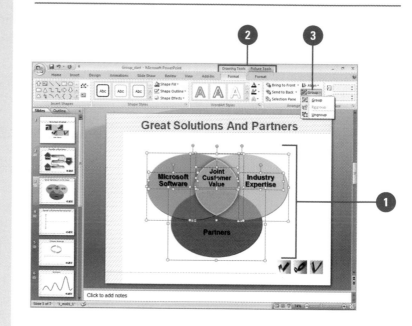

Ungroup a Drawing

1. Select the grouped object you want to ungroup.

2. Click the **Format** tab under Drawing or Picture Tools.

3. Click the **Group** button, and then click **Ungroup**.

See Also

See "Selecting Objects Using the Selection Pane" on page 142 for information on selecting "hard-to-select" objects.

Regroup a Drawing

1. Select one of the objects in the group of objects you want to regroup.

2. Click the **Format** tab under Drawing or Picture Tools.

3. Click the **Group** button, and then click **Regroup**.

Did You Know?

You can troubleshoot the arrangement of objects. If you have trouble selecting an object because another object is in the way, you can use the Selection pane to help you select it.

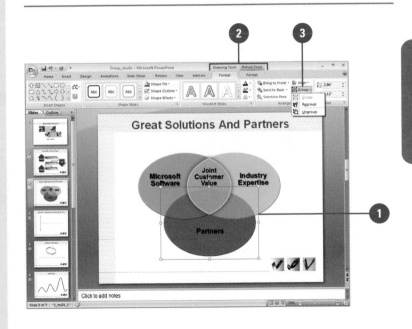

Inserting AutoShapes from the Clip Gallery ▶

In addition to drawing shapes, you can also insert AutoShapes, such as computers and furniture, from the Clip Art task pane. These AutoShapes are called **clips**. The Clip Art task pane gives you a miniature of each clip. You can click the clip you want to insert onto your slide or click the clip list arrow to select other options, such as previewing the clip or searching for similar clips. After you insert an AutoShape, you can add text to it. You can format the text in an AutoShape in the same way you format text in a word processing program.

Insert an AutoShape from the Clip Gallery

1. Click the **Insert** tab.

2. Click the **Clip Art** button.

3. Click the **Results should be** list arrow, and then select the **Clip Art** check box, if necessary.

4. Type **autoshape** in the Search for box.

5. Click **Go**.

6. Click the shape you want onto your slide. If necessary, use the scroll arrows to display more AutoShapes.

7. When you're done, click the **Close** button on the task pane.

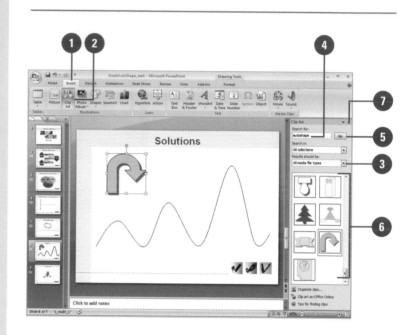

Find Similar AutoShapes in the Clip Gallery

1 Click the **Insert** tab.

2 Click the **Clip Art** button.

3 Type **autoshape** in the Search for box.

4 Click **Go**.

5 Point to the AutoShape in which you want to find a similar one.

6 Click the list arrow, and then click **Find Similar Style**.

The similar AutoShape styles appear in the results box.

7 When you're done, click the **Close** button on the task pane.

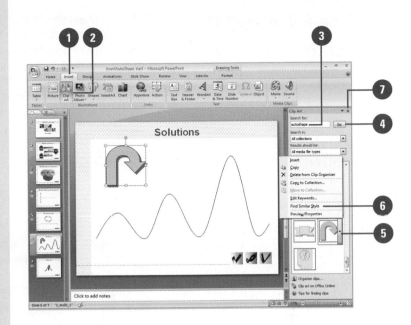

Adding a Shape to the Clip Organizer

After spending time creating an object, you might want to save it for use in future presentations. You can add any object you create to the Microsoft Clip Organizer—an organized collection of clip art, pictures, videos, and sounds that comes with PowerPoint. You can also find a picture in the Clip Organizer and use it as the basis for the logo for your home business. For example, you could use the basket of bread image for a home bakery.

Add Your Own Shape to the Clip Organizer

1. Select the drawing object you want to add to the Clip Organizer.

2. Click the **Copy** button on the Home tab.

3. Click the **Insert** tab, and then click the **Clip Art** button.

4. Click **Organize Clips** at the bottom of the Clip Art task pane.

5. Click the collection folder you want to add the clip to.

6. Click the **Edit** menu in the Clip Organizer, and then click **Paste**.

7. Click the **Close** button to close the Microsoft Clip Organizer.

Did You Know?

The AutoImport dialog box doesn't automatically open on first run. When Clip Organizer runs for the first time, it no longer calls the AutoImport dialog box (**New!**). However, you can click the File menu, point to Add Clips to Organizer, and then click Automatically to run it.

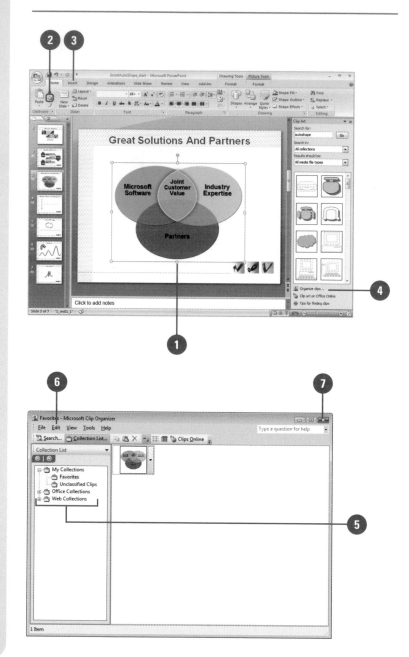

Inserting Pictures and Multimedia

5

Introduction

Although well-illustrated slides can't make up for a lack of content, you can capture your audiences' attention if your slides are vibrant and visually interesting. You can easily enhance a slide by adding a picture—one of your own or one of the hundreds that come with Microsoft Office PowerPoint 2007. If you have the appropriate hardware, such as a sound card and speakers, you can also include sound files and video clips in your presentation.

Microsoft Office comes with a vast array of ClipArt, and there are endless amounts available through other software packages or on the Web. When going online to look at clips, you can categorize them so that it's easier to find the best choice for your presentation. You can use the Microsoft Online Web site to search for and download additional clip art.

With all of your digital photos or scanned pictures, you can organize them in an album. Certain elements, such as adding text or oval frames, make cataloging your pictures an easier process. If you need to modify your pictures, you can resize them, compress them for storage, change their brightness or contrast, recolor them, or change their shape by cropping them.

WordArt is another feature that adds detail to your slide presentation. Available in other Office applications, WordArt can bring together your slides—you can change it s color, shape, shadow, or size. Because WordArt comes with so many style choices, time spent customizing your slides is minimal.

Another element that will give your presentation a real professional look and feel is the addition of movie clips or sounds. Imagine watching a slide show presentation with music playing at key points or starting a slide show with a movie clip that loosens up the audience.

What You'll Do

Insert Multimedia Clips

Add and Remove Clips

Organize Clips into Categories

Locate and Insert Clip Art

Access Clip Art on the Web

Insert a Picture

Examine Picture File Formats

Create a Photo Album

Add a Quick Style to a Picture

Apply a Shape and Border to a Picture

Apply Picture Effects

Modify Picture Size

Modify Picture Brightness and Contrast

Crop, Rotate and Recolor a Picture

Create and Format WordArt Text

Apply and Modify WordArt Text Effects

Insert Movies and Sounds

Record Sounds

Set Movie and Sound Play Options

Play Movies and Sounds

Inserting Multimedia Clips

Microsoft Certified Application Specialist

PP07S-2.3.4, PP07S-3.3.3

PowerPoint provides access to hundreds of professionally designed pieces of clip art. These clips include clip art, pictures, photographs, sounds, and videos. All Office 2007 programs includes **Microsoft Clip Organizer**, which organizes these objects into categories and gives you tools to help locate the clips you need quickly. You can extend the usefulness of the Clip Organizer by importing your own objects. The Clip Art task pane helps you search for clip art and access the clip art available in the Clip Organizer.

Clip Art

Clip art objects (pictures and animated pictures) are images made up of geometric shapes, such as lines, curves, circles, squares, and so on. These images, known as vector images, are mathematically defined, which makes them easy to resize and manipulate. A picture in the Microsoft Windows Metafile (.wmf) file format is an example of a vector image.

Pictures

Pictures, on the other hand, are not mathematically defined. They are **bitmaps**, images that are made up of dots. Bitmaps do not lend themselves as easily to resizing because the dots can't expand and contract when you enlarge or shrink your picture. You can create a picture using a bitmap graphics program such as Adobe Photoshop, Microsoft Paint, or Paint Shop Pro by drawing or scanning an image or by taking a digital photograph.

Sounds

A **sound** is a file that makes a sound. Some sounds play on your computer's internal speakers (such as the beep you hear when your operating system alerts you to an error), but others require a sound card and speakers. You can use the Windows accessory called **Windows Media Player** to listen to sound clips.

Videos

A **video** can be animated pictures, such as cartoons, or it can be digital video prepared with digitized video equipment. Although you can play a video clip on most monitors, if it has sound, you need a sound card and speakers to hear the clip.

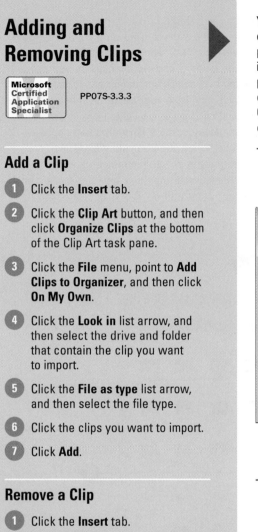
Adding and Removing Clips

Microsoft
Certified
Application
Specialist

PP07S-3.3.3

Add a Clip

1. Click the **Insert** tab.

2. Click the **Clip Art** button, and then click **Organize Clips** at the bottom of the Clip Art task pane.

3. Click the **File** menu, point to **Add Clips to Organizer**, and then click **On My Own**.

4. Click the **Look in** list arrow, and then select the drive and folder that contain the clip you want to import.

5. Click the **File as type** list arrow, and then select the file type.

6. Click the clips you want to import.

7. Click **Add**.

Remove a Clip

1. Click the **Insert** tab.

2. Click the **Clip Art** button, and then click **Organize Clips** at the bottom of the Clip Art task pane.

3. Point to the clip you want to remove, and then click the list arrow.

4. To delete the clip from all Clip Organizer categories, click **Delete from Clip Organizer**.

   To remove the clip from just one category, click **Delete** From the listed category.

You might want to add pictures and categories to the Clip Organizer for easy access in the future. You can import your own clips (pictures, photographs, sounds, and videos) into the Clip Organizer. For example, if you have a company logo that you plan to include in more than one presentation, add it to the Clip Organizer. You can also add groups of clips to the Clip Organizer. If you no longer need a picture in the Clip Organizer, you can remove it, which also saves space on your computer.

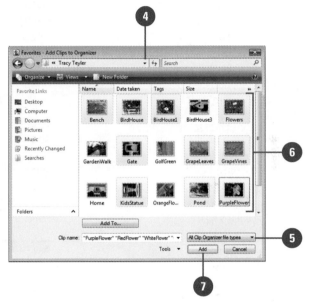

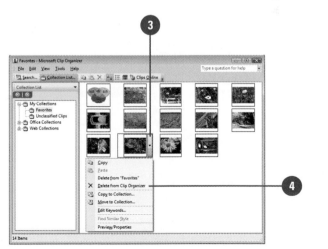

Organizing Clips into Categories

The clips that come with Microsoft Office PowerPoint 2007 are already organized, but if you've added clips without organizing them, it's probably hard to find what you need in a hurry. The Microsoft Clip Organizer sorts clip art images, pictures, sounds, and motion clips into categories. The Clip Organizer allows you to organize and select clips from Microsoft Office, from the Web, and from your personal collection of clips. To help you quickly locate a clip, you can place it in one or more categories. You can also assign one or more keywords to a clip and modify the description of a clip. When you add media files, Clip Organizer automatically creates new sub-collections under My Collections. These files are named after the corresponding folders on your hard disk. To help you find clips later on, Clip Organizer also creates search keywords based on the file's extension and folder name.

Categorize a Clip

1 Click the **Insert** tab.

2 Click the **Clip Art** button, and then click **Organize Clips** at the bottom of the Clip Art task pane.

3 In Clip Organizer, click the **File** menu, point to **Add Clips to Organizer**, and then click **On My Own**.

4 Locate the folder that contains the clip you want to add, and then select the clip.

5 Click the **Add To** button.

6 Click the collection to which you want to add the clip, or click **New** to create a new folder.

7 Click **OK**.

8 Click **Add**.

Did You Know?

You can create a new collection. In the Clip Organizer, click the File menu, click New Collection, type a new collection name, and then click OK.

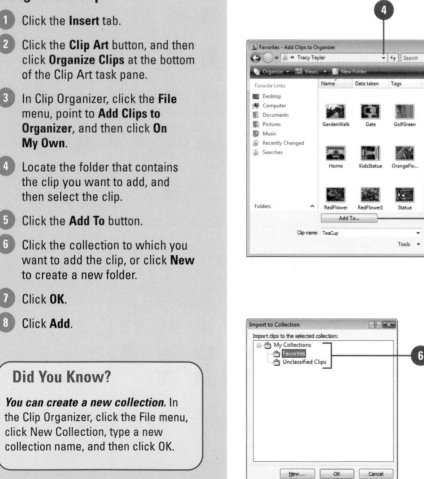

Change Clip Properties

1 Click the **Insert** tab.

2 Click the **Clip Art** button, and then click **Organize Clips** at the bottom of the Clip Art task pane.

3 To create a new collection folder, click the **File** menu, click **New Collection**, type a name, select a location, and then click **OK**.

4 In the Clip Organizer, find and point to the clip you want to categorize or change the properties of, click the list arrow, and then click one of the following:

- ◆ Click **Copy to Collection** to place a copy of the clip in another category.

- ◆ Click **Move to Collection** to move the clip to another category.

- ◆ Click **Edit Keywords** to edit the caption of the clip and to edit keywords used to find the clip.

5 Click the **Close** button to close the Clip Organizer dialog box.

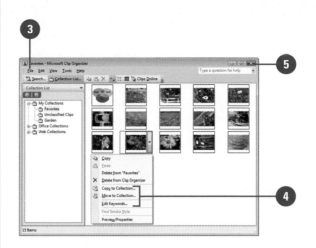

Create a new collection

Edit keywords

Did You Know?

You can change clip properties in the Clip Art task pane. In the Clip Art task pane, point to a clip, click the list arrow next to the clip, and then click Copy to Collection, Move to Collection, Edit Keywords, and Delete from Clip Organizer.

Locating and Inserting Clip Art

Microsoft Certified Application Specialist

PP07S-3.3.3

To add a clip art image to a slide, you can use a slide layout with a content placeholder and simply click the Insert Clip Art icon. Or click the Insert Clip Art button on the Insert tab to open the Clip Art task pane. The Clip Art task pane helps you search for clip art and access the clip art available in the Clip Organizer. You can limit search results to a specific collection of clip art or a specific type of media file. After you find the clip art you want, you can click it to insert it, or point to it to display a list arrow. Then click an available command, such as Insert, Find Similar Style, Edit Keywords, and Delete from Clip Organizer.

Locate Clip Art by Keyword

1 Click the **Insert** tab, and then click the **Clip Art** button.

2 Type the keyword(s) associated with the clip you are looking for.

To narrow your search, do one of the following:

◆ To limit search results to a specific collection of clip art, click the **Search In** list arrow, and then select the collections you want to search.

◆ To limit search results to a specific type of media file, click the **Results Should Be** list arrow, and then select the check box next to the types of clips you want to find.

3 Click **Go**.

Clips matching the keywords appear in the Results list.

4 Click the **Close** button on the task pane.

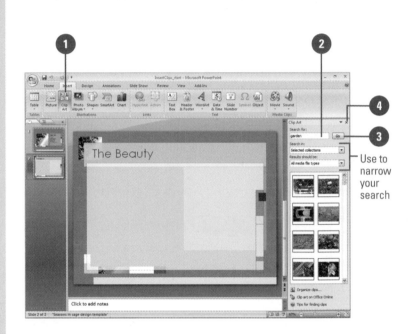

Use to narrow your search

Did You Know?

You can find similar clips. In the Clip Art task pane, click the list arrow next to the clip in which you want to find similar clips, and then click Find Similar Style.

Insert a Clip Art Image Using a Slide Layout

1. Click the **Home** tab.

2. Click the **New Slide** button arrow, and then click a slide layout that includes the clip art content placeholder.

3. In the content placeholder, click the **Insert Clip Art** icon.

4. In the Clip Art task pane, click the Search for box, type what you want to search for, and then click **Go**.

5. Click the clip you want.

6. Click the **Close** button on the task pane.

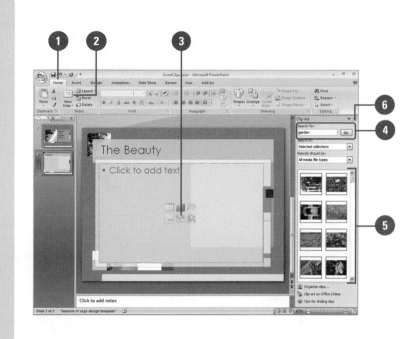

Insert a Clip Art Image Using the Insert Clip Art Task Pane

1. Click the **Insert** tab, and then click the **Clip Art** button.

2. In the Clip Art task pane, click in the Search for box, type what you want to search for, and then click **Go**.

3. Click the clip you want, and then resize it, if necessary.

4. Click the **Close** button on the task pane.

Did You Know?

You can drag a picture. You can also drag a picture from the Clip Art task pane to your slide.

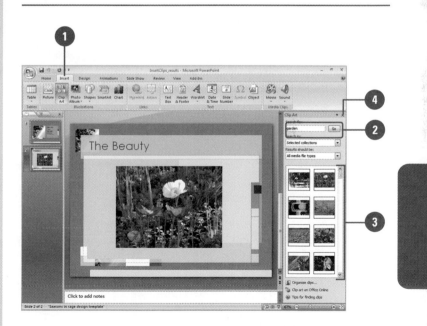

Accessing Clip Art on the Web

If you can't find the image that you want in the Clip Organizer, you can search for additional images in Clip art on Office Online, a clip gallery that Microsoft maintains on its Web site. To access Clip Art on Office Online, you can click the link at the bottom of the Clip Art task pane or click the Clips Online button on the Clip Organizer toolbar. This launches your Web browser and navigates you directly to the Office Online Web site, where you can access thousands of free clip art images.

Open Clips Online

1. Click the **Insert** tab.

2. Click the **Clip Art** button.

3. Click **Clip art on Office Online**.

4. Establish a connection to the Internet.

   Your Web browser displays the Microsoft Office Online Clip Art and Media Home Web page.

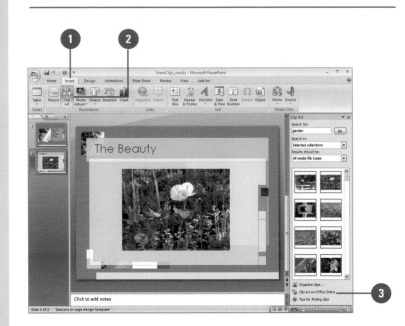

View Clips in a Category

1. If necessary, click the **Accept** button on the Clips Online Web page.

2. Scroll down to the Browse Clip Art And Media section, and then click the name of the category you want.

Search for a Clip

1. Click the **Search** list arrow on the Office Online Web page, and then select the media type you want: Clip Art, Photos, Animations, or Sounds.

2. Click the Search box.

3. Type a keyword.

4. Click the **Search** button.

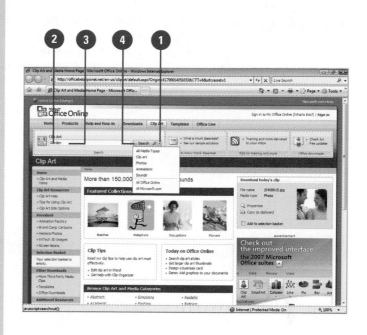

Download a Clip

1. Once you have displayed a list of clips on the Office Online Web page, select the check box below a clip to add it to your selection basket.

   You can select as many as you want. Clear the check box to deselect a clip.

2. Click Download 1 Item (will vary depending on the number of items you are downloading), review the Terms of Use, and then click Accept.

3. If a security virus warning dialog box appears, click **Yes**, and then click **Continue**.

4. Click **Download Now**, and then click **Open**.

5. The clip is stored on your hard disk and shown in your Clip Organizer where you can categorize it.

Inserting a Picture

Microsoft Certified Application Specialist

PP07S-1.2.2, PP07S-3.3.1

PowerPoint makes it possible for you to insert pictures, graphics, scanned photographs, art, photos, or artwork from a CD-ROM or other program into a slide. When you use the Picture button on the Insert tab, you specify the source of the picture. When you insert pictures from files on your hard disk drive, scanner, digital camera, or Web camera, PowerPoint allows you to select multiple pictures, view thumbnails of them, and insert them all at once, which speeds up the process.

Insert a Picture from a File

1. Click the **Insert** tab.

2. Click the **Picture** button.

3. Click the **Look in** list arrow, and then select the drive and folder that contain the file you want to insert.

4. Click the file you want to insert.

5. Click **Insert**.

   ◆ To link a picture file, click the **Insert** button arrow, and then click **Link to File**.

   ◆ To insert and link a picture file, click the **Insert** button arrow, and then click **Insert and Link**.

   TROUBLE? *If you see a red "x" instead of a picture or motion clip in your presentation, then you don't have a graphics filter installed on your computer for that clip.*

Did You Know?

You can change a picture. If you no longer want to use a picture, you can change it instead of deleting it and inserting another one. Select the picture, click the Change Picture button on the Format tab, select a picture, and then click Insert.

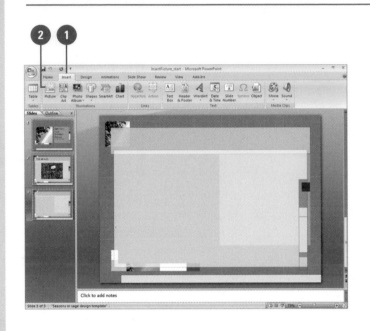

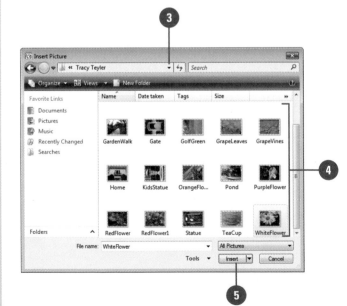

Examining Picture File Formats

The following table lists the default graphic formats available in PowerPoint. If the graphic format you need is not in the list, you can use Office Setup's maintenance feature to install additional graphic formats—such as Macintosh Graphics (PICT), Encapsulated Postscript (EPS), or WordPerfect Graphics (WPG)—using the Add or Remove Features option. See "Diagnosing and Repairing Problems" on page 28 for more information on using the maintenance feature.

Supported Graphic File Formats

Save As file type	Extension	Used to save a
GIF (Graphics Interchange Format)	.gif, .gfa	Slide as a graphic for use on Web pages; support 256 colors; best for scanned images and animation
JPEG (Joint Photographic Experts Group)	.jpeg, .jpg .jfif, .jpe	Slide as a graphic for use on Web pages; supports 16 millions colors; best for photographs
PNG (Portable Network Graphics)	.png	Slide as a graphic for use on Web pages; the future replacement for GIF, but not yet
TIFF (Tag Image File Format)	.tiff, .tif	Slide as a graphic for use in print; best for bitmaps; good at any resolution
Device Independent Bitmap	.bmp, .dib, .rle, .bmz	Slide as a graphic; colors are represented in a format independent of the output
Windows Metafile	.wmf	Slide as a 16-bit graphic (Windows 3.x and later)
Enhanced Windows Metafile	.emf	Slide as a 32-bit graphic (Windows 95 and later)

Add or Remove Feature

Creating a Photo Album

If you have a large collection of pictures, you can use PowerPoint to create a photo album. A PowerPoint photo album is a presentation that you can use to display your photographs and pictures. PowerPoint makes it easy for you to insert multiple pictures from your hard disk into your photo album. You can also customize the photo album by applying themes (**New!**) and using special layout options, such as oval frames and captions under each picture. When you setup captions in a photo album, PowerPoint automatically uses picture file name as caption placeholder text, which you can change later. You can also change the appearance of a picture in the photo album by adjusting rotation, contrast, and brightness.

Create a New Photo Album

1. Click the **Insert** tab.

2. Click the **Photo Album** button arrow, and then click **New Photo Album**.

3. Click **File/Disk**.

4. Click the **Look in** list arrow, and then select the drive and folder that contain the pictures you want to insert.

5. Select the pictures you wish to include in the new photo album.

    TIMESAVER *Hold down the Ctrl key to select multiple pictures.*

6. Click **Insert**.

7. Click the **Picture Layout** list arrow, and then click a picture layout.

8. Click the **Frame Shape** list arrow, and then click a frame shape.

9. If you want to change the picture order or remove one, click a picture, and then use the **Up**, **Down**, or **Remove** buttons.

10. Click **Create**.

11. Click the **Office** button, click **Save As**, and then type a file name.

12. Click **Save**.

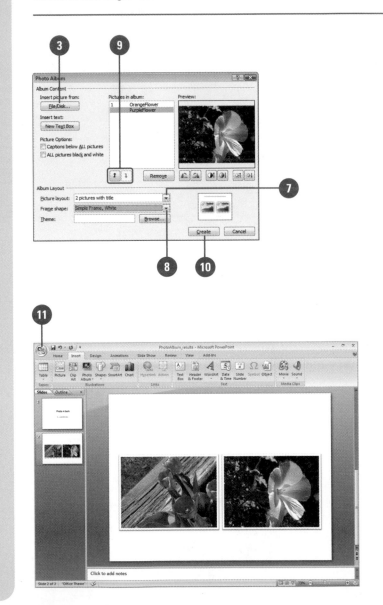

Edit a Photo Album

1. Open the photo album presentation.

2. Click the **Insert** tab.

3. Click the **Photo Album** button arrow, and then click **Edit Photo Album**.

4. To add captions, select the **Captions below ALL pictures** check box.

   TROUBLE? *If the check box is not available, you need to select another picture layout.*

5. To add a text box for spacing purposes, select the picture you want to use, and then click **New Text Box**.

6. To change the appearance of a picture, do one of the following:

   ◆ **Rotate.** Click these buttons to rotate the picture.

   ◆ **Contrast.** Click these buttons to increase or decrease contrast.

   ◆ **Brightness.** Click these buttons to increase or decrease brightness.

7. To apply a theme (**New!**), click **Browse**, locate and select a theme file, and then click **Select**.

8. Click **Update**.

Did You Know?

You can share your photo album with others. You can print it, publish it to the Web, or send it as an attachment in an e-mail.

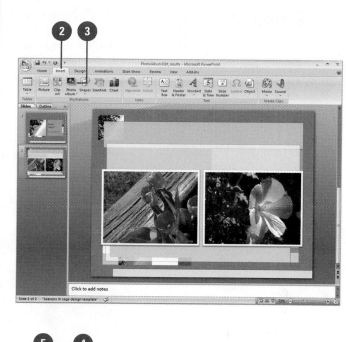

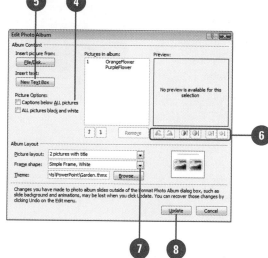

Adding a Quick Style to a Picture

Microsoft
Certified
Application
Specialist

PP07S-3.4.1

Instead of changing individual attributes of a picture—such as shape, border, and effects—you can quickly add them all at once with the Picture Quick Style gallery. The Picture Quick Style gallery (**New!**) provides a variety of different formatting combinations. To quickly see if you like a Picture Quick Style, point to a thumbnail in the gallery to display a live preview (**New!**) of it in the selected shape. If you like it, you can apply it.

Add a Quick Style to a Picture

1 Click the picture you want to change.

2 Click the **Format** tab under Picture Tools.

3 Click the scroll up or down arrow, or click the **More** list arrow in the Picture Styles group to see additional styles.

The current style appears highlighted in the gallery.

4 Point to a style.

A live preview (**New!**) of the style appears in the current shape.

5 Click the style you want from the gallery to apply it to the selected picture.

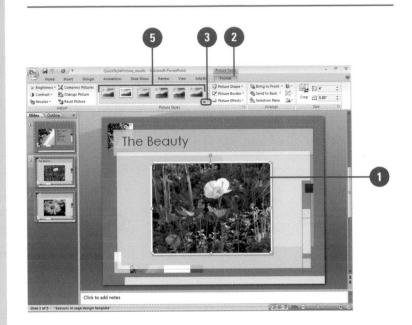

Did You Know?

You can save a shape as a picture in the PNG format. Right-click the shape, click Save as Picture, type a name, and then click Save.

You can copy the window or screen contents. To make a copy of the active window, press Alt+Print Scrn. To copy the entire screen as it appears on your monitor, press Print Scrn.

Applying a Shape to a Picture

After you insert a picture into your presentation, you can select it and apply one of PowerPoint's shapes to it (**New!**). The picture appears in the shape just like its been cropped. The Picture Shape gallery makes it easy to choose the shape you want to use. Live preview is not available with the Picture Shape gallery. You can try different shapes to find the one you want. If you don't find the one you want, you can use the Reset Picture button to return the picture back to it's original state.

Apply a Shape to a Picture

1. Click the picture you want to change.

2. Click the **Format** tab under Picture Tools.

3. Click the **Picture Shape** button.

4. Select the shape you want to apply to the selected picture.

Did You Know?

You can quickly return a picture back to its original form. Select the picture, click the Format tab, and then click the Reset Picture button.

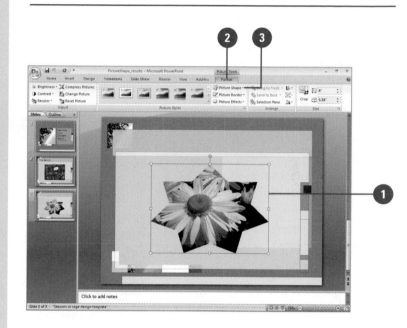

Applying a Border to a Picture

Microsoft
Certified
Application
Specialist

PP07S-3.4.1

After you insert a picture, you can add and modify the picture border by changing individual outline formatting using the Picture Border button on the Format tab under Picture Tools. The Picture Border button works just like the Shape Outline button, and provides similar options to add a border, select a border color, and change border width and style. You can try different border combinations to find the one you want. If you don't find one that works for you, you can use the No Outline command on the Picture Border gallery to remove it.

Apply a Border to a Picture

1. Click the picture you want to change.

2. Click the **Format** tab under Picture Tools.

3. Click the **Picture Border** button.

4. Click a color, or point to **Weight**, or **Dashes**, and then select a style, or click **More Lines** to select multiple options.

5. Drag a sizing handle to change the size or angle of the line or arrow.

Did You Know?

You can remove a border. Select the picture, click the Format tab, click the Picture Border button, and then click No Outline.

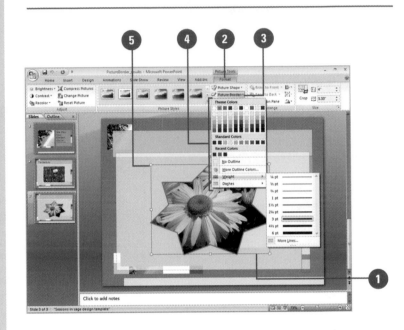

Applying Picture Effects

Microsoft Certified Application Specialist

PP07S-3.4.1

You can change the look of a picture by applying effects (**New!**), such as shadows, reflections, glow, soft edges, and 3-D rotations. You can also apply effects to a shape by using the Picture Effects gallery for quick results, or by using the Format Shape dialog box for custom results. From the Picture Effects gallery you can apply a built-in combination of 3-D effects or individual effects to a picture. To quickly see if you like a picture effect, point to a thumbnail in the Picture Effects gallery to display a live preview (**New!**) of it. If you like it, you can apply it. If you no longer want to apply a picture effect to an object, you can remove it. Simply, select the picture, point to the effect type on the Picture Effects gallery, and then select the No effect type option.

Add an Effect to a Picture

1. Click the picture you want to change.

2. Click the **Format** tab under Picture Tools.

3. Click the **Picture Effects** button, and then point to one of the following:

   ◆ **Preset** to select No 3-D, one of the preset types, or More 3-D Settings.

   ◆ **Shadow** to select No Shadow, one of the shadow types, or More Shadows.

   ◆ **Reflection** to select No Reflection or one of the Reflection Variations.

   ◆ **Glow** to select No Glow, one of the Glow Variations, or More Glow Colors.

   ◆ **Soft Edges** to select No Soft Edges or a point size to determine the soft edge amount.

   ◆ **3-D Rotation** to select No Rotation, one of the rotation types, or More 3-D Settings.

   When you point to an effect, a live preview (**New!**) of the style appears in the current shape.

4. Click the effect you want from the gallery to apply it to the selected shape.

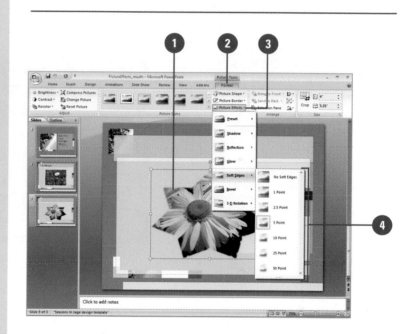

Modifying Picture Size

Microsoft
Certified
Application
Specialist

PP07S-3.5.1

Once you have inserted a picture, clip art and other objects into your presentation, you can adapt them to meet your needs. Perhaps the clip is too small to be effective, or you don't quite like the colors it uses. Like any object, you can resize or move the picture. You can use the sizing handles to quickly resize a picture or use height and width option in the Size group on the Format tab to resize a picture more precisely. If you want to set multiple options at the same time, you can use the Size and Position dialog box. You can make sure your pictures keep the same relative proportions as the original and provide the best scaling size for a slide show on a specific monitor size (**New!**).

Resize a Picture

1. Click the object you want to resize.

2. Drag one of the sizing handles to increase or decrease the object's size.

   ◆ Drag a middle handle to resize the object up, down, left, or right.

   ◆ Drag a corner handle to resize the object proportionally.

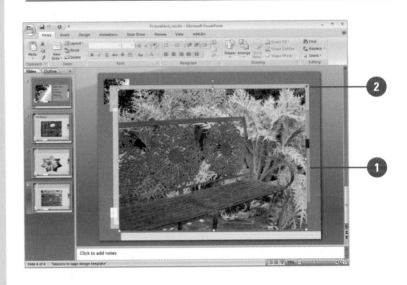

Resize a Picture Precisely

1. Click the object you want to resize.

2. Click the **Format** tab under Picture Tools.

3. Click the up and down arrows or enter a number (in inches) in the Height and Width boxes on the Ribbon and press Enter.

   If the **Lock aspect ratio** check box is selected in the Size and Position dialog box, height or width automatically changes when you change one of them. Click the **Size Dialog Box Launcher** to change the option.

Size Dialog Box Launcher

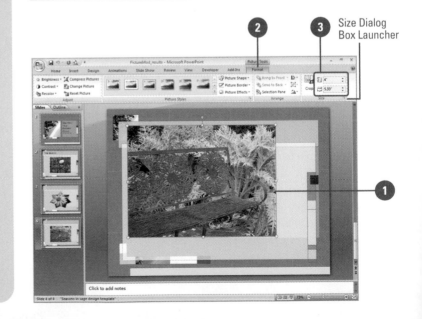

Precisely Scale a Picture

1. Click the object you want to resize.

2. Click the **Format** tab under Picture Tools.

3. Click the **Size Dialog Box Launcher**.

4. To keep the picture proportional, select the **Lock aspect ratio** check box.

5. To keep the picture the same relative size, select the **Relative to original picture size** check box.

6. To scale a picture for the best slide show look on a specific slide monitor, select the **Best scale for slide show** check box, and then select a resolution size.

7. Click the up and down arrows or enter a number in the Height and Width boxes in one of the following:

   ◆ **Size.** Enter a size in inches.

   ◆ **Scale.** Enter a percentage size.

   If the Lock aspect ratio check box is selected, height or width automatically changes when you change one of them.

8. If you want to remove your changes, click **Reset**.

9. Click **Close**.

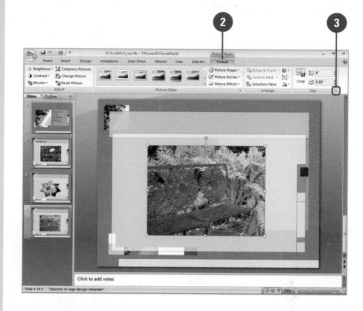

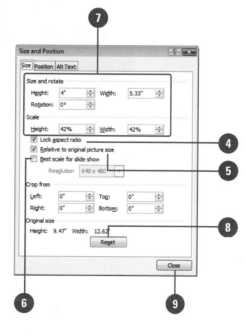

Compressing a Picture

PP07S-4.3.5

PowerPoint allows you to compress pictures in order to minimize the file size of the image. In doing so, however, you may lose some visual quality, depending on the compression setting. You can pick the resolution that you want for the pictures in a presentation based on where or how they'll be viewed (for example, on the Web or printed). You can also set other options, such as Delete Cropped Areas Of Picture, to get the best balance between picture quality and file size or automatically compress pictures when you save your presentation.

Compress a Picture

1. Click to select the pictures you want to compress.

2. Click the **Format** tab under Picture Tools.

3. Click the **Compress Pictures** button.

4. Select the **Apply to selected pictures only** check box to apply compression setting to only the selected picture. Otherwise, clear the check box to compress all pictures in your presentation.

5. Click **Options**.

6. Select or clear the **Automatically perform basic compression on save** check box.

7. Select or clear the **Delete cropped areas of pictures** check box to reduce file.

8. Click the **Print**, **Screen**, or **E-mail** option to specify a target output.

9. Click **OK** to close the Compression Settings dialog box.

10. Click **OK**.

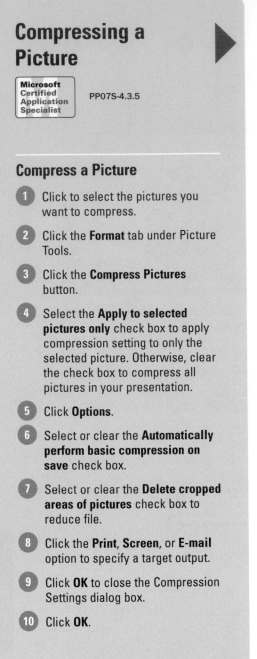

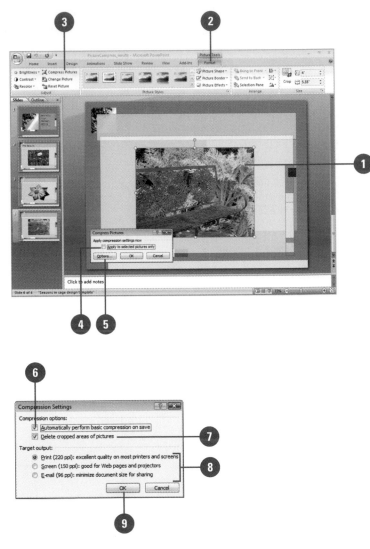

Modifying Picture Brightness and Contrast

Once you have inserted a picture, you can control the image's colors, brightness, and contrast using Picture tools. The brightness and contrast controls let you make simple adjustments to the tonal range of a picture. The brightness and contrast controls change a picture by an overall lightening or darkening of the image pixels. You can experiment with the settings to get the look you want. If you don't like the look, you can use the Reset Picture button to return the picture back to its original starting point.

Change Brightness

1. Click the picture whose brightness you want to increase or decrease.

2. Click the **Format** tab under Picture Tools.

3. Click the **Brightness** button, and then do one of the following:

   ◆ Click a positive brightness to lighten the object colors by adding more white, or click a negative brightness to darken the object colors by adding more black.

   ◆ Click **Picture Corrections Options** to set other specific brightness percentages.

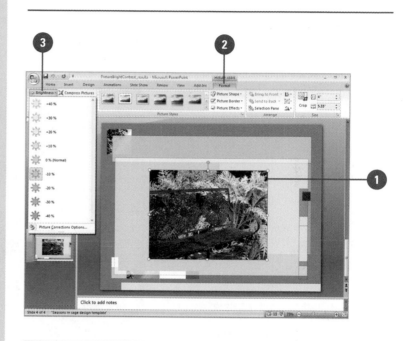

Change Contrast

1. Click the picture whose contrast you want to increase or decrease.

2. Click the **Format** tab under Picture Tools.

3. Click the **Contrast** button, and then do one of the following:

   ◆ Click a positive contrast to increase color intensity, resulting in less gray, or click a negative contrast to decrease color intensity, resulting in more gray.

   ◆ Click **Picture Corrections Options** to set other specific contrast percentages.

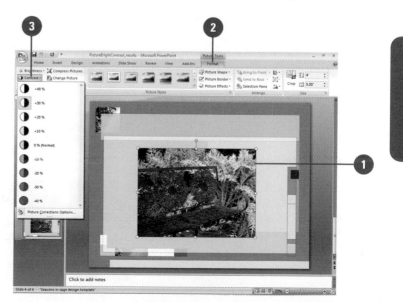

Recoloring a Picture

Microsoft Certified Application Specialist

PP07S-3.4.2

You can recolor clip art and other objects to match the color scheme of your presentation. For example, if you use a flower clip art as your business logo, you can change shades of pink in the spring to shades of orange in the autumn. The Recolor Picture Quick Style gallery (**New!**) provides a variety of different formatting combinations. To quickly see if you like a Recolor Picture Quick Style, point to a thumbnail in the gallery to display a live preview (**New!**) of it in the selected shape. If you like it, you can apply it. You can also use a transparent background in your picture to avoid conflict between its background color and your slide's background. With a transparent background, the picture takes on the same background as your slide presentation.

Recolor a Picture

1. Click the picture whose color you want to change.

2. Click the **Format** tab under Picture Tools.

3. Click the **Recolor** button.

4. Click one of the Color options.

   ◆ **No Recolor.** Click this option to remove a previous recolor.

   ◆ **Color Modes.** Click an option to apply a color type:

   Grayscale. Converts colors into whites, blacks and shades of gray between black and white.

   Sepia. Converts colors into very light gold and yellow colors like a picture from the old west.

   Washout. Converts colors into whites and very light colors.

   Black and White. Converts colors into only white and black.

   ◆ **Light and Dark Variations.** Click an option to apply an accent color in light or dark variations.

   ◆ **More Variations.** Point to this option to select a specific color.

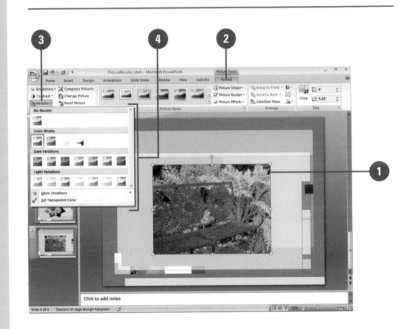

Light Variations

Dark Variations

Set a Transparent Background

1 Click the picture you want to change.

2 Click the **Format** tab under Picture Tools.

3 Click the **Recolor** button, and then click **Set Transparent Color**.

4 Move the pointer over the object until the pointer changes shape.

5 Click the color you want to set as transparent.

6 Move the pointer over the picture where you want to apply the transparent color, and then click to apply it.

7 When you're done, click outside the image.

Did You Know?

Why is the Set Transparent Color command dimmed? Setting a color as transparent works only with bitmaps. If you are working with an object that is not a bitmap, you will not be able to use this feature.

You can't modify some pictures in PowerPoint. If the picture is a bitmap (.BMP, .JPG, .GIF, or .PNG), you need to edit its colors in an image editing program, such as Adobe Photoshop, Microsoft Paint, or Paint Shop Pro.

You can reset a picture back to it's original state. Click the picture you want to reset, click the Format tab under Picture Tools, and then click the Reset Picture button.

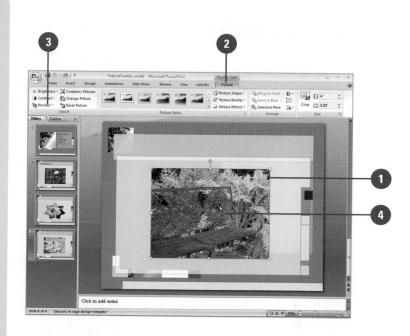

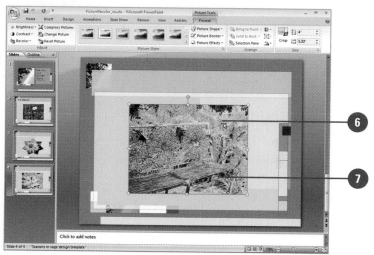

Cropping and Rotating a Picture

You can crop clip art to isolate just one portion of the picture. Because clip art uses vector image technology, you can crop even the smallest part of it and then enlarge it, and the clip art will still be recognizable. You can also crop bitmapped pictures, but if you enlarge the area you cropped, you lose picture detail. Use the crop button to crop an image by hand. You can also crop using the Size and Position dialog box, which gives you precise control over the dimensions of the area you want to crop. You can also rotate a picture by increments or freehand.

Crop a Picture Quickly

1. Click the picture you want to crop.
2. Click the **Format** tab under Picture Tools.
3. Click the **Crop** button.
4. Drag the sizing handles until the borders surround the area you want to crop.
5. Click outside the image when you are finished.

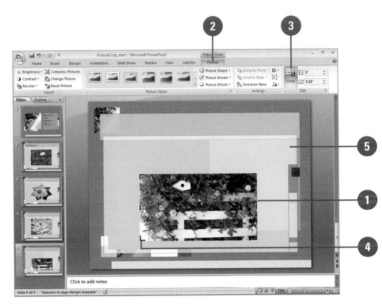

Redisplay a Cropped Picture

1. Click the picture you want to restore.
2. Click the **Format** tab under Picture Tools.
3. Click the **Crop** button.
4. Drag the sizing handles to reveal the areas that were originally cropped.
5. Click outside the image when you are finished.

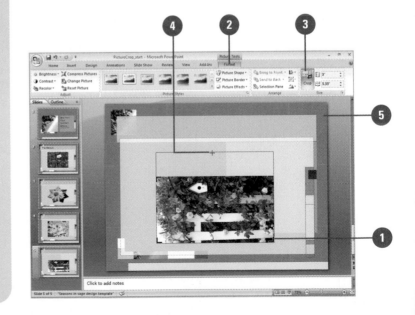

Crop a Picture Precisely

1. Click the object you want to crop.

2. Click the **Format** tab under Picture Tools.

3. Click the **Size Dialog Box Launcher**.

4. Adjust the values in the **Left**, **Right**, **Top**, and **Bottom** boxes to crop the image to the exact dimensions you want.

5. If you want to remove your changes, click **Reset**.

6. Click **Close**.

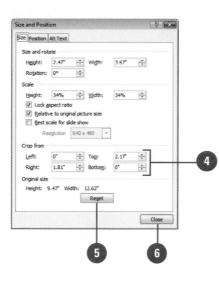

Rotate a Picture

1. Click the object you want to rotate.

2. Use one of the following methods:

   ◆ Position the pointer (which changes to the Free Rotate pointer) over the green rotate lever at the top of the object, and then drag to rotate the object.

   ◆ Click the **Home** tab, click the **Arrange** button, point to **Rotate**, and then click one of the rotate or flip commands.

3. Click outside the object to set the rotation.

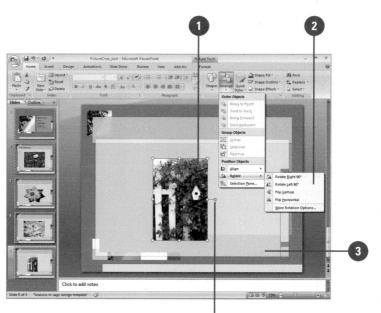

Free Rotate pointer

Creating WordArt Text

Microsoft
Certified
Application
Specialist

PP07S-2.2.7

The WordArt feature lets you create stylized text to draw attention to your most important words. Most users apply WordArt to short phrases or even just a word, such as *GROWING A GARDEN*. You should apply WordArt to a slide sparingly. Its visual appeal and unique look require uncluttered space. When you use WordArt, you can choose from a variety of text styles that come with the WordArt Quick Style gallery (**New!**), or you can create your own using tools in the WordArt Styles group. To quickly see if you like a WordArt Quick Style, point to a thumbnail in the gallery to display a live preview (**New!**) of it in the selected text. If you like it, you can apply it. You can also use the free angle handle (pink diamond) inside the selected text box to adjust your WordArt text angle.

Insert WordArt Text

1 Click the **Insert** tab.

2 Click the **WordArt** button, and then click one of the WordArt styles.

A WordArt text box appears on the slide with selected placeholder text.

3 Type the text you want WordArt to use.

4 If applicable, use the Font and Paragraph options on the Home tab to modify the text you entered.

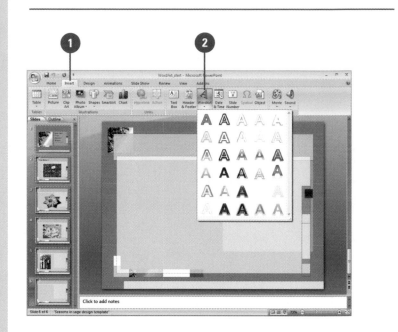

Did You Know?

You can convert text to WordArt. Select the text, click the Home tab, and then click the WordArt text style you want from the Ribbon.

You can remove WordArt text. Select the WordArt text you want to remove, click the Format tab, click the Quick Styles button, and then click Clear WordArt.

Edit WordArt Text

1. Click the WordArt object you want to edit.

2. Click to place the insertion point where you want to edit, and then edit the text.

3. Click outside the objects to deselect it.

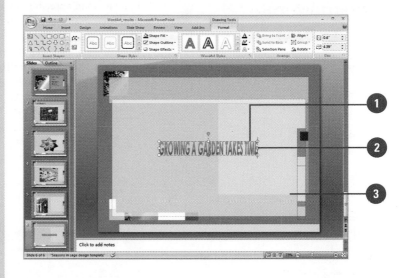

Adjust WordArt Text Angle

1. Click the WordArt object you want to change.

2. Drag the free angle handle (pink diamond) to adjust text angle in the direction you want.

3. When you're done, release the mouse button.

4. Click outside the object to deselect it.

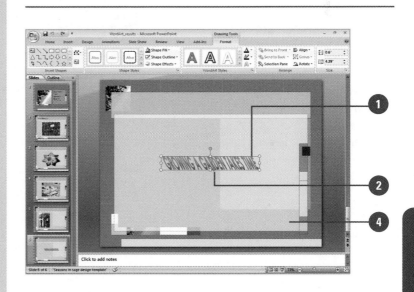

Formatting WordArt Text

Microsoft Certified Application Specialist

PP07S-2.2.2, PP07S-2.2.7

In addition to applying one of the preformatted WordArt styles, you can also create your own style by shaping your text into a variety of shapes, curves, styles, and color patterns. The WordArt Styles group gives you tools for changing the fill and outline of your WordArt text. To quickly see if you like a WordArt Style, point to a thumbnail in the gallery to display a live preview (**New!**) of it in the selected text. If you like it, you can apply it.

Apply a Different WordArt Style to Existing WordArt Text

1. Click the WordArt object whose style you want to change.

2. Click the **Format** tab under Drawing Tools.

3. Click the scroll up or down arrow, or click the **More** list arrow in the WordArt Styles group to see additional styles.

   The current style appears highlighted in the gallery.

4. Point to a style.

   A live preview (**New!**) of the style appears in the current shape text.

5. Click the style you want from the gallery to apply it to the selected shape.

Did You Know?

You can add more formatting to WordArt text. Select the WordArt object, click the Home tab, and then use the formatting button in the Font and Paragraph groups.

You can change the WordArt fill color to match the background. Click the WordArt object, right-click the object, click Format Shape, click the Background option, and then click Close.

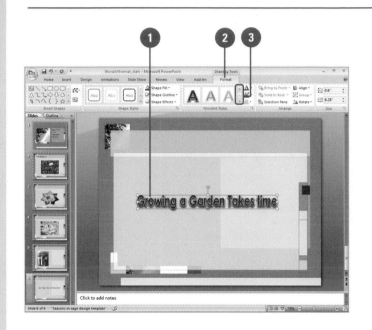

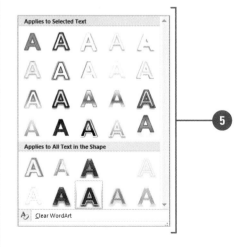

Apply a Fill to WordArt Text

1. Click the WordArt object you want to change.

2. Click the **Format** tab under Drawing Tools.

3. Click the **Text Fill** button, and then click or point to one of the following:

   ◆ **Color** to select a theme or standard color.

   ◆ **Picture** to select a picture file.

   ◆ **Gradient** to select No Gradient, one of the shadow types, or More Gradients.

   ◆ **Texture** to select one of the of the texture types, or More Textures.

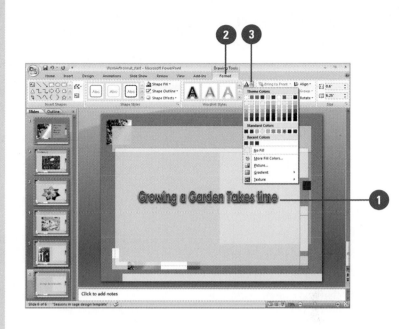

Apply an Outline to WordArt Text

1. Click the WordArt object you want to change.

2. Click the **Format** tab under Drawing Tools.

3. Click the **Text Outline** button.

4. Click a color, or point to **Weight** or **Dashes**, and then select a style.

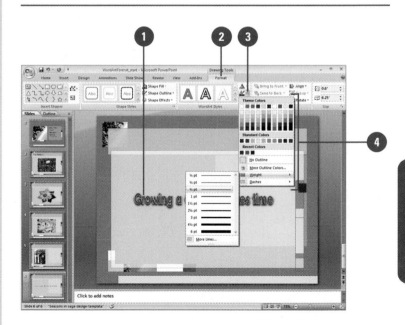

Applying WordArt Text Effects

Microsoft Certified Application Specialist

PP07S-2.2.7

You can change the look of WordArt text by applying effects (**New!**), such as shadows, reflections, glow, soft edges, 3-D rotations, and transformations. You can apply effects to a shape by using the Text Effects gallery for quick results. From the Text Effects gallery you can apply a built-in combination of 3-D effects or individual effects to WordArt text. To quickly see if you like the effect, point to a thumbnail in the Text Effects gallery to display a live preview (**New!**) of it. If you like it, you can apply it. If you no longer want to apply the effect, you can remove it. Simply, select the WordArt text, point to the effect type on the Text Effects gallery, and then select the No effect type option.

Apply an Effect to WordArt Text

1. Click the WordArt object you want to change.

2. Click the **Format** tab under Drawing Tools.

3. Click the **Text Effects** button, and then point to one of the following:

    ◆ **Shadow** to select No Shadow, one of the shadow types (Outer or Inner), or More Shadows.

    ◆ **Reflection** to select No Reflection or one of the Reflection Variations.

    ◆ **Glow** to select No Glow, one of the Glow Variations, or More Glow Colors.

    ◆ **Bevel** to select No Bevel, one of the bevel variations, or More 3-D Settings.

    ◆ **3-D Rotation** to select No Rotation, one of the rotation types (Parallel, Perspective, or Oblique), or More 3-D Settings.

    ◆ **Transform** to select No Transform, or one of the transform types (Follow Path or Warp).

    When you point to an effect, a live preview (**New!**) of the style appears in the current shape.

4. Click the effect you want from the gallery to apply it to the selected shape.

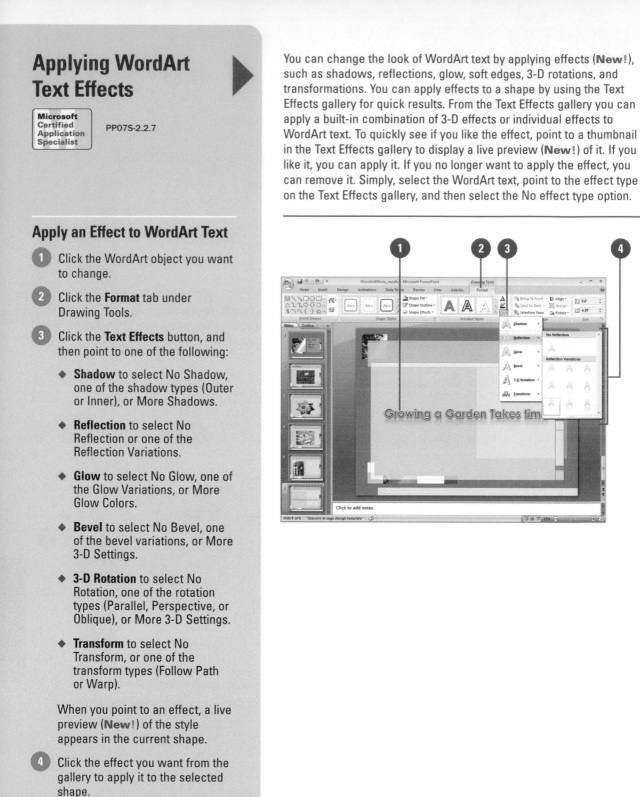

Modifying WordArt Text Position

You can apply a number of text effects to your WordArt objects that determine alignment and direction. The effects of some of the adjustments you make are more pronounced for certain WordArt styles than others. Some of these effects make the text unreadable for certain styles, so apply these effects carefully. You can apply effects to a shape by using the Format Shape dialog box for custom results. You can also use the free rotate handle (green circle) at the top of the selected text box to rotate your WordArt text.

Change WordArt Text Direction

1. Right-click the WordArt object you want to change, and then click **Format Shape**.

2. If necessary, click **Text Box**.

3. Click the **Vertical alignment** or **Horizontal alignment** list arrow, and then select an option: Top, Middle, Bottom, Top Center, Middle Center, or Bottom Center.

4. Click the **Text Direction** list arrow, and then select an option: **Horizontal**, **Rotate all text 90°**, **Rotate all text 270°**, or **Stacked**.

5. Click **Close**.

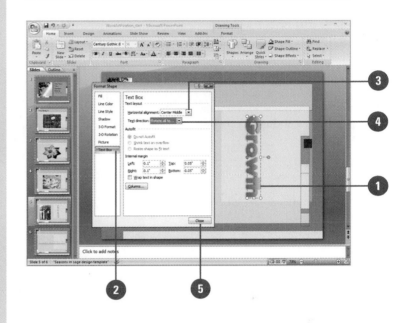

Rotate WordArt Text

1. Click the WordArt object you want to change.

2. Drag the free rotate handle (green circle) to rotate the object in any direction you want.

3. When you're done, release the mouse button.

4. Click outside the object to deselect it.

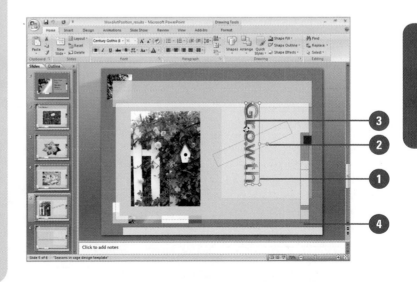

Inserting Movies and Sounds

Microsoft Certified Application Specialist

PP07S-2.3.4

You can insert movies or sounds into a presentation by inserting them from the Clip Art task pane or a file. Movies can be either animated pictures—also known as animated GIFs, such as cartoons—or they can be digital videos prepared with digitized video equipment. Movies and sounds are inserted as PowerPoint objects. When you insert a sound, a small icon appears representing the sound file. When you insert a movie or sound, PowerPoint asks you how you want it to start in a slide show. You can choose to have the movie or sound play automatically or when clicked.

Insert a Clip Organizer Movie or Sound

1. Click the **Insert** tab.

2. Click the **Movie** or **Sound** button arrow, and then click **Movie from Clip Organizer** or **Sound from Clip Organizer**.

3. Search for and click the media clip you want to insert.

   PowerPoint supports the following audio file formats (AIFF, AU, MP3, WAV, WMA), and video file formats (ASF, AVI, MPG or MPEG, WMV).

4. When a message is displayed, do one of the following:

   To play the media clip automatically when you go to the slide, click **Automatically**.

   To play the media clip only when you click it, click **When Clicked**.

5. When you're done, click the **Close** button on the task pane.

See Also

See "Creating Hyperlinks to External Objects" on page 248 for information on adding movie files, such as Adobe Director, Adobe Flash, or Apple QuickTime, which are not currently supported by PowerPoint 2007.

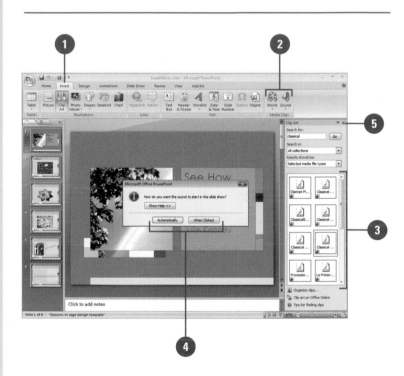

For Your Information

Playing a Non-Supported Movie

An Apple QuickTime movie (.mov) file, an Adobe Director movie file, or Flash movie file cannot be inserted into an Microsoft Office PowerPoint 2007 presentation. However, you still can play it externally from PowerPoint. To play one of these movies during your presentation, you can create a hyperlink or action button to the external file. If this doesn't work the way you want, you can also play a movie using an ActiveX control. You can also convert a QuickTime movie to a Microsoft Windows video (.avi) or other compatible file format using QuickTime Pro by Apple Computer.

Insert a Movie or Sound from a File

1. Click the **Insert** tab.

2. Click the **Movie** or **Sound** button arrow, and then click **Movie from File** or **Sound from File**.

3. Locate and select a movie or sound file.

4. Click **OK**.

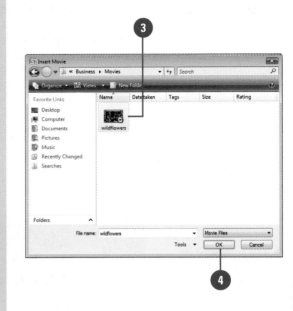

Insert a Movie on a New Slide

1. Click the **Home** tab.

2. Click the **New Slide** button arrow, and then click a slide layout with media content placeholder.

3. Click the **Insert Movie** icon in the media content placeholder.

4. Click the media clip you want to insert, and then click **OK**.

5. When the message is displayed, click **Automatically** or **When Clicked**.

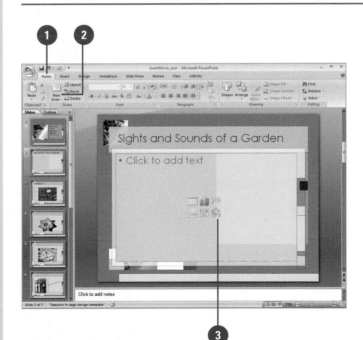

Did You Know?

You can quickly delete a movie or sound. Click the sound icon or movie image, and then press Delete.

Inserting CD Audio

If you have an audio CD with a music track you want to include in a slide show, you can insert it into your presentation. PowerPoint allows you to select the start and end point for the track, loop the audio playback, set the volume, and hide the sound icon during the slide show. Before you can insert or play CD audio tracks in your presentation, you need to make sure your audio CD is inserted into your CD/DVD player.

Insert CD Audio

1. Insert a CD into your CD/DVD player.

2. Click the **Insert** tab.

3. Click the **Sound** button arrow, and then click **Play CD Audio Track**.

4. Specify the starting and ending track, or starting and ending time you want.

5. To play continuously, select the **Loop Until Stopped** check box.

6. Click the **Volume** button, and then drag to set a volume.

7. To hide the CD icon, select the **Hide Sound Icon During Slide Show** check box.

8. Click **OK**.

9. When a message is displayed, do one of the following:

   To play the audio automatically when you go to the slide, click **Automatically**.

   To play the audio only when you click it, click **When Clicked**.

   A CD icon appears on the slide.

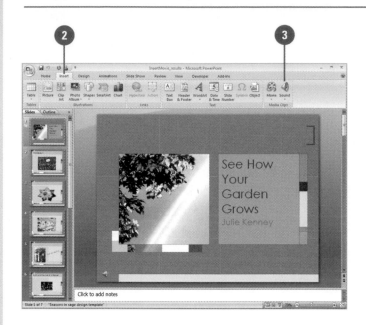

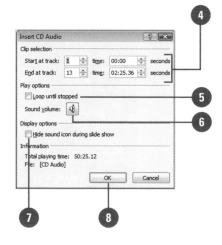

Recording Sounds

You can add voice narration or sound in a slide show when you are either creating a slide show for individuals who can't attend a presentation or archiving a meeting for presenters to review later and hear comments made during the presentation. If you want to add voice narration or sound to a slide, you can record a sound clip directly into PowerPoint. Before you can record sounds, you need a microphone, sound card, and speakers installed on your computer.

Record a Sound on a Slide

1 Click the **Insert** tab.

2 Click the **Sound** button arrow, and then click **Record Sound**.

3 Type a name for the sound.

4 Click the **Record** button (red dot).

5 Click the **Stop** button when you are finished.

6 Click **OK**.

A sound icon appears on the slide.

Did You Know?

You can delete a sound. Click the sound icon or CD icon, and then press Delete.

You can turn off sound narration. Click the Slide Show tab, click the Set Up Slide Show button, select the Show without narration check box, and then click OK.

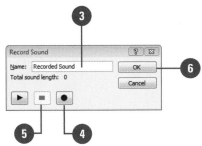

Setting Movie and Sound Play Options

After you insert movie, sound, or CD audio objects, you can set play options to determine how they will play back. You can change settings so they play continuously or just one time. Movies and sounds can play in either Normal view or Slide Show view. You can also view and play movies using the full screen. PowerPoint supports the following audio file formats (AIFF, AU, MP3, WAV, WMA), and video file formats (ASF, AVI, MPG or MPEG, WMV). To play sound and movies, you need to have Microsoft DirectShow or Microsoft Windows Media Player installed on your computer, which you can download from the Microsoft Web site.

Change Movie Play Options

1. Click the movie object you want to change options.

2. Click the **Options** tab under Movie Tools.

3. To adjust slide show volume, click the **Slide Show Volume** button, and then click an option: **Low**, **Medium**, **High**, or **Mute** (no audio).

4. Change the movie settings.

   ◆ To change the way a movie plays, click the **Play Movie** list arrow, and then select an option: **Automatically**, When Clicked, or **Play across slides**.

   ◆ To hide movie, select the **Hide During Slide Show** check box.

   ◆ To resize the movie to fit the screen, select the **Play Full Screen** check box.

   ◆ To play continuously, select the **Loop Until Stopped** check box.

   ◆ To automatically rewind the movie, select the **Rewind Movie After Playing** check box.

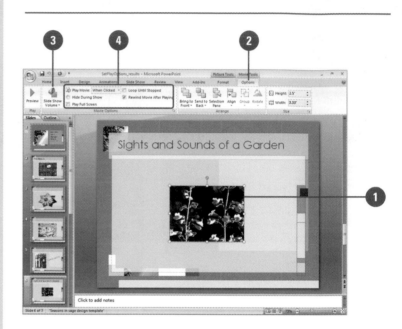

Change Sound Play Options

1 Click the sound or CD icon you want to change options.

2 Click the **Options** tab under Sound Tools.

3 To adjust slide show volume, click the **Slide Show Volume** button, and then click an option: **Low**, **Medium**, **High**, or **Mute** (no audio).

4 Change the sound settings.

- ◆ To hide sound or CD icon, select the **Hide During Slide Show** check box.

- ◆ To play continuously, select the **Loop Until Stopped** check box.

- ◆ To change the way a movie plays, click the **Play Sound** list arrow, and then select an option: **Automatically**, **When Clicked**, or **Play across slides**.

- ◆ To keep presentation file sizes down, enter a maximum sound file size for embedding a sound within the presentation.

  If you want to use sounds larger than this size, you need to link the external file to the presentation and keep the file with it.

- ◆ To set CD audio track start and end point, use the up and down arrows, or enter a track number or time.

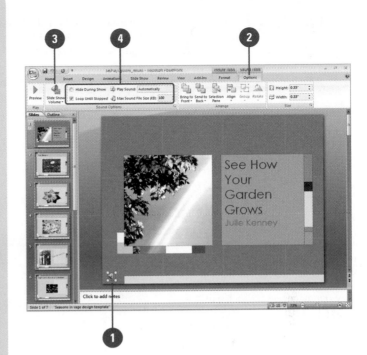

See Also

See "Linking and Embedding Sounds" on page 242 for information on when a sound is linked or embedded.

Playing Movies and Sounds

After you insert movie or sound objects, you can play them several different ways. Movies and sounds can play in either Normal view or Slide Show view during a slide show. You can modify them so they play continuously or just one time. Before you can play sounds, or sounds from video, you need a sound card and speakers installed on your computer.

Play a Movie or Sound

◆ To play a movie or sound in Normal view, double-click the movie object or sound icon.

◆ To play a movie or sound in Normal view, select the movie object or sound icon, click the **Options** tab, and then click the **Preview** button (**New!**).

◆ To play a movie, sound, or animated picture in Slide Show view, click the **Slide Show** button, and then display the slide with the media you want to play.

Depending on your play options, you may need to click the movie object or sound icon to play it.

◆ To stop a movie or sound, click a blank area of the slide. To pause a movie, click the movie.

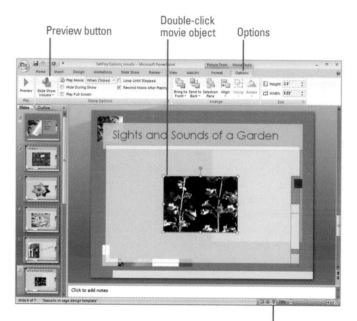

Preview button

Double-click movie object

Options

Slide show button

Did You Know?

You cannot insert a digital movie from a video DVD. PowerPoint 2007 is unable to add a movie from a video DVD. However, some third-party add-ins, such as PFCMedia, let you play a video DVD in a presentation.

You can delay the start of a movie. Click the movie, click the Animation tab, and then click the Custom Animation button. In the task pane, click the arrow next to the movie, and then click Effects Options. Click the Effects tab, click From Time (under Start Playing), and then enter the total number of seconds for the delay.

For Your Information

Having Problems Playing a Movie?

Movie files are always linked to a presentation, which means they are stored in an external location. When you move your presentation around, you need to move your movie files too. To avoid problems, the best place to store your movies is the same folder as your presentation. If your movie still doesn't play, you can do a few things: check the list of compatible movie file formats (see the Insert Movie dialog box), take out captions or subtitles, or reinsert it with a shorter path. If a movie plays white, the path exceeds 128 characters. If a movie plays black, your hardware accelerator is incompatible.

Inserting Charts and Related Material

Introduction

An effective presentation draws on information from many sources. Microsoft Office PowerPoint helps you seamlessly integrate information into your presentations using shared data from Office applications.

In PowerPoint and other Microsoft Office programs, you can insert SmartArt graphics (**New!**) to create diagrams that convey processes or relationships. PowerPoint offers a wide-variety of built-in SmartArt graphic types from which to choose, including graphical lists, process, cycle, hierarchy, relationship, matrix, and pyramid. Using built-in SmartArt graphics makes it easy to create and modify charts without having to create them from scratch. If you already have text on a slide, you can quickly convert your text to a SmartArt graphic.

Instead of adding a table of dry numbers, insert a chart. Charts add visual interest and useful information represented by lines, bars, pie slices, or other markers. Office uses Microsoft Excel (**New!**) to embed and display the information in a chart.

In PowerPoint, you can insert an object created in another program into a presentation using technology known as **object linking and embedding (OLE)**. OLE is a critical feature for many PowerPoint users because it lets you share objects among compatible programs when you create presentations. When you want to make any changes or enhancements to the objects, you can edit the inserted object without having to leave PowerPoint. OLE makes it easy to add graph and organization charts to present information visually. If you have information in other programs, such as Microsoft Office Word or Microsoft Office Excel, you can insert it in to your presentation with the help of OLE.

What You'll Do

Create SmartArt Graphics

Use the Same Text Pane with SmartArt Graphics

Modify, Resize and Format a SmartArt Graphic

Format a Shape in a SmartArt Graphic

Create and Modify an Organization Chart

Insert a Chart and Import Data

Select, Enter and Edit Chart Data

Modify the Data Worksheet

Select a Chart Type, Layout and Style

Format Chart Objects

Change the Chart Layout Objects

Save a Chart Template

Insert, Modify and Format a Table

Add a Quick Style and Effects to a Table

Share Information Among Documents

Embed and Link an Object or Sound

Insert a Microsoft Excel Chart, Word Document and Organization Chart

Creating SmartArt Graphics

Microsoft Certified Application Specialist

PP07S-3.1.1, PP07S-3.1.2

SmartArt graphics (**New!**) allow you to create diagrams that convey processes or relationships. PowerPoint offers a wide variety of built-in SmartArt graphic types, including graphical lists, process, cycle, hierarchy, relationship, matrix, and pyramid. Using built-in SmartArt graphics makes it easy to create and modify charts without having to create them from scratch. If you already have text on a slide, you can quickly convert your text to a SmartArt graphic. To quickly see if you like a SmartArt graphic layout, point to a thumbnail in the gallery to display a live preview (**New!**) of it in the selected shape. If you like it, you can apply it.

Create a SmartArt Graphic

1. Click the **Insert** tab.

2. Click the **SmartArt** button.

> **TIMESAVER** *In a content placeholder, you can click the SmartArt icon to start.*

3. In the left pane, click a category, such as All, List, Process, Cycle, Hierarchy, Relationship, Matrix, or Pyramid.

4. In the right pane, click a SmartArt graphic style type.

5. Click **OK**.

   The SmartArt graphic appears with a Text pane to insert text.

6. Label the shapes by doing one of the following:

   ◆ Type text in the [Text] box.

   You can use the arrow keys to move around the Text pane.

   ◆ Click a shape, and then type text directly into the shape.

7. When you're done, click outside of the SmartArt graphic.

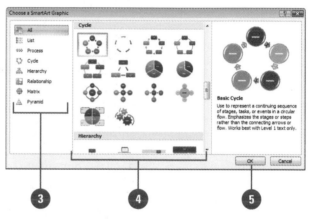

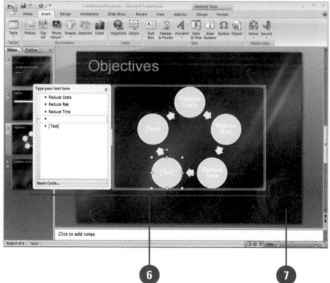

Convert Text to a SmartArt Graphic

1. Select the text box with the text you want to convert to a SmartArt graphic.

2. Click the **Home** tab.

3. Click the **Convert to SmartArt Graphic** button.

   The gallery displays layouts designed for bulleted lists.

4. To view the entire list of layout, click **More SmartArt Graphics**.

5. Point to a layout.

   A live preview (**New!**) of the style appears in the current shape.

6. Click the layout for the SmartArt graphic you want from the gallery to apply it to the selected shape.

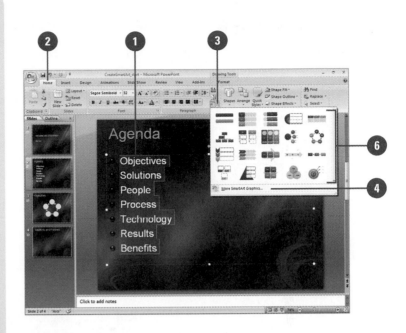

Did You Know?

You cannot drag text into the Text pane. Although you can't drag text into the Text pane, you can copy and paste text.

You can create a blank SmartArt graphic. In the Text pane, press Ctrl+A to select all the placeholder text, and then press Delete.

Shorter amounts of text work best for SmartArt graphics. Most of the layouts for SmartArt graphics work the best with smaller amounts of text. However, if you have larger amounts, layouts in the List category work better than others.

Placeholder text doesn't print or show during a slide show. Placeholder text in the SmartArt graphic doesn't print or show during a slide show.

SmartArt Graphic Purposes

Type	Purpose
List	Show non-sequential information
Process	Show steps in a process or timeline
Cycle	Show a continual process
Hierarchy	Show a decision tree or create an organization chart
Relationship	Illustrate connections
Matrix	Show how parts relate to a whole
Pyramid	Show proportional relationships up and down

Using the Text Pane with SmartArt Graphics

PP07S-3.2.1

After you create a layout for a SmartArt graphic, a Text pane (**New!**) appears next to your selected SmartArt graphic. The bottom of the Text pane displays a description of the SmartArt graphic. The Text pane and SmartArt graphic contain placeholder text. You can change the placeholder text in the Text pane or directly in the SmartArt graphic. The Text pane works like an outline or a bulleted list and the text corresponds directly with the shape text in the SmartArt graphic. As you add and edit content, the SmartArt graphic automatically updates, adding or removing shapes as needed while maintaining the design. If you see a red "x" in the Text pane, it means that the SmartArt graphic contains a fixed number of shapes, such as Counterbalance Arrows (only two).

Show or Hide the Text Pane

1. Click the SmartArt graphic you want to modify.

2. Click the **Design** tab under SmartArt Tools.

3. Do any of the following:

   ◆ **Show**. Click the **Text Pane** button, or click the control with two arrows along the left side of the SmartArt graphic selection to show the Text pane.

   ◆ **Hide**. Click the **Text Pane** button, click the **Close** button on the Text pane, deselect the SmartArt graphic.

   The Text Pane button toggles to show or hide the Text pane.

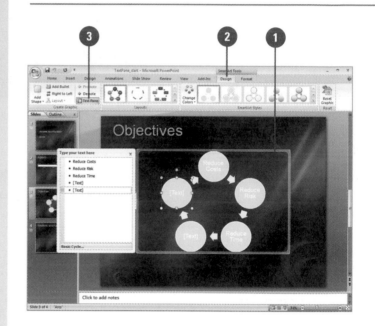

Did You Know?

You can resize the Text pane. To resize the Text pane, point to any edge (pointer changes to double-headed arrow), and then drag to resize it.

You can move the Text pane. To move the Text pane, drag the top of the pane. The Text pane location resets when you exit PowerPoint.

Work with Text in the Text Pane

1. Click the SmartArt graphic you want to modify.

2. Click the **Design** tab under SmartArt Tools.

3. If necessary, click the **Text Pane** button to show the Text pane.

4. Do any of the following tasks:

   ◆ **New line**. At the end of a line, press Enter.

   ◆ **Indent line right**. Press Tab, or click the **Promote** button.

   ◆ **Indent line left**. Press Shift+Tab, or click the **Demote** button.

   ◆ **Delete line**. Select the line text, and then press Delete.

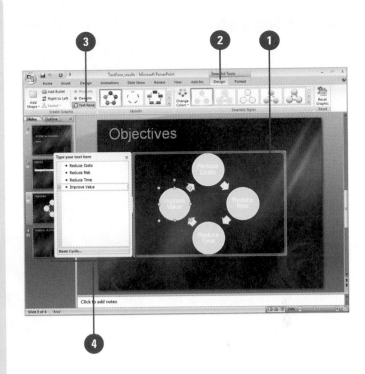

Did You Know?

You can format text in the Text pane. When you apply formatting to text in the Text pane, it doesn't display in the Text pane, but it does display in the SmartArt graphic.

You can remove a shape from a SmartArt graphic. Select the SmartArt graphic, click the shape you want to remove, and then press Delete.

Modifying a SmartArt Graphic

PP07S-3.2.6

After you create a SmartArt graphic, you can add, remove, change, or rearrange shapes to create a custom look. For shapes within a SmartArt graphic, you can change the shape from the Shape gallery or use familiar commands, such as Bring to Front, Send to Back, Align, Group, and Rotate, to create your own custom SmartArt graphic (**New!**). If you no longer want a shape you've added, simply select it, and then press Delete to remove it.

Add a Shape to a SmartArt Graphic

1. Select the shape in the SmartArt graphic you want to modify.

2. Click the **Design** tab under SmartArt Tools.

3. Click the **Add Shape** button to insert a shape at the end, or click the **Add Shape** button arrow, and then select the position where you want to insert a shape.

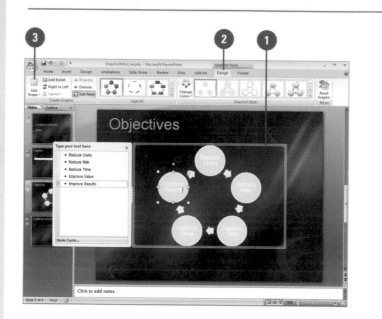

Change Shapes in a SmartArt Graphic

1. Select the shapes in the SmartArt graphic you want to modify.

2. Click the **Format** tab under SmartArt Tools.

3. Click the **Change Shape** button, and then click a shape.

Did You Know?

You can reset a SmartArt graphic back to its original state. Select the SmartArt graphic, click the Design tab under SmartArt Tools, and then click the Reset Graphic button.

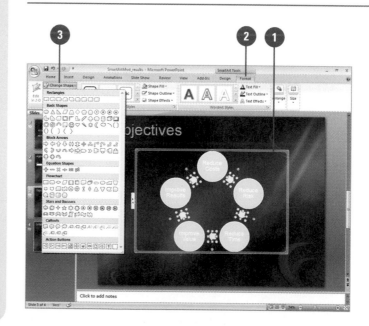

Resizing a SmartArt Graphic

Microsoft
Certified
Application
Specialist   PP07S-3.2.5

Resize a SmartArt Graphic

1. Select the shapes in the SmartArt graphic or the entire SmartArt graphic you want to modify.

2. Click the **Format** tab under SmartArt Tools.

3. Use one of the following methods:

   ◆ Drag a middle handle to resize the object up, down, left, or right.

   ◆ Drag a corner handle to resize the object proportionally.

   ◆ Click the **Size** button, and then specify the size you want.

   ◆ Click the **Larger** or **Smaller** button to increase or decrease the object in standard increments.

Did You Know?

You can arrange shapes in a SmartArt graphic. Select the shape in the SmartArt graphic, click the Format tab under SmartArt Tools, click the Arrange button, and then use any of the arrange button options: Bring to Front, Send to Back, Align, Group, or Rotate.

You can edit a SmartArt graphic shape in 2-D. Select the SmartArt graphic with the 3-D style, click the Format tab under SmartArt Tools, and then click the Edit in 2-D button.

You can change the size of individual shapes within a SmartArt graphic or of an entire SmartArt graphic. If the size of an individual shape within a SmartArt graphic changes, the other shapes in the graphic may also change based on the type of layout. When you resize a shape with text or increase or decrease text size, the text may automatically resize to fit the shape depending on the space available in the SmartArt graphic. When you resize an entire SmartArt graphic, shapes within it scale proportionally or adjust to create the best look.

Larger and Smaller buttons

Size button

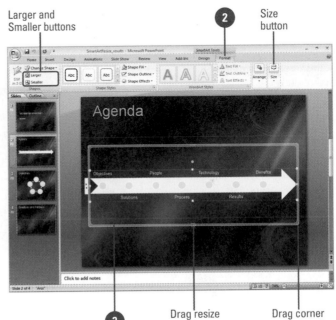

Drag resize handle

Drag corner resize handle

Formatting a SmartArt Graphic

If your current SmartArt graphics don't quite convey the message or look you want, you can use live preview (**New!**) to quickly preview layouts in the Quick Styles (**New!**) and Layout Styles (**New!**) groups and select the one you want. If you only want to change the color, you can choose different color schemes using theme colors by using the Change Color button (**New!**). If the flow of a SmartArt graphic is not the direction you want, you can change the orientation.

Apply a Quick Style to a SmartArt Graphic

1. Click the SmartArt graphic you want to modify.

2. Click the **Design** tab under SmartArt Tools.

3. Click the scroll up or down arrow, or click the **More** list arrow in the Quick Styles group to see additional styles.

   The gallery displays the current layout with different theme colors.

4. Point to a style.

   A live preview (**New!**) of the style appears in the current shape.

5. Click the layout for the SmartArt graphic you want from the gallery.

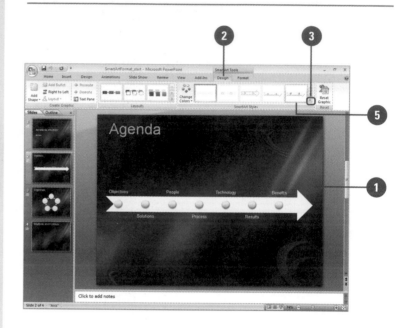

Change a SmartArt Graphic Orientation

1. Click the SmartArt graphic you want to modify.

2. Click the **Design** tab under SmartArt Tools.

3. Click the **Right to Left** button.

   The button toggles, so you can click it again to switch back.

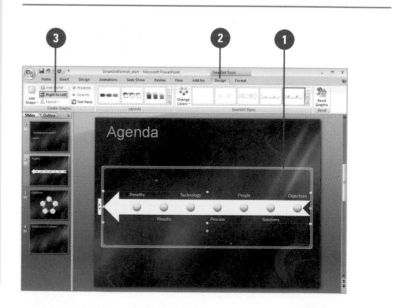

Change a SmartArt Graphic Layout

1. Click the SmartArt graphic you want to modify.

2. Click the **Design** tab under SmartArt Tools.

3. Click the scroll up or down arrow, or click the **More** list arrow in the Layout Styles group to see additional styles.

   The gallery displays layouts designed for bulleted lists.

4. To view the entire list of diagram layouts, click **More Layouts**.

5. Point to a layout.

   A live preview (**New!**) of the style appears in the current shape.

6. Click the layout for the SmartArt graphic you want from the gallery.

7. If you opened the entire list of layouts, click **OK**.

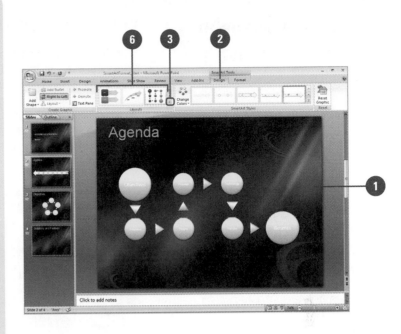

Change a SmartArt Graphic Colors

1. Click the SmartArt graphic you want to modify.

2. Click the **Design** tab under SmartArt Tools.

3. Click the **Change Colors** button.

   The gallery displays the current layout with different theme colors.

4. Point to a style.

   A live preview (**New!**) of the style appears in the current shape.

5. Click the layout for the SmartArt graphic you want from the gallery.

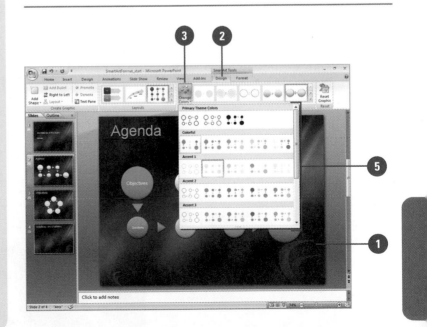

Formatting a Shape in a SmartArt Graphic

Microsoft Certified Application Specialist

PP07S-3.2.3

In the same way you can apply shape fills, outlines, and effects to a shape, you can also apply them to shapes in a SmartArt graphic. You can modify all or part of the SmartArt graphic by using the Shape Fill, Shape Outline, and Shape Effects buttons (**New!**). Shape Fill can be set to be a solid, gradient, texture or picture, or set the Shape Outline to be a solid or gradient (**New!**). In addition, you can change the look of a SmartArt graphic by applying effects (**New!**), such as glow and soft edges. If a shape in a SmartArt graphic contains text, you can use WordArt style galleries to modify shape text.

Apply a Shape Fill to a SmartArt Graphic

1. Select the shapes in the SmartArt graphic you want to modify.

   TIMESAVER *You can hold Ctrl while you click to select multiple shapes, or press Ctrl+A to select all the shapes.*

2. Click the **Format** tab under SmartArt Tools.

3. Click the **Shape Fill** button.

4. Click a color, **No Fill**, or **Picture** to select an image, or point to **Gradient**, or **Texture**, and then select a style.

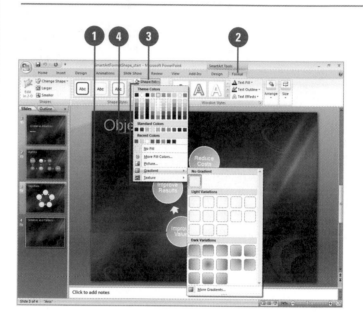

Apply a Shape Outline to a SmartArt Graphic

1. Select the shapes in the SmartArt graphic you want to modify.

2. Click the **Format** tab under SmartArt Tools.

3. Click the **Shape Outline** button.

4. Click a color or **No Outline**, or point to **Weight** or **Dashes**, and then select a style.

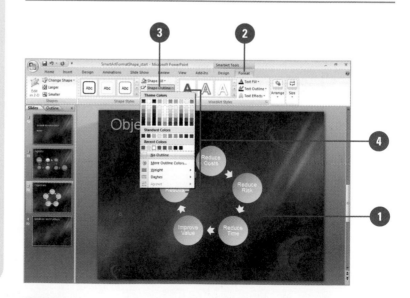

Apply a Shape Effect to a SmartArt Graphic

1. Select the shapes in the SmartArt graphic you want to modify.

2. Click the **Format** tab under SmartArt Tools.

3. Click the **Shape Effects** button, and then point to one of the following:

   ◆ **Preset** to select No 3-D, one of the preset types, or More 3-D Settings.

   ◆ **Shadow** to select No Shadow, one of the shadow types, or More Shadows.

   ◆ **Reflection** to select No Reflection or one of the Reflection Variations.

   ◆ **Glow** to select No Glow, one of the Glow Variations, or More Glow Colors.

   ◆ **Soft Edges** to select No Soft Edges or a point size to determine the soft edge amount.

   ◆ **Bevel** to select No Bevel, one of the bevel types, or More 3-D Settings.

   ◆ **3-D Rotation** to select No Rotation, one of the rotation types, or More 3-D Settings.

   When you point to an effect, a live preview (**New!**) of the style appears in the current shape.

4. Click the effect you want from the gallery to apply it to the selected shape.

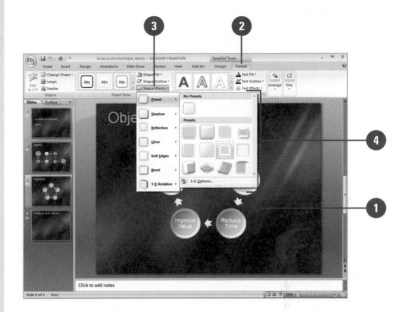

See Also

See "Formatting WordArt Text" on page 178 for information on applying WordArt styles to a SmartArt graphic.

Creating an Organization Chart

An organization chart shows the reporting relationships between individuals in an organization. For example, you can show the relationship between a manager and employees within a company. You can create an organization chart using a SmartArt graphic (**New!**) or using Microsoft Organization Chart. If you're creating a new organization chart, a SmartArt graphic is your best choice. If you need to match an existing organization chart from a previous version of PowerPoint, Microsoft Organization Chart is your best choice. A SmartArt graphic organization chart makes it easy to add shapes using the graphic portion or the Text pane.

Create an Organization Chart Using a SmartArt Graphic

1. Click the **Insert** tab.

2. Click the **SmartArt** button.

3. In the left pane, click **Hierarchy**.

4. In the right pane, click a SmartArt organization chart type.

5. Click **OK**.

   The SmartArt graphic appears with a Text pane to insert text.

6. Label the shapes by doing one of the following:

   ◆ Type text in the [Text] box.

   You can use the arrow keys to move around the Text pane.

   ◆ Click a shape, and then type text directly into the shape.

7. To add shapes from the Text pane, place the insertion point at the beginning of the text where you want to add a shape, type the text you want, press Enter, and then to indent the new shape, press Tab or to de-indent, press Shift+Tab.

8. When you're done, click outside of the SmartArt graphic.

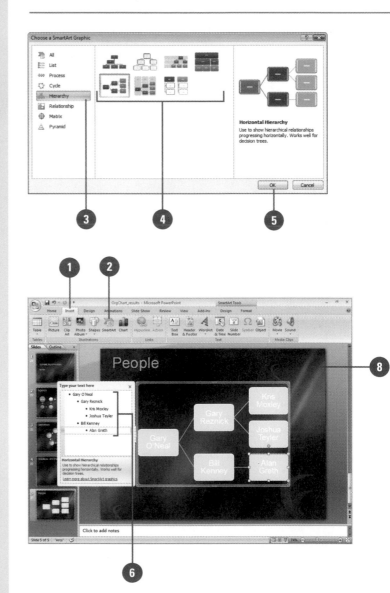

Add a Shape to an Organization Chart

1. Select the shapes in the SmartArt graphic you want to modify.

2. Click the **Design** tab under SmartArt Tools.

3. Click the shape with the layout you want to change.

4. Click the **Add Shape** button arrow, and then select the option you want:

   ◆ **Add Shape After or Add Shape Before.** Inserts a shape at the same level.

   ◆ **Add Shape Above or Add Shape Below.** Inserts a shape one level above or below.

   ◆ **Add Assistant.** Inserts a shape above, but it's displayed at the same level at the end in the Text pane.

5. When you're done, click outside of the SmartArt graphic.

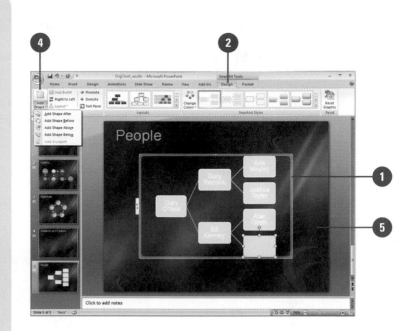

Did You Know?

You can create organization charts using other methods. You can also use Office Visio 2007 or Organization Chart (also known as Microsoft Organization Chart 2.0), which was used in Power-Point 2003 or earlier. Click the Object button in the Text group on the Insert tab to insert an organization chart.

Modifying an Organization Chart

Like any SmartArt graphic, you can add special effects—such as soft edges, glows, or 3-D effects, and animation—to an organization chart. If your organization chart doesn't quite look the way you want, live preview (**New!**) can help you preview layouts in the Quick Styles (**New!**) and Layout Styles (**New!**) groups and select the one you want. If you only want to change the color, you can choose different color schemes using theme colors by using the Change Color button (**New!**).

Change the Layout or Apply a Quick Style to an Organization Chart

1. Click the SmartArt graphic you want to modify.

2. Click the **Design** tab under SmartArt Tools.

3. Click the scroll up or down arrow, or click the **More** list arrow in the Layouts group or Quick Styles group to see additional styles.

   The gallery displays different layouts or the current layout with different theme colors.

4. Point to a style.

   A live preview (**New!**) of the style appears in the current shape.

5. Click the layout or style for the SmartArt graphic you want from the gallery.

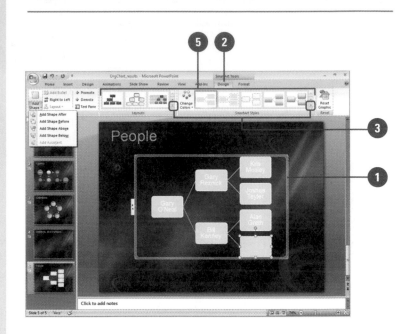

Did You Know?

You can change organization chart lines to dotted lines. Right-click the line you want to modify, click Format Object, click Line Style, click Dash type, click a style, and then click Close.

Modify an Organization Chart Layout Using a SmartArt Graphic

1. Select the shapes in the SmartArt graphic you want to modify.

2. Click the **Design** tab under SmartArt Tools.

3. Click the shape with the layout you want to change.

4. Click the **Organization Chart Layout** button, and then select the option you want:

   ◆ **Standard.** Traditional top down chart.

   ◆ **Both.** Relational left and right chart.

   ◆ **Left Hanging** or **Right Hanging.** Left or right hanging down chart.

5. When you're done, click outside of the SmartArt graphic.

Did You Know?

You can change the colors of an organization chart. Click the SmartArt graphic you want to modify, click the Design tab under SmartArt Tools, click the Change Colors button, and then click the color theme you want.

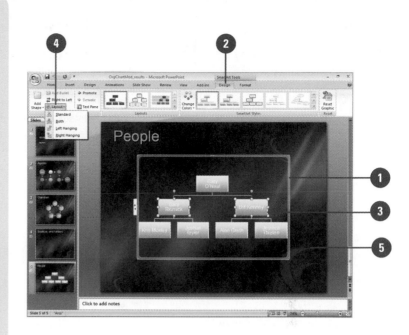

Inserting a Chart

Instead of adding a table of dry numbers, insert a chart. Charts add visual interest and useful information represented by lines, bars, pie slices, or other markers. PowerPoint uses Microsoft Excel (**New!**) to embed and display the information in a chart: the **worksheet**, a spreadsheet-like grid of rows and columns that contains your data; and the **chart**, the graphical representation of the data. A worksheet contains cells to hold your data. A **cell** is the intersection of a row and column. A group of data values from a row or column of data makes up a **data series**. Each data series has a unique color or pattern on the chart.

Insert and Create a Chart

1. Click the **Insert** tab.

2. Click the **Chart** button.

   TIMESAVER *In a content placeholder, you can click the Chart icon to start.*

3. In the left pane, click a category, such as Column, Line, Pie, Bar, Area, X Y (Scatter), Stock, Surface, Doughnut, Bubble, and Radar.

4. In the right pane, click a chart style type.

5. Click **OK**.

   A Microsoft Excel worksheet opens and tiles next to your PowerPoint presentation. The worksheet contains sample data, and the presentation contain a chart.

6. Replace the sample data in the datasheet with your own data.

7. Edit and format the data in the datasheet as appropriate.

8. Click the **Close** button on the Excel worksheet to close it and view the chart in PowerPoint.

9. If necessary, change the chart type, and format the chart.

10. When you're done, click outside of the chart.

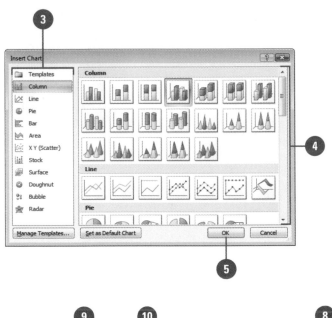

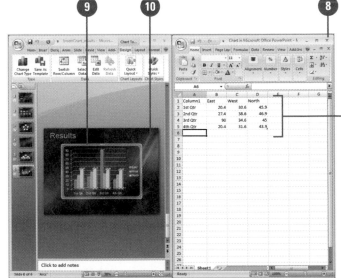

Open and View Chart Data

1 Click the chart you want to modify.

A chart consists of the following elements.

◆ **Data markers**. A graphical representation of a data point in a single cell in the datasheet. Typical data markers include bars, dots, or pie slices. Related data markers constitute a data series.

◆ **Legend**. A pattern or color that identifies each data series.

◆ **X-axis**. A reference line for the horizontal data values.

◆ **Y-axis**. A reference line for the vertical data values.

◆ **Tick marks**. Marks that identify data increments.

2 Click the **Design** tab under Chart Tools.

3 Click the **Edit Data** button.

A Microsoft Excel worksheet opens and tiles next to your PowerPoint presentation.

4 To close the worksheet and view the chart, click the **Close** button on the Excel worksheet and return to PowerPoint.

Did You Know?

You can create a chart from a slide layout. To create a chart on a new slide, click the Add Slide button on the Home tab, choose a slide layout with the content or chart option from the gallery, and then click the chart icon in the placeholder to add the chart and worksheet.

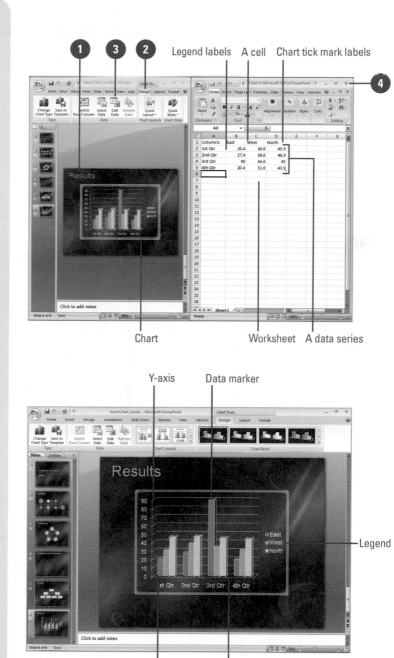

Legend labels A cell Chart tick mark labels

Chart   Worksheet   A data series

Y-axis   Data marker

Legend

X-axis   Tick mark

Selecting Chart Data

Use Microsoft Excel worksheet to edit your data. Select the data first in the worksheet. If you click a cell to select it, anything you type replaces the contents of the cell. If you double-click the cell, however, anything you type is inserted at the location of the cursor. You can select one cell at a time, or you can manipulate blocks of adjacent data called **ranges**. For example, the sample data below is a range.

Select Data in the Worksheet

1. Click the chart you want to modify, and then click the **Edit Data** button on the Design tab under Chart Tools.

2. Use one of the following to select a cell, row, column, or datasheet.

   ◆ To select a cell, click it.

   ◆ To select an entire row or column, click the row heading or column heading button.

   ◆ To select a range of cells, drag the pointer over the cells you want to select, or click the upper-left cell of the range, press and hold Shift, and then click the lower-right cell. When you select a range of cells, the active cell is white, and all other selected cells are outlined in black.

3. To close the worksheet and view the chart, click the **Close** button on the Excel worksheet and return to PowerPoint.

Did You Know?

You can get help with Microsoft Excel. Get help specific to Microsoft Excel by clicking the Help button on the Ribbon or by pressing F1 when you are in Excel.

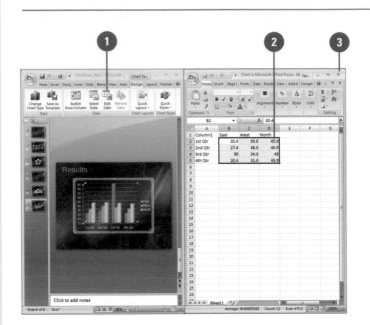

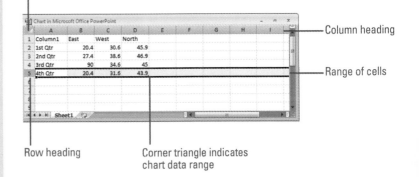

Click to select the entire worksheet

Column heading

Range of cells

Row heading

Corner triangle indicates chart data range

Entering Chart Data

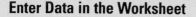

You can enter chart data in the worksheet either by typing it or by inserting it from a different source. The worksheet is designed to make data entry easy, so direct typing is best when you're entering brief, simple data. For more complex or longer data, and when you're concerned about accuracy, insert and link your data to the chart. When you first insert a chart, the worksheet contains sample labels and numbers. If you're entering data by typing, click a cell to make it the active cell, and then select the sample information and replace it with your own.

Enter Data in the Worksheet

1. Click the chart you want to modify, and then click the **Edit Data** button on the Design tab under Chart Tools.

2. To delete the sample data, click the upper-left heading button to select all the cells, and then press Delete.

3. Click the cell to make it active.

4. Type the data you want to enter in the cell.

5. Press Enter to move the insertion point down one row or press Tab to move the insertion point right to the next cell.

6. If necessary, select the data you want for the chart, click the Design tab, click the **Resize Table** button, and then click **OK**.

7. To close the worksheet and view the chart, click the **Close** button on the Excel worksheet and return to PowerPoint.

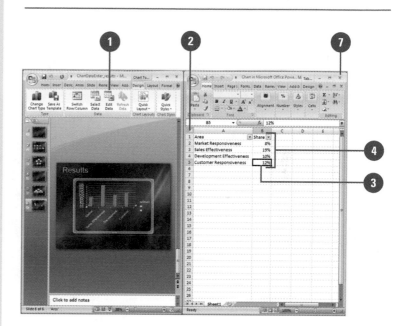

Did You Know?

You can turn automatic completion of cell entries on or off. Excel completes text entries that you start to type. Click the Office button, click Excel Options, click Advanced in the left pane, select or clear Enable AutoComplete for cell values check box, and then click OK.

Editing Chart Data

You can edit chart data in an Excel worksheet one cell at a time, or you can manipulate a range of data. If you're not sure what data to change to get the results you want, use the Edit Data Source dialog box (**New!**) to help you. You can work with data ranges by series, either Legend or Horizontal. The Legend series is the data range displayed on the axis with the legend, while the Horizontal series is the data range displayed on the other axis. Use the Collapse Dialog button to temporarily minimize the dialog to select the data range you want. After you select your data, click the Expand Dialog button to return back to the dialog box.

Edit Data in the Worksheet

1 Click the chart you want to modify, and then click the **Edit Data** button on the Design tab under Chart Tools.

2 To delete the sample data, click the upper-left heading button to select all the cells, and then press Delete.

3 In the worksheet, use any of the following methods to edit cell contents:

◆ To replace the cell contents, click the cell, type the data you want to enter in the cell. It replaces the previous entry.

◆ To edit the cell content, double-click the selected cell where you want to edit.

Press Delete or Backspace to delete one character at a time, and then type the new data.

4 Press Enter to move the insertion point down one row or press Tab to move the insertion point right to the next cell.

5 To close the worksheet and view the chart, click the **Close** button on the Excel worksheet and return to PowerPoint.

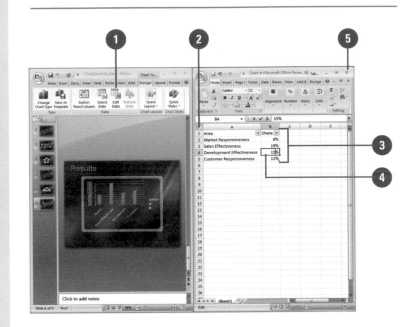

Edit the Data Source

1. Click the chart you want to modify, and then click the **Select Data** button on the Design tab under Chart Tools.

2. In the Select Data Source dialog box, use any of the following:

   IMPORTANT *Click the* **Collapse Dialog** *button to minimize the dialog, so you can select a range in the worksheet. Click the* **Expand Dialog** *button to maximize it again.*

   ◆ **Chart data range.** Displays the data range in the worksheet of the plotted chart.

   ◆ **Switch Row/Column.** Click to switch plotting the data series in the chart from rows or columns.

   ◆ **Add.** Click to add a new Legend data series to the chart.

   ◆ **Edit.** Click to make changes to a Legend or Horizontal series.

   ◆ **Remove.** Click to remove the selected Legend data series.

   ◆ **Move Up and Move Down.** Click to move a Legend data series up or down in the list.

   ◆ **Hidden and Empty Cells.** Click to plot hidden worksheet data in the chart and determine what to do with empty cells.

3. Click **OK**.

4. To close the worksheet and view the chart, click the **Close** button on the Excel worksheet and return to PowerPoint.

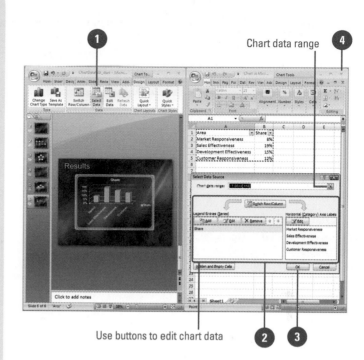

Chart data range

Use buttons to edit chart data

Importing Data

Microsoft Excel makes it easy to insert data from other sources, such as a plain text file, Microsoft Access database, or a Microsoft Excel worksheet. You have control over how much of the data in a file you want to insert, and, in the case of an imported text file, you can indicate how Excel should arrange your data once it is imported.

Import Data into the Worksheet

1 Click the chart you want to modify, and then click the **Edit Data** button on the Design tab under Chart Tools.

2 In Excel, click the cell where you want the data to begin. You cannot select cells already used in a PowerPoint chart. If you want, delete them first.

3 Click the **Data** tab.

4 Click the **Get External Data** button arrow, and then click the button with the type of data you want to import.

5 Double-click the file that contains the data you want to import.

6 If you are importing a text file, follow the Text Import Wizard steps, and then click **Finish**.

7 If you are importing Excel data, select the sheet that contains the data you want to import in the Import Data Options dialog box.

◆ Select the option how you want to view this data in your workbook: **Table**, **PivotTable Report**, **PivotChart and PivotTable Report**, or **Only Create Connection**.

◆ Select where you want to put the data. Click the **New worksheet** option or click the **Existing worksheet** option, and then specify a cell or range of data.

8 Click **OK**.

The Text Import Wizard

Paste Data into the Worksheet

1. In the source program, open the file that contains the data you want to paste.

2. Select the data you want to paste.

3. Click the **Home** tab.

4. Click the **Copy** button.

5. Switch to PowerPoint, and then click the Microsoft Excel chart.

6. Click the **Edit Data** button on the Design tab under Chart Tools.

7. If necessary, switch to the datasheet and clear its contents.

8. Paste the data into the datasheet using one of the following methods.

   ◆ To paste the data without linking it, click the **Home** tab, and then click the **Paste** button.

   ◆ To link the data, click the Home tab, click the **Paste** button arrow, click **Paste Link**, and then click **OK**.

9. If necessary, select the data you want for the chart, click the **Design** tab, click the **Resize Table** button, and then click **OK**.

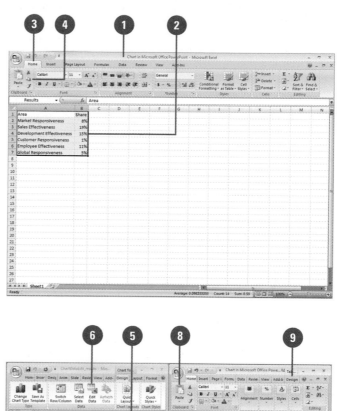

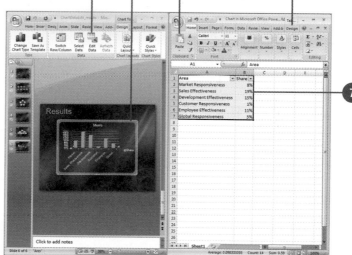

Did You Know?

You can switch the data series around. In PowerPoint, click the chart, click the Design tab under Chart Tools, click the Switch Row/Column button.

Office pastes charts from PowerPoint as a picture. If you paste a chart from PowerPoint into a program other than PowerPoint, Word, or Excel, the chart is pasted as a picture. A workaround is to copy the chart from Excel.

Modifying the Data Worksheet

After you enter or edit data in the worksheet, you might need to change the column widths to fit the data. If you see ##### in a cell, it means there is not enough room in the column to display the data. You need to increase the column width to display the data. If you need to change one column, you can use the mouse to quickly change the column width. To uniformly change several columns to the same column width, you can use the Column Width command on the Format menu. You may need to reformat the datasheet itself—its size and how it displays the data—to make it easier to read. For example, you can format numbers in currency, accounting, percentage, and scientific formats. You can also change the fonts used in the graph.

Change the Width of a Column

◆ To increase or decrease the width of a column, show the data in the worksheet, position the pointer on the vertical line to the right of the column heading, and then drag the pointer until the column is the correct width.

◆ To adjust a datasheet column to display the widest data entered (also known as Best Fit), show the data in the worksheet, position the pointer on the line to the right of the column heading, and then double-click to adjust the column width.

  If a series of number signs (#) appears in a cell, it means the cell is not wide enough to display the entire cell contents. Widen the column to view the data.

Double-click the line to the right of the column heading to resize the column to the widest entry.

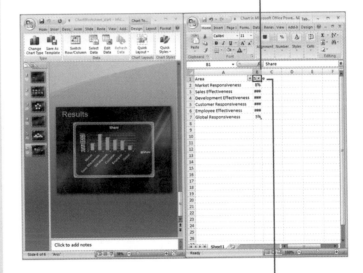

Drag the pointer until the column is the correct width.

Did You Know?

You can specify a precise column width. Click a cell in the column you want to format, click the Home tab, click the Cells button, click the Format button, and then click Width to enter a column width, click Standard Width to change the standard column width, or click AutoFit Selection to change the column to the smallest size possible to fit the data.

Insert Cells, Rows, and Columns

1. In the worksheet, select the cells you want to modify.

2. Click the **Home** tab.

3. Click where you want to insert cells:

   ◆ To insert a column, click the column heading to the right of where you want the new column.

   ◆ To insert a row, click the row heading below where you want the new row.

   ◆ To insert a single cell, click an adjacent cell.

4. Click the **Insert Cells** button arrow, and then click the insert option you want.

Format the Worksheet

1. In the worksheet, select the cells you want to modify.

2. Click the **Home** tab.

3. Use the options on the Ribbon to make the formatting changes you want.

   ◆ To apply a theme, click the **Cell Styles** button, and then click the style you want.

   ◆ To format individual attributes, use the options in the Font and Alignment groups to make the formatting changes you want.

   ◆ To format numbers, use the options in the Number groups to make the formatting changes you want.

Click to apply cell styles

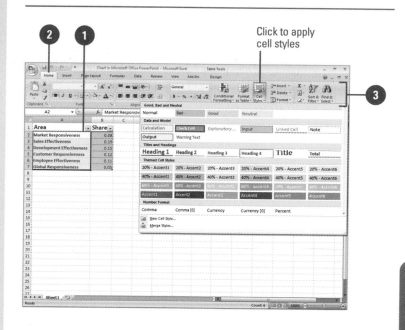

Selecting a Chart Type, Layout, and Style

Microsoft
Certified
Application
Specialist

PP07S-3.6.2

Your chart is what your audience sees, so make sure to take advantage of PowerPoint's pre-built chart layouts and styles (**New!**) to make the chart appealing and visually informative. Start by choosing the chart type that is suited for presenting your data. There are a wide variety chart types, available in 2-D and 3-D formats, from which to choose. For each chart type, you can select a predefined chart layout and style to apply the formatting you want. If you want to format your chart beyond the provided formats, you can customize a chart. Save your customized settings so that you can apply that chart formatting to any chart you create.

Change a Chart Type

1. Select the chart you want to change.

2. Click the **Design** tab under Chart Tools.

3. Click the **Change Chart Type** button.

4. Click the chart type you want.

5. Click **OK**.

Did You Know?

You can reset chart formatting. Click the chart you want to reset, click the Format tab under Chart Tools, and then click Reset to Match Style.

You can delete a chart. Click the chart object, and then press Delete.

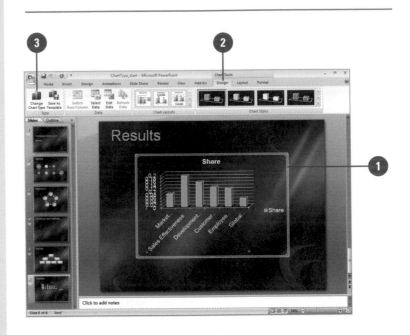

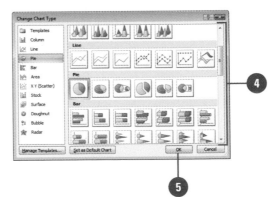

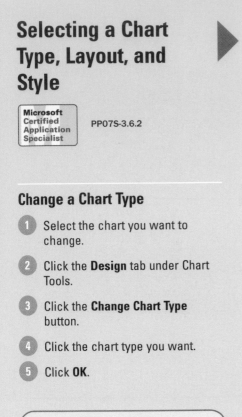

Apply a Chart Layout

1. Select the chart you want to change.

2. Click the **Design** tab under Chart Tools.

3. Click the scroll up or down arrow, or click the **More** list arrow in the Chart Layouts group to see variations of the chart type.

4. Click the chart layout you want.

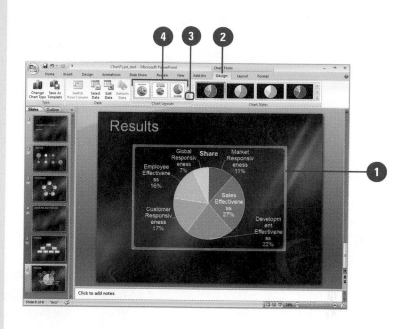

Apply a Chart Style

1. Select the chart you want to change.

2. Click the **Design** tab under Chart Tools.

3. Click the scroll up or down arrow, or click the **More** list arrow in the Chart Styles group to see color variations of the chart layout.

4. Click the chart style you want.

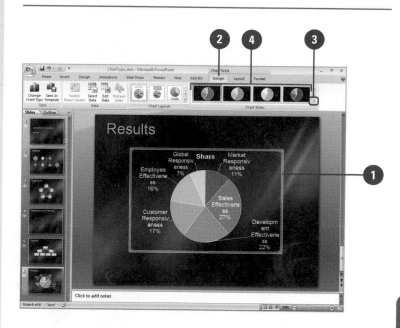

Formatting Chart Objects

Microsoft Certified Application Specialist

PP07S-3.6.2, PP07S-3.6.3

Chart objects are the individual elements that make up a chart, such as an axis, the legend, or a data series. The **plot area** is the bordered area where the data are plotted. The **chart area** is the area between the plot area and the chart object selection box. Before you can format a chart object, you need to select it first. You can select a chart object directly on the chart or use the Chart Elements list arrow on the Ribbon. Once you select a chart object, you can use options on the Format tab to modify them. In the same way you can apply shape fills, outlines, and effects to a shape, you can also apply them to shapes in a chart.

Select a Chart Object

1. Select the chart you want to change.

2. Click the **Format** tab under Chart Tools.

3. Click the **Chart Elements** list arrow.

4. Click the chart object you want to select.

   When a chart object is selected, selection handles appear.

   TIMESAVER *To select a chart object, click a chart element directly in the chart.*

5. Use the Home, Design, Layout, or Format tabs to change the selected chart element.

Did You Know?

You can enlarge a chart object to select it. Increase the zoom percentage to enlarge your view before using the mouse pointer to select chart objects.

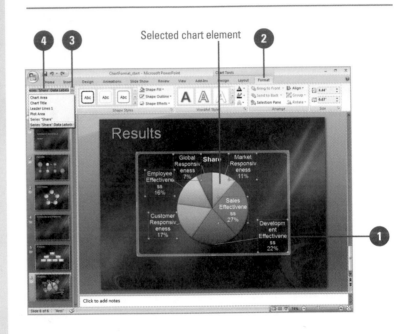

Selected chart element

Change a Chart Object Style

1. Select the chart or a chart element you want to change.

   When a chart object is selected, selection handles appear.

2. Click the **Format** tab under Chart Tools.

3. Click the **Format Selection** button.

4. Select the options you want. The available options change depending on the chart object.

5. Click **Close**.

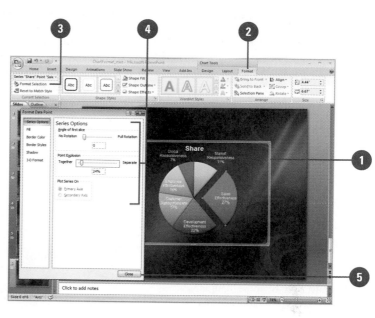

Apply a Shape Styles to a Chart Object

1. Select the chart element you want to modify.

2. Click the **Format** tab under Chart Tools.

3. Click the **Shape Fill**, **Shape Outline**, or **Shape Effects** button, and then click or point to an option.

   ◆ **Fill.** Click a color, No Fill, or Picture to select an image, or point to Gradient, or Texture, and then select a style.

   ◆ **Outline.** Click a color or No Outline, or point to Weight, or Dashes, and then select a style.

   ◆ **Effects.** Point to an effect category (Preset, Shadow, Reflection, Glow, Soft Edges, Bevel, or 3-D Rotations), and then select an option.

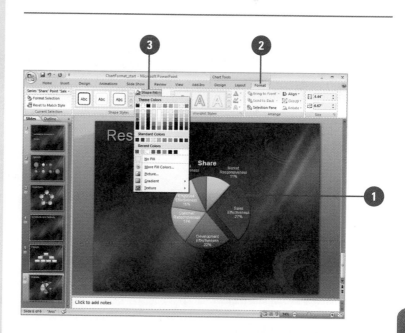

Changing the Chart Layout Objects

Microsoft Certified Application Specialist   PP07S-3.6.4

The layout of a chart typically comes with a chart title, axis titles, data labels, and a legend. However, you can also include other elements, such as data labels, and a data table. You can show, hide, or change the positions chart elements to achieve the look you want. You can also change the chart display by showing axis or gridlines with different measurements. Format the background of a chart by showing or hiding the chart wall or floor with a default color fill, or by changing the 3-D view of a chart.

Change Chart Labels

1. Select the chart or a chart element you want to change.

2. Click the **Layout** tab under Chart Tools.

3. Click any of the following buttons:

   ◆ **Chart Title** to show, hide, or position the chart title.

   ◆ **Axis Title** to show, hide, or position the text used to label each axis.

   ◆ **Legend** to show, hide, overlay, or position the chart legend.

   ◆ **Data Labels** to add, remove, or position data labels.

   ◆ **Data Table** to add a data table to the chart.

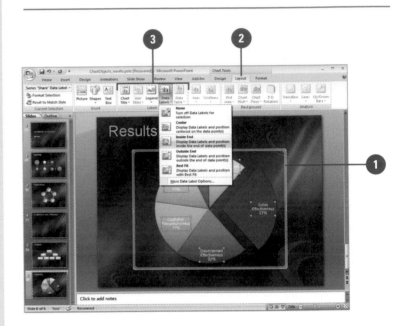

Did You Know?

You can insert a picture into a chart. Select the chart, click the Layout tab under Chart Tools, click the Picture button arrow, click Picture from File, or Clip Art, then select the picture you want.

You can insert a shape into a chart. Select the chart, click the Layout tab under Chart Tools, click the Shape button, click the shape you want, and then draw the shape.

For Your Information

Using Advanced Chart Analysis Techniques

PowerPoint offers a number of advanced charting techniques to create a chart with data analysis. You can add trendlines derived from regression analysis to show a trend in existing data and make predictions; create a moving average, a sequence of averages from grouped data points, that smooths the fluctuations in data so you can more easily identify trends; add error bars that express the degree of uncertainty attached to a given data series; add drawing objects, including arrows, text boxes, and pictures, to your charts; fill chart elements such as bars, areas, and surfaces with textures, imported pictures, or gradient fills; and animate bars, data points, or other chart data for added multimedia impact. To use advanced chart analysis techniques, select the chart or a chart element you want to change, click the Layout tab under Chart Tools, and then use the Trendline, Lines, Up/Down Bars, or Error Bars buttons in the Analysis group.

Change Chart Axis

1. Select the chart or a chart element you want to change.

2. Click the **Layout** tab under Chart Tools.

3. Click any of the following buttons:

   ◆ **Axis** to change the formatting and layout of each axis.

   ◆ **Gridlines** to show or hide major or minor gridlines.

4. If necessary, select the options you want, and then click **Close**.

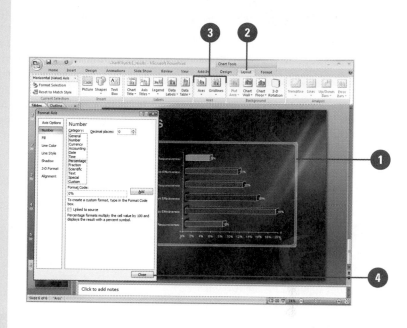

Change Chart Background

1. Select the chart or a chart element you want to change.

2. Click the **Layout** tab under Chart Tools.

3. Click any of the following buttons:

   ◆ **Plot Area** to show or hide the plot area.

   ◆ **Chart Wall** to show or hide the chart wall with the default color fill.

   ◆ **Chart Floor** to show or hide the chart floor with the default color fill.

   ◆ **3-D View** to change the 3-D viewpoint of the chart.

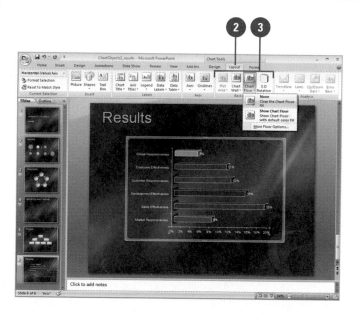

Saving a Chart Template

A chart template file (.crtx) (**New!**) saves all the customization you made to a chart for use in other presentations. You can save any chart in a presentation as a chart template file and use it to form the basis of your next presentation chart, which is useful for standard company financial reporting. Although you can store your template anywhere you want, you may find it handy to store it in the Templates/Charts folder that PowerPoint and Microsoft Office uses to store its templates. If you store your design templates in the Templates/Charts folder, those templates appear as options when you insert or change a chart type using My Templates (**New!**). When you create a new chart or want to change the chart type of an existing chart, you can apply the new chart template.

Create a Custom Chart Template

1. Click the chart you want to save as a template.

2. Click the **Design** tab under Chart Tools.

3. Click the **Save As Template** button.

4. Make sure the Charts folder appears in the Save in box.

   Microsoft Office templates are typically stored in the following location:

   Windows Vista. C:/Users/*your name*/AppData/Microsoft/ Roaming/Templates/Charts.

   Windows XP. C:/Documents and Settings/*your name*/Application Data/Microsoft/Templates/Charts.

5. Type a name for the chart template.

6. Click **Save**.

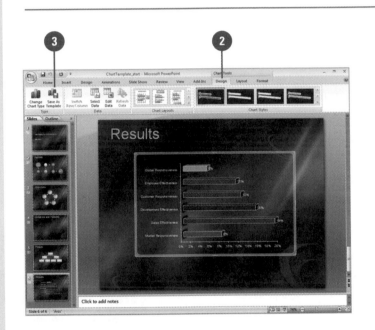

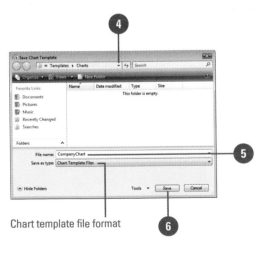

Chart template file format

Apply a Chart Template

 Use one of the following methods:

◆ **New chart.** Click the **Insert** tab, and then click **Insert Chart**.

◆ **Change chart.** Select the chart you want to change, click the **Design** tab under Chart Tools, and then click the **Change Chart Type** button.

2 In the left pane, click **Templates**.

3 Click the custom chart type you want.

4 Click **OK**.

Did You Know?

You can manage chart templates in the Charts folder. In the Chart Type dialog box, you can click the Manage Templates button to open the Charts folder and move, copy, or delete chart templates (.crtx). When you're done, click the Close button to return back to the Chart Type dialog box, and then click Cancel.

You can set a chart as the default. If you use the same chart template over and over again, you can set a chart as the default when creating a new chart. In the Chart Type dialog box, click Template in the left pane, select the chart you want to use, click Set as Default Chart, and then click Cancel.

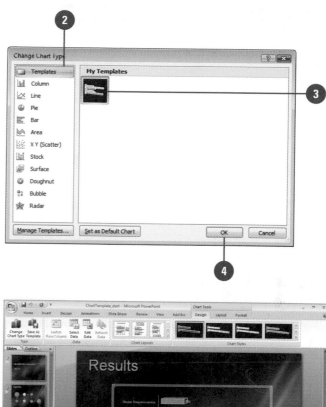

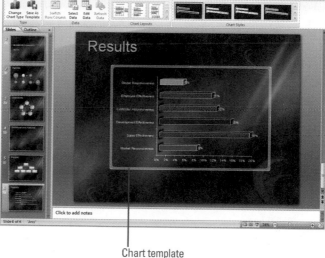

Chart template

Inserting a Table

A **table** neatly organizes information into rows and columns, now up to a maximum of 75x75 (**New!**). The intersection of a column and row is called a **cell**. Enter text into cells just as you would anywhere else in PowerPoint, except that pressing the Tab key moves you from one cell to the next. PowerPoint tables behave much like tables in Word. You can insert tables by specifying a size, or drawing rows and columns to create a custom table. If you like to use Microsoft Excel worksheets, you can also insert and create an Excel table in your presentation.

Insert a Table Quickly

1. In Normal view, display the slide to which you want to add a table.

2. Click the **Insert** tab.

3. Click the **Table** button, and then drag to select the number of rows and columns you want, or click **Insert Table**, enter the number of columns and rows you want, and then click **OK**.

4. Release the mouse button to insert a blank grid in the document.

5. When you're done, click outside of the table.

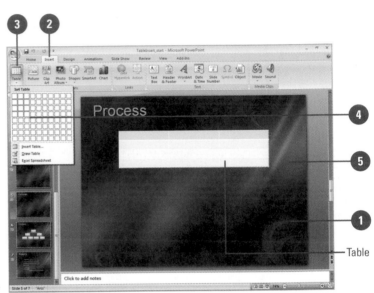

Table

Draw a Table

1. In Normal view, display the slide to which you want to add a table.

2. Click the **Insert** tab.

3. Click the **Table** button, and then click **Draw Table**.

4. Drag the table size you want.

5. Drag horizontal lines to create rows and vertical lines to create columns.

6. When you're done, click outside of the table.

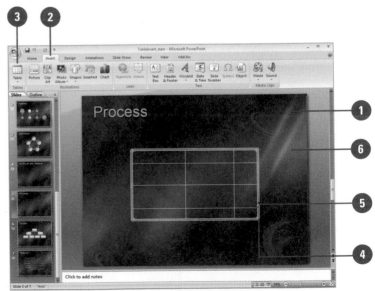

Insert an Excel Table

1. In Normal view, display the slide to which you want to add a table.

2. Click the **Insert** tab.

3. Click the **Table** button, and then click **Insert Excel Spreadsheet**.

   An Excel worksheet appears on your slide.

4. If necessary, drag the lower-right corner sizing handle to enlarge the size of the worksheet.

5. When you're done, click outside of the table.

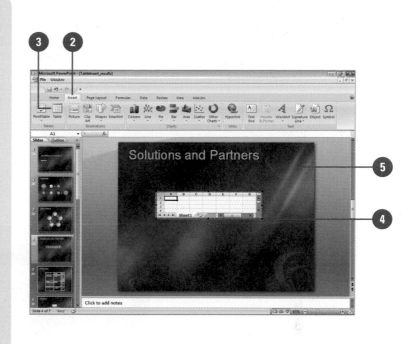

Enter Text and Move Around a Table

The insertion point shows where text you type will appear in a table. Choose one of the following after you type text in a cell.

◆ Press Enter to start a new paragraph within that cell.

◆ Press Tab to move the insertion point to the next cell to the right (or to the first cell in the next row).

◆ Use the arrow keys or click anywhere in the table to move the insertion point to a new location.

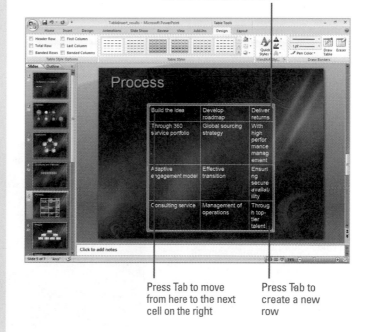

Press Tab to move from here to the first cell in the next row

Press Tab to move from here to the next cell on the right

Press Tab to create a new row

Modifying a Table

Microsoft Certified Application Specialist

PP07S-3.7.3

After you create a table or begin to enter text in one, you might want to add more rows or columns to accommodate the text you are entering in the table. PowerPoint makes it easy for you to format your table. You can change the alignment of the text in the cells (by default, text is aligned on the left of a cell). You can also modify the appearance and size of the cells and the table.

Insert and Delete Columns and Rows

1. Click in a table cell next to where you want the new column or row to appear.

2. Click the **Layout** tab under Table Tools.

3. To insert columns and rows, click **Insert Above**, **Insert Below**, **Insert Left**, or **Insert Right** buttons.

4. To delete columns and rows, click the **Delete** button, and then click **Delete Columns** or **Delete Rows**.

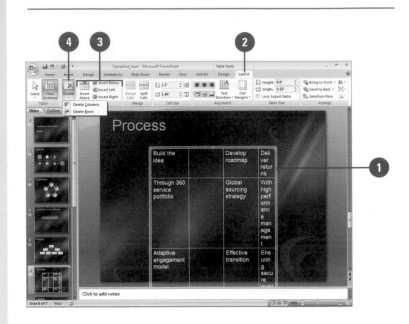

Change Cells Margins and Table Sizes

1. Select the text you want to align in the cells, rows, or columns.

2. Click the **Layout** tab under Table Tools.

3. To resize the table manually, drag a corner or middle resize handle.

   To set a specific size for the table, click the **Table Size** button, and then specify a height and width. To keep the size proportional, select the **Lock Aspect Ratio** check box.

4. To change margins, click the **Cell Margins** button, and then click a cell size margin option: Normal, None, Narrow, Wide, or Custom Margins.

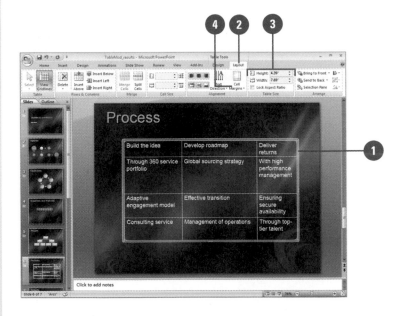

Adjust Row Height and Column Width

1. Move the pointer over the boundary of the row or column you want to adjust until the pointer changes into a resizing pointer.

2. Drag the boundary to adjust the row or column to the size you want.

> ### Did You Know?
>
> *You can merge or split cells.* Select the cells you want to merge or the cell you want to split, and then click the Merge Cells or Split Cells button in the Merge group on the Layout tab.

Align Text Within Cells, Rows, and Columns

1. Select the text you want to align in the cells, rows, or columns.

2. Click the **Layout** tab under Table Tools.

3. To align text in a cell, row or column, click one of the alignment buttons in the Alignment group: **Align Left**, **Center**, **Align Right**, **Align Top**, **Center Vertically**, or **Align Bottom**.

4. To evenly distribute the height and width of the selected row and columns, select the row or column, and then click **Distribute Rows** or **Distribute Columns**.

5. To change the direction of text in a cell, select a cell, row or column, click the **Text Direction** button, and then select an option.

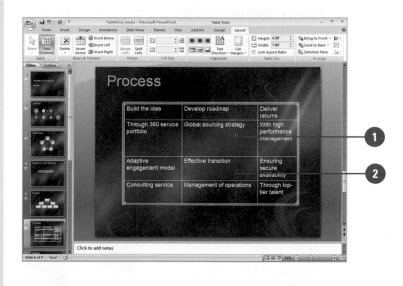

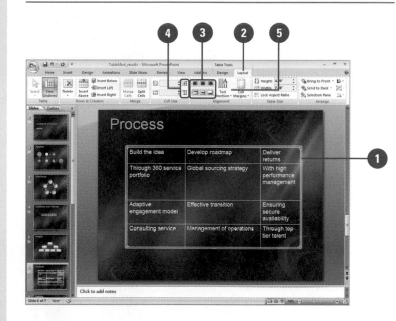

Formatting a Table

When you create a table, you typically include a header row or first column to create horizontal or vertical headings for your table information. You can use Quick Style options (**New!**), such as a header or total row, first or last column, or banded rows and columns, to show or hide a special row and column formatting. The Total Row option displays a row at the end of the table for column totals. The Banded Row or Banded Column option formats even rows or columns differently from odd rows or columns to make a table easier to view. You can also insert a picture into a table to create a more polished look.

Format Table Columns

1. Click the table you want to change.

2. Click the **Design** tab under Table Tools.

3. Select any of the following row and column check box options:

   ◆ **First Column** to format the first column of the table as special.

   ◆ **Last Column** to format the last column of the table as special.

   ◆ **Banded Column** to format even columns differently than odd columns.

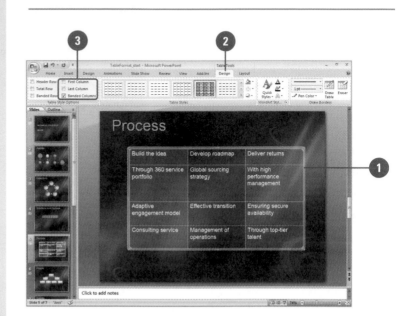

Format Table Rows

1. Click the table you want to change.

2. Click the **Design** tab under Table Tools.

3. Select any of the following row and column check box options:

   ◆ **Header Row** to format the top row of the table as special.

   ◆ **Total Row** to format the bottom row of the table for column totals.

   ◆ **Banded Rows** to format even rows differently than odd rows.

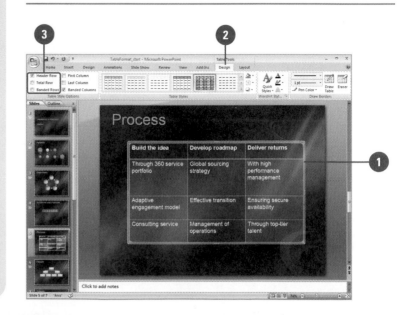

Add Pictures to a Table

1. Select the cells where you want to insert a picture, and then right-click one of the selected cells.

2. Click **Format Shape**.

3. In the left pane, click **Fill**.

4. Click **Picture or texture fill** option.

5. Click **File**.

6. Click the **Look in** list arrow, and then select the drive and folder that contain the file you want to insert.

7. Click the file you want to insert.

8. Click **Insert**.

9. Select or clear the **Tile picture as texture** check box.

10. Click **Close**.

Did You Know?

You can add or remove lines from a table. Select the table you want to change, and then click the Design tab under Table Tools. In the Draw Borders group. Select a pen style, weight, and color. Click the Draw Table button, and then drag the pencil pointer from one boundary to another to add cells. Click the Eraser button, and then click on a border to erase a cell. Press ESC when you're done.

You can show or hide gridlines in a table. Select the table you want to change, click the Layout tab under Table Tools, and then click Show Gridlines to toggle it on and off.

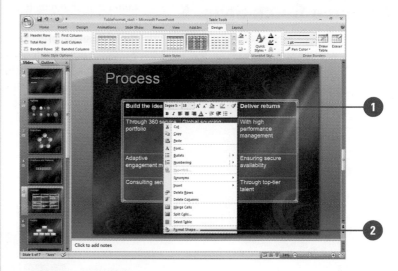

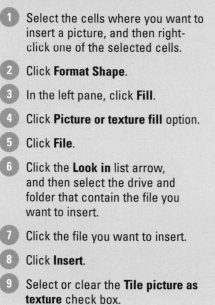

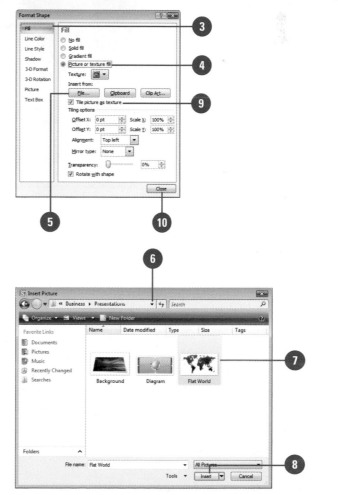

Adding a Quick Style to a Table

Microsoft
Certified
Application
Specialist

PP07S-3.7.2

Instead of changing individual attributes of a table, such as shape, border, and effects, you can quickly add them all at once with the Table Quick Style gallery. The Table Quick Style gallery (**New!**) provides a variety of different formatting combinations. To quickly see if you like a Table Quick Style, point to a thumbnail in the gallery to display a live preview (**New!**) of it in the selected shape. If you like it, you can apply it. In addition to applying one of the preformatted table from the Table Quick Style gallery, you can also create your own style by shaping your text into a variety of shapes, curves, styles, and color patterns.

Add a Quick Style to a Table

1. Click the table you want to change, or select the cells you want to modify.

2. Click the **Design** tab under Table Tools.

3. Click the scroll up or down arrow, or click the **More** list arrow in the Table Styles group to see additional styles.

   The current style appears highlighted in the gallery.

   TIMESAVER *Click the gallery title bar arrow to narrow down the list of styles: All, Document Matching, Light, Medium, or Dark.*

4. Point to a style.

   A live preview (**New!**) of the style appears in the current shape.

5. Click the style you want from the gallery to apply it to the selected table.

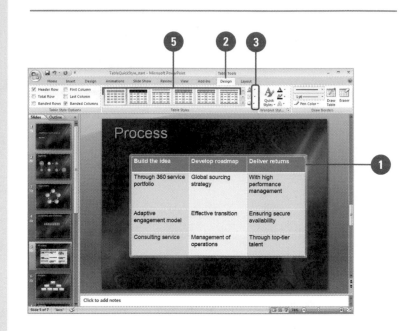

Did You Know?

You can clear table formatting. Select the table you want to change, click the Design tab under Table Tools, click the More list arrow in the Table Styles group, and then click Clear Table.

Apply a Fill to a Table

1. Click the table you want to change, or select the cells you want to modify.

2. Click the **Design** tab under Table Tools.

3. Click the **Shading** button, and then click or point to one of the following:

   ◆ **Color** to select a theme or standard color.

   ◆ **Picture** to select a picture file.

   ◆ **Gradient** to select No Gradient, one of the shadow types, or More Gradients.

   ◆ **Texture** to select one of the of the texture types, or More Textures.

   ◆ **Table Background** to select a theme or standard color.

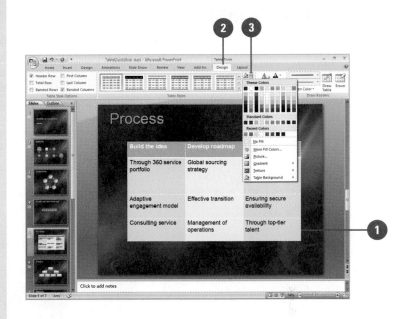

Apply an Outline to a Table

1. Click the table you want to change, or select the cells you want to modify.

2. Click the **Design** tab under Table Tools.

3. Click the **Border** button.

4. Click a border option, such as No Border, All Borders, Outside Borders, Inside Horizontal Border, Inside Vertical Border, Diagonal Down Border, or Diagonal Up Border.

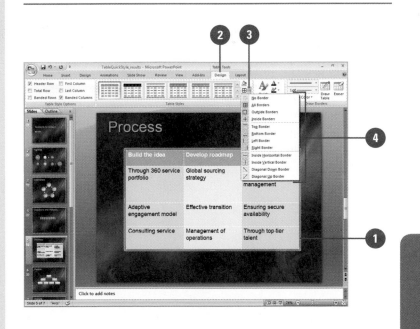

Applying Effects to a Table

You can change the look of a table by applying effects (**New!**), such as shadows, reflections, glow, soft edges, 3-D rotations, and transformations. Apply effects to a table by using the Table Effects gallery for quick results. From the Table Effects gallery you can apply a built-in combination of 3-D effects or individual effects to a table. To quickly see if you like the effect, point to a thumbnail in the Table Effects gallery to display a live preview (**New!**) of it. If you like it, you can apply it. If you no longer want to apply the effect, you can remove it. Simply, select the table, point to the effect type on the Table Effects gallery, and then select the No effect type option.

Apply an Effect to a Text

1. Click the table you want to change.

2. Click the **Design** tab under Table Tools.

3. Click the **Tables Effects** button, and then point to one of the following:

   ◆ **Cell Bevel** to select No Bevel or one of the bevel variations.

   ◆ **Shadow** to select No Shadow, one of the shadow types (Outer or Inner), or More Shadows.

   ◆ **Reflection** to select No Reflection or one of the Reflection Variations.

   When you point to an effect, a live preview (**New!**) of the style appears in the current shape.

4. Click the effect you want from the gallery to apply it to the selected shape.

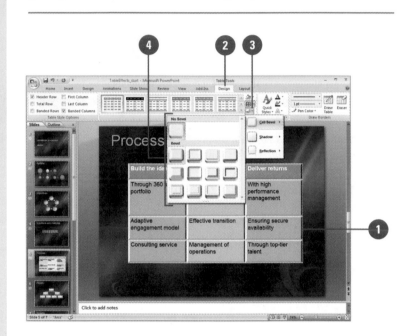

Sharing Information Among Documents

Object linking and embedding (OLE) is a familiar innovation in personal computing. OLE lets you insert an object created in one program into a document created in another program. Terms that you'll find useful in understanding how you can share objects among documents include:

Embedding and Linking	
Term	**Definition**
Source program	The program that created the original object
Source file object	The file that contains the original
Destination program	The program that created the document into which you are inserting the object
Destination file	The file into which you are inserting the object

For example, if you place an Excel chart in your PowerPoint presentation, Excel is the source program and PowerPoint is the destination program. The chart is the source file; the presentation is the destination file. There are three ways to share information in Windows programs: pasting, embedding, and linking.

Pasting

You can cut or copy an object from one document and then paste it into another using the Cut, Copy, and Paste commands on the source and destination program ribbons.

Embedding

When you **embed** an object, you place a copy of the object in the destination file, and when you activate the object, the tools from the in which it was created (the **source program**) become available in your presentation. For example, if you insert and then click an Excel chart in your PowerPoint presentation, the Excel ribbon replaces the PowerPoint ribbon, so you can edit the chart if necessary. With embedding, any changes you make to the chart in the presentation do not affect the original file.

Linking

When you link an object, you insert a representation of the object itself into the **destination file**. The tools of the source program are available, and when you use them to edit the object you've inserted, you are actually editing the source file. Moreover, any changes you make to the source file are reflected in the destination file. You can edit the linked object from either file, although changes are stored in the source file. For example, you might link an Excel chart to a Word document and a PowerPoint slide so you can update the chart from any of the files. If you break the link between a linked object and its source file, the object becomes embedded.

Embedding and Linking an Object

PP07S-2.2.1, PP07S-2.3.2

You can embed or link objects in several ways. If you are creating a new object you want to embed or link, use the Insert Object button. If you want to embed an existing file, you can also use Insert Object and specify whether you want to also link the object. If your object is already open in its source program, you can copy the object, and in some cases, paste it onto a slide, automatically embedding it. Finally, you can use the Paste Special command to **paste link** a copied object—pasting and linking it at the same time.

Insert a New Object

1. Click the **Insert** tab, and then click **Insert Object** button.

2. Click the **Create new** option.

3. Click the type of object you want to insert.

4. Click **OK**.

5. Use the source program tools to edit the object.

6. When you're done, click outside the object.

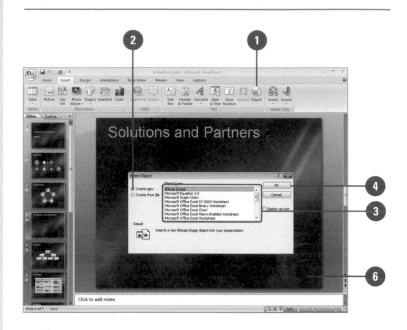

Insert a File

1. Click the **Insert** tab, and then click **Insert Object** button.

2. Click the **Create from file** option.

3. Click **Browse**.

4. Click the **Look in** list arrow, and then select the file you want to insert, and then click **OK**.

5. To embed the object, clear the **Link** check box, if necessary. To link it, select the **Link** check box.

6. Click **OK**.

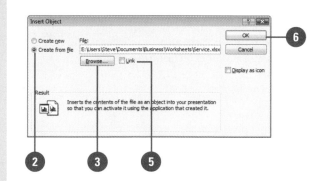

Paste Link an Object

1. In the source program, select the object you want to paste link.

2. Click the **Home** tab.

3. Click the **Cut** or **Copy** button.

4. Switch to your presentation.

5. Click the **Home** tab.

6. Click the **Paste** button arrow, and then click **Paste Special**.

7. Click the **Paste link** option.

8. Click the object type you want.

9. Click **OK**.

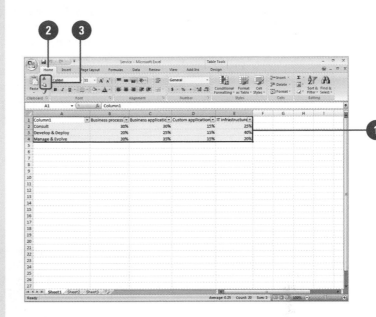

Did You Know?

You can paste text in different formats. The Paste Special command allows you to paste text on the Clipboard to other parts of a presentation or other documents in different formats: HTML Format, Formatted Text (RTF), or Unformatted Text.

You can insert objects as icons. In the Insert Object dialog box, select the Display As Icon check box. If you insert an object as an icon, you can double-click the icon to view the object. This is especially handy for kiosk presentations.

You can work with embedded objects. If you click an embedded object, you simply select it. You can then resize it in PowerPoint. If you double-click an embedded object, you activate it and the source toolbars and menus appear.

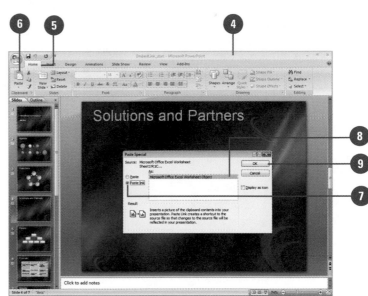

Modifying Links

When you modify a linked object, it is usually updated in the destination document. However, if it doesn't automatically update, you can update the link manually. All Office 2007 programs give you some control over the links you have established. You can convert a linked object to another object type. For example, if you linked an Excel 2007 worksheet to a PowerPoint 2007 presentation, and then later wanted to save it as a PowerPoint 97-2003 presentation, you can convert the linked Excel object to an Excel 97-2003 worksheet.

Edit a Linked Object

1. Open the presentation that contains the links you want to update.

2. Double-click the object.

   The source program opens.

3. Make changes you want.

4. Click the **Office** button (or **File** menu, depending on the program), and then click **Exit** *program name* (or *Exit to return to program name*).

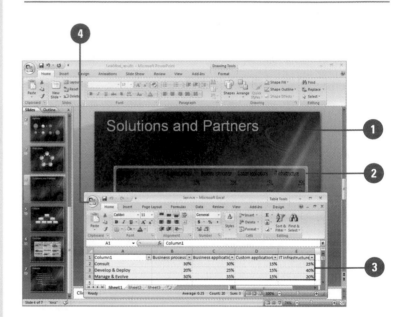

Did You Know?

You can change the source of a linked object. Double-click the linked object to open it, close the original file, open a new one, place the data you want in the file, and then save and exit the source program.

You can update the source of a linked object. Open the source file directly from the source program (not through PowerPoint), make the changes you want, and then save and exit the program. Open PowerPoint with the linked object. Double-click the object, and then exit the program to update the object in PowerPoint.

Convert a Linked Object

1. Right-click the linked object whose file type you want to convert.

2. Point to **Linked *x* Object**, where *x* is Worksheet, Equation, or some file type, depending on the object type.

3. Click **Convert**.

4. Click the new object type you want.

5. Click **OK**.

Did You Know?

You can reconnect a broken link. After you break the connection to a linked object, you must reinsert the object into your presentation to reconnect.

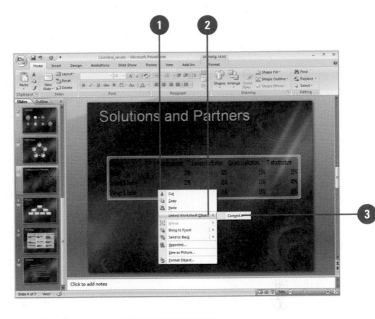

For Your Information

Reducing the Size of Embedded Objects

If you no longer need to edit an embedded object, you can reduce the size of the object in PowerPoint by removing the OLE related data and compressing the picture. OLE objects include a Windows® Metafile (WMF) picture of the image. PowerPoint normally compresses images very efficiently, but it can't compress images in WMFs, so copying and pasting or dragging images into your files can make your files quite large. To remove the OLE data, right-click the embedded object, point to Grouping on the shortcut menu, and then click Ungroup. Next, right-click the image again, point to Grouping on the shortcut menu, and then click Regroup. Ungrouping throws away the OLE data and leaves just the picture in a form that PowerPoint can now compress. Remember, once you ungroup the embedded object, you cannot restore the OLE data without creating a new embedded object.

Inserting a Microsoft Excel Chart

If you need to create chart for backwards compatibility with Power-Point 97-2003, you can embed an Excel object for Excel 97-2003. An embedded object is an object that maintains a direct connection to its original program, known as the source program. After you insert an embedded object, you can easily edit it by double-clicking it, which opens the program in which it was originally created. Embedding objects increases the file size of a presentation because the embedded object is stored in the presentation. To reduce the file size of the presentation, you can link an object instead of embedding it. A linked object appears in the slide, but it actually contains a "link" back to the original file, known as the source document. When you link an object, the original object is stored in its source document, where it was created. You must have Microsoft Excel installed on your computer to insert an Excel chart or worksheet.

Insert a New Excel Chart

1. Click the **Insert** tab, and then click **Insert Object** button.

2. Click the **Create new** option.

3. Click **Microsoft Office Excel Chart**.

4. Click **OK**.

5. Use the source program tools to edit the object.

6. When you're done, click outside the object.

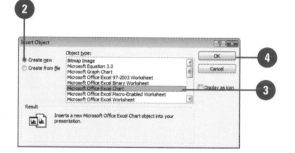

> **Did You Know?**
>
> **You can drag a chart from Excel to PowerPoint.** Open both Excel and PowerPoint, select the chart in Excel, and then drag it into PowerPoint. If the PowerPoint presentation is not visible, drag the chart to the presentation button on the taskbar to display PowerPoint.

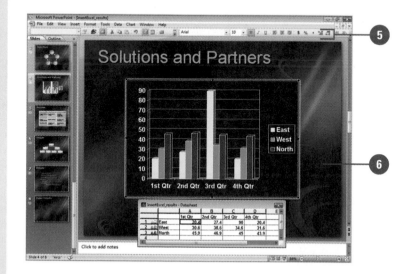

Import a Microsoft Excel Worksheet or Chart

1. Display the slide on which you want to insert the Excel chart.

2. Click the **Insert** tab, and then click **Insert Object** button.

3. Click the **Create from file** option, click the **Browse** button, locate and select the chart you want, and then click **OK**.

4. To link the chart, click the **Link** check box.

5. Click **OK**.

6. If necessary, edit the worksheet using the Excel tools.

7. When you're done, click outside the worksheet.

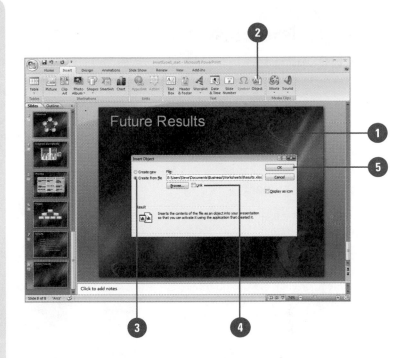

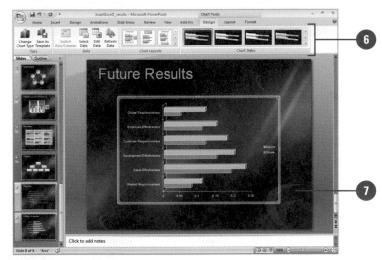

Inserting a Microsoft Word Document

If you need to create a chart for backwards compatibility with Power-Point 97-2003, you can embed a Word document object for Word 97-2003. You can insert a Microsoft Word table into PowerPoint by inserting the document as an embedded object in a slide. When you insert a new or existing Word document, a Microsoft Word document opens in the PowerPoint slide. A Ribbon will also open which assists you in creating and formatting the document. Double-click your embedded object to open Word and edit the document. You must have Microsoft Word installed on your computer to insert a Word document.

Insert a Word Document

1. Click the **Insert** tab, and then click **Insert Object** button.

2. Click the **Create new** option, and then click **Microsoft Word 97-2003 Document**, or click the **Create from file** option, click the **Browse** button, and then locate and select the file you want.

3. Click **OK**.

   A Microsoft Word document opens in the PowerPoint slide.

4. Use the commands on the Ribbon to create or modify the document that you want.

5. When you're done, click outside of the object.

See Also

See "Sharing Information Among Documents" on page 231 for more information about an embedded object.

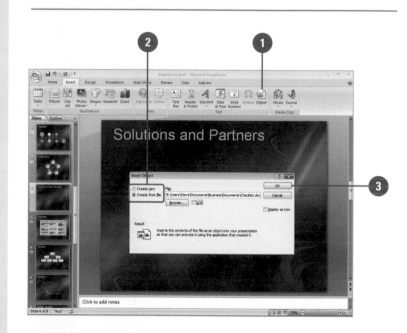

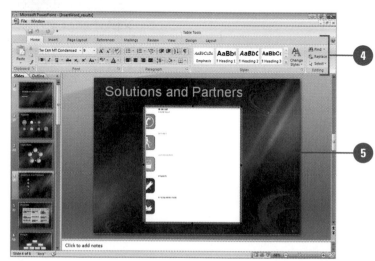

Inserting a Microsoft Organization Chart

If you need to match an existing organization chart from a previous version of PowerPoint, or create a chart layout for Co-Manager, Vertical, and Multiple Manager, then Microsoft Organization Chart is your best choice. Microsoft Organization Chart is an add-in for Microsoft Office 2007 programs, which you need to install. You can insert an Organization Chart using the Insert Object button on the Insert tab. When you create an organization chart, a sample chart appears. You can add text, add shapes, and format the chart boxes and connecting lines. To convert an existing organization chart from a previous version of PowerPoint, simply double-click the chart, and PowerPoint converts it.

Create an Organization Chart Using an Embedded Object

1. Click the **Insert** tab, and then click **Insert Object** button.

2. Click the **Create new** option.

3. Click **Microsoft Organization Chart**.

4. Click **OK**.

5. To add text, click a chart box, and then type a name or text you want.

6. Click the chart box to which you want to attach the new chart box.

7. Click the **Insert Shape** button list arrow on the Organization Chart toolbar, and then click a shape option.

   ◆ **Coworker.** Places the shape next to the selected shape and connect it to the same manager shape.

   ◆ **Subordinate.** Places the new shape below the selected shape and to connect it to the selected shape.

   ◆ **Assistant.** Places the new shape below the selected shape with an elbow connector.

8. When you're done, click anywhere outside the org chart.

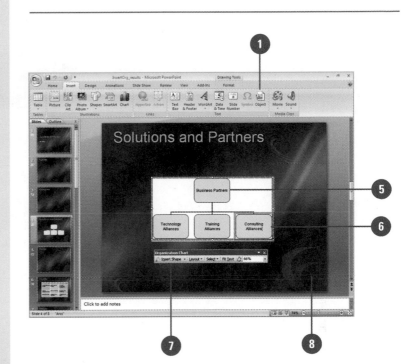

Modifying a Microsoft Organization Chart

In Microsoft Organization Chart, you can change the chart style, rearrange chart boxes, or edit names in the chart boxes to match the organization of the company. The current chart type appears in the traditional style, one manager at the top with subordinates below. You can use the AutoFormat button on the Organization Chart toolbar to change the chart style. You can also change the chart box color, shadow, border style, border color, or border line style. Remember to use formatting wisely and keep in mind the overall design of your presentation.

Change the Layout

1. Double-click the organization chart, if necessary, to open the chart.

2. Select the top chart box of the branch to which you want to apply a new layout. The chart box should have subordinates or assistants.

3. Click the **Layout** list arrow on the Organization Chart toolbar, and then select a new layout.

4. When you're done, click anywhere outside the org chart.

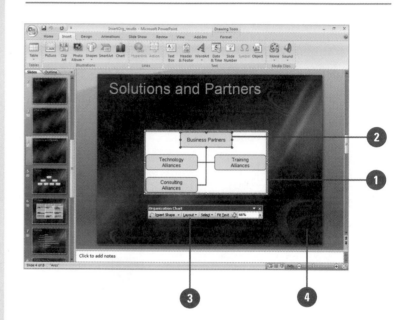

Did You Know?

You can use the Default Chart Style when modifying. Format changes such as coloring and line style can only be made to the Default chart style, not the predesigned styles.

You can delete a chart box. If you add a chart box in the wrong place, you can delete it by first selecting the chart box and then pressing the Delete key.

You can align text in a chart box. Align the text in a chart box by selecting text in the chart box, and then clicking the Left, Center, or Right button on the Formatting toolbar.

Select and Deselect Chart Boxes

To	Do this
Select a single chart box	Click a chart box using the arrow pointer
Select a set of chart boxes	Click the Select list arrow on the Organization Chart toolbar, and then click the set you want
Select one or more levels of chart boxes	Click a chart box in the level you want to select, click the Organization Chart tool bar, click Level
Deselect a chart box	Click outside the chart box

Rearrange a Chart Box

1. Double-click the organization chart, if necessary, to open the chart.

2. Make sure the chart box you want to move is not selected.

3. Position the mouse over the chart box you want to move. The pointer changes to a four-headed arrow.

4. Drag the chart box over an existing chart box.

5. Release the mouse button when the chart box is in the correct position.

6. When you're done, click anywhere outside the org chart.

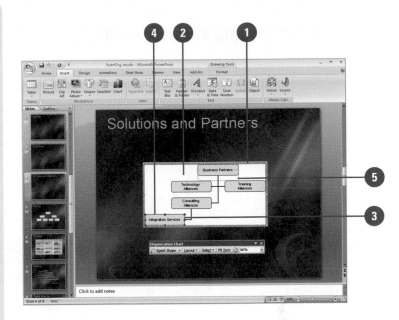

Change the Chart Style

1. Double-click the org chart, if necessary, to open the org chart.

2. Click the **AutoFormat** button on the Organization Chart toolbar.

3. Select a Diagram Style from the Organization Chart Style Gallery.

4. Click **OK**.

5. When you're done, click anywhere outside the org chart.

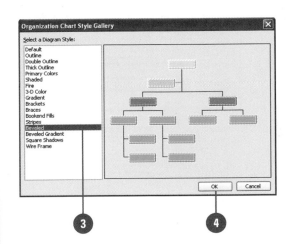

Linking and Embedding Sounds

When you insert a sound into a presentation, PowerPoint checks the file size of the sound to determine whether to link or embed it. Linking stores the sound file externally, while embedding stores the sound file within the presentation.

In PowerPoint Options, you can set the file size you want (100KB is recommended). If the sound file is less than the file size you indicate, the sound is embedded. If the file size is greater, the sound is linked with the exception of a WAV file, which is always embedded. To set the file size, click the Office button, click PowerPoint Options, click

Advanced, scroll down to under Save, enter a file size in KB, and then click OK. To determine if a sound is embedded or linked, click the sound icon, click the Sounds tab, and then click the Edit Sound Object Dialog Box Launcher. In the dialog box, you see either [Contained in presentation] for an embedded sound or a path to the sounds for a linked sound.

If you have an embedded sound in a presentation and don't have the sound file, you can save the presentation as a Web page, which save the sound as a file.

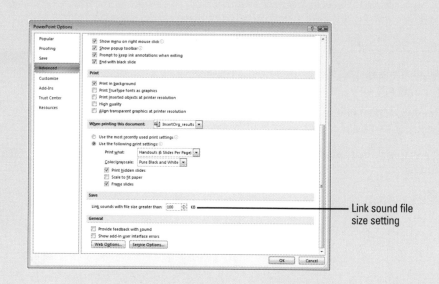

Link sound file size setting

Creating a Web Presentation

7

Introduction

Microsoft Office PowerPoint provides you with the tools you need to create and save your presentation as a Web page and to publish it on the Web. The Save As command allows you to format your presentation in **Hypertext Markup Language (HTML)**, a simple coding system used to format documents for an intranet or the Internet. Saving your presentation in HTML format means you can use most Web browsers to view your presentation. Any presentation can easily be saved as a Web document and viewed in a Web browser. By saving your PowerPoint presentations as Web pages, you can share your data with others via the Internet.

Incorporating action buttons and hyperlinks within your presentation adds an element of connectivity to your work. If you add action buttons to your slides, you can click a button in a slide show to jump instantly to another slide, presentation, or program file. If you add hyperlinks to objects, you can jump to Internet and intranet locations. You can also customize your hyperlink by adding sound to it.

A digital signature adds authentication to your presentation. When customers, clients, employees or others see the digital stamp, it is a sign that the information is valid. When you have a presentation, the signature is assigned to the file. If the presentation has been converted to a Web page, the signature is assigned to a macro project.

Microsoft Office Online offers tips, software updates, tools, and general information to help you work with your PowerPoint presentation.

What You'll Do

Add Action Buttons

Add Hyperlinks to Objects

Create Hyperlinks to External Objects

Insert Hyperlinks

Use and Removing Hyperlinks

Save a Presentation as a Web Page

Save a Presentation as a Single File Web Page

Save Slides as Web Graphics

Change Web Page Options

Open a Web Page

Preview a Web Page

Get Documents from the Web

Access Office Information on the Web

Explore XML

Save an XML Presentation

Open an XML Presentation

Adding Action Buttons

When you create a self-running presentation to show at a kiosk, you might want a user to be able to move easily to specific slides or to a different presentation altogether. To give an audience this capability, insert **action buttons**, such as Back, Forward, Home, Help, or Return, which a user can click to jump to a different slide or presentation. Clicking an action button activates a **hyperlink**, a connection between two locations in the same document or in different documents.

Insert an Action Button

1. Click the **Home** or **Insert** tab.

2. Click the **Shapes** button, and then choose the action button (at the bottom) you want, such as Back, Forward, Home, Information, Return, Movie, Document, Sound, or Help.

3. Drag the pointer to insert the action button, and then release the mouse button when the action button is the size you want.

4. Fill in the hyperlink settings you want as needed.

5. Click **OK**.

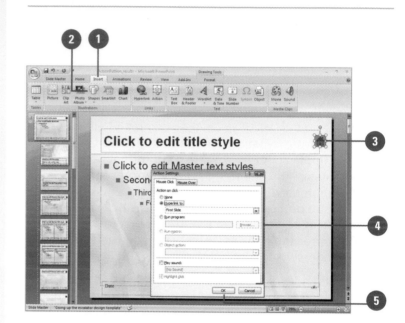

Test an Action Button

1. Click the **Slide Show View** button.

2. Display the slide containing the action button.

3. Click the action button.

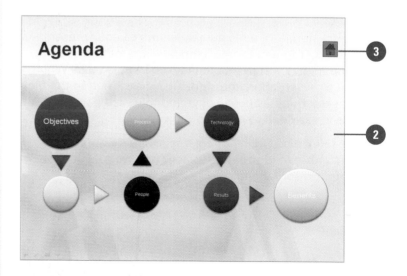

244

Create an Action Button to Go to a Specific Slide

1. Click the **Home** or **Insert** tab.

2. Click the **Shapes** button, and then click the **Custom** action button (at the bottom far right).

3. Drag the pointer to insert the action button on the slide.

4. Click the **Hyperlink To** option, click the list arrow, and then click **Slide** from the list of hyperlink destinations.

5. Select the slide you want the action button to jump to.

6. Click **OK**.

7. Click **OK**.

8. Select the action button object, and then type the name of the slide the action button points to.

9. Click outside the action button to deselect it.

10. Run the slide show and test the action button.

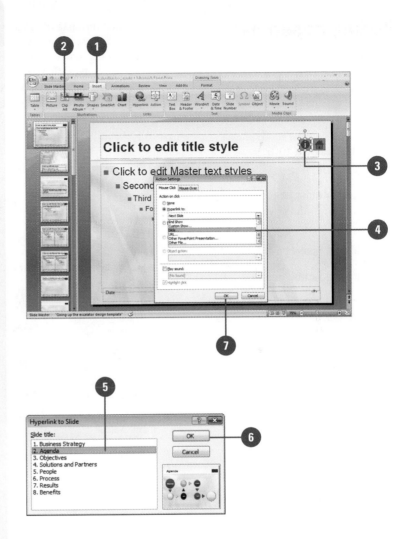

Did You Know?

You can insert the Return action button to help navigate the slide show. If you want to return to the slide you were previously viewing, regardless of its location in the presentation, insert the Return action button.

You can create a square action button. Press and hold Shift as you drag to create a square action button.

Adding Hyperlinks to Objects

Add a Hyperlink to a Slide Object

① Click the object (not within a SmartArt graphic) you want to modify.

② Click the **Insert** tab.

③ Click the **Action** button.

④ Click the **Mouse Click** or **Mouse Over** tab.

⑤ Click the **Hyperlink to** option.

⑥ Click the **Hyperlink to** list arrow.

⑦ Click a destination for the hyperlink.

⑧ Click **OK**.

⑨ Run the slide show and test the hyperlink by pointing to or clicking the object in the slide show.

Did You Know?

You can edit a hyperlink quickly. Right-click the object with the hyperlink, and then click Edit Hyperlink.

You can highlight a click or mouse over. When you click or move over a hyperlink, you can highlight the object. In the Action Settings dialog box, select the Highlight Click or Highlight When Mouse Over check box.

You can turn one of the objects on your slide into an action button so that when you click or move over it, you activate a hyperlink and jump to the new location. You can point hyperlinks to almost any destination, including slides in a presentation and Web pages on the Web. Use the Action Settings dialog box to add sound to a hyperlink. You can add a default sound such as Chime, Click, or Drum Roll, or select a custom sound from a file.

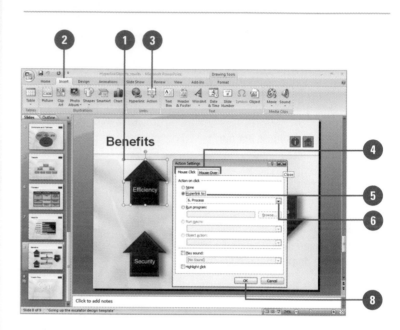

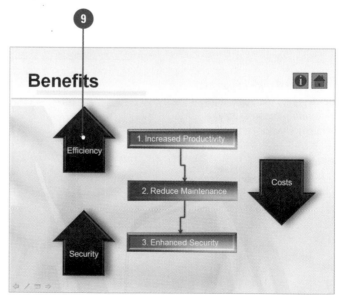

Add a Sound to a Hyperlink

1. Click the object (not within a SmartArt graphic) you want to modify.

2. Click the **Insert** tab.

3. Click the **Action** button.

4. Click the **Mouse Click** or **Mouse Over** tab.

5. Select the **Play Sound** check box.

6. Click the **Play Sound** list arrow, and then click the sound you want to play when the object is clicked during the show.

   ◆ **Custom Sound.** Or scroll to the bottom of the Play Sound list, and then click Other Sound, locate and select the sound you want to use, and then click OK.

7. Click **OK**.

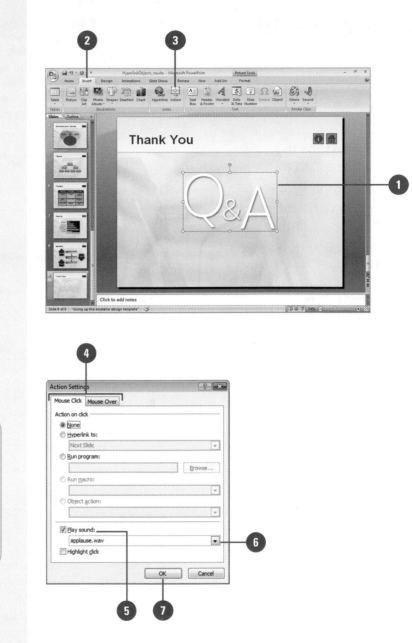

Did You Know?

You can create an action button for a sound. Click the Slide Show menu, point to Action Buttons, click the Sound action button, drag to create the sound action button, click the Play Sound list arrow, select the sound you want, and then click OK.

Creating Hyperlinks to External Objects

PP07S-2.3.3

You can create hyperlinks in your presentation that access other sources, such as another presentation, a file, a Web site, or even a program. This feature is especially useful for kiosk presentations, where you want to make information available to your audience, even if you can't be there to provide it. Depending on your audience, you can set a hyperlink to be activated by clicking the hyperlink with the mouse or by moving the mouse over the hyperlink.

Create a Hyperlink to Another Presentation

1. Click the object (not within a SmartArt graphic) you want to modify.

2. Click the **Insert** tab, and then click the **Action** button.

3. Click the **Hyperlink To** option.

4. Click the list arrow, and then click **Other PowerPoint Presentation** from the list of hyperlinks.

5. Locate and select the presentation you want, and then click **OK**.

6. Select the slide you want to link to.

7. Click **OK**, and then click **OK** again.

Create a Hyperlink to an External File

1. Click the object (not within a SmartArt graphic) you want to modify.

2. Click the **Insert** tab, and then click the **Action** button.

3. Click the **Hyperlink To** option.

4. Click the list arrow, and then click **Other File** in the list of hyperlinks.

5. Locate and select the file on your computer, and then click OK.

6. Click **OK**, and then click **OK** again.

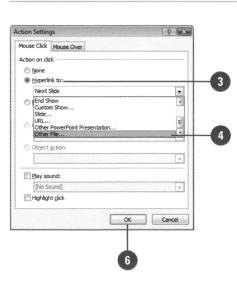

Create a Hyperlink to a Web Page

1. Click the object (not within a SmartArt graphic) you want to modify.

2. Click the **Insert** tab, and then click the **Action** button.

3. Click the **Hyperlink to** option.

4. Click the **Hyperlinks to** list arrow, and then click URL.

5. Enter the URL of the Web page.

6. Click **OK**.

7. Click **OK** again.

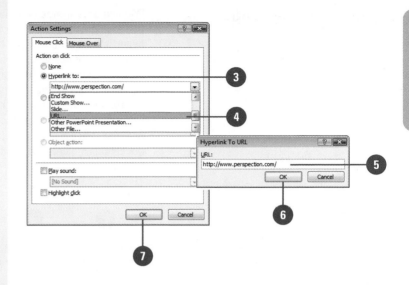

Create a Hyperlink to a Program

1. Click the object (not within a SmartArt graphic) you want to modify.

2. Click the **Insert** tab, and then click the **Action** button.

3. Click the **Run Program** option.

4. Click **Browse**, and then locate and select the program you want.

5. Click **OK**.

6. Click **OK** again.

Did You Know?

You can use Mouse Over instead of Mouse Click. Set a hyperlink to be activated by clicking the hyperlink with the mouse or by moving the mouse over the hyperlink. To set a hyperlink to be activated by moving the mouse over it, click the Mouse Over tab in the Action Settings dialog box.

Inserting Hyperlinks

Microsoft
Certified
Application
Specialist

PP07S-2.3.3

When you reference information included earlier in a presentation, you had to duplicate material or add a footnote. Now you can create a **hyperlink**—a graphic object or colored, underlined text that you click to move (or **jump**) to a new location (or **destination**). The destination can be in the same presentation, another file on your computer or network, or a Web page on your intranet or the Internet. PowerPoint inserts an absolute link—a hyperlink that jumps to a fixed location—to an Internet destination. Office inserts a relative link—a hyperlink that changes when the hyperlink and destination paths change—between documents. You must move the hyperlink and destination together to keep the link intact.

Insert a Hyperlink Within a Presentation

1. Click where you want to insert the hyperlink, or select the text or object you want to use as the hyperlink.

2. Click the **Insert** tab.

3. Click the **Insert Hyperlink** button.

4. Click **Place In This Document**.

5. Click a destination in the document.

   The destination can be a PowerPoint slide, slide title, or custom show.

6. Type the text you want to appear as the hyperlink.

7. Click **ScreenTip**.

8. Type the text you want to appear when someone points to the hyperlink.

9. Click **OK**.

10. Click **OK**.

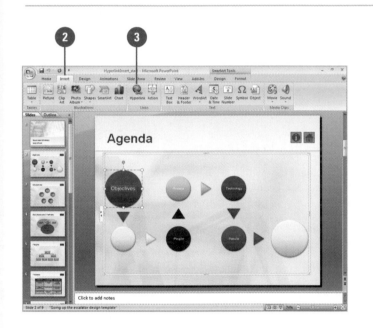

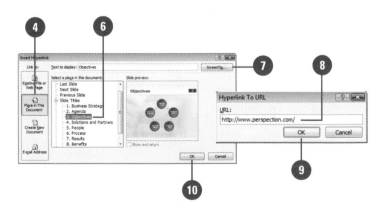

Insert a Hyperlink Between Documents

1. Click where you want to insert the hyperlink, or select the text or object you want to use as the hyperlink.

2. Click the **Insert** tab.

3. Click the **Insert Hyperlink** button.

4. Click **Existing File Or Web Page**.

5. Enter the name and path of the destination file or Web page.

   ◆ Or click the **Bookmark** button; select the bookmark, and then click **OK**.

6. Type the text you want to appear as the hyperlink, if available.

7. Click **ScreenTip**.

8. Type the text you want to appear when someone points to the hyperlink.

9. Click **OK**.

10. Click **OK**.

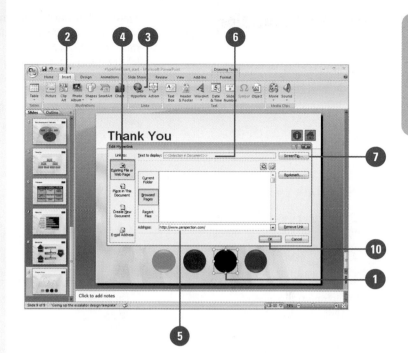

Did You Know?

You can create a hyperlink to send e-mail messages. Click where you want to insert the hyperlink, click the Insert tab, click the Insert Hyperlink button on the Insert tab, click E-Mail Address, enter the recipients e-mail address, enter a subject, enter the hyperlink display text, and then click OK.

For Your Information

Understanding Web Addresses and URLs

Every Web page has a **uniform resource locator** (URL), a Web address in a form your browser program can decipher. Like postal addresses and e-mail addresses, each URL contains specific parts that identify where a Web page is located. For example, the URL for Perspection's Web page is http://www.perspection.com where "http://" shows the address is on the Web and "www.perspection.com" shows the computer that stores the Web page. As you browse various pages, the URL includes their folders and file names.

Using and Removing Hyperlinks

Hyperlinks connect you to information in other documents. Rather than duplicating the important information stored in other documents, you can create hyperlinks to the relevant material. When you click a hyperlink for the first time (during a session), the color of the hyperlink changes, indicating that you have accessed the hyperlink. If a link becomes outdated or unnecessary, you can easily revise or remove it. PowerPoint repairs broken links. Whenever you save a presentation with hyperlinks, PowerPoint checks the links and repairs any that aren't working. For example, if a file was moved, PowerPoint updates the location.

Use a Hyperlink

1. In Slide Show view, position the mouse pointer (which changes to a hand pointer) over any hyperlink.

2. Click the hyperlink.

   Depending on the type of hyperlink, the screen

   - Jumps to a new location within the same document.

   - Jumps to a location on an intranet or Internet Web site.

   - Opens a new file and the program in which it was created.

   - Opens Outlook and displays a new e-mail message.

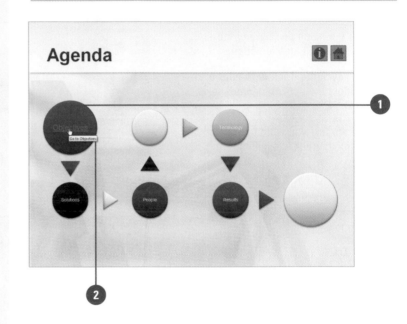

Edit a Hyperlink

1. Right-click the hyperlink you want to edit, and then click **Edit Hyperlink**.

2. If you want, change the display text.

3. If you want, click **ScreenTip**, edit the custom text, and then click **OK**.

4. If necessary, change the destination.

5. Click **OK**.

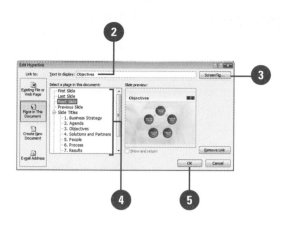

Remove a Hyperlink

1. Right-click the hyperlink you want to remove.

2. Click **Remove Hyperlink**.

   TIMESAVER *Drag the I-beam pointer across the hyperlink to select it, and then press Ctrl+Shift+F9 to delete a hyperlink.*

3. If necessary, delete the text or object.

Did You Know?

You can format a hyperlink. You can change the look of a hyperlink just as you do other text—select it and apply attributes. Select the hyperlink, click the Home tab, and then use WordArt styles, and formatting buttons, such as Bold, Italic, Underline, Font, and Font Size. You can also use Shape styles on the Format tab under Drawing Tools.

Saving a Presentation as a Web Page

**Microsoft
Certified
Application
Specialist**

PP07S-4.3.6

PowerPoint allows you to save any presentation as a Web page. Web pages use **Hypertext Markup Language** (HTML)—a simple coding system that specifies the formats a Web browser uses to display the document. You can save a file as an HTML or HTM file by using the Save As command. A presentation saved as a Web page consists of an HTML file and a folder that stores supporting files, such as a file for each graphic, slide, and so on. PowerPoint selects the appropriate graphic format for you based on the image's content. Once you save the file in HTML format, you can publish the Web page. To publish a Web page means to place a copy of the presentation in HTML format on the Web. You can publish a complete presentation, a custom show, a single slide, or a range of slides.

Save a Presentation as a Web Page

1. Click the **Office** button, and then click **Save As**.

2. Click the **Save as type** list arrow, and then click **Web Page.**

3. If you want to save the file in another folder, click the **Save in** list arrow, and then select a location for your Web page.

4. To change the title of your Web page, click **Change Title**, type the new title in the Set Page Title box, and then click **OK.**

5. Click **Save.**

Did You Know?

What is a Web server? A Web server is a computer on the Internet or intranet that stores Web pages.

Save and Publish a Presentation as a Web Page

1. Click the **Office** button, and then click **Save As**.

2. Click the **Save as type** list arrow, and then click **Web Page**.

3. If you want to save the file in another folder, If you want to save the file in another folder, click the **Save in** list arrow, and then select a location for your Web page.

4. To change the title of your Web page, click **Change Title**, type the new title in the Set Page Title box, and then click **OK**.

5. Click **Publish**.

6. Select the publishing options you want, including slides and notes to publish, browser support, and if you want to publish a copy.

7. Select the **Open published Web page in browser** check box.

8. Click **Publish**.

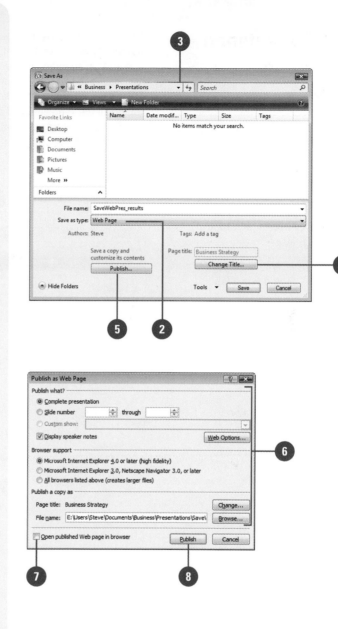

Did You Know?

You can use Microsoft.Net Passport. When you click the Publish button in the Save As dialog box, you may be prompted to sign-in for Microsoft.Net Passport.

You can hide the outline in a Web presentation. When you save a presentation as a Web page, the outline is displayed like a table of contents by your browser. To hide it, click the Web Options button in the Publish as Web Page dialog box, click the General tab, clear the Add slide navigation controls check box, and then click OK.

Saving a Presentation as a Single File Web Page

A single file Web page saves all the elements of a Web site, including text and graphics, into a single file. When you save a document as a single file Web page, all the Web site elements are stored together in one file in the MHTML format, which is supported by Internet Explorer 4.0 or later. A single file makes it easy to manage the Web site. When you move the Web site, you don't need to worry about forgetting linked files stored in another folder. A single file also makes it easy to send an entire Web site as an e-mail attachment.

Save a Presentation as a Single File Web Page

1. Click the **Office** button, and then click **Save As**.

2. Click the **Save as type** list arrow, and then click **Single File Web Page**.

3. Click the **Save in** list arrow, and then select a location for the file.

4. Type a name for the file.

5. Click **Save**.

   The Web page is saved as a single file.

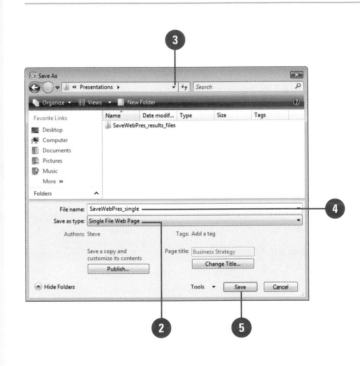

Saving Slides as Web Graphics

Microsoft
Certified
Application
Specialist

PP07S-4.3.6

As you develop a Web site, you can incorporate slides from any of your PowerPoint presentations. You can save any slide in a presentation in the GIF, JPEG, or PNG Web graphic format. **Graphics Interchange Format (GIF)** is a form of compression for line drawings or other artwork. Office converts to GIF such images as logos, graphs, line drawings, and specific colored objects. **Joint Photographic Experts Group (JPEG)** is a high-quality form of compression for continuous tone images, such as photographs. Office converts to JPEG such images as photographs or other images that have many shades of colors. **Portable Network Graphics Format** is a new bit-mapped graphics format similar to GIF.

Save a PowerPoint Slide as a Web Graphic

1. Open the PowerPoint presentation with the slide you want to save as a Web graphic, and then display the slide.

2. Click the **Office** button, and then click **Save As**.

3. Click the **Save as type** list arrow, and then click **GIF Graphics Interchange Format**, **JPEG File Interchange Format**, or **PNG Portable Network Graphics Format**.

4. Click the **Save in** list arrow, and then select a location for the file.

5. Type a name for the file.

6. Click **Save**.

7. Click **Every Slide** or **Current Slide Only**.

See Also

See "Saving a Presentation with Different Formats" on page 24 and "Saving Slides in Different Formats" on page 289 for information on saving files with different file formats.

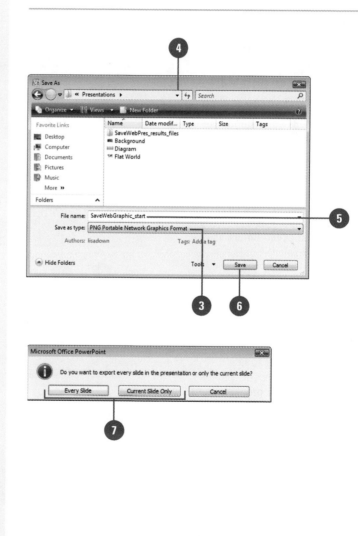

Changing Web Page Options

When you save or publish a presentation as a Web page, you can change the appearance of the Web page by changing PowerPoint's Web options. You can set Web options to add slide navigation buttons, change Web page colors, show slide transitions and animations in the browser window, and resize graphics to fit the display of the browser window. Web pages are saved using the appropriate international text encoding so users on any language system are able to view the correct characters.

Change Web Page Options

1. Click the **Office** button, and then click **PowerPoint Options**.

2. In the left pane, click **Advanced**.

3. Click **Web Options**.

4. Click the **General** tab.

5. Click the options you want to use when you save or publish a Web page.

   ◆ To add slide navigation controls and change the Web page colors, select the **Add slide navigation controls** check box, and then click the **Colors** list arrow and select a color scheme.

   ◆ To show slide transitions and animations, select the **Show slide animation while browsing** check box.

   ◆ To allow graphics to fit in different size browser windows, select the **Resize graphics to fit browser window** check box.

6. Click **OK**.

7. Click **OK**.

Opening a Web Page

After saving a presentation as a Web page, you can open the Web page, an HTML file, in PowerPoint. This allows you to quickly and easily switch from HTML to the standard PowerPoint format and back again without losing any formatting or functionality. For example, if you create a formatted chart in a PowerPoint presentation, save the presentation file as a Web page, and then reopen the Web page in PowerPoint, the chart will look the same as the original chart in PowerPoint. PowerPoint preserves the original formatting and functionality of the presentation.

Open a Presentation as a Web Page in PowerPoint

1. Click the **Office** button, and then click **Open**.

2. Click the **Files of type** list arrow, and then click **All Web Pages**.

3. Click the **Look in** list arrow, and then select the folder where the file is located.

4. Click the Web presentation file.

5. Click **Open**.

◆ To open the Web page in your browser, click the **Open** button arrow, and then click **Open in Browser**.

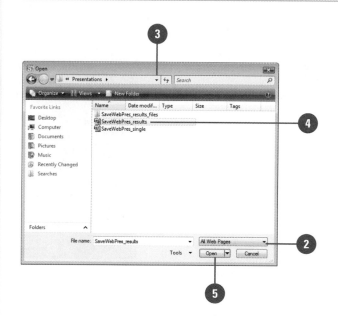

Did You Know?

You can change the appearance of Web pages and Help Viewer window. In the Internet Options dialog box for Windows, click Accessibility on the General tab, select the Ignore colors specified on Web pages check box, and then click OK. In the Internet Properties dialog box, click Colors to select text and background colors or Fonts to change text style.

Previewing a Web Page

It is a good idea to preview your page before publishing it to the Web. Previewing a Web page shows you what the page will look like once it's posted on the Internet. When you display a Web presentation in a Web browser, a **navigation bar** appears with toolbar buttons to make it easy to navigate through the Web presentation. You can also view your presentation as a Web page one slide at a time, in full-screen mode, as an outline, or as the slide master.

Preview a Web Page

1. Open the presentation file you want to view as a Web page.

2. Click the **Web Page Preview** button on the Quick Access Toolbar. If necessary, use PowerPoint Options to add the button to the Quick Access Toolbar.

   Your Web browser opens, displaying your Web page.

3. Click the **Next Slide** or **Previous Slide** button on the navigation bar to move from slide to slide.

4. Click the **Full Screen Slide Show** button on the navigation bar to display the presentation in slide show, and press ESC to exit.

5. Click the **Expand/Collapse Outline** button on the navigation bar to display more or less outline detail.

6. Click the **Close** button to quit the browser and return to PowerPoint.

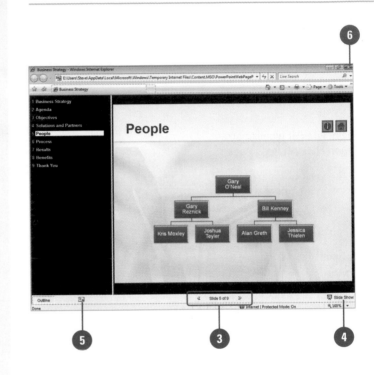

Did You Know?

You can show animation and transition effects while viewing your presentation in a browser. Click the Office button, click PowerPoint Options, click Advanced in the left pane, click Web Options, select the Show Slide Animation While Browsing check box, click OK, and then Click OK again.

View an Individual Slide

1. Start your Web browser.

2. Click the **File** menu, and then click **Open**.

   If necessary, click **Browse** to help you locate your Web presentation.

3. Locate and open the folder containing your Web presentation files.

   Be sure you are opening the presentation folder, not the presentation itself.

4. Double-click the file slide000X, where "X" is the number of the slide.

5. Click **OK**.

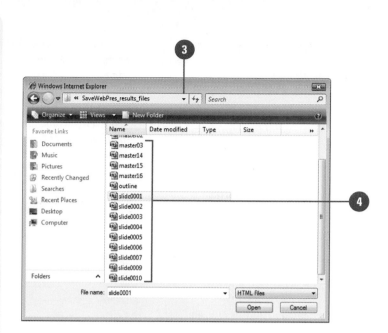

View a Presentation in Full-Screen Mode

1. Start your Web browser.

2. Click the **File** menu, and then click **Open**.

3. Locate and open the folder containing your Web presentation.

4. Double-click the file FULLSCREEN.

5. Click **OK**.

Did You Know?

You can view a Web presentation outline in a browser. Start your Web browser, click the File menu, click Open, locate and open the folder containing your Web presentation, double-click the file OUTLINE, and then click OK.

Getting Documents from the Web

File Transfer Protocol (FTP) is an inexpensive and efficient way to transfer files between your computer and others on the Internet. You can download or receive from another computer any kind of file, including text, graphics, sound, and video files. To download a file, you need an ID and password to identify who you are. Anonymous FTP sites are open to anyone; they usually use *anonymous* as an ID and your *e-mail address* as a password. You can also save the FTP site address to revisit the site later.

Add or Modify FTP Locations

1. Click the **Office** button, and then click **Open**.

2. Click the **Look in** list arrow, and then click **Add/Modify FTP Locations** (in Windows XP).

3. Type the complete address for an FTP site.

4. Type your e-mail address as the password.

5. Click **Add**.

6. Click **OK**.

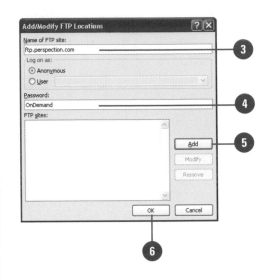

Access an FTP Site

1. Click the **Office** button, and then click **Open**.

2. Click the **Look in** list arrow, and then click **FTP Locations** (in Windows XP).

3. Click the FTP site to which you want to log in.

4. Select a Log on as option.

5. Enter a password (your E-mail address or personal password).

6. Click **OK**.

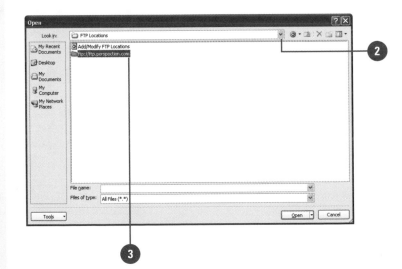

Accessing Office Information on the Web

New information about programs comes out with great frequency. You have access to an abundance of information about PowerPoint and other programs in the Office Suite from Microsoft. This information is constantly being updated. Answers to frequently asked questions, user forums, and update offers are some of the types of information you can find about Microsoft Office. You can also find out about conferences, books, and other products that help you learn just how much you can do with your Office software.

Find Online Office Information

1. Click the **Office** button, and then click **PowerPoint Options**.

2. In the left pane, click **Resources**.

3. Click **Go Online**.

   Your Web browser opens, displaying the Microsoft Office Online Web page.

4. Click a hyperlink of interest.

5. Click the **Close** button to quit the browser and return to PowerPoint.

Exploring XML

Introduction

XML (Extensible Markup Language) is a platform-independent universal language that enables you to create documents in which data is stored independently of the format so you can use the data more seamlessly in other forms. XML is a markup language just like HTML. You mark up a document to define the structure, meaning, and visual appearance of the information in the document.

When you mark up a document, using XML or HTML, you use codes called **tags** that define the appearance or structure of the document. In HTML, the tags define the appearance and location of your data, while in XML, the tags define the structure and meaning of your data. For a HTML document, the tags determine where titles, text, and information goes in a document. For a XML document, the tags defines the kind of data, which makes it possible to reuse or exchange data. The

You cannot use HMTL in place of XML. However, you can wrap your XML data in HTML tags and display it in a Web page. HTML is limited to a predefined set of tags, while XML allows you to create tags that describe your data and its structure. This makes XML an extensible markup language.

In order to share XML data among programs and operating systems, it needs to be **well-formed**, which means it conforms to a standard set of XML rules. In addition to well-formed data, XML also uses schemas and transforms. A **schema** is an XML file (.xsd extension instead of the typical .xml) with a set of rules that defines the elements and content used in an XML document. XML schemas are created by developers who understand XML. The schema is used to validate the data in an XML document and help prevent corrupted data. After you validate an

XML data file with a schema, you can apply a **transform** that allows you to reuse the data in different forms, such as a document or worksheet, or exchange the data with a data system, such as a database. The XML data file, schema, and transform make up the components of a XML system.

Microsoft Office XML

XML is supported in Microsoft Office 2007 through PowerPoint, Word, and Excel. Each of these Office programs uses XML (**New!**) as the default file format. XML allows you to work with the Office interface and create XML documents, without ever knowing the XML language. In Word and Excel, you can use the Developer tab to work with XML structure, schema, and documents. In Access and Excel, you can import and export XML data. Office programs can work with schemas, transforms, and data from other suppliers as long as the XML is well-formed.

XML Benefits

The XML format significantly reduces file sizes, provides enhanced file recovery, and allows for increased compatibility, confidentially, sharing, reuse, and transportability. The XML format uses ZIP and other compression methods to reduce the file size by as much as 75%. Since XML separates the data from the structure and meaning, it's easier for Office program to recover data or remove sensitive information. In fact, you can even open a damaged file in Microsoft Notepad to recover some of the information. The XML format is also royalty free, which makes it more available.

Saving an XML Presentation

When you save a presentation, PowerPoint 2007 saves it by default (**New!**) in a XML file format (.pptx). PowerPoint allows you to work with the easy-to-use Office interface, and create and save documents as XML, without ever knowing the XML language. The XML format significantly reduces file sizes, provides enhanced file recovery, and allows for increased compatibility, sharing, reuse, and transportability.

Save an XML Presentation

1. Click the **Office** button, and then click **Save As**.

2. Click the **Save in** list arrow, and then click the drive or folder where you want to save the file.

3. Type a presentation file name.

4. If necessary, click the **Save as type** list arrow, and then click **PowerPoint Presentation**.

5. Click **Save**.

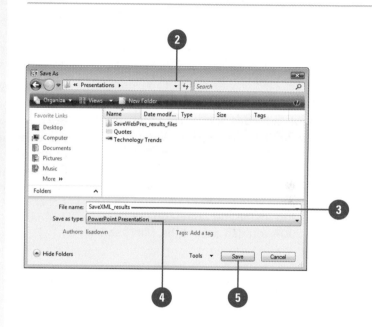

For Your Information

Understanding Extensions: PPTX vs. PPTM

PowerPoint 2007 files with the default "x" at the end of the extension (.pptx) cannot contain Visual Basic for Application (VBA) macros or ActiveX controls, which decreases the security risks associated with files that contain embedded code. PowerPoint 2007 files with an "m" at the end of the extension (.pptm) contain VBA macros and ActiveX controls. The embedded code is even stored in a separate section within the .pptm file to make it easier to isolate if necessary. The two different extensions make it easier for antivirus software to identify potential threats and block documents with unwanted macros or controls.

Opening an XML Presentation

Open XML in Earlier Versions

If you saved a presentation with PowerPoint 2007 in the default XML format (.pptx) and a co-worker wanted to open it up in an earlier version of PowerPoint, you have two different options. You can either save the presentation again using the PowerPoint 97-2003 file format, or use converters to open it in the earlier PowerPoint version.

Microsoft provides converters you can use with Office 2000, Office XP, and Office 2003 programs—with the latest Service Pack installed—to open up Office 2007 files. To use the converters, you go to the Microsoft Office Downloads and Updates Web site, and then download and install the Compatibility Pack for Office 2007. You can access the Microsoft

Office Web site from PowerPoint 2007. Click the Office button, click PowerPoint Options, click Resources in the left pane, and then click Check for Updates. If you try to open a PowerPoint 2007 file in an earlier version before you install the converters, the earlier program provides you with instructions to download and install the Compatibility Pack.

After you install the converters, earlier versions of PowerPoint automatically convert and open PowerPoint 2007 presentations, so you can edit and save them. Remember that some of the new PowerPoint 2007 features, such as SmartArt graphics and WordArt style, are not recognized in earlier versions. Some objects are converted to bitmaps to maintain their appearance.

Finalizing a Presentation and Its Supplements

Introduction

As you finish developing your presentation in PowerPoint, you can add some last-minute enhancements that will help with your delivery of the slide show. By creating a summary slide in the beginning of your presentation, your audience will know the scope of your presentation. Before finalizing your presentation, you should make sure that you embed truetype fonts into your presentation. This will ensure that your slide show appears correctly, regardless of the fonts installed on the various computers that you might be using.

Handouts are printed materials that you supply to your audience. Typically, handouts include an outline for the audience to follow as you speak, a copy of the slides in your presentation (printed one or more slides to a page), or a set of pages with blank lines next to reduced images of the slides for note taking. PowerPoint gives you many options for printing handouts, including editing and formatting them with the Handout Master. Most speakers feel more comfortable giving a presentation with a script in front of them, and you can easily create one in Notes Page view. With **speaker notes**, you can control the success of your presentation delivery.

As you take your presentation to various clients, it may be necessary to translate your slide show into another language. You might also want to export your notes to Microsoft Office Word to further customize them. You can save your slides in different formats—you might want to save them as part of a Web page, or maybe a different version of PowerPoint for other clients. PowerPoint allows you to save a presentation as an XPS or PDF file (**New!**), which are secure fixed-layout formats you can send to others. You can also preview your presentation before printing or print as black and white or color to review your presentation in different print formats.

What You'll Do

Change Page Setup Options

Prepare Handouts and Speaker Notes

Customize Notes Pages

Change Proofing Options

Check Spelling and Use Custom Dictionaries

Insert Research Material

Find the Right Words

Use the English Assistant

Translate and Change Text to Another Language

Export Notes and Slides to Word

Document Presentation Properties

Check Compatibility

Save Slides in Different Formats

Save Outline Text as a Document

Create a PDF and XPS Document

Select Printing Options

Preview a Presentation

Print a Presentation and Outline

Changing Page Setup Options

Microsoft Certified Application Specialist

PP07S-1.4.1, PP07S-1.4.3

Before you print a presentation, you can use the Page Setup dialog box to set the proportions of your presentation slides—standard and wide screen (**New!**)—and their orientation on the page. You can also control slide numbering in the Number Slides From box. For a new presentation, PowerPoint opens with default slide page settings: on-screen slide show, landscape orientation, and slides starting at number one. Notes, handouts, and outlines are printed in portrait orientation.

Control Slide Size

1. Click the **Design** tab.

2. Click the **Page Setup** button.

3. Click the **Slides sized for** list arrow.

4. Click the size you want.

   ◆ **On-Screen Show** for slides that fit computer monitor with ratios of 4:3 (standard), 16:9 (wide screen HDTV's) (**New!**), or 16:10 (wide screen laptops) (**New!**).

   ◆ **Letter Paper** for slides that fit on 8.5-by-11-inch paper.

   ◆ **Ledger Paper** for slides that fit on 11-by-17-inch paper.

   ◆ **A3 Paper**, **A4 Paper**, **B4 (ISO) Paper**, or **B5 (ISO) Paper** for slides that fit on international paper.

   ◆ **35mm Slides** for 11.25-by-7.5-inch slides.

   ◆ **Overhead** for 10-by-7.5-inch slides that fit transparencies.

   ◆ **Banner** for 8-by-1-inch slides that are typically used as advertisements on a Web page.

   ◆ **Custom** to enter the measurements you want in the width and height boxes.

5. Click **OK**.

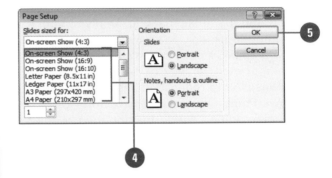

For Your Information

Using Portrait and Landscape Together

In PowerPoint, you can have only one slide orientation in a presentation. However, if you want to use portrait and landscape slide orientation in the same presentation, you can do it by creating a link between two presentations. For best results, place both presentations in the same folder on your computer. First, you create a link from the first presentation to the second presentation, and then create a link from the second presentation back. See "Creating Hyperlinks to External Objects" on page 248 for instructions on creating a link to another presentation.

Customize Slide Proportions

① Click the **Design** tab.

② Click the **Page Setup** button.

③ Enter a specific width in inches.

④ Enter a specific height in inches.

⑤ Click **OK**.

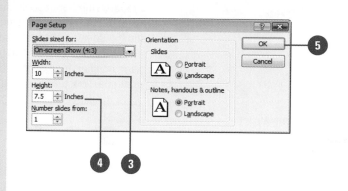

Change Slide Orientation

① Click the **Design** tab.

② Click the **Page Setup** button.

TIMESAVER *Click the Design tab, and then click the Slide Orientation button, and then click Portrait or Landscape.*

③ To orient your slides, click the **Portrait** or **Landscape** option.

④ To orient your notes, handouts, and outline, click the **Portrait** or **Landscape** option in the Notes, Handouts & Outline area.

⑤ Click **OK**.

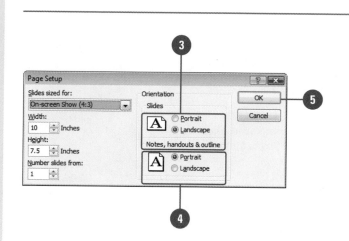

Preparing Handouts

Microsoft
Certified
Application
Specialist

PP07S-4.4.1

Prepare your handouts in the Print dialog box, where you can specify what to print. You can customize your handouts by formatting them in the handout master first, using the formatting and drawing tools. You can also add a header and footer to include the date, slide number, and page number, for example. In the Print dialog box, you can choose to print one, two, three, four, six, or nine slides per page.

Format the Handout Master

1. Click the **View** tab.

2. Click the **Handout Master** button.

3. Click the **Slides per page** button, and then select an option with how many slides you want per page.

4. Select or clear the **Header**, **Date**, **Footer**, or **Page Number** check boxes to show or hide handout master placeholders.

5. To add a background style, click the **Background Styles** button, and then click a style.

6. Use the formatting tools on the Home tab or drawing tools on the Format tab to format the handout master placeholders.

7. Click the **Close Master View** button.

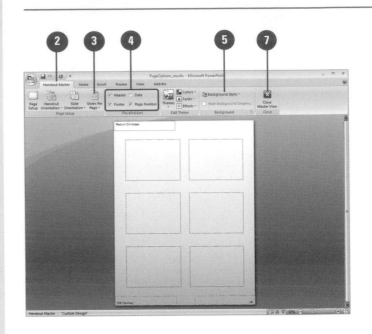

Did You Know?

What are the dotted rectangles in the handout master? The dotted rectangles are placeholders for slides and for header and footer information.

You can add headers and footers to create consistent handouts. Headers and footers you add to the handout master are also added to notes pages and the printed outline.

Add Headers and Footers to Handouts

1. Click the **Insert** tab.

2. Click the **Header & Footer** button.

3. Click the **Notes and Handouts** tab.

4. Enter the information you want to appear on your handouts.

5. Click **Apply To All**.

Print Handouts

1. Click the **Office** button, and then click **Print**.

2. Click the **Print What** list arrow, and then click the option you want.

   ◆ Click **Slides** to print one slide per page.

   ◆ Click **Handouts**, and then click the **Slides per page** list arrow to select one of the six options: one, two, three, four, six, or nine slides per page.

3. Click an **Order** option.

4. Click **OK**.

Did You Know?

You can add a frame around printed slides. Click the Office button, click Print, select the Frame Slides check box, and then click OK.

Preparing Speaker Notes

You can add speaker notes to a slide in Normal view using the Notes pane. Also, every slide has a corresponding **notes page** that displays a reduced image of the slide and a text placeholder where you can enter speaker's notes. Once you have created speaker's notes, you can reference them as you give your presentation, either from a printed copy or from your computer. You can enhance your notes by including objects on the notes master.

Enter Notes in Normal View

1. Click on the slide for which you want to enter notes.

2. Click to place the insertion point in the Notes pane, and then type your notes.

> ### Did You Know?
>
> ***You can view more of the Notes pane.***
> To see more of the Notes pane in Normal view, point to the top border of the Notes pane until the pointer changes to a double-headed arrow, and then drag the border until the pane is the size you want.

Enter Notes in Notes Page View

1. Switch to the slide for which you want to enter notes.

2. Click the **View** tab.

3. Click the **Notes Pages** button.

4. If necessary, click the **Zoom** list arrow, and then increase the zoom percentage to better see the text you type.

5. Click the text placeholder.

6. Type your notes.

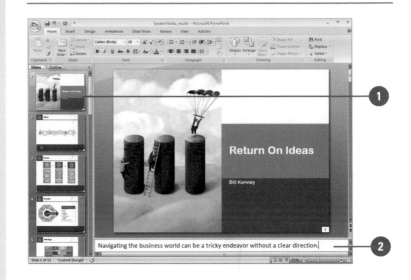

Reduced image of slide

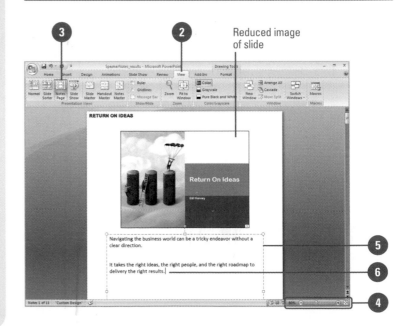

272

Format the Notes Master

1 Click the **View** tab.

2 Click the **Notes Master** button.

3 Select or clear the **Header**, **Slide Image**, **Footer**, **Date**, **Body** or **Page Number** check boxes to show or hide notes master placeholders.

4 To add a background style, click the **Background Styles** button, and then click a style.

5 If you want, add objects to the notes master that you want to appear on every page, such as a picture or a text object.

6 Use the formatting tools on the **Home** tab or drawing tools on the **Format** tab to format the handout master text placeholders.

7 To add a header and footer, click the **Insert** tab, and then click the **Header & Footer** button.

8 Click the **Close Master View** button.

Did You Know?

Why don't the objects on the Notes master appear in the Notes pane in Normal view? The objects that you add to the Notes master will appear when you print the notes pages. They do not appear in the Notes pane of Normal view or when you save your presentation as a Web page.

You export notes and slides to Microsoft Office Word. Click the Send to Microsoft Word button on the Quick Access Toolbar (add it if necessary), click the page layout option you want for handouts, click the Paste Link option if you want to create a link, and then click OK.

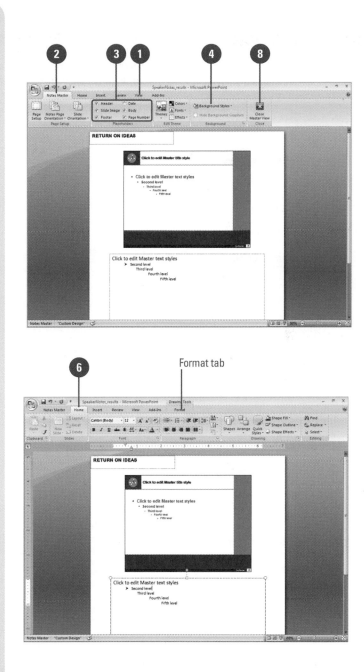

Format tab

Customizing Notes Pages

You can add dates, numbering, and header and footer text to your notes pages just as you do to your slides. If you have removed objects from the master and decide you want to restore them, you can reapply any of the master placeholders (the slide image, the date, header, and so on) without affecting objects and text outside the placeholders. Moreover, if you delete the slide placeholder or text placeholder from a notes page, you can easily reinsert it.

Add a Header and Footer to Notes Pages

1. Click the **Insert** tab.

2. Click the **Header & Footer** button.

3. Click the **Notes and Handouts** tab.

4. Add the header and footer information you want.

5. Click **Apply To All**.

Reinsert Notes Placeholders on the Notes Master

1. Click the **View** tab.

2. Click the **Notes Master** button.

3. Select the **Header**, **Slide Image**, **Footer**, **Date**, **Body** or **Page Number** check boxes in the Placeholder group corresponding to the placeholders you want to reinsert.

4. Click the **Close Master View** button.

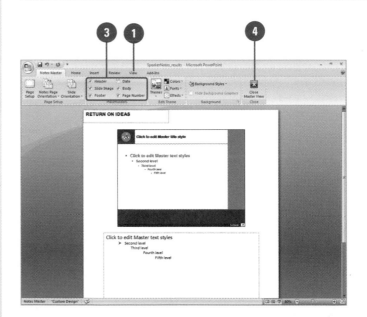

Changing Proofing Options

You can customize the way PowerPoint and Microsoft Office spell check a presentation by selecting proofing settings in PowerPoint Options. Some spelling options apply to PowerPoint, such as Check Spelling as you Type, while other options apply to all Microsoft Office programs (**New!**), such as Ignore Internet and File Addresses, and Flag Repeated Words. If you have ever mistakenly used their instead of *there*, you can use contextual spelling to fix it (**New!**). While you work in a presentation, you can can set options to have the spelling check search for mistakes in the background.

Change Spelling Options for All Microsoft Programs

1. Click the **Office** button, and then click **PowerPoint Options**.

2. In the left pane, click **Proofing**.

3. Select or clear the Microsoft Office spelling options you want.

    ◆ **Ignore words in UPPERCASE**.

    ◆ **Ignore words that contain numbers**.

    ◆ **Ignore Internet and file addresses** (**New!**).

    ◆ **Flag repeated words** (**New!**).

    ◆ **Enforce accented uppercase in French** (**New!**).

    ◆ **Suggest from main dictionary only** (**New!**). Select to exclude your custom dictionary.

4. Select or clear the PowerPoint spelling options you want.

    ◆ **Check spelling as you type**.

    ◆ **Use contextual spelling** (**New!**). Select to correct the usage errors like the use of *their* vs *there*.

    ◆ **Hide spelling errors** (**New!**). Clear to displays errors with a red wavy line. If you select this, you must also select Check spelling as you type (above).

5. Click **OK**.

Checking Spelling

As you type, a red wavy line appears under words not listed in PowerPoint's dictionary (such as misspellings, names, technical terms, or acronyms) or duplicate words (such as *the the*). You can correct these errors as they arise or after you finish the entire presentation. PowerPoint's spelling checker checks the spelling of the entire presentation, including all slides, outlines, notes pages, and handout pages. You can use the Spelling button on the Review tab to check the entire presentation using the Spelling dialog box, or when you encounter a wavy red line under a word, you can right-click the word and choose the correct spelling or add it to your custom dictionary from the list on the shortcut menu.

Check Spelling All at Once

1. Click the **Review** tab.

2. Click the **Spelling** button.

   TIMESAVER *To open the Spelling dialog box, right-click a misspelled word, and then click Spelling.*

3. If the Spelling dialog box opens, choose an option:

   ◆ Click **Ignore** to skip the word, or click **Ignore All** to skip every instance of the word.

   ◆ Click a suggestion, and then click **Change** or **Change All**.

   ◆ Select the correct word, and then click **AutoCorrect** to add it to the AutoCorrect list.

   ◆ Click **Add** to add a word to your dictionary, so it doesn't show up as a misspelled word in the future.

   ◆ If no suggestion is appropriate, click in the presentation and edit the text yourself. Click **Resume** to continue.

4. PowerPoint will prompt you when the spelling check is complete, or you can click **Close** to end the spelling check.

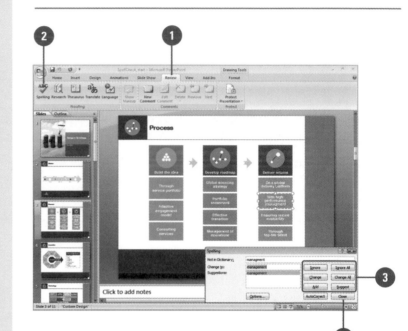

Correct Spelling as You Type

1. Right-click a word with a red wavy underline.

   TIMESAVER *In the Spelling dialog box, click Options.*

2. Choose an option:

   ◆ Click the correct spelling.

   ◆ Click **Ignore All** to skip any other instances of the word

   ◆ Click **Add to Dictionary** to include it in your custom dictionary.

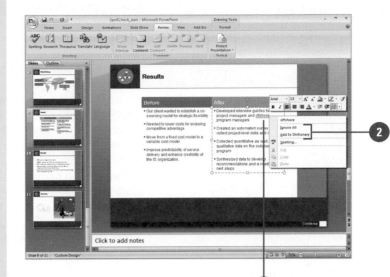

See Also

See "Changing Proofing Options" on page 275 for information on setting options to correct spelling as you type.

Did You Know?

You can make spell check ignore text or an entire style. Select the word or phrase that you want to mark. Click the Review tab, click the Set Language button, select the Do not check spelling check box, and then click OK.

You can mark a word as a foreign language word. If spell check identifies correct words as misspellings, the words might not be identified with the correct language. Select the foreign word or phrase that you want to mark. Click the Review tab, click the Set Language button, click the foreign language, and then click OK.

Using Custom Dictionaries

Before you can use a custom dictionary, you need to enable it first. You can enable and manage custom dictionaries by using the Custom Dictionaries dialog box (**New!**). In the dialog box, you can change the language associated with a custom dictionary, create a new custom dictionary, or add or remove existing custom dictionary. If you need to manage dictionary content, you can also change the default custom dictionary to which the spelling checker adds words, as well as add, delete, or edit words. All the modifications you make to your custom dictionaries are shared with all your Microsoft Office programs, so you only need to make changes once (**New!**). If you mistakenly type an obscene or embarrassing word, such as *ass* instead of *ask*, spell check will not catch it because both words are spelled correctly. You can avoid this problem by using an exclusion dictionary (**New!**). When you use a language for the first time, Office automatically creates an exclusion dictionary. This dictionary forces the spelling checker to flag words you don't want to use.

Use a Custom Dictionary

1. Click the **Office** button, and then click **PowerPoint Options**.

2. In the left pane, click **Proofing**.

3. Click **Custom Dictionaries**.

4. Select the check box next to **CUSTOM.DIC (Default)**.

5. Click **Dictionary language**, and then select a language for a dictionary.

6. Click the options you want:

   ◆ Click **Edit Word List** to add, delete, or edit words.

   ◆ Click **Change Default** to select a new default dictionary.

   ◆ Click **New** to create a new dictionary.

   ◆ Click **Add** to insert an existing dictionary.

   ◆ Click **Remove** to delete a dictionary.

7. Click **OK** to close the Custom Dictionaries dialog box.

8. Click **OK**.

Find and Modify the Exclusion Dictionary

1. In Windows Explorer, go to the folder location where the custom dictionaries are stored.

   ◆ **Windows Vista.** C:\Users*user name*\AppData\Roaming\Micro soft\UProof

   ◆ **Windows XP.** C:\Documents and Settings*user name*\Application Data\Microsoft\UProof

   TROUBLE? *If you can find the folder, change folder settings to show hidden files and folders.*

2. Locate the exclusion dictionary for the language you want to change.

   ◆ The file name you want is ExcludeDictionary *Language Code Language LCID*.lex.

      For example, ExcludeDictionary EN0409.lex, where EN is for English.

   Check PowerPoint Help for an updated list of LCID (Local Identification Number) number for each language.

3. Open the file using Microsoft Notepad or WordPad.

4. Add each word you want the spelling check to flag as misspelled. Type the words in all lowercase and then press Enter after each word.

5. Save and close the file.

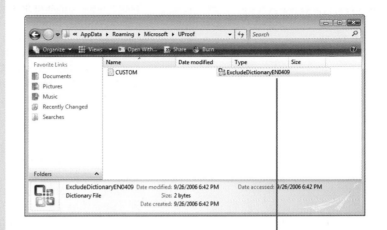

Inserting Research Material

With the Research task pane, you can access data sources and insert research material right into your text without leaving your PowerPoint presentation. The Research task pane can help you to access electronic dictionaries, thesauruses, research sites, and proprietary company information. You can select one reference source or search in all reference books. This research pane allows you to quickly and easily find information and incorporate it into your work.

Research a topic

1. Click the **Review** tab.

2. Click the **Research** button.

3. Type the topic you would like to research.

4. Click the list arrow, and then select a reference source, or click **All Reference Books**.

5. To customize which resources are used for translation, click **Research options**, select the reference books and research sites you want, and then click **OK**.

6. Click the **Start Searching** button (green arrow).

7. Point to the information in the Research task pane that you want to copy.

8. Click the list arrow, and then click **Copy**.

9. Paste the information into your presentation.

10. When you're done, click the **Close** button on the task pane.

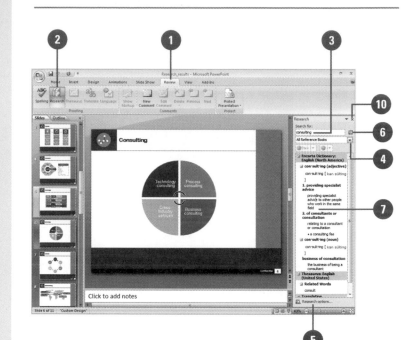

Did You Know?

You can search for more related words. In the Research task pane, click one of the words in the list of results.

Finding the Right Words

Repeating the same word in a presentation can reduce a message's effectiveness. Instead, replace some words with synonyms or find antonyms. If you need help finding exactly the right words, use the shortcut menu to quickly look up synonyms or search a Thesaurus for more options. This feature can save you time and improve the quality and readability of your presentation. You can also install a Thesaurus for another language. Foreign language thesauruses can be accessed under Research Options on the Research task pane.

Use the Thesaurus

1. Select the text you want to translate.

2. Click the **Review** tab.

3. Click the **Thesaurus** button.

4. In the Search For list, select a **Thesaurus**, if necessary.

TIMESAVER *Right-click the word you want to look up, point to Synonyms, and then click a synonyms word or Thesaurus.*

5. Point to the word in the Research task pane.

6. Click the list arrow, and then click one of the following:

   ◆ **Insert** to replace the word you looked up with the new word.

   ◆ **Copy** to copy the new word and then paste it within the presentation.

7. When you're done, click the **Close** button on the task pane.

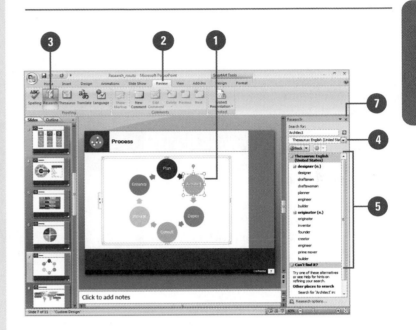

Using the English Assistant

The English Assistant (**New!**) is a Microsoft Office Online service that helps people, for whom English is a second language, write professional English text. The English Assistant provides tools for spelling, explanation, and usage. It also provides suggestions for synonyms and collocations (the association between two words that are typically or frequently used together), and related example sentences.

Use the English Assistant

1. Click the **Review** tab.

2. Click the **Research** button.

3. Click the **All Reference Books** list arrow, and then click **English Assistant (PRC)** or **English Assistant (Japan)**.

4. If the English assistances are not available, click **Research options**, select the assistances you want, and then click **OK**.

5. Type the word or phrase in the Search for box, and then click the **Start Searching** button (green arrow).

6. Point to the information in the Research task pane that you want to copy.

7. Click the list arrow, and then click **Copy**.

8. Paste the information into your presentation.

9. When you're done, click the **Close** button on the task pane.

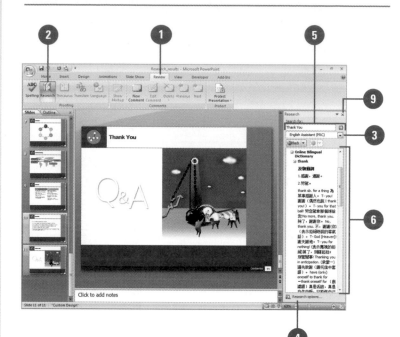

Translating Text to Another Language

With the Research task pane, you can translate single words or short phrases into different languages by using bilingual dictionaries. The Research task pane provides you with different translations and allows you to incorporate it into your work. If you need to translate an entire document for basic subject matter understanding, Web-based machine translations services are available. A machine translation is helpful for general meaning, but may not preserve the full meaning of the content.

Research a Topic

1. Select the text you want to translate.

2. Click the **Review** tab.

3. Click the **Translate** button.

   If this is the first you have used translation services, click **OK** to install the bilingual dictionaries and enable the service.

4. If necessary, click the list arrow, and then click **Translation**.

5. Click the **From** list arrow, and then select the language of the selected text.

6. Click the **To** list arrow, and then select the language you want to translate into.

7. To customize which resources are used for translation, click **Translation options**, select the look-up options you want, and then click **OK**.

8. Right-click the translated text in the Research task pane that you want to copy, and then click **Copy**.

9. Paste the information into your presentation.

10. When you're done, click the **Close** button on the task pane.

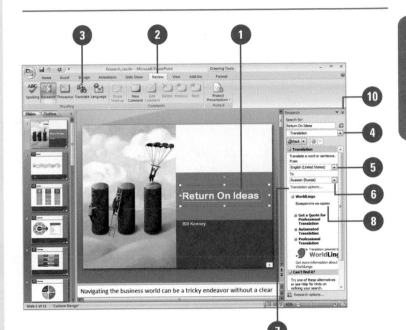

Changing Text to a Language

If your text is written in more than one language, you can designate the language of selected text so spell check uses the right dictionary. For international Microsoft Office users, you can change the language that appears on their screens by enabling different languages. Users around the world can enter, display, and edit text in all supported languages. You'll be able to use PowerPoint in your native language.

Mark Text as a Language

1. Select the text you want to mark.

2. Click the **Review** tab.

3. Click the **Language** button.

4. Click the language you want to assign to the selected text.

5. To skip this text during spell checking, select the **Do not check spelling** check box.

6. Click **OK**.

See Also

See "Using Multiple Languages" on page 400 for information on adding and enabling languages.

Did You Know?

There is a Multilingual AutoCorrect.
Office supports an AutoCorrect list for each language. For example, the English AutoCorrect list capitalizes all cases of the single letter "i;" in Swedish however, "i" is a preposition and is not capitalized.

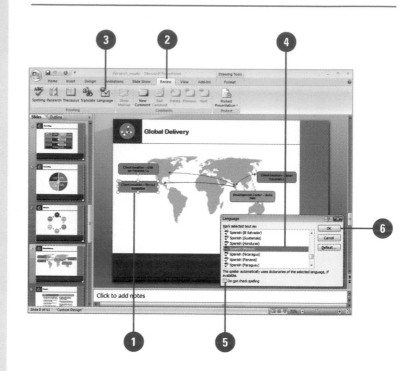

Exporting Notes and Slides to Word

You can send both your notes and slides to Word so that you can use a full array of word processing tools. This is especially handy when you are developing more detailed materials, such as training presentations and manuals. By default, PowerPoint pastes your presentation into a Word document. If you change the presentation after sending it to Word, the changes you make to the presentation are not reflected in the Word document. If you click the Paste Link option in the Send to Microsoft Office Word dialog box, however, you create a link between the Word document and the presentation, and changes you make in one are reflected in the other.

Create Handouts in Word

① Click the **Office** button, point to **Publish**, and then click **Create Handouts in Microsoft Office Word**.

② Click the page layout option you want for handouts.

③ To create a link to the presentation, click the **Paste Link** option.

④ Click **OK**.

Word starts, creates a new document, and inserts your presentation slides with the page layout you selected.

⑤ Print the document in Word, editing and saving it as necessary.

⑥ When you're done, click the **Close** button to quit Word.

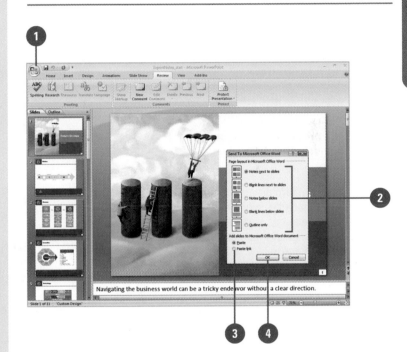

Documenting Presentation Properties

PP07S-4.3.2

PowerPoint automatically documents presentation properties while you work—such as file size, save dates, and various statistics—and allows you to document other properties, such as title, author, subject, key-words, category, and status. You can view or edit standard document properties or create advanced custom properties by using the **Document Information Panel (New!)**, which is actually an XML-based Microsoft InfoPath 2007 form hosted in PowerPoint. You can use document properties—also known as metadata—to help you manage and track files; search tools can use the metadata to find a presentation based-on your search criteria. If you associate a document property to an item in the document, the document property updates when you change the item.

View and Edit Standard Presentation Properties

1. Click the **Office** button, point to **Prepare**, and then click **Properties**.

2. Click the **Document Properties** arrow, and then click **Standard**, if necessary.

3. Enter the standard properties, such as author, title, subject, keywords, category, status, and comments, in the Document Information Panel.

4. Click the **Close** button on the Document Information Panel.

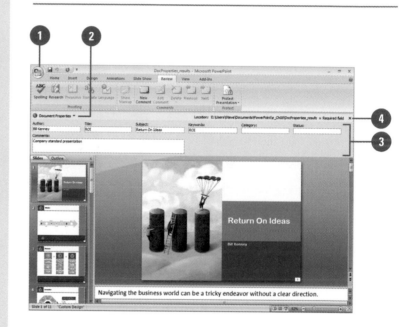

Did You Know?

Your Document Information Panel might look different. If you save your document to a SharePoint library or a document management server, your Document Information Panel might have additional properties.

You can view document properties when you open or save a file. In the Open or Save As dialog box, select the document you want, click the arrow next to the Views, and then click Details to view file size and last changed date, or click Properties to view all information.

Display Advanced Properties

1. Click the **Office** button, point to **Prepare**, and then click **Properties**.

2. Click the **Document Properties** arrow, and then click **Advanced Properties**.

3. Click the tabs to view and add information:

   ◆ **General**. To find out file location or size.

   ◆ **Summary**. To add title and author information for the presentation.

   ◆ **Statistics**. To display the number of slides, paragraphs, words and other details about the presentation.

   ◆ **Contents**. To display slide titles and information about fonts and design templates used in the presentation.

4. Click **OK**.

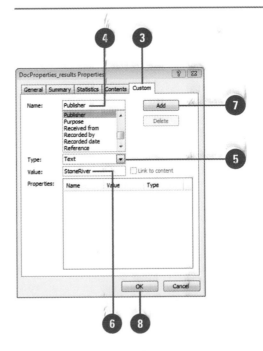

Customize Properties

1. Click the **Office** button, point to **Prepare**, and then click **Properties**.

2. Click the **Document Properties** arrow, and then click **Advanced Properties**.

3. Click the **Custom** tab.

4. Type the name for the custom property or select a name from the list.

5. Select the data type for the property you want to add.

6. Type a value for the property.

7. Click **Add**.

8. Click **OK**.

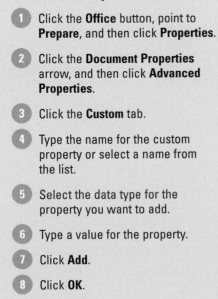

Checking Compatibility

The Compatibility Checker (**New!**) identifies the potential loss of functionality when you save a PowerPoint 2007 presentation in the PowerPoint 97-2003 Presentation file format. The Compatibility Checker generates a report that provides a summary of the potential losses and the number of occurrences in the presentation. Use the report information to determine what caused each message and for suggestions on how to change it. If the loss is due to a new feature in PowerPoint 2007—such as custom layouts or Quick Styles applied to shapes, pictures, and WordArt—you might be able to simply remove the effect or feature. In other cases, you might not be able to do anything about it. To maintain a visual appearance, SmartArt graphics and other objects with new effects are converted to bitmaps to preserve their overall look and cannot be edited.

Check Presentation Compatibility

① Click the **Office** button, point to **Prepare**, and then click **Run Compatibility Checker**.

Office checks compatibility of the presentation for non supported features in earlier versions of PowerPoint.

② View the compatibility summary information, so you can make changes, as necessary.

③ To have the compatibility checker check the presentation when PowerPoint save the file, select the **Check compatibility when saving this presentation** check box.

④ Click **OK**.

Saving Slides in Different Formats

Microsoft Certified Application Specialist

PP07S-4.3.6

You can save PowerPoint presentations in a number of formats so that many different programs can access them. For example, you might want to save a presentation slide as a Web graphic image in the .jpg or .gif format to use in a Web page that you can view in a Web browser. Or you can save a presentation slide as a graphic image that you can open in a graphics editor. When you're saving presentation slides, PowerPoint asks if you want to save the current slide only or all the slides in your presentation, which can be a big timesaver.

Save a Slide as a Graphic Image

1. In Normal view, display the slide you want to save.

2. Click the **Office** button, point to **Save As**, and then click **Other Formats**.

3. Click the **Save as type** list arrow, and then click the graphics format you want to use (i.e. .jpeg or .gif).

4. Click the **Save in** list arrow, and then click the drive or folder where you want to save the file.

5. Type a file name.

6. Click **Save**.

7. Click **Every Slide** to save all slides as separate graphic image files, or click **Current Slide Only** to save just the current slide. If necessary, click **OK**.

> ### See Also
>
> *See "Examining Picture File Formats" on page 161 for information on the different graphic file formats.*

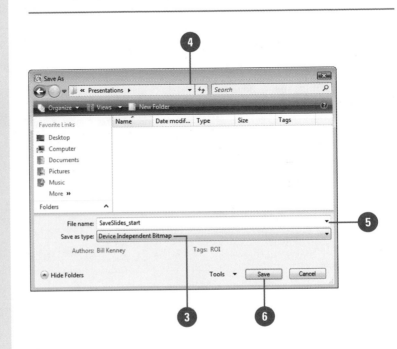

Saving Outline Text as a Document

When you need the text portion of a presentation for use in another program, you can save the presentation text in a format called Rich Text Format (RTF). Saving an outline in RTF allows you to save any formatting that you made to the presentation text in a common file format that you can open in other programs. As long as Microsoft Office Word is installed on your computer, you can export a presentation outline directly from PowerPoint into a report in Word with the Send to Microsoft Word feature. PowerPoint launches Word and sends or copies the outline in the presentation to a blank Word document.

Save a Presentation as an Outline

1. Click the **Office** menu, point to **Save As**, and then click **Other Formats**.

2. Click the **Save as type** list arrow, and then click **Outline/RTF**.

3. Click the **Save in** list arrow, and then click the drive or folder where you want to save the file.

4. Type the file name.

5. Click **Save**.

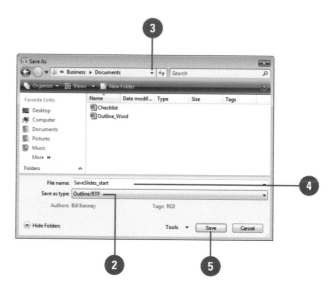

Send a Outline to Word

1. Click the **Office** button, point to **Publish**, and then click **Create Handouts in Microsoft Office Word**.

   If necessary, use PowerPoint Options to add the button to the Quick Access Toolbar.

2. Click the **Outline Only** option.

3. Click **OK**.

   Microsoft Office Word starts, creating a new document, and inserts the presentation slide information you selected.

Creating a PDF Document

Portable Document Format (PDF) is a fixed-layout format developed by Adobe Systems that retains the form you intended on a computer monitor or printer. A PDF is useful when you want to create a document primarily intended to be read and printed, yet hard to modify. PowerPoint allows you to save a presentation as a PDF file (**New!**), which you can send to others for review in an e-mail. To view a PDF file, you need to have Acrobat Reader—free downloadable software from Adobe Systems—installed on your computer. Depending on which edition of Microsoft Office 2007 you have installed, you might need to download and install the Publish as PDF or XPS add-in for Microsoft Office 2007.

Save a Presentation as a PDF Document

1. Click the **Office** button, point to **Save As**, and then click **PDF or XPS**.

    On first run, click **Find add-ins for other formats** to install the option.

2. Click the **Save as type** list arrow, and then click **PDF.**

3. Click the **Save in** list arrow, and then click the drive or folder where you want to save the file.

4. Type a PDF file name.

5. To open the file in Adobe Reader after saving, select the **Open file after publishing** check box.

6. Click the **Standard** or **Minimize size** option to specify how you want to optimize the file.

7. Click **Options**.

8. Select the publishing options you want, such as what to publish, and whether to include non-printing information, or PDF options.

9. Click **OK**.

10. Click **Publish**.

11. If necessary, install Adobe Acrobat Reader and related software as directed.

Creating an XPS Document

XML Paper Specification (XPS) is a secure fixed-layout format developed by Microsoft that retains the form you intended on a monitor or printer. An XPS is useful when you want to create a document primarily intended to be read and printed, yet hard to modify. PowerPoint allows you to save a presentation as an XPS file (**New!**), which you can send to others for review in an e-mail. XPS includes support for digital signatures and is compatible with Windows Rights Management for additional protection. The XPS format also preserves live links with documents, making files fully functional. To view an XPS file, you need to have a viewer—free downloadable software from Microsoft Office Online—installed on your computer. Depending on which edition of Microsoft Office 2007 you have installed, you might need to download and install the Publish as PDF or XPS add-in for Microsoft Office 2007.

Save a Presentation as an XPS Document

1. Click the **Office** button, point to **Save As**, and then click **PDF or XPS**.

   On first run, click **Find add-ins for other formats** to install the option.

2. Click the **Save as type** list arrow, and then click **XPS Document.**

3. Click the **Save in** list arrow, and then click the drive or folder where you want to save the file.

4. Type an XPS file name.

5. To open the file in viewer after saving, select the **Open file after publishing** check box.

6. Click the **Standard** or **Minimize size** option to specify how you want to optimize the file.

7. Click **Options**.

8. Select the publishing and XPS options you want, such as whether to include non-printing information.

9. Click **OK**.

10. Click **Publish**.

11. If necessary, click **Install** to download and install the Microsoft .NET Framework.

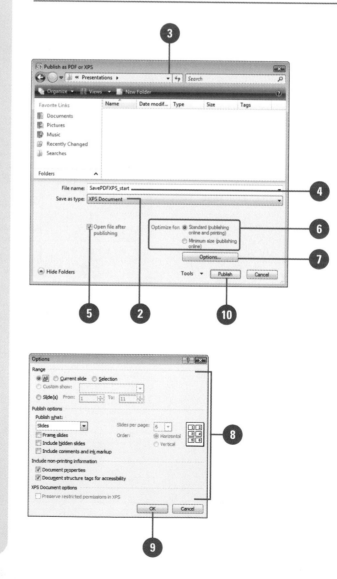

292

Selecting Printing Options

You can customize the way PowerPoint prints presentations and supplements by selecting printing settings in PowerPoint Options. These PowerPoint preferences determine the internal process of printing a presentation. You can set options that allow you to print a presentation while you continue to work and provide you with the best quality print out. If you use the same print options most of the time, you can set print preferences in PowerPoint Options to save you some time.

Change Printing Options

1. Click the **Office** button, and then click **PowerPoint Options**.

2. In the left pane, click **Advanced**.

3. Select or clear the printing options you do or don't want.

   - **Print in background**. Select to print as you continue to work.

   - **Print TrueType fonts as graphics**. Select to print fonts as vector graphic for better print quality.

   - **Print inserted objects at printer resolution**. Select to print charts and tables with the best print quality.

   - **High Quality**. Select to print with the highest color and resolution settings available.

   - **Align transparent graphics at printer resolution**. Select to print transparent graphics at the printer set resolution.

4. Click the **When printing this document** list arrow, and then click the presentation in which you want to set print options.

5. Click the option you want for the specified presentation:

   - **Use the most recent used print settings**.

   - **Use the following print settings**. Similar to the Print dialog box.

6. Click **OK**.

Previewing a Presentation

Print preview allows you to see how your presentation will look before you print it. While in print preview, you have the option of switching between various views, such as notes, slides, outlines, and handouts. You can even view your presentation in landscape or portrait. If you are using a black and white printer, you can preview your color slides in pure black and white or grayscale in print preview to verify that they will be legible when you print them.

Preview Your Presentation

1. Click the **Office** button, point to **Print**, and then click **Print Preview**.

   If you are printing to a grayscale printer, your slides are shown in grayscale using print preview.

2. Click the **Print what** list arrow on the Print Preview tab, and then click an option in the list.

3. To preview the next or previous slide, click the **Next Page** or **Previous Page** button.

4. To change the view, click the **Zoom** or **Fit to Window** buttons.

5. To change other options, click the **Options** button, and then select the options you want.

6. When you're done, click the **Close Print Preview** button.

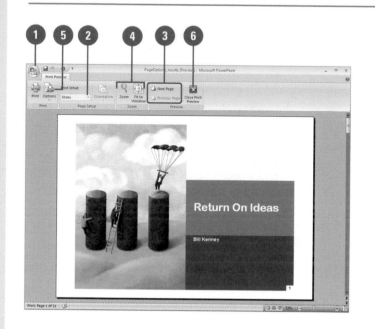

> ## See Also
>
> See "Printing a Presentation" on page 296 for information on printing a presentation.

Change Preview Options

1. Click the **Office** button, point to **Print**, and then click **Print Preview**.

2. Click the **Options** button, and then choose any of the following:

   ◆ **Header and Footer.** Click to change header and footer.

   ◆ **Color/Grayscale.** Click to change print color.

   ◆ **Scale to Fit Paper.** Click to scale slide to fit paper.

   ◆ **Frame Slides.** Click to add a frame to slides.

   ◆ **Print Hidden Slides**. Click to print hidden slides.

   ◆ **Print Comments and Ink Markup.** Click to print review comments and mark ups.

   ◆ **Printing Order.** Point to select a printing order.

3. When you're done, click the **Close Print Preview** button.

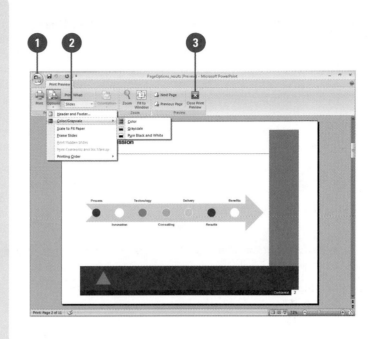

Preview Slides in Pure Black and White or Grayscale

1. Click the **View** tab.

   ◆ Or, if in Print Preview, click the Options button, and then point to **Color/Grayscale**.

2. Click the **Pure Black and White** or **Grayscale** button.

3. On the Black and White or Grayscale tab, click the button with the specific color method you want to use.

4. When you're done, click the **Back To Color View** button.

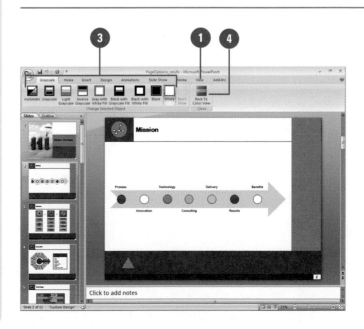

Printing a Presentation

Microsoft Certified Application Specialist PP07S-4.4.2

You can print all the elements of your presentation—the slides, outline, notes, and handouts—in either color or black and white. PowerPoint makes it easy to print your presentation; it detects the type of printer that you choose—either color or black and white—and then prints the appropriate version of the presentation. For example, if you select a black and white printer, your presentation will be set to print in shades of gray (grayscale). The Print dialog box also offers standard Windows features, giving you the option to print multiple copies, specify ranges, access printer properties, and print to a file.

Print a Presentation

1. Click the **Office** button, and then click **Print**.

2. Click the **Name** list arrow, and then select a printer.

3. Click the **Print what** list arrow, and then click what you want to print.

4. Change settings in the Print dialog box as necessary.

5. Click **OK**.

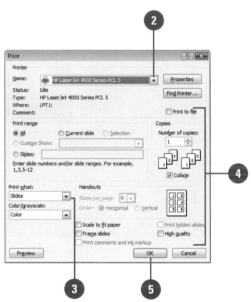

Did You Know?

You can quickly print a presentation. Use the Quick Print command on the Print submenu (on the Office menu) only when you want to bypass the Print dialog box. If you need to make selections in the Print dialog box, use the Print command on the Office menu.

Print a Custom Show

1 Click the **Office** button, and then click **Print**.

2 Click the **Custom Show** option.

3 Click the **Custom Show** list arrow, and then click the custom show you want to print.

4 Change settings in the Print dialog box as necessary.

5 Click **OK**.

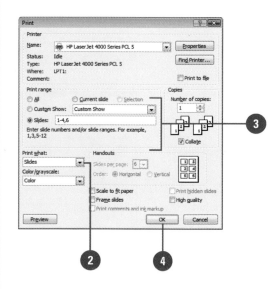

Print a Single Slide or a Range of Slides

1 Click the **Office** button, and then click **Print**.

2 If necessary, click the **Print what** list arrow, and then click **Slides**.

3 Select the range of slides you want to print.

4 Click **OK**.

Printing an Outline

Microsoft Certified Application Specialist

PP07S-4.4.2

When you print an outline, PowerPoint prints the presentation outline as shown in Outline view. What you see in the Outline pane is what you get on the printout. PowerPoint prints an outline with formatting according to the current view setting. Set your formatting to display only slide titles or all of the text levels, and choose to display the outline with or without formatting. From the Print dialog box you can choose to preview your outline before printing.

Print an Outline

1. In Outline pane, format your outline the way you want it to be printed.

   ◆ Display only slide titles or all text levels.

   ◆ Display with or without formatting. Right-click the outline, and then click **Show Text Formatting**.

2. Click the **Office** button, and then click **Print**.

3. Click the **Print what** list arrow, and then click **Outline View**.

4. To view the outline before printing and access more print options, click **Preview**, and then click the **Close Print Preview** button (the print dialog box closes).

5. Click **OK**.

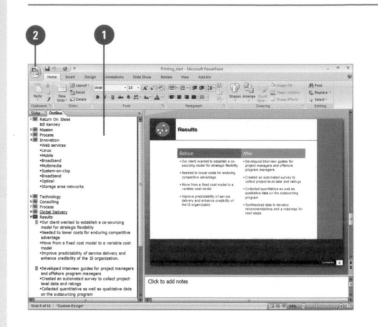

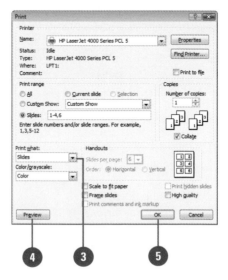

Did You Know?

You can scale slides to fit your paper when you print. Click the Office button, click Print, select the Scale To Fit Paper check box, and then click OK.

See Also

See "Inserting and Developing an Outline" on page 48 for more information on saving a presentation as an outline.

Preparing a Slide Show

9

Introduction

Microsoft Office PowerPoint provides many tools to help you coordinate your slide show as a complete multimedia production. After all your effort to create your presentation, the final details could be the lasting memory of your slide show.

Before you can deliver a slide show, you need to select the type of show you want. Will your show be presented by a speaker, or be self running? Will your show include narration or animation? These are some of the details you will need to set up for your slide show. Some presentations include slides that are appropriate for one audience but not for another. PowerPoint lets you create custom slide shows that include only a selection of slides, in whatever order you want, intended for a given audience.

After setting up your slide show requirements, you can add other special features to customize your show. Elements such as creating transitions between slides, adding special visual, sound, and animation effects. Using animations—effects that animate your slide elements, such as text flying in from the right or fading text after it's been shown, can increase the interest in your slide show.

PowerPoint includes tools that let you time your presentation to make sure that it is neither too long nor too short. You can set the timing of your slides as you rehearse your slide show. To make sure each slide has enough time on the screen. You might want to add a narration to your slide show or a music clip to play during a planned coffee break in your presentation. You can also create a self-running presentation to package for off-site clients or to run at a trade show.

What You'll Do

Create Slide Transitions

Add Animation

Use Specialized Animation

Coordinate Multiple Animations

Animate a SmartArt Graphic

Add Slide Timings

Record a Narration

Set Up a Slide Show

Create a Custom Slide Show

Create a Self-Running Presentation

Work with Fonts

Save a Presentation as a Slide Show

Creating Slide Transitions

Microsoft
Certified
Application
Specialist

PP07S-1.4.2

If you want to give your presentation more visual interest, you can add transitions between slides. For example, you can create a fading out effect so that one slide fades out as it is replaced by a new slide, or you can have one slide appear to push another slide out of the way. You can also add sound effects to your transitions, though you need a sound card and speakers to play them. To quickly see if you like a transition, point to one in the Transition Quick Style gallery to display a live preview (**New!**) of it. When you add a transition effect to a slide, the effect takes place between the previous slide and the selected slide.

Specify a Transition

1. In Normal view, click the **Slides** tab.

2. Click the slide(s) to which you want to add a transition effect.

3. Click the **Animations** tab.

4. Click the scroll up or down arrow, or click the **More** list arrow in the Transition To This Slide group to see additional transitions.

5. Point to a transition to view a live preview (**New!**), and then click the transition effect you want.

   ◆ To remove a slide transition, click No Transition.

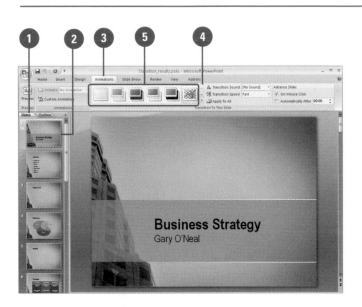

Apply a Transition to All Slides in a Presentation

1. Click the **Animations** tab.

2. Click the scroll up or down arrow, or click the **More** list arrow in the Transition To This Slide group to see additional transitions.

3. Click the transition effect you want.

4. Click the **Apply To All** button.

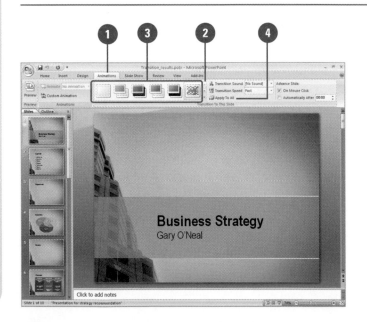

Set Transition Effect Speeds

1 In Normal or Slide Sorter view, click or display the slide whose transition effect you want to edit.

2 Click the **Animations** tab.

3 Click the **Transition Speed** list arrow, and then click **Slow**, **Medium**, or **Fast**.

4 To apply the settings to all slides, click the **Apply To All** button.

> ### Did You Know?
>
> **You can quickly view a slide's transition quickly in Slide Sorter view.** In Slide Sorter view, click a slide's transition icon to view the transition effect.

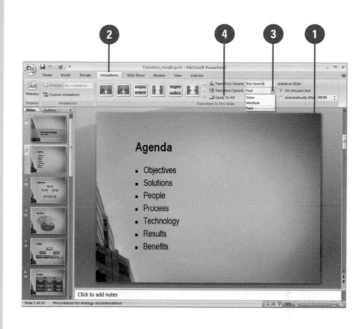

Add Sound to a Transition

1 In Normal or Slide Sorter view, click or display the slide to which you want to add a transition sound.

2 Click the **Animations** tab.

3 Click the **Transition Sound** list arrow, and then click a sound you want, or choose an option:

◆ Click **[No Sound]** or **[Stop Previous Sound]** to specify the command.

◆ Click **Other Sound** to select a sound file.

◆ Click **Loop Until Next Sound** to toggle the sound loop option.

4 To apply the settings to all slides, click the **Apply To All** button.

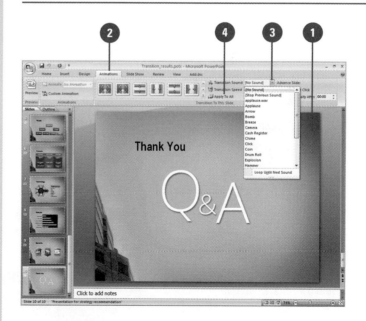

Adding Animation

Microsoft
Certified
Application
Specialist

PP07S-2.4.1

You can use animation to introduce objects onto a slide one at a time or with special animation effects. For example, a bulleted list can appear one bulleted item at a time, or a picture or chart can fade in gradually. The easiest way to apply animation effects is to use commands on the Animations tab. To quickly see if you like an animation, point to a name in the Animate list to display a live preview (**New!**) of it. If you like it, you can apply it. You can also design your own **customized animations**, including those with your own special effects and sound elements.

Apply a Standard Animation Effect to Text or an Object

1. Select the text or object you want to animate.

2. Click the **Animations** tab.

3. Click the **Animate** list arrow, and then point to an animation.

   A live preview (**New!**) of the style appears in the current shape.

4. Click the animation you want.

Preview an Animation

1. In Normal view, display the slide containing the animation you want to preview.

2. Click the **Animations** tab.

3. Click the **Preview** button.

Did You Know?

You can view a slide's animation quickly in Slide Sorter view. In Slide Sorter view, click a slide's animation icon to view the animation.

Apply a Customized Animation

1. In Normal view, select the object you want to animate.

2. Click the **Animations** tab.

3. Click the **Custom Animations** button.

4. In the Custom Animation task pane, click **Add Effect**, point to a category, and then choose an effect from the animation list.

5. Use the Modify Effect options in the Custom Animation task pane to further modify the effect.

6. Click the **Play** button to see the animation effect.

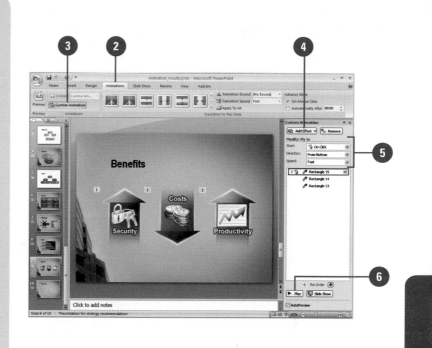

Add Sound to an Animation

1. In Normal view, select the object you want to animate.

2. Click the **Animations** tab.

3. Click the **Custom Animations** button.

4. In the Animation Order list, click the list arrow of the animation to which you want to add a sound, and then click **Effect Options**.

5. Click the **Sound** list arrow, and then click the sound effect you want.

   ◆ To add your own sound, click **Other Sound** from the list, select the sound you want, and then click **OK**.

6. Click **OK**.

7. Click the **Play** button to hear the animation effect.

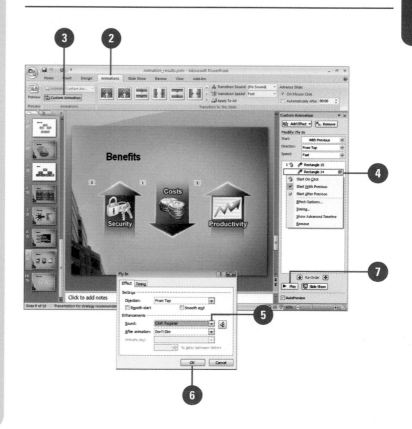

Using Specialized Animations

Microsoft Certified Application Specialist   PP07S-2.4.3

Using specialized animations, you can apply animations specific to certain objects. For example, for a text object, you can introduce the text on your slide all at once or by word or letter. Similarly, you can introduce bulleted lists one bullet item at a time and apply different effects to older items, such as graying the items out as they are replaced by new ones. You can animate charts by introducing chart series or chart categories one at a time.

Animate Text

1. In Normal view, select the text object you want to animate.

2. Click the **Animations** tab, and then click the **Custom Animation** button.

3. In the Custom Animation task pane, click **Add Effect**, point to a category, and then choose an effect from the animation list.

4. In the Animation Order list, click the list arrow of the animation, and then click **Effect Options**.

5. Click the **Animate Text** list arrow, and then click the effect you want.

6. Click **OK**, and then click **Play**.

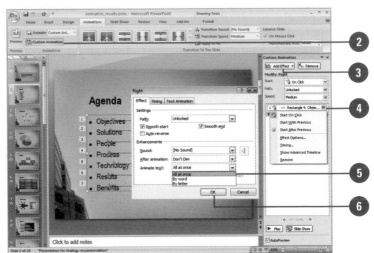

Animate Bulleted Lists

1. In Normal view, select the bulleted text you want to animate.

2. Click the **Animations** tab, and then click the **Custom Animation** button.

3. In the Custom Animation task pane, click **Add Effect**, point to a category, and then choose an effect from the animation list.

4. In the Animation Order list, click the list arrow of the animation, and then click **Effect Options**.

5. Click the **Text Animation** tab, click the **Group Text** list arrow, and then click at what paragraph level bulleted text will be animated.

6. Click **OK**, and then click **Play**.

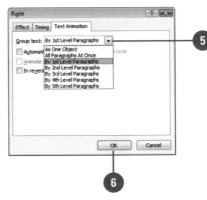

Dim Text After Its Animated

1. In Normal view, select the text you want to animate.

2. Click the **Animations** tab, and then click the **Custom Animation** button.

3. In the Custom Animation task pane, click **Add Effect**, point to a category, and then choose an effect from the animation list.

4. In the Animation Order list, click the list arrow of the animation, and then click **Effect Options**.

5. Click the **After Animation** list arrow, and then click the dim text color or option you want.

6. Click **OK**, and then click **Play** to see the animation effect.

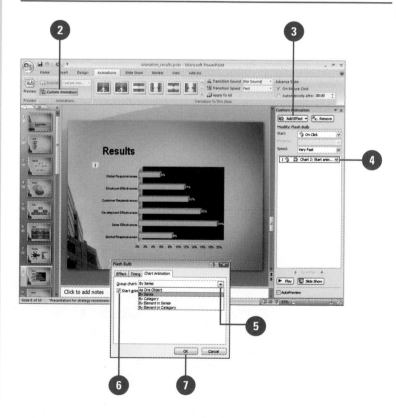

Animate Chart Elements

1. In Normal view, select the chart you want to animate.

2. Click the **Animations** tab, and then click the **Custom Animation** button.

3. In the Custom Animation task pane, click **Add Effect**, point to a category, and then choose an effect from the animation list.

4. In the Animation Order list, click the list arrow of the animation, and then click **Effect Options**.

5. Click the **Chart Animation** tab, click the **Group Chart** list arrow, and then click the order you want to introduce chart elements.

6. Select the **Animate Grid And Legend** check box to animate the chart grid and legend.

7. Click **OK**, and then click **Play** to see the animation effect.

Coordinating Multiple Animations

PP07S-2.4.2, PP07S-2.4.3

The Custom Animation task pane helps you keep track of your presentation's animations by listing all animated objects in a single location. Use these lists if your slides contain more than one animation, because they help you determine how the animations will work together. For example, you can control the animation of each object, the order each object appears, the time between animation effects, and remove unwanted animations.

Add Multiple Animation Effects to Slide Objects

1. In Normal view, select the slide object you want to animate.

2. Click the **Animations** tab, and then click the **Custom Animation** button.

3. Click the **Add Effect** button, point to a category (**Entrance**, **Emphasis**, **Exit**, or **Motion Paths**), and then choose an animation effect.

4. Click the **Start**, **Direction**, or **Speed** list arrow, and then select the option you want.

5. Repeat Steps 1 through 4 to create multiple animation effects.

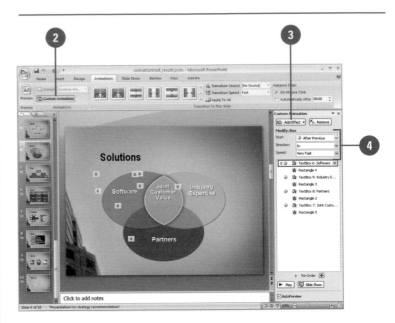

Modify the Animation Order

1. In Normal view, select the slide object you want to animate.

2. Click the **Animations** tab, and then click the **Custom Animation** button.

3. In the Animation Order list, click an animation.

4. Click the **Re-Order Up** or **Down** arrow button.

5. Click the **Play** button.

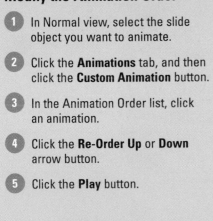
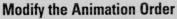
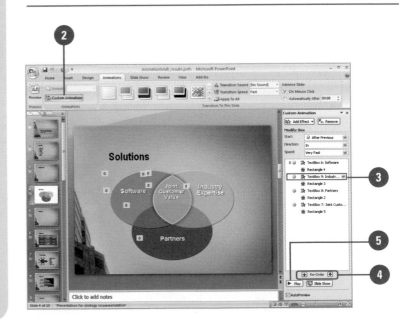

Set Time Between Animations

1. In Normal view, select the slide object you want to animate.

2. Click the **Animations** tab, and then click the **Custom Animation** button.

3. In the Animation Order list, click the list arrow of an animation, and then click **Timing**.

4. Click the **Start** list arrow, and then click **After Previous**.

5. Use the **Delay** arrows to select the number of seconds between this animation and the previous event.

6. Click **OK**.

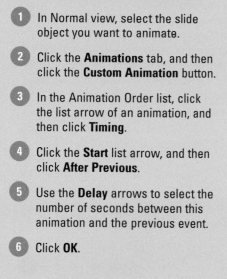

Remove an Animation

1. In Normal view, select the slide object you want to animate.

2. Click the **Animations** tab, and then click the **Custom Animation** button.

3. Click the animation you want to remove from the Animation Order list, and then click the list arrow.

4. Click **Remove**.

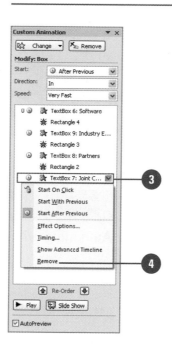

Did You Know?

You can show animation and transition effects while viewing your presentation in a browser. Click the Office button, click PowerPoint Options, click Advanced. Click Web Options, click the Show Slide Animation While Browsing check box, and then click OK. Click OK again to close the PowerPoint Options dialog box.

Animating a SmartArt Graphic

PP07S-2.4.2, PP07S-2.4.3

SmartArt graphics (**New!**) allow you to create diagrams that convey processes or relationships. You can add animation to a SmartArt graphic to show information in phases on a slide one at a time or with special animation effects. The easiest way to apply animation effects to a slide show is to use animation commands on the Animations tab. To quickly see if you like a animation, point to a name in the Animate list to display a live preview (**New!**) of it. If you like it, you can apply it. You can also design your own customized animations, including those with your own special effects and sound elements.

Animate a SmartArt Graphic

1. Select the SmartArt graphic you want to animate.

2. Click the **Animations** tab.

3. Click the **Animate** list arrow, and then point to an animation.

   A live preview (**New!**) of the style appears in the current shape.

4. Click the animation you want under one of the animation types (commands vary depending on the SmartArt graphic):

   ◆ **No Animation.** Removes the animation effect.

   ◆ **As one object.** Animates the SmartArt object as a whole.

   ◆ **All at once.** Animates all shapes at the same time.

   ◆ **One by one.** Animates each shape individually one at a time.

   ◆ **By branch (one by one).** Animates all shapes in the same branch at the same time.

   ◆ **By level (at once).** Animates all shapes in the same level at the same time.

   ◆ **Custom Animation.** Opens the Custom Animation task pane.

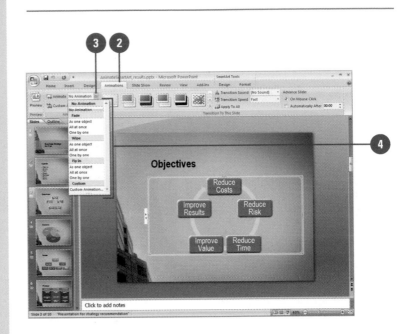

For Your Information

Animating with SmartArt Graphics Differences

Animations you apply to a SmartArt graphic are different from the ones you apply to text, shapes, or WordArt. Connecting lines between shapes are associated with the second shape and not animated individually. Shapes in a SmartArt graphic animate in the order the shapes appear. When you convert a diagram created in an earlier version of PowerPoint to a SmartArt graphic, you might loose some animation settings.

Apply a Customized Animation to a SmartArt Graphic

1. Select the SmartArt graphic you want to animate.

2. Click the **Animations** tab.

3. Click the **Custom Animations** button.

4. In the Custom Animation task pane, click **Add Effect**, point to a category, and then choose an effect from the animation list.

5. Use the Modify Effect options in the Custom Animation task pane to further modify the effect.

6. Click the **Play** button to see the animation effect.

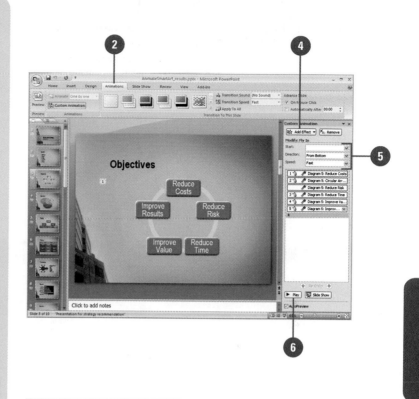

Reverse the Order of a SmartArt Graphic Animation

1. Select the SmartArt graphic you want to reverse.

2. Click the **Animations** tab.

3. Click the **Custom Animations** button.

4. In the Animation Order list, click the list arrow of the animation to which you want to reverse, and then click **Effect Options**.

5. Click the **SmartArt Animation** tab.

6. Select the **Reverse order** check box.

7. Click **OK**, and then click **Play** to see the animation effect.

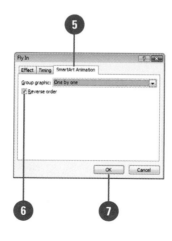

Adding Slide Timings

PP07S-4.5.2

Use PowerPoint's timing features to make sure that your presentation is not too long or too fast. You can specify the amount of time given to each slide or use Rehearse Timings, which ensures that your timings are legitimate and workable. By rehearsing timings, you can vary the amount of time each slide appears on the screen. If you want the timings to take effect, make sure the show is set to use timings in the Set Up Show dialog box.

Set Timings Between Slides

1. Click the slide(s) to which you want to set slide timings.

2. Click the **Animations** tab.

3. Select the **Automatically After** check box.

4. Enter the time (in seconds) before the presentation automatically advances to the next slide after displaying the entire slide.

5. To apply the settings to all slides, click the **Apply To All** button.

Did You Know?

You can use the mouse to control slide timings. In Slide Show View, a mouse click always advances a slide, even if the set timing has not elapsed, and holding down the mouse button prevents a timed transition from occurring until you release the mouse button.

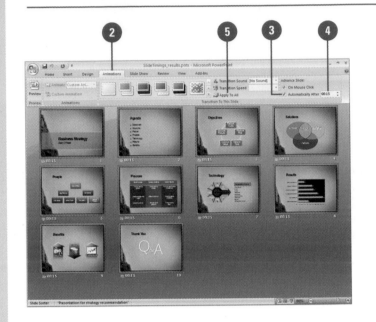

Create Timings Through Rehearsal

1. Click the **Slide Show** tab.

2. Click the **Rehearse Timings** button.

3. As the slide show runs, rehearse your presentation by clicking or pressing Enter to go to the next transition or slide.

4. When you're done, click **Yes** to accept the timings.

5. To test timings, start the slide show and note when the slides advance too quickly or too slowly.

6. Review and edit individual timings in Slide Sorter view.

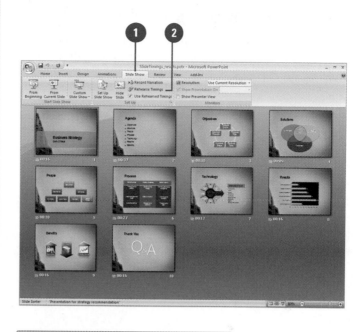

Edit Timings

1. Click the **Slide Sorter View** button.

2. Click the slide whose timing you want to change.

3. Click the **Animations** tab.

4. Enter a new value in the Seconds box.

5. Press Enter or click anywhere in the presentation to save the new timing.

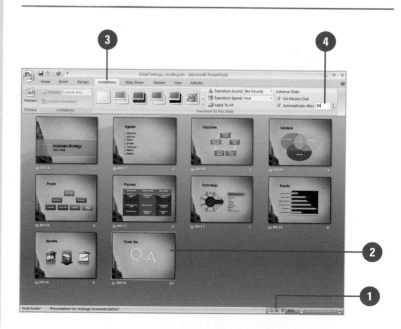

Recording a Narration

Microsoft Certified Application Specialist

PP07S-4.5.2, PP07S-4.5.5

If you are creating a self-running presentation, you might want to add a narration to emphasize the points you make. PowerPoint lets you record your own narration as you rehearse your slide show. You can record a narration before you run a slide show, or you can record it during the presentation and include audience comments. As you record the narration, you can pause or stop the narration at any time. When you play back a narration, the recording is synchronized with the presentation, including all slide transitions and animations. You can also delete a voice narration, as with any other PowerPoint object. You will need a microphone and a computer with a sound card to record the narration.

Record a Narration

1. Click the **Slide Show** tab.

2. Click the **Record Narration** button.

3. Click **Set Microphone Level**.

4. Set the microphone level you want.

5. Click **OK**.

6. Click **Change Quality**.

7. Click the **Name** list arrow, and then click the recording quality you want.

8. Click **OK**.

9. If necessary, select the **Link narrations in** check box to insert the narration as a linked object.

10. Click **OK**.

See Also

See "Recording Sounds" on page 185 for information on adding music or other sounds to a presentation.

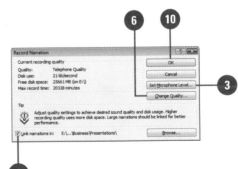

11. If necessary, click **Current Slide** or **First Slide**.

12. Speak clearly into the microphone attached to your computer and record your narration for each slide.

13. Click **Save** when prompted to save slide timings along with your narration.

14. Rerun the slide show and verify that your narration has been recorded along with the automatic timings.

Did You Know?

You can pause narration. Right-click anywhere on the screen, and then click Pause Narration.

You can resume narration. Right-click anywhere on the screen, and then click Resume Narration.

You can show a presentation without narration. To show a presentation with narration on a computer without sound hardware installed, click the Slide Show tab, click the Set Up Show button, and then select the Show without narration check box to avoid problems running the presentation.

Setting Up a Slide Show

Microsoft Certified Application Specialist

PP07S-4.5.1, PP07S-4.5.5

PowerPoint offers several types of slide shows appropriate for a variety of presentation situations, from a traditional big-screen slide show to a show that runs automatically on a computer screen at a conference kiosk. When you don't want to show all of the slides in a PowerPoint presentation to a particular audience, you can specify only a range of slides to show, or you can hide individual slides. You can also save a presentation to open directly into Slide Show view or run continuously.

Set Up a Show

1. Click the **Slide Show** tab.

2. Click the **Set Up Slide Show** button.

3. Choose the show type you want.

   ◆ Click the **Presented by a speaker** option to run a full screen slide show.

   ◆ Click the **Browsed by an individual** option to run a slide show in a window and allow access to some PowerPoint commands.

   ◆ Click the **Browsed at a kiosk** option to create a self-running, unattended slide show for a booth or kiosk.

4. Select or clear the following check boxes:

   ◆ **Loop continuously until 'Esc'**. Select to replay the slide show again until you stop it.

   ◆ **Show without narration.** Select to not play narration.

   ◆ **Show without animation.** Select to not play animation.

5. Select the **Manually** or **Using timings, if present** option, where you can advance the slides manually or automatically.

6. Click the **Slide show** list arrow, and then select the display resolution you want (**New!**).

7. Click **OK**.

Frequently Asked Questions

How Do You Choose a Screen Resolution?

The quality of a display system depends on its screen resolution, how many pixels it can display, and how many bits are used to represent each pixel. The screen resolution signifies the number of dots (pixels) on the entire screen. A higher screen resolution, such as 1024 by 768, makes items appear smaller, while a lower screen resolution, such as 640 by 480, makes items appear larger, which can help make a slide show eraser to view.

Show a Range of Slides

1. Click the **Slide Show** tab.

2. Click the **Set Up Show** button.

3. Click the **From** option.

4. Enter the first and last slide numbers of the range you want to show.

5. Click **OK**.

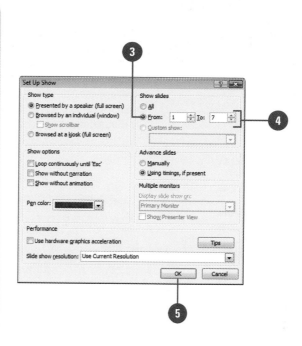

Hide Slides

1. In Slide Sorter view, or Normal view, select or display the slide you want to hide.

2. Click the **Slide Show** tab.

3. Click the **Hide Slide** button.

   The slide number in the Slide pane or Slide Sorter view appears with circle and a line through it.

4. To show a hidden slide, click it, click the **Hide Slide** button again.

Did You Know?

You can run a slide show continuously. Open the presentation you want to run, click the Slide Show tab, click the Set Up Show button, select the Loop Continuously Until 'Esc' check box, and then click OK.

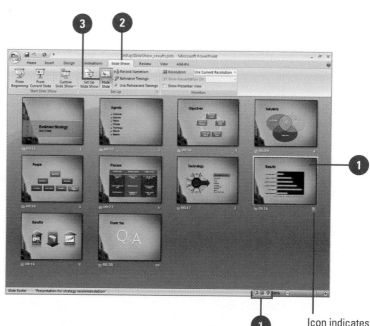

Icon indicates hidden slide

Creating a Custom Slide Show

If you plan to present a slide show to more than one audience, you don't have to create a separate slide show for each audience. Instead, you can create a custom slide show that allows you to specify which slides from the presentation you will use and the order in which they will appear. You can also edit a custom show which you've already created. Add, remove, and rearrange slides in a custom show to fit your various needs.

Create a Custom Slide Show

1. Click the **Slide Show** tab.

2. Click the **Custom Slide Show** button, and then click **Custom Shows**.

3. Click **New**.

4. Type a name for the show.

5. Click the slide(s) you want, and then click **Add**. To remove a slide, select it in the Slides In Custom Show list, and then click **Remove**.

6. Click **OK**.

7. Click **Close**.

Show a Custom Slide Show

1. Click the **Slide Show** tab.

2. Click the **Custom Slide Show** button, and then click **Custom Shows**.

3. Click the custom slide show you want to run.

4. Click **Show**.

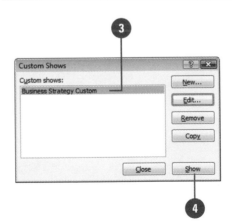

Edit a Custom Slide Show

1. Click the **Slide Show** tab.

2. Click the **Custom Slide Show** button, and then click **Custom Shows**.

3. Click the show you want to edit.

4. Click **Edit**.

5. To add a slide, click the slide in the Slides in presentation list and then click the **Add** button. The slide appears at the end of the Slides in custom show list.

6. To remove a slide from the show, click the slide in the Slides in custom show list, and then click **Remove**.

7. To move a slide up or down in the show, click the slide in the Slides In Custom Show list, and then click the **Up Arrow** or **Down Arrow** button.

8. Click **OK**.

9. Click **Close**.

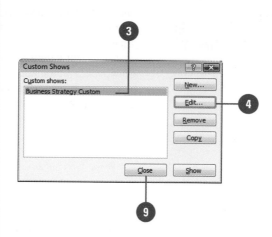

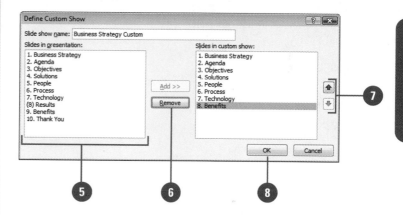

Did You Know?

You can delete a custom slide show. Click the Slide Show tab, click the Custom Slide Show button, click Custom Shows, click the show you want to delete, click Remove, and then click Close.

You can use the Set Up Show command to display a custom slide show. Click the Slide Show tab, click the Set Up Show button, click the Custom Show option, click the Custom Show list arrow, select the custom slide show, and then click OK.

Creating a Self-Running Presentation

Microsoft Certified Application Specialist   PP07S-4.5.5

Self-running slide shows are a great way to communicate information without needing someone to run the show. You might want to set up a presentation to run unattended in a kiosk at a trade show or place it on your company's Intranet to run at the user's convenience. The slides will advance automatically, or a user can advance the slides or activate hyperlinks. You can use the Set Up Show dialog box to select the Browsed at a Kiosk (Full Screen) and other related options to create a self-running slide show.

Set Up a Self-Running Slide Show

1 Click the **Slide Show** tab.

2 Click the **Set Up Slide Show** button.

3 Click the **Browsed at a kiosk (full screen)** option.

The Loop continuously until 'Esc' option is selected and grayed out.

4 Select the **Manually** or **Using timings, if present** option, where you can advance the slides manually or automatically.

5 Select additional show options check boxes as appropriate.

6 Click the **Slide show** list arrow, and then select the display resolution you want, such as 640x480, 1024x768, or User Current Resolution (**New!**).

7 Click **OK**.

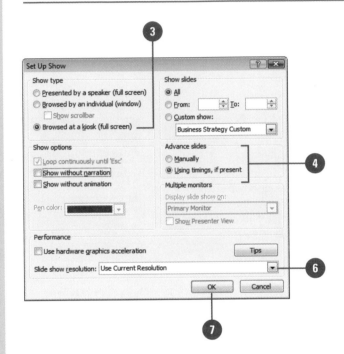

Did You Know?

Certain tools are active in a self-navigating show. A self-navigating show turns off all navigation tools except action buttons and other action settings available to the user.

Working with Fonts

PowerPoint offers an assortment of tools for working with the fonts in your presentation. If you are using nonstandard fonts, you can embed the fonts you use so they "travel" with your presentation. Then, if the computer you use to show your presentation does not have all your fonts installed, the presentation quality will not suffer.

Embed TrueType Fonts in a Presentation

① Click the **Office** button, and then click **PowerPoint Options**.

TIMESAVER *If you're in the Save As dialog box, click the Tools button arrow, and then click Save Options.*

② In the left pane, click **Save**.

③ Click the list arrow next to Preserve fidelity when sharing this presentation, and then select the presentation you want to embed fonts.

④ Select the **Embed fonts in the file** check box.

⑤ Click the option you want.

◆ **Embed only the characters used in the presentation (best for reducing file size).**

◆ **Embed all characters (best for editing by other people).**

⑥ Click **OK**.

Did You Know?

Embedding fonts increase the presentation size. When you embed all characters in a presentation, you embed all the characters in the font set, and the increase file size.

Frequently Asked Questions

What's the Difference Between the Fonts?

There are two basic types of fonts: scalable and bitmapped. A **scalable font** (also known as **outline font**) is based on a mathematical equation that creates character outlines to form letters and numbers of any size. The two major scalable fonts are Adobe's Type 1 PostScript and Apple/Microsoft's TrueType or OpenType. Scalable fonts are generated in any point size on the fly and require only four variations for each typeface. A **bitmapped font** consists of a set of dot patterns for each letter and number in a typeface for a specified type size. Bitmapped fonts are created or prepackaged ahead of time and require four variations for each point size used in each typeface. Although a bitmapped font designed for a particular font size will always look the best, scalable fonts eliminate storing hundreds of different sizes of fonts on disk.

Saving a Presentation as a Slide Show

PP07S-4.3.6

When you're giving a professional slide show presentation, you might not want your audience to see you start it from PowerPoint. Instead, you can save a presentation as a PowerPoint Show to open directly into Slide Show view. You can use the Save As dialog box to save a presentation as a PowerPoint Show (.ppsx) or PowerPoint Macro-Enabled (.ppsm). After you save a presentation as a PowerPoint Show file, you can create a shortcut to it on your desktop and then simply double-click the PowerPoint Show file to start it directly in Slide Show view.

Save a Presentation as a PowerPoint Show

1. Click the **Office** button, point to **Save As**, and then click **PowerPoint Show**.

2. Click the **Save in** list arrow, and then click the drive or folder where you want to save the file.

3. Type a presentation show file name.

4. Click the **Save as type** list arrow, and then click **PowerPoint Show** or **PowerPoint Macro-Enabled Show**.

5. Click **Save**.

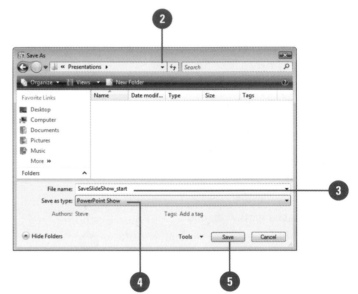

Presenting a Slide Show

10

Introduction

When you're done preparing your slide show, it's time to consider how to show it to your audience. Microsoft Office PowerPoint gives you several ways to give and share your presentations. When you are presenting the show in person, you can use PowerPoint's slide navigation tools to move around your presentation. You can move forward and backward or move to a specific slide by using various navigation keys on the keyboard and on-screen Slide Show tools.

As you're presenting your slide show, you can highlight key ideas by using the mouse as a pointer or pen/highlighter. By annotating your slide show, you can give extra emphasis on a topic or goal for your audience. Annotations can be saved as enhancements to your presentation for later. If you are presenting a slide show using a second monitor or projection screen, PowerPoint includes the tools you need to properly navigate the display equipment.

If you are taking your presentation to another site, you might not need the entire PowerPoint package. Rather than installing PowerPoint on the sites' computer, you can pack your presentation into one compressed file, storing it on a CD. Once you reach your destination, you can expand the compressed file onto your client's computer and play it, regardless of whether that computer has PowerPoint installed.

What You'll Do

Start a Slide Show

Navigate a Slide Show

Annotate a Slide Show

Deliver a Show on Multiple Monitors

Package a Presentation on CD

Show a Presentation with the PowerPoint Viewer

Customize the PowerPoint Viewer

Show Multiple Presentations

Starting a Slide Show

Once you have set up your slide show, you can start the show at any time. As you run your slide show, you can use the Slide Show toolbar, or Pop-up toolbar, to access certain PowerPoint commands without leaving Slide Show view. If your show is running at a kiosk, you might want to disable this feature.

Start a Slide Show and Display the Slide Show Toolbar

1. Click the **Slide Show** tab.

   TIMESAVER *Click the Slide Show View button on the Status bar to start a slide show quickly from the current slide.*

2. Click the **From Beginning** or **From Current Slide** button.

3. Move the mouse pointer to display the Slide Show toolbar.

4. Click a button on the Slide Show toolbar to move to the next or previous slide, or navigate the slide show, or end the show.

   TIMESAVER *Press Esc to stop a slide show.*

See Also

See "Setting Up a Slide Show" on page 314 for information on preparing a slide show.

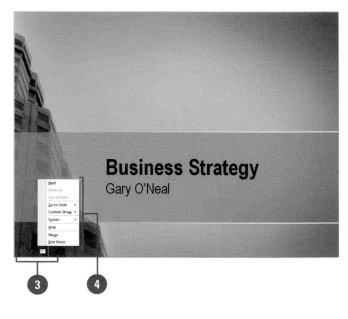

Set Slide Show Options

1. Click the **Office** button, and then click **PowerPoint Options**.

2. In the left pane, click **Advanced**.

3. Select the slide show and pop-up toolbar check box options you want.

   ◆ **Show menu on right mouse click.** Select to show a shortcut menu when you right-click a slide during a slide show.

   ◆ **Show popup toolbar.** Select to show the popup toolbar at the bottom of a full screen presentation.

   ◆ **Prompt to keep ink annotations when exiting.** Select to be prompted to save your changes when you write on slides during a slide show.

   ◆ **End with black slide.** Select to insert a black slide at the end of the presentation.

4. Click **OK**.

Navigating a Slide Show

Microsoft
Certified
Application
Specialist

PP07S-4.5.3

In Slide Show view, you advance to the next slide by clicking the mouse button, pressing the Spacebar, or pressing Enter. In addition to those basic navigational techniques, PowerPoint provides keyboard shortcuts that can take you to the beginning, the end, or any particular slide in your presentation. You can also use the navigation commands on the shortcut menu to access slides in custom slide shows. After a period of inactivity during a normal full-screen slide show, PowerPoint hides the pointer and Slide Show toolbar.

Go to a Specific Slide

1. In Slide Show view, move the mouse to display the Slide Show toolbar, and then click the **Slide** button.

   TIMESAVER *Right-click a slide to display a shortcut menu.*

2. Point to **Go to Slide**, and then click the title of the slide to which you want to go.

Did You Know?

You can add speaker notes in Slide Show. In Slide Show view, right-click a blank area on the slide, point to Screen, click Speaker Notes, type your notes, and then click Close.

You can switch to another program in Slide Show. In Slide Show view, right-click a blank area on the slide, point to Screen, and then click Switch Programs. Use the taskbar to switch between programs.

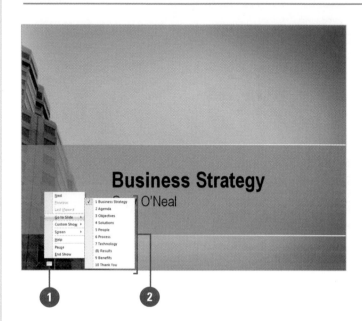

Use Slide Show View Navigation Shortcuts

◆ Refer to the adjacent table for information on Slide Show view navigation shortcuts.

Slide Show View Shortcuts

Action	Result
Mouse click	Moves to the next slide
Right-mouse click	Moves to the previous slide (only if the Shortcut Menu On Right-Click option is disabled)
Press Enter	Moves to the next slide
Press Home	Moves to the first slide in the show
Press End	Moves to the last slide in the show
Press Page Up	Moves to the previous slide
Press Page Down	Moves to the next slide
Enter a slide number and press Enter	Moves to the slide number you specified when you press Enter
Press B	Displays a black screen; press again to return
Press W	Displays a white screen; press again to return
Press Esc	Exits Slide Show view

Go to a Custom Slide Show

1️⃣ In Slide Show view, right-click a slide.

2️⃣ Point to **Custom Show**.

3️⃣ Click the custom slide show that you want to go to.

See Also

See "Creating a Custom Slide Show" on page 316 for information on creating a custom slide show.

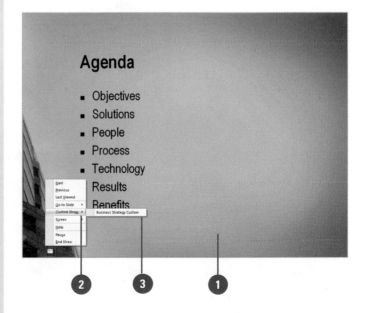

Annotating a Slide Show

Microsoft Certified Application Specialist

PP07S-4.5.3

When you are presenting your slide show, you can turn your mouse pointer into a pen tool to highlight and circle your key points. If you decide to use a pen tool, you might want to set its color to match the colors in your presentation. When you are finished, you can turn the pen back to the normal mouse pointer. Mark ups you make on a slide with the pen tool during a slide show can be saved with the presentation, and then turned on or off when you re-open the presentation for editing.

Change Pointer Options

1 In Slide Show view, move the mouse to display the Slide Show toolbar.

2 Click the **Pen** button, point to **Arrow Options**, and then click a pointer option.

- **Automatic** hides the pointer until you move the mouse.

- **Visible** makes the pointer visible.

- **Hidden** makes the pointer invisible throughout the presentation.

Use a Pen During the Slide Show

1 In Slide Show view, move the mouse to display the Slide Show toolbar.

2 Click the **Pen** button, and then click or point to an option.

- A writing tool (**Ballpoint Pen**, **Felt Tip Pen**, or **Highlighter**).

- **Ink Color** to select an ink color.

3 Drag the mouse pointer to draw on your slide presentation with the pen or highlighter.

4 To remove ink, click the **Pen** button, and then click **Eraser** for individual ink, or click **Erase All Ink on Slide** for all ink.

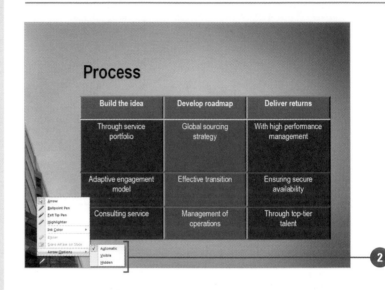

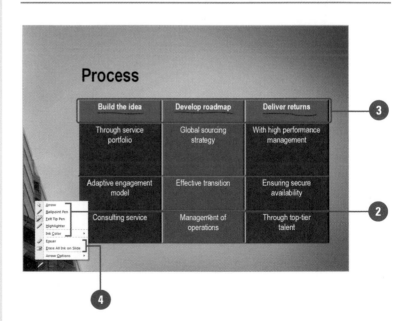

Save Annotations and Turn Them On and Off

1. In Slide Show view, right-click a slide.

2. Point to **Pointer Options**.

3. Click a pen or highlighter, and then make an annotation on a slide.

4. Right-click the slide, and then click **End Show**.

5. Click **Keep** when asked if you want to keep your ink annotations for editing.

6. In Normal view, click the **Review** tab.

7. Click the **Show Markup** button.

   The annotations disappear from the slide.

8. Click the **Office** button, click **Close**, and then click **Yes** to save the changes.

   When you re-open this presentation, you can view the Mark ups in Normal or Slide Sorter view, and then turn them off or on.

Did You Know?

You can quickly turn the pen back to the mouse pointer. To turn the pen back to the normal mouse pointer, right-click a slide in Slide Show view, point to Pointer Options, and then click Arrow.

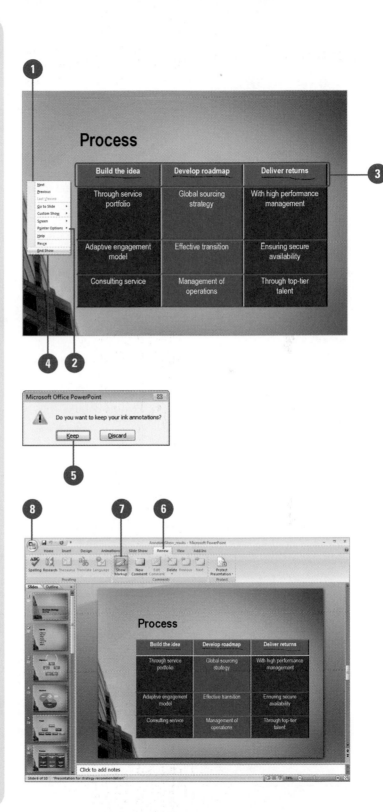

Delivering a Show on Multiple Monitors

If your computer is connected to two monitors, you can view a slide show on one monitor while you control it from another. This is useful when you want to control a slide show and run other programs that you don't want the audience to see. When you display your slide show on multiple monitors, you can present it using PowerPoint's Presenter Tools in the Presenter view, which allows presenters to have their own view that is not visible to the audience. In addition to including details about what bullet or slide is coming next, this view also enables you to see your speaker notes and lets you jump directly to any slide. You can only use Presenter view and run the presentation from one monitor.

Turn on Multiple Monitor Support

1. In Display Settings in your Windows Control Panel, turn on multiple monitor support.

   Click the monitor icon for the presenter's monitor, and then select the **Extend the desktop onto this monitor** check box (Vista).

2. In PowerPoint, click the **Slide Show** tab.

3. Click the **Set Up Slide Show** button.

4. Select the **Show Presenter View** check box.

5. Click the **Display slide show on** list arrow, and then select the monitor where you want to display the slide show.

6. Click **OK**.

Did You Know?

There are requirements to run two monitors? You must have dual-monitor hardware installed (either two video cards, or multiple monitor capabilities, like a laptop) and be using Windows 2000 with SP3 (or later; recommended for Windows XP or Vista). PowerPoint only supports the use of two monitors.

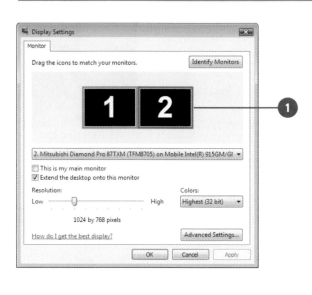

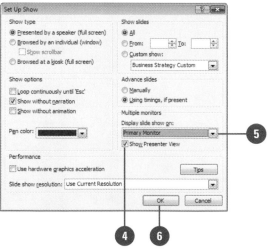

Present a Slide Show On Two Monitors in Presenter View

1 Click the **Slide Show** tab.

2 Click the **Resolution** list arrow, and then click the screen size you want to project the slide show.

3 Click the **Show Presentation On** list arrow, and then click the name of the monitor on which you want to project the slide show.

4 Select the **Use Presenter View** check box.

5 In Presenter view, use the navigation tools to deliver the presentation on multiple monitors.

◆ **Slide thumbnails.** Click to select slides out of sequence and create a customized presentation.

◆ **Preview text.** Shows you want your next click will add to the screen, such as a new slide or the next bullet in a list.

◆ **Slide number and elapsed time.** Shows you the current slide number and elapsed show time.

◆ **Speaker notes.** Read speaker's notes shown in large, clear type as a script.

◆ **Pointer Options.** Click to select pen type, ink color, erase and arrow options (**New!**).

◆ **Slide Show.** Click to navigate to other locations in the presentation.

6 If necessary, press Esc or click the **Close** button to exit Presenter View.

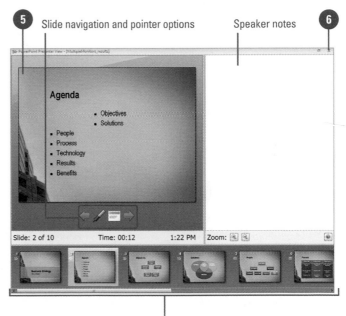

Slide navigation and pointer options   Speaker notes

Slide thumbnails

Packaging a Presentation on CD

Microsoft
Certified
Application
Specialist

PP07S-4.5.4

The Package for CD feature allows you to copy one or more presentations and all of the supporting files, including linked files, on CD. You can choose packaging options to automatically or manually run your presentations. The PowerPoint Viewer is a program included on the packaged CD used to run presentations on computers that don't have Microsoft PowerPoint installed. If you are packaging your presentation for use on your laptop computer, a DVD, or a network, you can use Package for CD to package your presentation to a folder or a network. PowerPoint doesn't support direct burning to DVDs, so you need to use DVD burning software to import the presentation files and create a DVD. Before you package your presentation, you can inspect it for hidden data and personal information (**New!**).

Package a Presentation on CD

1. Click the **Office** button, point to **Publish**, and then click **Package for CD**.

2. Type a name for the CD.

3. To add additional files to the CD, click **Add Files**, select the files you want, and then click **Add**.

4. Click **Options**.

5. Click the package type option you want.

6. To link any external files, select the **Linked files** check box.

7. To ensure fonts are available on the play back computer, select the **Embedded TrueType fonts** check box.

8. If you want, type a password to open or modify the presentation.

9. To remove data, select the **Inspect presentation for inappropriate or private information** check box.

10. Click **OK**.

11. Click **Copy to CD**, and then follow the CD writer instructions.

    If a message alert appears, click the buttons you want to complete the process.

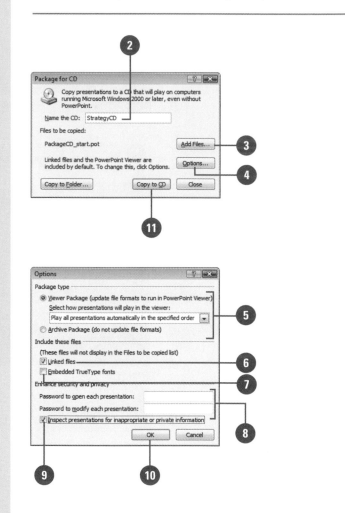

Package a Presentation to a Folder

1. Click the **Office** button, point to **Publish**, and then click **Package for CD**.

2. Type a name for the folder.

3. To add additional files to the folder, click **Add Files**, select the files you want, and then click **Add**.

4. Click **Options**.

5. Click the package type option you want.

6. To link any external files, select the **Linked files** check box.

7. To ensure fonts are available on the play back computer, select the **Embedded TrueType fonts** check box.

8. If you want, type a password to open or modify the presentation.

9. To remove data, select the **Inspect presentation for inappropriate or private information** check box.

10. Click **OK**.

11. Click **Copy to Folder**, specify a folder location, and then click **OK**.

12. Click Browse to select the complete path to the folder location you want.

13. Click **OK**.

    If a message alert appears, click the buttons you want to complete the process.

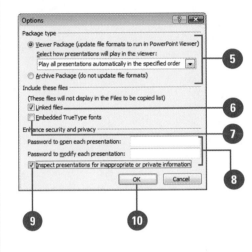

Showing a Presentation with the PowerPoint Viewer

The PowerPoint Viewer is a program used to run presentations on computers that don't have Microsoft PowerPoint installed. This Viewer is used as part of the Package for CD feature, but you can also use the Viewer independently. The PowerPoint Viewer is installed when you install PowerPoint. However, you can download it from the Microsoft Office Online Web site in the downloads section if you need it on the road. If a presentation contains password protection, the PowerPoint Viewer prompts you for a password. The PowerPoint Viewer 2007 supports all presentations created using PowerPoint 2000 or later. You can run the PowerPoint Viewer 2007 on Microsoft Windows XP Service Pack 2 (or later).

Show a Presentation with the PowerPoint Viewer

1. Click the **Start** button, point to **All Programs**, click **Microsoft Office**, and then click **Microsoft Office PowerPoint Viewer 2007**.

   TROUBLE? *If the viewer is not available on the Start menu, open Windows Explorer, and then search for the pptview.exe file, which you can double-click to start the program.*

2. If necessary on first run, click **Accept** for the license agreement.

3. If you want to open a specific file type, click the **Files of type** list arrow, and then click a file type.

4. If the file is located in another folder, click the **Look in** list arrow, and then navigate to the file.

5. Select the presentation you want to show.

6. Click **Open**.

7. Navigate the slide show.

8. To stop the show, press Esc at any time or click **Cancel** at the end to close the PowerPoint Viewer.

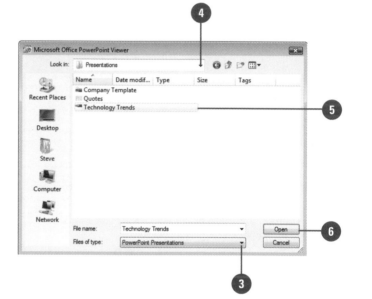

Customizing the PowerPoint Viewer

You can use the Run command within Microsoft Windows to customize the way the PowerPoint Viewer 2007 starts and functions. In the Run dialog box, you can enter a command to start the PowerPoint Viewer without the startup splash screen, at a specific slide, and using a playlist (showing consecutive presentations). You can also show the Open dialog box at the end of the show and print a presentation. The command you enter uses switches and parameters to perform the functions you want. A switch determines the function you want to perform. In the command-line, the switch appears after the program name (PPTVIEW.EXE) with a a space, followed by a slash (/) and the name of the switch. The switch is followed in some cases by a space and a parameter, which gives direction. A parameter is typically a file name. For example, "c:*path to folder*\PPTVIEW.EXE /N3 "pres.pptx"", where "c:*path to folder*\PPTVIEW.EXE" is the command, /N3 is the switch, and "pres.pptx" is the parameter. The path to folder is the location where the PPTVIEW.EXE file is stored. It's typically located in "c:\programs files\microsoft office\office 12\PPTVIEW.EXE"

Use the Run Command to Start the PowerPoint Viewer

1 Click the **Start** button, and then click **Run** (XP), or point to **All Programs**, point to **Accessories**, and click **Run** (Vista).

2 Refer to the adjacent table for commands to enter.

You can use only one switch at a time. Quotation marks are required if there are spaces in the path or file name; they are optional there are no spaces.

3 Click **OK**.

Command-line Switches

Switch	Action
/D	Show the Open dialog box when presentation ends. Example: "c:*path to folder*\PPTVIEW.EXE" /D
/L	Read a playlist of PowerPoint presentations contained within a text file. Example: "c:*path to folder*\PPTVIEW.EXE" /L "playlist.txt"
/N#	Open the presentation at a specified slide number. Example: "c:*path to folder*\PPTVIEW.EXE" /N3 "pres.pptx"
/S	Start the Office PowerPoint Viewer 2007 without showing the splash screen. Example: "c:*path to folder*\PPTVIEW.EXE" /S
/P	Send the presentation to a printer and print the file. Example: "c:*path to folder*\PPTVIEW.EXE" /P "pres.pptx"

Did You Know?

You can create a shortcut to reuse a command-line switch. Right-click the Windows desktop, point to New, click Shortcut. In the wizard, type the full path to the Viewer or click Browse to find it, add a switch and parameter to the path command-line, click Next, type a shortcut name, click Finish.

Showing Multiple Presentations

If you want to deliver more than one slide show at a time, you can create and use a playlist. A **playlist** is a simple text file than contains a list of presentation file names in the order that you want to deliver them. File names in a playlist file need to include the full path to the presentation unless they are located in the same location as the PowerPoint Viewer. It is not possible to add command-line switches to the presentation file name in the playlist.

Create and Show a Playlist

 Open a text editor, such as Notepad or WordPad.

 Type the presentations files you want to use on separate lines.

If the presentation files are not in the same location as the Viewer, be sure to include full paths.

 Save the text file with the name you want, such as playlistpres.txt, and then exit the program.

To avoid problems, place the text file, and presentation files in the same folder as the PowerPoint Viewer.

 Click the **Start** button, and then click **Run** (XP), or point to **All Programs**, point to **Accessories**, and click **Run** (Vista).

 Type "c:*path to folder*\ PPTVIEW.EXE" /L "playlistpres.txt"

Quotation marks are required if there are spaces in the path or file name; they are optional when there are no spaces.

 Click **OK**.

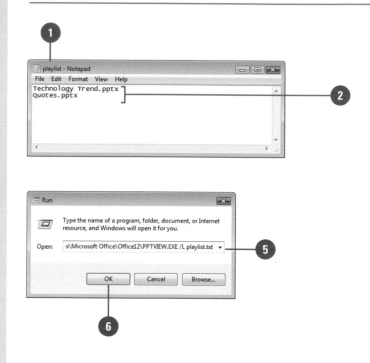

> ## See Also
>
> *See "Customizing the PowerPoint Viewer" on page 333 for information on using the Run command, command-line switches, and parameters.*

Reviewing and Securing a Presentation

11

Introduction

When you've developed content in your presentation and want feedback, you can electronically send a PowerPoint presentation to reviewers so that they can read, revise, and comment on the presentation without having to print it. Instead of reading handwritten text or sticky notes on your printout, you can get clear and concise feedback right in your presentation.

Adding a password to protect your presentation is not only a good idea for security purposes, it's an added feature to make sure that changes to your presentation aren't accidentally made by unauthorized people. Not only can you guard who sees your presentation, you can set rights on who can add changes and comments to your presentation. You can also add restricted access known as **Information Rights Access (IRM)**. IRM is a tool that is available with all Microsoft Office applications that restricts a file being sent through e-mail to other users.

The **Trust Center (New!)** is a place where you set security options and find the latest technology information as it relates to document privacy, safety, and security from Microsoft. The Trust Center allows you to set security and privacy settings—Trusted Publishers, Trusted Locations, Add-ins, ActiveX Settings, Macro Settings, Message Bar, and Privacy Options—and provides links to Microsoft privacy statements, a customer improvement program, and trustworthy computing practices. If you receive a security warning when you open a presentation, you can set options in the Trust Center to enable macro or active content. If you trust the content provider, you can add the trusted publishers or location to alleviate the warning in the future.

After you finish making changes to your presentation, you can quickly send it to another person for review using e-mail or an Internet Fax service.

What You'll Do

Add and Edit Comments in a Presentation

Inspect Documents

Add Password Protection to a Presentation

Restrict Presentation Access

Add a Digital Signature

Avoid Harmful Attacks

Use the Trust Center

Select Trusted Publishers and Locations

Set Add-In, ActiveX and Macro Security Options

Change Message Bar Security Options

Set Privacy Options

Work with Office Safe Modes

Mark a Presentation as Read-Only

Review a Presentation for Review Using E-Mail

Send a Presentation by Internet Fax

Adding Comments to a Presentation

Microsoft
Certified
Application
Specialist

PP07S-4.1.1, PP07S-4.1.2

When you review an Office document, you can insert comments to the author or other reviewers. **Comments** are like electronic adhesive notes tagged with your name. They typically appear in yellow boxes in PowerPoint. You can use comments to get feedback from others or to remind yourself of revisions you plan to make. A comment is visible only when you show comments using the Show Markup button and place the mouse pointer over the comment indicator. You can attach one or more comments to a letter or word on a slide, or to an entire slide. When you insert a comment, PowerPoint create a comment thumbnail with your initials and a number, starting at 1, and a comment box with your user name and date. When you're reviewing a presentation, you can use the Show Markup button on the Review tab to show and hide comments and saved annotations during a slide show.

Insert a Comment

1. Click the slide where you want to insert a comment or select an object.

2. Click the **Review** tab.

3. Click the **New Comment** button.

4. Type your comment in the comment box or pane.

5. Click outside the comment box.

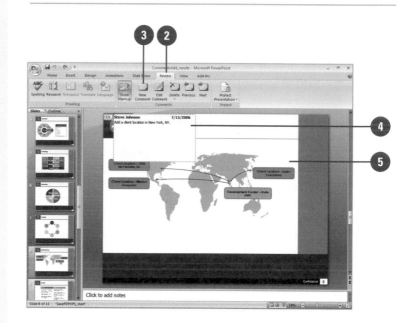

Did You Know?

You can move a comment. Drag it to a new location on the same slide.

You can show annotations. During a slide show you can add annotations to a slide, which you can save. When you show markups in PowerPoint, annotations are included. You can select, move, and delete them.

My reviewer initials and name are incorrect. You can change them in PowerPoint Options. Click the Office button, click PowerPoint Options, click Popular, enter your User name and Initials in the boxes provided, and then click OK.

Read a Comment

1. Click the **Review** tab.

2. Click the **Show Markup** button to show all comments.

   The Show Markup button toggles to show (button highlighted) or hide (button not highlighted) comments and annotations.

3. Point to the comment box.

4. Read the comment.

5. Click the **Previous** or **Next** button to read another comment.

6. When you reach the end of the presentation, click **Continue** to start at the beginning again or **Cancel**.

Did You Know?

You cannot merge PowerPoint 2007 comments back into a PowerPoint 2003 presentation. If you use PowerPoint 2003 or earlier to send your presentation for review, reviewers who use Office PowerPoint 2007 can view and add commands to your presentation, but you cannot merge their comments into your presentation.

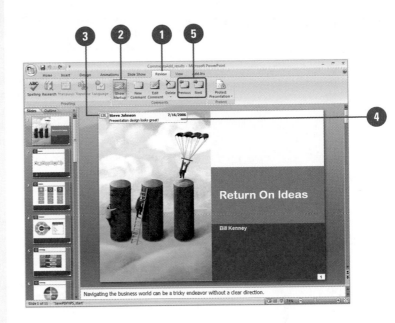

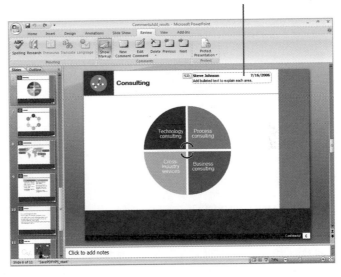

Next comment

Editing Comments in a Presentation

PowerPoint uses a different color comment for each reviewer, which is based on the User name and Initials settings in PowerPoint Options. When you add or edit a comment, the color of the review comment changes to the reviewer's color, and changes the comment name and date. You can use the Previous and Next button to quickly review each comment. When you're done, you can delete one comment at a time, all the comments on a slide, or all the comments in the presentation. If you want to save the text in a comment, you can save it to the Clipboard and then paste it into another document.

Change Reviewers

1. Click the **Office button**, and then click **PowerPoint Options**.

2. In the left pane, click **Popular**.

3. Enter a User name and Initials.

4. Click **OK**.

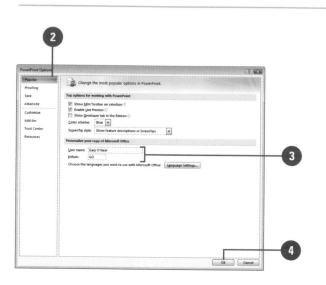

Edit a Comment

1. Click the **Review** tab.

2. Click the **Show Markup** button.

3. Right-click the comment, and then click **Edit Comment**.

   TIMESAVER *Double-click the comment box to open and edit it.*

4. Make your editing changes.

   If you're a different reviewer, the comment color and name changes to reflect the reviewer.

5. Click outside the comment box.

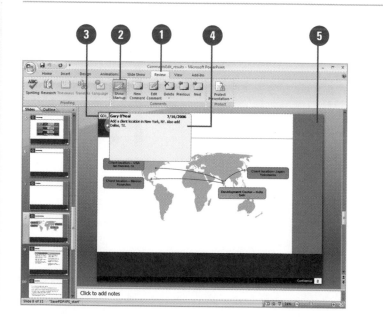

Delete a Comment

1. Click the **Review** tab.

2. Click the **Show Markup** button.

3. Click the comment you want to remove.

4. Click the **Delete Comment** button arrow, and then click one of the options:

   ◆ **Delete** to remove the selected comment.

   ◆ **Delete All Markup on the Current Slide** to remove all comments on the current slide.

   ◆ **Delete All Markup in this presentation** to remove all comments.

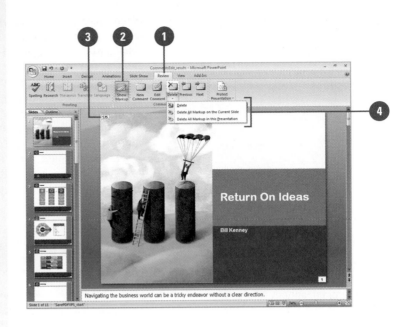

Copy Comment Text

1. Click the **Review** tab.

2. Click the **Show Markup** button.

3. Right-click the comment you want to copy, and then click **Copy Text**.

   All the text in the comment is copied to the Clipboard, including the person who wrote the comment and the date.

4. Paste the comment text where you want.

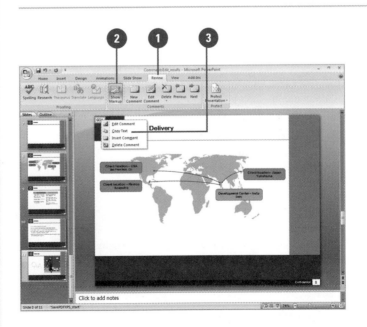

Inspecting Documents

**Microsoft
Certified
Application
Specialist**

PP07S-4.3.2

While you work on your presentation, PowerPoint automatically saves and manages personal information and hidden data to enable you to collaborate on creating and developing a presentation with other people. The personal information and hidden data includes comments, revision marks, versions, ink annotations, document properties, invisible content, off-slide content, presentation notes, document server properties, and custom XML data. The **Document Inspector (New!)** uses inspector modules to find and remove any hidden data and personal information specific to each of these modules that you might not want to share with others. If you remove hidden content from your presentation, you might not be able to restore it by using the Undo command, so it's important to make a copy of your presentation before you remove any information.

Inspect a Document

1. Click the **Office** button, click **Save As**, type a name to save a copy of the original, specify a folder location, and then click **Save**.

2. Click the **Office** button, point to **Prepare**, and then click **Inspect Document**.

3. Select the check boxes with the content you want to find and remove:

   ◆ **Comments and Annotations.** Includes comments and ink annotations.

   ◆ **Document Properties and Personal Information.** Includes metadata document Properties (Summary, Statistics, and Custom tabs), the file path for publishing Web pages, document server properties, and content type information.

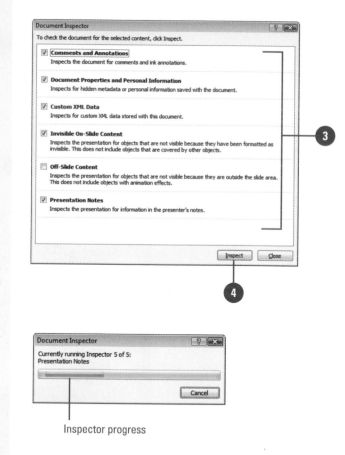

Inspector progress

Did You Know?

What is metadata? Metadata is data that describes other data. For example, text in a presentation is data, while the number of slides is metadata.

- ◆ **Custom XML Data.** Includes any custom XML data.

- ◆ **Invisible On-Slide Content.** Includes objects formatted as invisible. Doesn't include objects covered by other objects.

- ◆ **Off-Slide Content.** Includes objects (such as clip art, text boxes, graphics, and table) off the slide area.

- ◆ **Presentation Notes.** Includes text entered in the Notes section. Doesn't include pictures in the Notes section.

④ Click **Inspect**.

⑤ Review the results of the inspection.

⑥ Click **Remove All** for each inspector module in which you want to remove hidden data and personal information.

TROUBLE? *Before you click Remove All, be sure you want to remove the information. You might not be able to restore it.*

⑦ Click **Close**.

Adding Password Protection to a Presentation

Microsoft Certified Application Specialist PP07S-4.2.1

You can assign a password and other security options so that only those who know the password can open the presentation, or to protect the integrity of your presentation as it moves from person to person. At times, you will want the information to be used but not changed; at other times, you will want only specific people to be able to view the presentation. Setting a presentation as read-only is useful when you want a presentation, such as a company-wide bulletin, to be distributed and read, but not changed. Password protection takes effect the next time you open the presentation.

Add Password Protection to a Presentation

1. Open the presentation you want to protect.

2. Click the **Office** button, and then click **Save As**.

3. Click **Tools**, and then click **General Options**.

4. Type a password in the Password To Open box (encrypted) or the Password To Modify box (not encrypted).

   IMPORTANT *It's critical that you remember your password. If you forget your password, Microsoft can't retrieve it.*

5. Select or clear the **Remove automatically created personal information from this file on save** check box.

   Personal information includes author, title, subject, manager, company, and other hidden data, such as invisible content, off-slide content, reviewer's names, notes, and custom XML Data.

6. Click **OK**.

7. Type your password again.

8. Click **OK**.

9. Click **Save**, and then click **Yes** to replace existing presentation.

General Options

General Options

File encryption settings for this document

Password to open: ●●●●

File sharing settings for this document

Password to modify: ●●●●

Privacy options

☑ Remove automatically created personal information from this file on save

Macro security

Adjust the security level for opening files that might contain macro viruses, and specify the names of trusted macro developers.   [Macro Security...]

[OK]   [Cancel]

Confirm Password

Reenter password to open:

●●●●

Caution: If you lose or forget the password, it cannot be recovered. It is advisable to keep a list of passwords and their corresponding document names in a safe place. (Remember that passwords are case-sensitive.)

[OK]   [Cancel]

For Your Information

Using a Strong Password

Hackers identify passwords as strong or weak. A strong password is a combination of uppercase and lowercase letters, numbers, and symbols, such as Grea8t!, while a weak one doesn't use different character types, such as Hannah1. Be sure to write down your passwords and place them in a different location.

Open a Presentation with Password Protection

1. Click the **Office** button, click **Open**, navigate to a presentation with password protection, and then click **Open**.

2. Click **Read Only** if you do not wish to modify the presentation, or type the password in the Password dialog box.

3. Click **OK**.

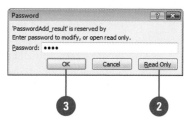

Change or Remove the Password Protection

1. Click the **Office** button, click **Open**, navigate to a presentation with password protection, and then click **Open**.

2. Type the password in the Password dialog box, and then click **OK**.

3. Click the **Office** button, click **Save As**, click **Tools**, and then click **General Options**.

4. Select the contents in the Password To Modify box or the Password To Open box.

5. Choose the option you want.

   ◆ **Change password.** Type a new password, click OK, and then retype your password.

   ◆ **Delete password.** Press Delete.

6. Click **OK**.

7. Click **Save**, and then click **Yes** to replace existing presentation.

For Your Information

Encrypting a Presentation

For added security, you can apply file encryption to a presentation file. File encryption scrambles your password to protect your presentation from unauthorized people breaking into the file. To set password protection using file encryption, click the Office button, point to Prepare, and then click Encrypt Document. Type a password, click OK, type the password again, and then click OK. All you need to do is remember the password. If you forget it, you can't open the file. Password protection takes effect the next time you open the presentation.

Restricting Presentation Access

Microsoft Certified Application Specialist

PP07S-4.3.3

Information Rights Management (IRM) in Office 2007 programs provides restricted access to Office documents. In Outlook, you can use IRM to restrict permission to content in presentations from being forwarded, printed, copied, faxed, or edited by unauthorized people. You can also enforce corporate polices and set file expirations. IRM uses a server to authenticate the credentials of people who create or receive presentations or e-mail with restricted permission. For Microsoft Office users without access to one of these servers, Microsoft provides a free trial IRM service, which requires a .NET Passport. If you want to view or change the permissions for a presentation, click Change Permission in the Message Bar or click the IRM icon button in the Status bar (**New!**). If someone tries to access a restricted presentation, a message appears with the author's address or Web site address so the individual can request permission.

Set Up Information Rights Management

1. Click the **Office** button, point to **Prepare**, point to **Restrict Permission**, and then click **Manage Credentials**.

2. Click **Yes** to download and install IRM. Follow the wizard instructions to install IRM software.

    Upon completion, the Service Sign-Up Wizard opens.

3. Click the **Yes, I Want To Sign Up For This Free Trial Service From Microsoft** option.

4. Click **Next**, and then follow the remaining instructions to create a .NET Passport and complete the service sign-up.

    You'll need to select a certificate type, either Standard or Temporary

5. Click **Finish**.

6. Select a user account with the credentials you want to use.

7. Select or clear the **Always use this account** check box.

8. Click **Cancel** or **OK** to restrict permission.

Create a Presentation with Restricted Permission

1. Open the presentation you want to restrict permission.

2. Click the **Office** button, point to **Prepare**, point to **Restrict Permission**, and then click **Restrict Access**.

    TIMESAVER *Click the Protect Presentation button on the Review tab to access the same commands.*

3. If necessary, click the user with the permissions to create or open restricted content, and then click **OK**. If expired, click **OK**, and then click **Add** to renew it.

4. Select the **Restrict permission to this Presentation** check box.

5. Enter e-mail addresses or click the **Read** or **Change** button to select users from your Address Book.

6. Click **More Options**.

7. Select the check boxes with the specific permissions you want.

8. Click **OK**.

    The Message Bar appears with the current rights management, along with a **Change Permission** button, which you can use to change presentation permissions.

Did You Know?

You can unrestrict access to a presentation. Click the Office button, point to Prepare, point to Restrict Permission, and then click Unrestricted Access.

You can change permission. Click Change Permission in the Message Bar, or click the IRM icon on the Status bar.

Adding a Digital Signature

Microsoft Certified Application Specialist

PP07S-4.2.1

After you've finished a presentation, you might consider adding a digital signature—an electronic, secure stamp of authentication on a document. Before you can add a digital signature, you need to get a **digital ID**, or **digital certificate**, which provides an electronic way to prove your identity, like a drivers license. A digital certificate checks a public key to validate a private key associated with a digital signature. To assure a digital signature is authentic, it must have a valid (non expired or revoked) certificate issued by a reputable certification authority (CA), and the signing person must be from a trusted publisher. If you need a verified authenticate digital certificate, you can obtain one from a trusted Microsoft partner CA. If you don't need a verified digital certificate, you can create one of your own. If someone modifies the file, the digital signature is removed and revoked. If you're not sure if a presentation is digitally signed, you can use the Signatures task pane to view or remove valid signatures.

Create an Digital ID

1. Click the **Office** button, point to **Prepare**, and then click **Add a Digital Signature**.

2. If an alert message appears, click **Signature Services from the Office Marketplace** to open an informational Web site where you can sign up for a digital certificate, or click **OK** to create your own.

   If you don't want to see this dialog box again, select the **Don't show this message again** check box.

3. If necessary, click **OK** and verify your Rights Management account credentials using your .NET password.

4. If you don't have a digital ID, click the option to get an ID from a Microsoft Partner or create your own, and then click **OK**.

5. Enter your name, e-mail address, organization name, and geographic location.

6. Click **Create**.

   You can sign a document, or click **Cancel**.

Add a Digital Signature to a Document

1. Click the **Office** button, point to **Prepare**, and then click **Add a Digital Signature**.

2. To change the digital signature, click **Change**, select the one you want, and then click **OK**.

3. Enter the purpose for signing this document.

4. Click **Sign**.

5. If necessary, click **OK**.

View or Remove Signatures

1. Click the **Signature** icon on the Status bar.

   The Signatures task pane appears, displaying valid signatures in the presentation. Invalid signatures are no longer automatically removed (**New!**).

2. Point to a signature, and then click the list arrow.

3. To see signature details, click **Signature Details**, select a signature, click **View**, click **OK** when you're done, and then click **Close**.

4. To remove a signature, point to a signature, click the list arrow, click **Remove Signature**, click **Yes**, and then if necessary click **OK**.

5. Click the **Close** button on the task pane.

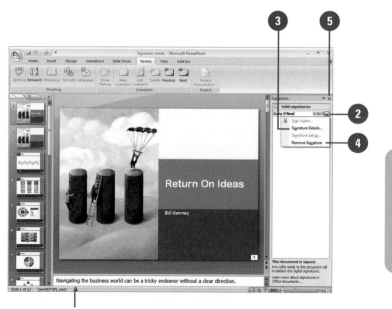

Signature icon

Avoiding Harmful Attacks

Spreading Harmful Infections

Many viruses and other harmful attacks spread through file downloads, attachments in e-mail messages, and data files that have macros, ActiveX controls, add-ins, or Visual Basic for Applications (VBA) code attached to them. Virus writers capitalize on people's curiosity and willingness to accept files from people they know or work with, in order to transmit malicious files disguised as or attached to benign files. When you start downloading files to your computer, you must be aware of the potential for catching a computer virus, worm, or Trojan Horse. Typically, you can't catch one from just reading a mail message or downloading a file, but you can catch one from installing, opening, or running an infected program or attached code.

Understanding Harmful Attacks

Phishing is a scam that tries to steal your identity by sending deceptive e-mail asking you for bank and credit card information online. Phishers spoof the domain names of banks and other companies in order to deceive consumers into thinking that they are visiting a familiar Web site.

Phishers create a Web address that looks like a familiar Web address but is actually altered. This is known as a **homograph**. The domain name is created using alphabet characters from different languages, not just English. For example, the Web site address "www.microsoft.com" looks legitimate, but what you can't see is that the "i" is a Cyrillic character from the Russian alphabet.

Don't be fooled by spoofed Web sites that look like the official site. Never respond to requests for personal information via e-mail; most companies have policies that do not ask for your personal information through e-mail. If you get a suspicious e-mail, call the institution to investigate and report it.

Spam is unsolicited e-mail, which is often annoying and time-consuming to get rid of. Spammers harvest e-mail addresses from Web pages and unsolicited e-mail. To avoid spam, use multiple e-mail addresses (one for Web forms and another for private e-mail), opt-out and remove yourself from e-mail lists. See the Microsoft Windows and Microsoft Outlook Help system for specific details.

Spyware is software that collects personal information without your knowledge or permission. Typically, spyware is downloaded and installed on your computer along with free software, such as freeware, games, or music file-sharing programs. Spyware is often associated with **Adware** software that displays advertisements, such as a pop-up ad. Examples of spyware and unauthorized adware include programs that change your home page or search page without your permission. To avoid spyware and adware, read the fine print in license agreements when you install software, scan your computer for spyware and adware with detection and removal software (such as Ad-aware from Lavasoft), and turn on Pop-up Blocker. See the Microsoft Windows Help system for specific details.

Avoiding Harmful Attacks Using Office

There are a few things you can do within any Office 2007 program to keep your system safe from the infiltration of harmful attacks.

1) Make sure you activate macro, ActiveX, add-in, and VBA code detection and notification. You can use the Trust Center to help protect you from attached code attacks. The Trust Center checks for trusted publisher and code locations on your computer and provides security options for add-ins, ActiveX controls, and macros to ensure the best possible protection. The Trust Center displays a security alert in the Message Bar when it detects a potentially harmful attack.

2) Make sure you activate Web site spoofing detection and notification. You can use the Trust Center to help protect you from homograph attacks. The *Check Office documents that are from or link to suspicious Web sites* check box under Privacy Options in the Trust Center is on by default and continually checks for potentially spoofed domain names. The Trust Center displays a security alert in the Message Bar when you have a document open and click a link to a Web site with an address that has a potentially spoofed domain name, or you open a file from a Web site with an address that has a potentially spoofed domain name.

3) Be very careful of file attachments in e-mail you open. As you receive e-mail, don't open or run an attached file unless you know who sent it and what it contains. If you're not sure, you should delete it. The Attachment Manager provides security information to help you understand more about the file you're opening. See the Microsoft Outlook Help system for specific details.

Avoiding Harmful Attacks Using Windows

There are a few things you can do within Microsoft Windows to keep your system safe from the infiltration of harmful attacks.

1) Make sure Windows Firewall is turned on. Windows Firewall helps block viruses and worms from reaching your computer, but it doesn't detect or disable them if they are already on your computer or come through e-mail. Windows Firewall doesn't block unsolicited e-mail or stop you from opening e-mail with harmful attachments.

2) Make sure Automatic Updates is turned on. Windows Automatic Updates regularly checks the Windows Update Web site for important updates that your computer needs, such as security updates, critical updates, and service packs. Each file that you download using Automatic Update has a digital signature from Microsoft to ensure its authenticity and security.

3) Make sure you are using the most up-to-date antivirus software. New viruses and more virulent strains of existing viruses are discovered every day. Unless you update your virus-checking software, new viruses can easily bypass outdated virus checking software. Companies such as McAfee and Symantec offer shareware virus checking programs available for download directly from their Web sites. These programs monitor your system, checking each time a file is added to your computer to make sure it's not in some way trying to change or damage valuable system files.

4) Be very careful of the sites from which you download files. Major file repository sites, such as FileZ, Download.com, or TuCows, regularly check the files they receive for viruses before posting them to their Web sites. Don't download files from Web sites unless you are certain that the sites check their files for viruses. Internet Explorer monitors downloads and warns you about potentially harmful files and gives you the option to block them.

Using the Trust Center

The **Trust Center (New!)** is a place where you set security options and find the latest technology information as it relates to document privacy, safety, and security from Microsoft. The Trust Center allows you to set security and privacy settings—Trusted Publishers, Trusted Locations, Add-ins, ActiveX Settings, Macro Settings, Message Bar, and Privacy Options—and provides links to Microsoft privacy statements, a customer improvement program, and trustworthy computing practices. The Trust Center also provides a link to open the Windows Security Center on your computer.

View the Trust Center

1. Click the **Offic**e button, and then click **PowerPoint Options**.

2. In the left pane, click **Trust Center**.

3. Click the links in which you want online information at the Microsoft Online Web site.

   ◆ **Show the Microsoft Office PowerPoint privacy statement.** Opens a Microsoft Web site detailing privacy practices.

   ◆ **Microsoft Office Online privacy statement.** Opens a Microsoft Web site detailing privacy practices.

   ◆ **Customer Experience Improvement Program.** Opens the Microsoft Customer Experience Improvement Program (CEIP) Web site.

   ◆ **Microsoft Windows Security Center.** Opens Windows Security Center on your computer.

   ◆ **Microsoft Trustworthy Computing.** Opens a Microsoft Web site detailing security and reliability practices.

4. When you're done, close your Web browser or dialog box, and return to PowerPoint.

5. Click **OK**.

Selecting Trusted Publishers and Locations

The Trust Center security system continually checks for external potentially unsafe content in your documents. Hackers can hide Web beacons in external content—images, linked media, data connections and templates—to gather information about you or cause problems. When the Trust Center detects potentially harmful external content, the Message Bar appears with a security alert and options to enable or block the content. Trusted publishers are reputable developers who create application extensions, such as a macro, ActiveX control, or add-in. The Trust Center uses a set of criteria—valid and current digital signature, and reputable certificate—to make sure publishers' code and source locations are safe and secure. If you are sure that the external content is trustworthy, you can add the content publisher and location to your trusted lists (**New!**), which allows it to run without being checked by the Trust Center.

Modify Trusted Publishers and Locations

1. Click the **Office** button, and then click **PowerPoint Options**.

2. In the left pane, click **Trust Center**.

3. Click **Trust Center Settings**.

4. In the left pane, click **Trusted Publishers**.

5. Select a publisher, and then use the **View** and **Remove** buttons to make the changes you want.

6. In the left pane, click **Trusted Locations**.

7. Select a location, and then use the **Add new location**, **Remove**, and **Modify** buttons to make the changes you want.

8. Select or clear the **Allow trusted locations on my network (not recommended)** check box.

9. Select or clear the **Disable all Trusted Locations, only files signed by Trusted Publishers will be trusted** check box.

10. Click **OK**.

11. Click **OK**.

Setting Add-in Security Options

An add-in, such as smart tags, extends functionality to Microsoft Office programs (**New!**). An add-in can add buttons and custom commands to the Ribbon. When an add-in is installed, it appears on the Add-Ins tab of an Office program and includes a special ScreenTip that identifies the developer. Since add-ins are software code added to Microsoft Office programs, hackers can use them to do malicious harm, such as spreading a virus. The Trust Center uses a set of criteria—valid and current digital signature, reputable certificate and a trusted publisher—to make sure add-ins are safe and secure. If it discovers a potentially unsafe add-in, it disables the code and notifies you in the Message Bar. If the add-in security options are not set to the level you need, you can change them in the Trust Center.

Set Add-in Security Options

1. Click the **Office** button, and then click **PowerPoint Options**.

2. In the left pane, click **Trust Center**.

3. Click **Trust Center Settings**.

4. In the left pane, click **Add-ins**.

5. Select or clear the check boxes you do or don't want.

   ◆ **Require Application Add-ins to be signed by Trusted Publisher.** Select to check for a digital signature on the .dll file.

   ◆ **Disable notification for unsigned add-ins (code will remain disabled).** Only available if the above check box is selected. Select to disable unsigned add-ins without notification.

   ◆ **Disable all Application Add-ins (may impair functionality).** Select to disable all add-ins without any notifications.

6. Click **OK**.

7. Click **OK**.

Setting ActiveX Security Options

An ActiveX control provides additional functionality, such as a text box, button, dialog box, or small utility program. ActiveX controls are software code, so hackers can use them to do malicious harm, such as spreading a virus. You can use the Trust Center to prevent ActiveX controls from harming your computer (**New!**). If the ActiveX security options are not set to the level you want, you can change them in the Trust Center. If you change ActiveX control settings in one Office program, it effects all Microsoft Office programs. The Trust Center uses a set of criteria—checks the kill bit and Safe for Initialization (SFI) settings—to make sure ActiveX controls run safely.

Change ActiveX Security Settings

1. Click the **Office** button, and then click **PowerPoint Options**.

2. In the left pane, click **Trust Center**.

3. Click **Trust Center Settings**.

4. In the left pane, click **ActiveX Settings**.

5. Click the option you want for ActiveX in documents not in a trusted location.

   ◆ Disable all controls without notification.

   ◆ Prompt me before enabling Unsafe for Initialization controls with additional restrictions and Save for Initialization (SFI) controls with minimal restrictions (default).

   ◆ Prompt me before enabling all controls with minimal restrictions.

   ◆ Enable all controls with restrictions and without prompting (not recommended, potentially dangerous controls can run).

6. Click **OK**.

7. Click **OK**.

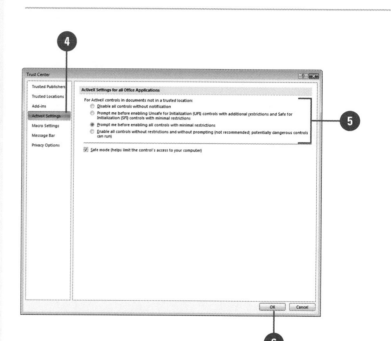

Setting Macro Security Options

A macro allows you to automate frequently used steps or tasks to save time and work more efficiently. Macros are written using VBA (Visual Basic for Applications) code, which opens the door to hackers to do malicious harm, such as spreading a virus. The Trust Center uses a set of criteria—valid and current digital signature, reputable certificate and a trusted publisher—to make sure macros are safe and secure. If the Trust Center discovers a potentially unsafe macro, it disables the code and notifies you in the Message Bar. You can click Options on the Message Bar to enable it or set other security options. If the macro security options are not set to the level you need, you can change them in the Trust Center (**New!**).

Change Macro Security Settings

1. Click the **Office** button, and then click **PowerPoint Options**.

2. In the left pane, click **Trust Center**.

3. Click **Trust Center Settings**.

4. In the left pane, click **Macro Settings**.

5. Click the option you want for macros in documents not in a trusted location.

   ◆ Disable all macros without notification.

   ◆ Disable all macros with notification (default).

   ◆ Disable all macros except digitally signed macros.

   ◆ Enable all macros (not recommended, potentially dangerous code can run).

6. If you're a developer, select the **Trust access to the VBA project object model** check box.

7. Click **OK**.

8. Click **OK**.

Changing Message Bar Security Options

The Message Bar (**New!**) displays security alerts when Office detects potentially unsafe content in an open document. The Message Bar appears below the Ribbon when a potential problem arises. The Message Bar provides a security warning and options to enable external content or leave it blocked. If you don't want to receive alerts about security issues, you can disable the Message Bar.

Modify Message Bar Security Options

1. Click the **Office** button, and then click **PowerPoint Options**.

2. In the left pane, click **Trust Center**.

3. Click **Trust Center Settings**.

4. In the left pane, click **Message Bar**.

5. Click the option you want for showing the Message bar.

   ◆ Show the Message Bar in all applications when content has been blocked (default).

   This option is not selected if you selected the Disable all macros without notification check box in the Macros pane of the Trust Center.

   ◆ Never show information about blocked content.

6. Click **OK**.

7. Click **OK**.

Setting Privacy Options

Privacy options in the Trust Center allow you to set security settings that protect your personal privacy online. For example, the *Check Office documents that are from or link to suspicious Web sites* option checks for spoofed Web sites and protects you from phishing schemes (**New!**). If your kids are doing research online using the Research task pane, you can set Privacy Options to enable parental controls and a password to block sites with offensive content.

Set Privacy Options

1 Click the **Offic**e button, and then click **PowerPoint Options**.

2 In the left pane, click **Trust Center**.

3 Click **Trust Center Settings**.

4 In the left pane, click **Privacy Options**.

5 Select or clear the check boxes you do or don't want.

◆ **Search Microsoft Office Online for Help content when I'm connected to the Internet.** Select to get up-to-date Help content.

◆ **Update featured links from Microsoft Office Online.** Select to get up-to-date headlines and featured templates.

◆ **Download a file periodically that helps determine system problems.** Select to have Microsoft request error reports, update trouble-shooting help, and accept downloads from Office Online.

◆ **Sign up for the Customer Experience Improvement Program.** Select to sign-up.

◆ **Check Microsoft Office documents that are from or link to suspicious Web sites.** Select to check for spoofed Web sites.

6 Click **OK**.

7 Click **OK**.

Set Parental Controls for Online Research

1. Click the **Office** button, and then click **PowerPoint Options**.

2. In the left pane, click **Trust Center**.

3. Click **Trust Center Settings**.

4. In the left pane, click **Privacy Options**.

5. Click **Research Options**.

6. Click **Parental Control**.

7. Select the **Turn on content filtering to make services block offensive results** check box.

8. Select the **Allow users to search only the services that can block offensive results** check box, if necessary.

9. Enter a password, so users cannot change these settings.

10. Click **OK**, retype the password, and then click **OK**.

11. Click **OK**.

12. Click **OK**.

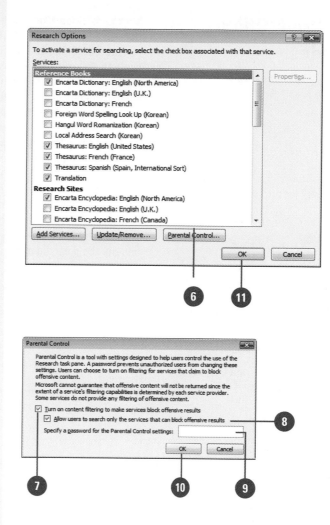

Working with Office Safe Modes

Microsoft Office 2007 uses two types of safe modes—Automated and User-Initiated (**New!**)—when it encounters a program problem. When you start an Office 2007 program, it automatically checks for problems, such as an extension not properly loading. If the program is not able to start the next time you try, the programs starts in **Automated Safe mode**, which disables extensions—macros, ActiveX controls, and add-ins—and other possible problem areas. If you're having problems and the Office program doesn't start in Automated Safe mode, you can start the program in **User-Initiated Safe mode**. When you start an Office program in Office Safe mode, not all features are available. For instance, templates can't be saved, AutoCorrect list is not loaded, Smart tags are not loaded, preferences cannot be saved, restricted permission (IRM) can't be used, and all command-line options are ignored except /a and /n. Before you can use Office Safe mode, you need to enable it in the Trust Center. When you're in safe mode, you can use the Trust Center to find out the disabled items and enable them one at a time to help you pin point the problem.

Enable Safe Mode

1. Click the **Office** button, and then click **PowerPoint Options**.

2. In the left pane, click **Trust Center**.

3. Click **Trust Center Settings**.

4. In the left pane, click **ActiveX Settings**.

5. Select the **Safe Mode (Helps limit the control's access to your computer)** check box.

6. Click **OK**.

7. Click **OK**.

See Also

See "Diagnosing and Repairing Problems" on page 28 for information on fixing problems with a Microsoft Office 2007 program.

Start User-Initiated Safe Mode

1. Click the **Start** button on the taskbar, point to **All Programs**, and then click **Microsoft Office**.

2. Press and hold Ctrl, and then click **Microsoft Office PowerPoint 2007**.

> ### Did You Know?
>
> **You can use the Run dialog box to work in Safe mode.** At the command prompt, you can use the */safe* parameter at the end of the command-line to start the program.

View Disabled Items

1. Click the **Office** button, and then click **PowerPoint Options**.

2. In the left pane, click **Add-ins**.

3. Click the **Manage** list arrow, and then click **Disabled Items**.

4. Click **Go**.

5. In the dialog box, you can select an item, click **Enable** to activate and reload the add-in, and then click **Close**.

Marking a Presentation as Read-Only

As a precaution to prevent readers and reviews from making accidental changes, you can use the Mark as Final command (**New!**) to make a PowerPoint 2007 presentation read-only. The Mark as Final command disables or turns off typing, editing commands, and proofing marks, and sets the *Status property* field in the Document Information Panel to Final. The Mark as Final command is not a security option; it only prevents changes to the presentation while it's turned on and it can be turned off by anyone at any time.

Mark a Presentation as Final

1. Click the **Office** button, point to **Prepare**, and then click **Mark as Final**.

2. Click **OK**, and then click **OK** again, if necessary.

   The presentation is marked as final and then saved.

3. If necessary, click **OK** and verify your Right Management account credentials using your .NET password.

   The Mark as Final icon appears in the Status bar to indicate the presentation is currently marked as final.

   IMPORTANT *A PowerPoint 2007 presentation marked as final is not read-only when opened in an earlier version of Microsoft PowerPoint.*

Did You Know?

You can enable editing for a presentation marked as final. Click the Office button, point to Prepare, and then click Mark as Final again to toggle off the Mark as Final feature.

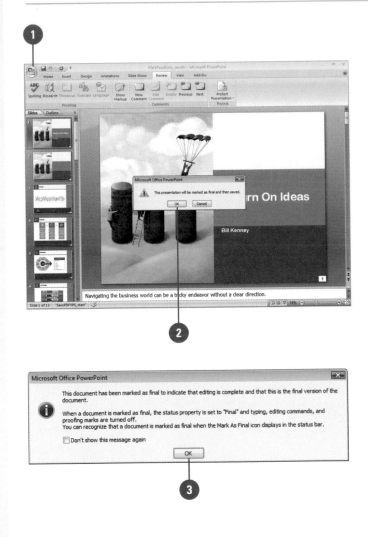

Sending a Presentation for Review Using E-Mail

After you finish making changes to a presentation, you can quickly send it to another person for review using e-mail. PowerPoint allows you to send presentations out for review as an attachment, either a presentation, PDF, or XPS document, using e-mail from within the program so that you do not have to open your e-mail program. An e-mail program, such as Microsoft Outlook, needs to be installed on your computer before you begin. When you send your presentation out for review, reviewers can add comments and then send it back to you.

Send a Presentation for Review Using E-Mail

1. Click the **Office** button, point to **Send**, and then click **E-mail**, **E-mail as PDF Attachment**, or **E-mail as XPS Attachment**.

2. If the Compatibility Checker appears, click **Continue** or **Cancel** to stop the operation.

    IMPORTANT *To complete the following steps, you need to have an e-mail program installed on your computer and an e-mail account set-up.*

    An e-mail message opens in Microsoft Outlook with your presentation attached. The subject line contains the file name of the presentation that you are sending.

3. Enter your recipients and subject (appears with presentation name by default).

    ◆ To add recipients from your address book or contacts list, click **To**, click the recipient names, click **To**, **Cc**, or **Bcc** **until you're done**, and then click **OK**.

4. Enter a message for your reviewer with instructions.

5. Click the **Send** button.

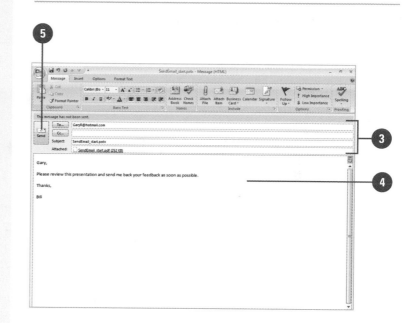

Sending a Presentation by Internet Fax

If you are a member of an online fax service, such as eFax, InterFAX, MyFax, or Send2Fax, you can use PowerPoint to send and receive faxes over the Internet directly from within your Microsoft Office program. If you're not a member, a Web site can help you sign up. You also need to have Microsoft Outlook and Word installed to use the fax service and Outlook must be open to send your fax. If Outlook is not open and you send the fax, it will be stored in your Outbox and not sent until you open Outlook again.

Send a Presentation by Internet Fax

1. Click the **Office** button, point to **Send**, and then click **Internet Fax**.

2. If you're not signed up with an Internet Fax service, click **OK** to open a Web page and sign up for one. When you're done, return to PowerPoint, and then repeat Step 1.

3. If the Compatibility Checker appears, click **Continue** or **Cancel** to stop the operation.

    An e-mail message opens in Microsoft Outlook with your presentation attached as a .tif (image) file.

4. Enter a Fax Recipient, Fax Number and Subject (appears with presentation name by default).

    ◆ You can enter a fax number from your address book. Country codes in your address book must begin with a plus sign (+).

    ◆ To send your fax to multiple recipients, click Add More, and then enter fax information.

5. In the Fax Service pane, choose the options you want.

6. Complete the cover sheet in the body of the e-mail message.

7. Click the **Send** button.

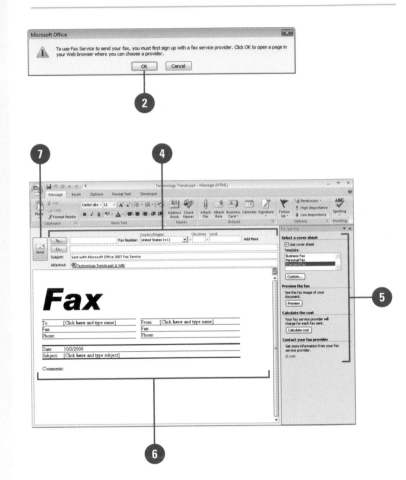

Working Together on Office Documents

12

Introduction

Microsoft Office Groove 2007 is a new addition to the Microsoft Office 2007 Enterprise system that enables teams to set up collaborative workspaces. With Office Groove 2007 (**New!**), you can bring the team, tools, and information together from any location to work on a project. After creating documents with Microsoft Office programs, you can use Groove for file sharing, document reviews, co-editing and co-reviewing Word documents, and for co-viewing PowerPoint presentations.

Instead of using a centralized server—like Office SharePoint Server 2007—to store information and manage tasks, Office Groove stores all your workspaces, tools, and data right on your computer. You don't need to connect to a network to access or update information. While you're connected to the Internet, Groove automatically sends the changes you make in a workspace to your team member's computers, and any changes they make get sent to you. Office Groove uses built-in presence awareness, alerts, and unread marks to see who is working online and what team members are doing without having to ask.

Office Groove uses tools and technology from other Microsoft Office system products to help you work together and stay informed. With the Groove SharePoint Files tool, you can check out documents from Microsoft Office SharePoint 2007 into a Groove workspace, collaborate on them, and then check them back in when you're done. With the Groove InfoPath Forms tool, you can import form solutions created in Office InfoPath 2007, or design your own.

If you have access to an Office SharePoint 2007 site, you can use the Document Management task pane directly from PowerPoint to access many Office SharePoint Server 2007 features. For example, you can create a slide library on a SharePoint site to exchange presentation sides (**New!**).

What You'll Do

Configure and Launch Groove

View the Groove Window

Set General Preferences

Create a Groove Workspace

Invite Others to a Workspace

Deal with Groove Alerts

Share Files in a Workspace

Hold a Discussion

Add Tools to a Workspace

Set Calendar Appointments

Manage Meetings

Work with Forms

Track Issues

Create a Picture Library

Add a Contact

Send a message and Chat with Others

Share Files with SharePoint

Share Files with Synchronizing Folders

Work with a Shared Workspace

Publish Slides to a Library

Configuring Groove

The first time you launch Microsoft Office Groove 2007, the Account Configuration Wizard appears, asking you to create a new Groove account or use an existing one already created on another computer. During the wizard process, you'll enter your Groove Account Configuration Code—for network purposes only—and Groove Account Information, including name, e-mail address, and password. If you want your Groove account to be listed in a Public Groove Directory, you can also select that option during the wizard process.

Start, Configure, and Exit Groove

1. For the first time, click the **Start** button, point to **All Programs**, click **Microsoft Office**, and then click **Microsoft Office Groove 2007**.

2. Click the **Create a new Groove account** option.

3. Click **Next**.

4. Click the Account Configuration Code option you want, and then click **Next**.

5. Enter account information, including name, e-mail address, and password.

6. Click **Next**.

7. Click an option to list your account in the Public Groove Directory, either **No Listing** (default), **Name Only**, and **All Contact Information**.

8. Click **Finish**.

9. Click **Yes or No** to watch a movie about Groove.

10. To exit Groove, click the **Close** button on the title bar.

Did You Know?

You can use your account on another computer. Click the Options menu, click Invite My Other Computers, click OK, and then copy the account file for use on another computer.

Launching Groove

Microsoft Groove 2007 allows teams to securely work together over the Internet or corporate network as if they were in the same location. Teams using Groove can remotely work with shared files and content, even when they are offline. You can launch Groove 2007 from the Start menu or from the notification area. When you start Groove, the Launchbar window opens, displaying two tabs: one for creating and managing workspaces, and one for adding and managing contacts. If you are having difficulty launching Groove, check to make sure Groove is configured as a Windows Firewall exception.

Launch Groove from the Start Menu and Login

1. Click the **Start** button on the taskbar, point to **All Programs**, click **Microsoft Office**, and then click **Microsoft Office Groove 2007**.

    TIMESAVER *Click the Groove icon in the notification area, and then click Open Groove.*

2. Enter your password, and then click **Login**.

3. To logoff, click the **File** menu, and then click **Log Off Account**.

Add Groove as a Firewall Exception

1. In Windows, click **Start**, and then click **Control Panel**.

2. Double-click the **Windows Firewall** icon.

3. Click the **Exceptions** tab.

4. Click **Add Program**.

5. Click **Browse**, navigate to the Programs Files folder, Microsoft Office folder, Office 12 folder, click **Groove.exe**, and then click **Open**.

6. Click **OK**.

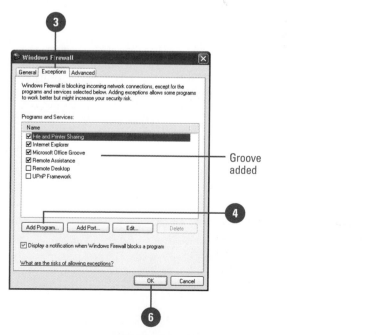

Groove added

Viewing the Groove Window

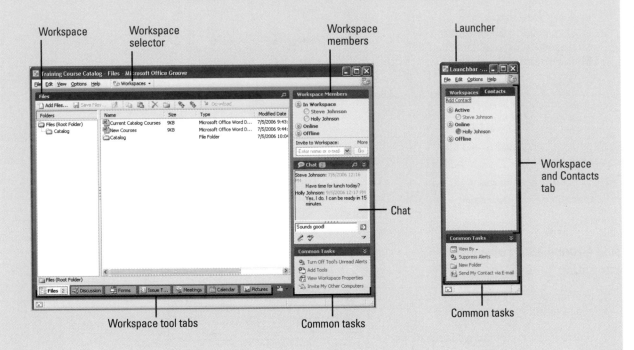

Workspace

Workspace selector

Workspace members

Launcher

Workspace and Contacts tab

Chat

Workspace tool tabs

Common tasks

Common tasks

Setting General Preferences

Groove makes it easy to set program preferences all in one place by using the Preferences dialog box. You can select from six different tabs —Identities, Account, Security, Alerts, Options, and Synchronization—to specify startup and application settings, alert levels, communication policies, file and workspace restrictions, account privileges, and identity information. The Options tab allows you to set general preferences to startup Groove and related applications, like Launchbar and Workspace Explorer, and scan for viruses.

Set General Preferences

1. In the Launchbar, click the **Options** menu, and then click **Preferences**.

2. Click the **Options** tab.

3. Select or clear the **Launch Groove when Windows starts up** and the **Integrate messenger Contacts** check boxes.

4. Click an application (Launchbar or Workspace Explorer by default), and then click **Settings**, select start up and display options, and then click **OK**.

5. Select or clear the **Discard Groove messages from unknown contacts** check box.

6. Select or clear the **Send e-mail invitations using Microsoft Outlook** check box.

7. Specify the online presence settings you want.

8. Select or clear the **Scan incoming and outgoing files for viruses** check box.

9. Click **OK**.

Did You Know?

You can set workspace properties. In the workspace, click View Workspace Properties under Command Tasks, click the tab and select the properties you want, and then click OK.

Creating a Groove Workspace

A Groove workspace is a special site template that provides you with tools to share and update documents and to keep people informed about the current status of the documents. After you create a workspace, you can use Files and Discussion Tools to share files, exchange messages, and collaborate with a team. In a Groove workspace, you can point to the Files or Discussion tab to display the contacts currently using a tool.

Create a Workspace

1. In the Launchbar, click the **File** menu, point to **New**, and then click **Workspace**.

2. Click a workspace option:

   ◆ **Standard.** Select to display the Groove Workspace Explorer and initially include the Files and Discussion Tools.

   ◆ **File Sharing.** Select to share the contents of a folder in your Windows system.

   ◆ **Template.** Select to display the Groove Workspace Explorer with the selected tools you want. Click Browse to visit a Groove Web site, where you can download templates.

3. Type a new name for the workspace.

4. Click **OK**.

   The new workspace opens in another window.

Did You Know?

You can delete a workspace. In the workspace, click the File menu, point to Delete Workspace, and then click From This Computer or For All Members.

You can save a workspace as a template or back it up. In the workspace, click the File menu, point to Save Workspace As, and then click Template or Archive.

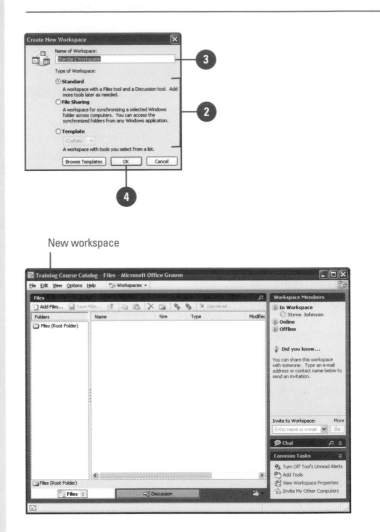

New workspace

Inviting Others to a Workspace

Before you can invite someone to a Groove workspace, they need to be a Groove user. Each person you invite to a Groove workspace needs to have a role, either Manager, Participant, or Guest. Each role comes with a set of permissions that allow a user to perform certain tasks. Mangers can invite others, edit existing files, and delete files or the entire workspace. Participants can edit and delete files. Guests can view existing data, but not make changes. After you send an invitation to join a workspace, check for Groove alerts in the notification area to see if the user has accepted your invitation.

Invite Users to a Workspace

1. Open the workspace, click the **Options** menu, and then click **Invite to Workshop**.

2. Click the **To** list arrow, and then select a user.

   If the user you want is not there, click **Add More**, click **Search for User**, type part of the user's name, click **Find**, select the user's name you want, and then click **Add**, and then click **OK**.

3. Click the **Role** list arrow, and then click a role: **Manager**, **Participant**, or **Guest**.

4. Enter a message.

5. Select the **Require acceptance confirmation** check box as a security recommendation.

6. Click **Invite**.

   Monitor your Groove alerts for status and acceptance.

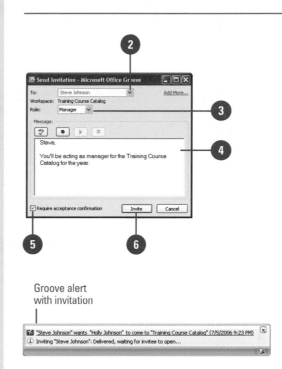

Groove alert
with invitation

> ### Did You Know?
>
> *You can change workspace roles and permissions.* In the Launchbar, click Set Roles under Common Tasks. To adjust permissions for a tool, right-click the tool tab, and then click Properties/Permissions.

Dealing with Groove Alerts

Groove alerts appear as blinking messages in the lower right corner of Windows. You can check for Groove alerts by resting the pointer on the Groove icon in the notification area. Groove alerts notify you about updates and work status. For example, Groove sends you an alert when someone accepts an invitation to a workspace, sends a message, changes an existing file or adds a new file. If you're getting more alerts than you want, you can set alert options in the Preferences dialog box.

Check for Groove Alerts

1. Look for a blinking message or Groove icon in the notification area.

2. Point to the **Groove** icon in the notification area to display the alert.

3. Click the alert to open Groove.

Set Alert Options

1. In the Launchbar, click the **Options** menu, and then click **Preferences**.

2. Click the **Alerts** tab.

3. Drag the slider to select an alert level:

   ◆ **Auto.** Similar to the High alert level, but auto-dismissed ignored unread alerts.

   ◆ **High.** Highlight unread content with an icon and display an alert for all unread content.

   ◆ **Medium.** Highlight unread content with an icon.

   ◆ **Off.** Don't display an alert for new or modified content.

4. Specify the number of days you want to keep unread alerts from being removed.

5. Click **OK**.

Sharing Files in a Workspace

The Files Tool in Groove allows you to share and collaborate on different types of files, including files from Microsoft Office programs. All team members of a workspace can open files that appear in the Files Tool. When a team member opens, changes, and saves a file to the workspace, Groove automatically updates the file for all other team members. When several team members work on the same file at the same time, the first person to save changes to the workspace updates the original file. If another team member saves changes to the original version, Groove creates a second copy with the editor's name.

Share Files in a Workspace

1. In Launchbar, double-click the workspace you want to share.

2. Click the **Files** tab.

3. Click the **Add Files** button.

4. Locate and select the files you want to add to the workspace.

5. Click **Open**.

   The selected files appear in the file list in the workspace.

Manage Tools

◆ **New Files**. Select a folder, click the File menu, point to New, and then click a file type.

◆ **Open Files**. Double-click it, make and save changes, and then click Yes or No to save changes in Groove.

◆ **Delete Files**. Right-click, and then click Delete.

◆ **New Folder**. Select a folder, click the File menu, point to New, click Folder, type a name, and then press Enter.

◆ **Alerts**. Right-click a folder or file, click Properties, click the Alerts tab, drag slider, and then click OK.

Workspace file options

Holding a Discussion

The Discussion Tool in Groove allows users to post an announcement, news item, or other information for everyone working together in a standard workspace. Team members can add and view discussion items as a threaded conversation. Since the discussions are entered into a different area than the shared document, users can modify the document without affecting the collaborative discussion. Users can add changes to read-only documents and allow multiple users to simultaneously create and edit discussion items.

Start and Participate in a Discussion

1. In Launchbar, double-click the workspace from which you want to hold a discussion.

2. Click the **Discussion** tab.

3. Click the **New** button, and then click **Topic**.

   A new topic opens.

4. Type the Subject.

5. Click the **Category** list arrow, and then select a category.

   If the category you want is not available, click the plus (+) sign, enter a category name, and then click OK.

6. Enter a message in the discussion box.

7. Click **Save** to post the message or click **Save and Create Another** to post and create a new topic.

   The new discussion is displayed in the workspace.

8. To participate in a discussion, double-click the discussion within the workspace in order to respond.

   When you're online, Groove synchronizes the discussion, so all workspace participants can see all new postings and topics.

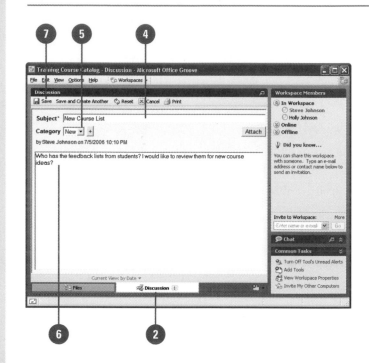

Adding Tools to a Workspace

Like many other Office programs, Groove allows you to add functionality. Groove already comes with the Files and Discussion Tools. You can add other tools, such as InfoPath Forms, Issue Tracking, or SharePoint Files. The InfoPath Tool allows you to collect and view data. The Issue Tracking Tool lets you report on and track the status of issues and incidents. If you have access to an Office or Windows SharePoint Server, the SharePoint Files Tool allows you to synchronize files on a workspace with those on a SharePoint site, document library, or folder.

Add Other Tools to a Workspace

1. In Launchbar, double-click the workspace you want to open.

2. Under Command Tasks, click **Add Tools**.

   TIMESAVER *Click the Add a tool to this workspace button, and then click the tool you want.*

3. Select the check box next to each tool you want to add.

4. Click **OK**.

   A button tab for each tool appears at the bottom of the workspace.

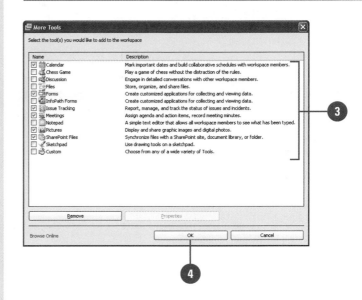

Manage Tools

- **Delete**. Right-click the tool tab, click Delete, and then click Yes.

- **Rename**. Right-click the tool tab, click Rename, enter a new name, and then click OK.

- **Move**. Drag a tool tab name to the left or right.

- **Open in Window**. Right-click the tool tab, and then click Open in New Window.

- **Properties**. Right-click the tool tab, and then click Properties. Click a tab—General, Permissions, Alerts—to view or change properties.

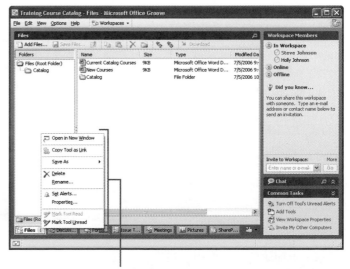

Tool options

Setting Calendar Appointments

Using the Calendar Tool, you can manage your time by doing much more than circling dates. The Calendar collects important information for team members by providing them with critical dates for the completion of a project. Among its many features, the Groove Calendar lets you schedule and manage project appointments and customize the Calendar view to help everyone stay on track.

Add an Appointment

1. In Launchbar, double-click the workspace you want to open, and then click the **Calendar** tab.

2. Click the **New Appointment** button.

   TIMESAVER *To create an appointment with pre-selected dates and times, drag across the range of dates and times you want.*

3. Enter an appointment subject.

4. Fill in the start and end date and a start and end time.

5. Click **OK**.

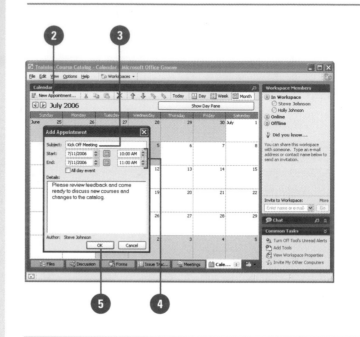

Manage Appointments and the Calendar

◆ **View**. Point to an appointment to display a text window.

◆ **Delete**. Select the appointment, and then press Delete.

◆ **Edit**. Double-click the appointment, make changes, and then click OK.

◆ **Navigate**. Click Navigate Previous or Next Appointment buttons on the toolbar, or click Navigate Previous or Next Unread buttons on the toolbar.

◆ **Navigate Calendar Days**. Click the Previous/Next buttons in the Calendar's title bar.

◆ **Change Calendar Display**. Click the Day, Week, or Month icons.

Navigate days   Change display

Managing Meetings

The Groove Meetings Tool helps you organize, conduct, and record meetings. Every Groove meeting includes a Meeting profile (start and end times, location, and description), Attendees list, Agenda, Minutes, and Actions, which are displayed as tabs for easy access. You can use a wizard to quickly create a meeting, and then manage all aspects of it.

Create a Meeting

1. In Launchbar, double-click the workspace you want to open, and then click the **Meetings** tab.

2. Click the **New Meeting** button to start the wizard.

3. Enter the subject, start and end times, location and details.

4. Click **OK**.

5. Use the **Attendees** tab to select meeting attendees and appoint a chairperson and minutes-taker.

Manage a Meeting

◆ **Agenda**. Click the Agenda tab, click New Topic, fill in the form, and then click OK.

◆ **Action Items**. Click the Actions tab, click New Action Item, fill in the form, and then click OK.

◆ **Record Minutes**. Click the Minutes tab, click Edit, type in text or click Insert Agenda, and then save or discard your work.

◆ **Attendees**. Click the Attendees tab, click Edit, make changes, and then click Save and Close.

◆ **Navigate**. Click the Date of range options button, and then select a range of dates, or click the Previous/Next arrows.

◆ **Attachments**. Select a profile, agenda, or action, click Edit, click Attachments list arrow, and then click Add, Delete, Save all, or file name you want to open.

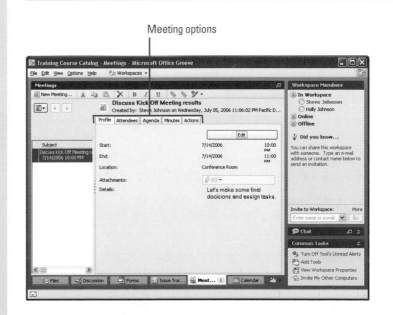

Meeting options

Working with Forms

If you need to collect data as part of your project, you can use the Groove Forms Tool to create custom forms in the workspace window, or use the InfoPath Forms Tool to import forms you have already created using Microsoft Office InfoPath 2007. With Designer Access privileges, you can use the Groove Forms Tool to name the form, choose the fields, select the form style, and create a form view to view the data. You create and layout form elements in the design sandbox, which multiple team members can use to help with the design. Like working with files in Groove, your form designs are stored locally until you publish them back to the workspace.

Create a Form and View

1. In Launchbar, double-click the workspace you want to open, and then click the **Forms** tab.

2. Click the **Designer** button, and then click **Create New Form**.

   ◆ On first run, click **Start Here**.

3. On the Basics tab, enter form name.

4. Select the check boxes with the system fields you want.

5. To create new fields, click **Create New Field** in the left pane, click the field type you want, click **Next**, click a property in the left pane, enter information or select options, and then click **Finish**.

6. Click the **Style Form** button, and then select a style.

7. Click **Column Number** button, and then select a number.

8. Select other options for defining the behavior of the fields and form.

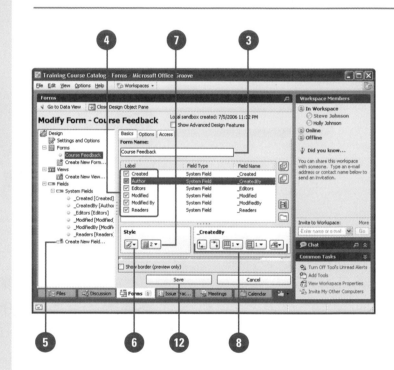

Did You Know?

You can revise a form. In the workspace, click the Forms tab, click the Designer button, point to Modify Form, click a form name, make changes, click Save, and then click Publish Sandbox to update the workspace.

9. In the left pane, click **Create New View**.

10. Click the **Basics** tab, and then enter a view name.

11. Select the check boxes with the fields you want, and other options.

12. Click **Save**.

13. Click the **Publish Sandbox** or **Discard Sandbox** button.

Did You Know?

You can change form settings and access. In the workspace, click the Forms tab, click the Designer button, point to Modify Form, click a form name, click the Options or Access tab, select options, click Save, and then click Publish Sandbox.

Create and Manage a Form Record

1. In Launchbar, double-click the workspace you want to open, and then click the **Forms** tab.

2. Click the **New** button, and then click the form name.

3. Enter form data.

4. Click the **Save** or **Save and Create Another** button.

5. To edit a form record, double-click it, make changes, and then click **Update**.

6. To delete a form record, click the form record, and then click the **Delete** button.

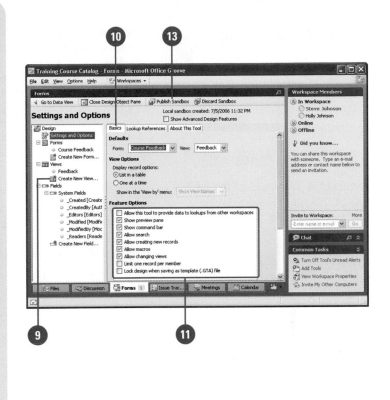

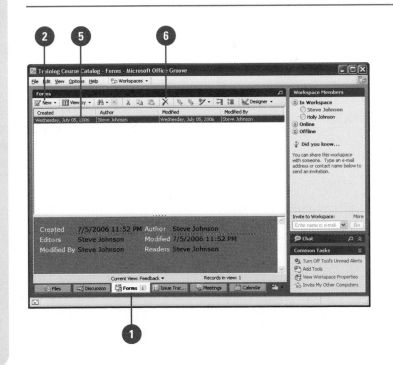

Tracking Issues

Tracking issues is useful for managing all phases of issue reporting and response tracking. Users can create reports, assign ownership, and track status over time. Issue Tracking is a tool designed using the Groove Forms Tool, which includes two basic form types: Issue and Response. The Issue form records issue information, owner assignment, and tracks status. The Response form records a response to an issue record.

Track Issues Using Forms

① In Launchbar, double-click the workspace you want to open, and then click the **Issue Tracking** tab.

② Click the **New** button, and then click **Issue**.

③ Click the **Original Report** tab.

④ Enter a title for the issue.

⑤ Click the list arrow next to each, and then select or add an item.

   ◆ Category.

   ◆ Subcategory.

   ◆ Originated by: Organization.

   ◆ Individual.

⑥ Enter a description.

⑦ If you want to attach a file and work with it, use the Attachment buttons.

⑧ Click the **Current Status** tab.

⑨ Click the list arrow next to each, and then select or add an item.

   ◆ Status.

   ◆ Priority.

   ◆ Assigned to: Organization.

   ◆ Individual.

⑩ Enter ongoing remarks.

⑪ Click the **Save** or **Save and Create Another** button.

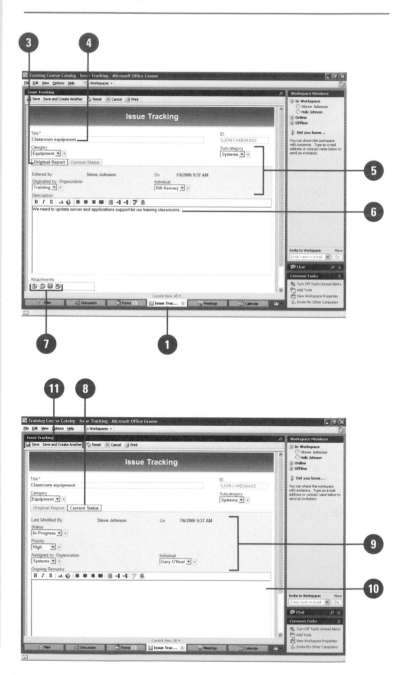

Manage Tools

◆ **Edit**. Double-click the issue, make changes, and then click Update.

◆ **Delete**. Select the issue record, and then click the Delete button on the toolbar.

◆ **Update Assignments**. As a manager, click the Run Macros button on the toolbar, and click Update Assignment - manager only.

◆ **Sort**. Click the column heading you want to sort by.

◆ **View by**. Click the View By button on the toolbar, and then select a view, such as Assignment, Category, Originator, Priority, and Status.

◆ **Search**. Click the Search button on the toolbar, click Search, enter the search criteria you want, and then click Search.

When you're done with the results, click the **Clear Results** button on the toolbar.

Did You Know?

You can set alerts for tools. In the workspace, click any tool tab, click Set Tool Alerts under Command Tasks, drag the slider to select an alert level, and then click OK. To turn alerts off, click Turn Off Tool's Unread Alerts under Common Tasks.

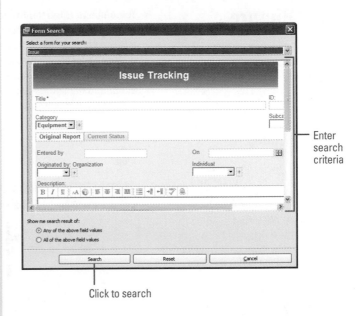

Enter search criteria

Click to search

Creating a Picture Library

You can add the Groove Pictures Tool to a workspace to display and share picture files in JPEG (.jpg) or bitmap (.bmp) format. You can view a list of picture files that you or other team members have added to the Pictures Tool. The list also includes status information about the picture files, such as type, size, modified date, and last editor. The Pictures Tool automatically scales all pictures you add to fit the current size of the picture viewer window.

Add and View Pictures

1. In Launchbar, double-click the workspace you want to open, and then click the **Pictures** tab.

2. To add pictures, click **Add Pictures**, and then drag and drop files into the list or copy and paste files into the list.

3. To show or hide pictures details, click the **Show Pictures Details** or **Hide Picture Details** button.

4. To view pictures, click the **Previous** or **Next** buttons.

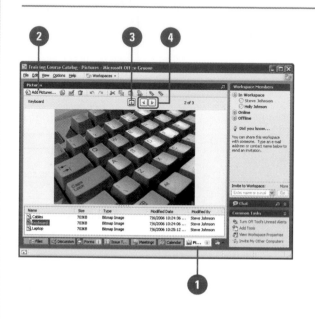

Manage Pictures

◆ **Edit**. Right-click a picture, and then click Open. Your graphics program opens. Edit and save the picture, and then Yes to update in Groove.

◆ **Rename**. Select the picture, click the Rename button on the toolbar, type a new name, and then click OK.

◆ **Export**. Select the picture file, click the Export button on the toolbar, select a location, and then click Save.

◆ **Delete**. Select one or more pictures, and then press Delete.

Toolbar to manage pictures

Adding a Contact

In order to send messages or have a chat with other Groove team members, you need to add them as contacts. In the Launchbar, you can quickly and easily check for the online presence of a contact. By default, each contact appears on the Contacts tab based on status, either Active, Online, or Offline. Each icon next to a contact also indicates whether the member is online, away or offline. In a Groove workspace, you can point to the Files or Discussion tab to display the contacts currently using a tool.

Add a Contact

1. In Launchbar, click the **Contacts** tab.

2. Click the **Add Contact** button.

   The Find User window opens.

3. Type part of the user's name.

4. Click **Find**.

5. Select the user's name you want to add as a contact.

6. Click **Add**.

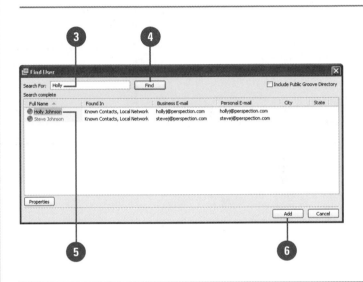

Check the Presence of a Contact

◆ In the Launchbar, click the **Contacts** tab. By default, each contact appears in the Launchbar based on status, either Active, Online, or Offline. Each icon next to a contact also indicates whether the member is online, away or offline.

   TIMESAVER *To change order, click the Options menu, point to View Contacts By, and then click a sort method.*

◆ In a Groove workspace, the tabs at the bottom of the workspace display the number of people who are actively using the tool, either Files or Discussion. To see the names of the people using a Tool, point to the tab.

Contacts

Sending a Message

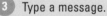

You can send messages to other Groove contacts at any time even if you or your contact are not online. If you or your contact are offline, Groove sends the message and alerts you of delivery, when it's opened, and when your contact replies as soon as you and your contact are online.

Send a Message

1 In Launchbar, click the **Contacts** tab.

2 Right-click a contact, and then click **Send Message**.

The Send Message window opens.

TIMESAVER *Press Shift-Shift to open a new instant message window or bring up your next unread instant message from your inbox.*

3 Type a message.

4 Click **Send**.

An alert appears, indicating your message was sent. Monitor Groove alerts for more message status.

Receive and Reply to a Message

1 When a Groove alert appears, indicating you have received a message, click it.

2 Enter your reply to the message.

3 Click **Send**.

An alert appears, indicating your message was sent. Monitor Groove alerts for more message status.

When the original sender received back the message, the sender can Reply, Forward, or Close the message.

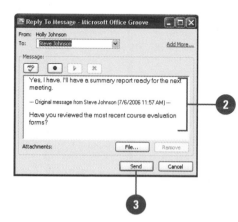

Chatting with Others

A chat is an ongoing conversation you type and send, or post. Each Groove workspace includes a chat tool, where you can communicate with others in real time or offline. The number of team members currently involved in a chat appears on the title bar. When you post a new message in the chat tool, a Groove alert notifies other team members. As each team members post messages in a workspace chat, the ongoing conversation is saved in the workspace for reference until the workspace is deleted.

Chat with Other Workspace Team Members

1. In Launchbar, double-click the workspace you want to open, and then click **Expand Chat** button next to Chart, if necessary.

   IMPORTANT *If you are using Groove on a Tablet PC, the chat window may open by default in Ink mode. To switch to Text mode, click the Options menu (Down Arrow), and then click Switch to Text Mode.*

2. Click in the blank box at the bottom of the chat tool, located on the right side of the workspace, and then type a message.

3. To check spelling, click the **Check Spelling** button, and then correct any mistakes.

4. Click **Go**.

   Your message is added to the ongoing conversation.

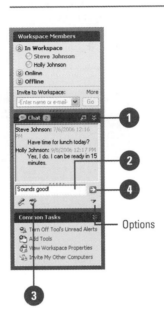

Options

Did You Know?

You can use a microphone. With a microphone installed on your computer, click the Microphone button, and then reply to the Audio Tuner wizard questions.

Sharing Files with SharePoint

If you have access to an Office or Windows SharePoint Server 3.0 site, (workspace collaboration using a Web server), you can synchronize file content between Groove and SharePoint libraries. Groove uses the SharePoint Files Tool as a centralized location to work on SharePoint files and with people outside your workspace. The SharePoint Files Tool synchronizes data with workspace members in the same way as the standard File Tool. The one who sets up the SharePoint connection is the synchronizer, and is typically the workspace Owner. The synchronizer has two options: manual or automatic based on a time interval. Simply double-click a SharePoint file to edit it in its native program. As the synchronizer, you can also check out/in files to avoid conflicts with other SharePoint users while you edit a file.

Set Up a SharePoint Connection

1. In Launchbar, double-click the workspace you want to open, and then click the **SharePoint Files** tab.

2. Click **Setup**.

3. Enter the SharePoint Server Web address, and then press Enter.

   See your Network Administrator for specifics.

4. Click the library in which you want to connect.

5. Click **Select**.

   All the files in the SharePoint library are synchronized with the Groove workspace.

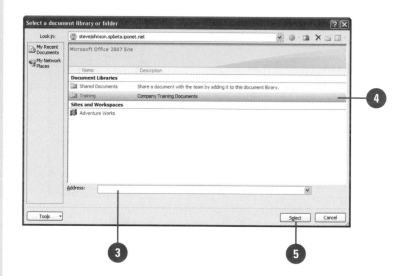

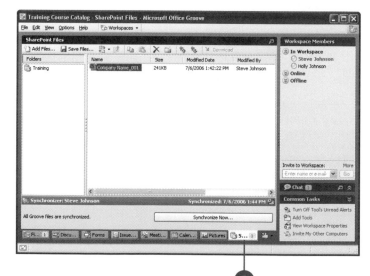

Did You Know?

You can get more information about SharePoint. To download a complete chapter about Office SharePoint, go to *www.perspection.com*.

You can set file permissions for SharePoint files. In the workspace, right-click the SharePoint Files tab, click Properties, click the Permissions tab, select a role, select the permissions you want, and then click OK.

Check Out and In Files to Edit

1. In Launchbar, double-click the workspace you want to open, and then click the **SharePoint Files** tab.

2. Select the file you want to check out.

3. Click the **Check In/Out** button on the toolbar, and then click **Check Out from SharePoint**.

4. To edit a file, double-click the file to open it in its native program, make changes, save and close it.

5. In Groove, click **Yes** to save changes.

6. Click the **Check In/Out** button on the toolbar, and then click **Check In from SharePoint**.

7. Describe your changes, and then click **OK**.

Synchronize Files

1. In Launchbar, double-click the workspace you want to open, and then click the **SharePoint Files** tab.

2. To set synchronization options, click the **Calendar** icon, click the **Manually** or **Automatically** option, and then if necessary, specify an interval, and then click **OK**.

3. To manually synchronize files, click **Synchronize Now**.

   The Preview Synchronization dialog box opens.

4. Click **Synchronize Now**.

   Resolve any conflicts that arise. If necessary, click Resolve, select another file version, and then click OK.

Sharing Files with Synchronizing Folders

Instead of using the File Tool in Groove, you can use Groove Folder Synchronization (GFS) in Windows to make sure all changes within a folder are shared between users and kept up-to-date. You create GFS folders in your Windows file system using Windows Explorer. GFS folders are separate from workspaces and currently have a 2 gigabyte size limit. Files shared in Groove workspaces are stored in an encrypted format, while files in a GFS folder are only encrypted during transmission between computers. Any new files added to a synchronized folder are automatically shared with other team members to ensure a secure environment. In Windows Explorer, you can use the Groove Folder Synchronization pane to view the details of the file sharing workspace, view members of the workspace, send workspace invitations, and set workspace and folder properties.

Synchronize Local Folders

1. In Windows Explorer, click the folder you want to share as a GFS folder.

2. Click the **Folder Sync** button.

   The Groove Folder Synchronization pane replaces the Windows Folder pane.

3. Click **Start synchronizing** *foldername*.

4. Click **Synchronize Now**, if necessary, to continue from the preview synchronization.

5. Click **Yes** to confirm the folder share.

6. Use commands in the Groove Folder Synchronization pane to view the details of the file sharing workspace, view members of the workspace, send workspace invitations, mark folders read or unread, and set workspace and folder properties.

7. In Groove, click the **Workspace** tab to access the GFS folder, and view read and unread files.

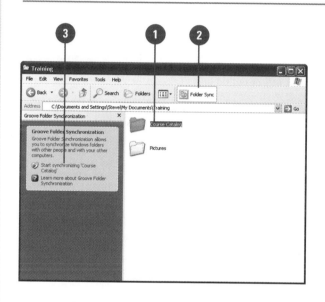

Working with a Shared Workspace

A **Document Workspace** is an Office SharePoint site template that provides you with tools to share and update documents and to keep people informed about the current status of the documents. Using icons on the Document Management task pane, you can connect to an Office SharePoint Server directly from PowerPoint. Each icon displays different information relating to your document: Status, Members, Tasks, Document, and Links. Users can show current tasks, view the status of a document, see the availability of a document, display properties of a document, and list additional resources, folders, and privileges.

Work with a Shared Workspace

1. In PowerPoint, open the presentation you want to share.

2. Click the **Office** button, point to **Publish** (to create) and then click **Create Document Server**, or point to **Server** (to modify), and then click **Document Management Server**.

3. To create a workspace, type a name for the site, type the URL or network location, and then click **Create**.

4. Use the Document Management task pane tools.

   ◆ **Status**. Displays the checked-in/checked-out status of your current document.

   ◆ **Members**. Shows you who is online from your Team Members Group. You can add new members and send e-mail message to members.

   ◆ **Tasks**. Shows you the tasks assigned for this document and the completion status. You can add new tasks, create alerts, and view workflow tasks.

   ◆ **Documents**. Displays the name and workspace of the selected document. You can add new documents and folders, and alert me about documents.

   ◆ **Links**. Displays links to files, folders, and resources. You can add new links and alerts.

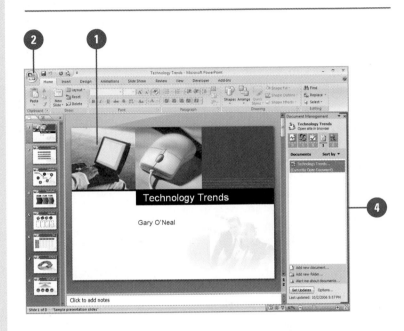

Publishing Slides to a Library

You can publish one or more slides (**New!**) directly from PowerPoint 2007 to a Slide Library on a network running Office SharePoint Server 2007 or to a folder location on your computer or network to store, share, track, and reuse later. Before you can publish slides to a Slide Library, you need to create a Slide Library on the Office SharePoint Server (with at least Designer permissions), where you can also identify the online location for the publishing process. When you publish slides to a Slide Library to a SharePoint Server, team members can use the Reuse Slides task pane (**New!**) to quickly insert the ones they want into presentations. When you make changes to slides in a Slide Library, the next time you open your presentation locally with the reused slides, PowerPoint notifies you there is a change.

Publish Slides to a SharePoint Document Library

1. In PowerPoint, click the **Office** button, point to **Publish**, and then click **Publish Slides**.

2. Select the check boxes next to the slides you want to publish, or click **Select All** to select all the slides.

   PowerPoint automatically names each slide file by using the presentation name and a unique ID number in sequential order.

3. To show only selected slides, select the **Show Only Selected Slides** check box.

4. To rename a slide file name, click the existing file name, and then type a new name.

5. To include a description, click in the description area, and then type a description.

6. Click the **Publish To** list arrow, click a location, or click **Browse** to select a SharePoint Slide Library location.

   To display the Slide Library location, display the library on the SharePoint site, click Settings, and then click Slide Library Settings.

7. Click **Publish**.

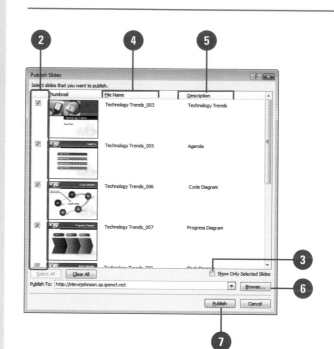

Reuse Published Slides

1. In PowerPoint, open the presentation, and then click the **Home** tab.

2. Click the **New Slide** button arrow, and then click **Reuse Slides**.

3. If the presentation you want is not available, click **Browse**, click **Browse Slide Library**, locate and select the shortcut to the library you want, and then click **Select**.

4. Click a slide to insert it, or right-click a slide, and then click **Insert All Slides**.

5. To be notified when a slide change happens, select the slide, and then select the **Tell me when this slide changes** check box.

6. When you're done, click the **Close** button on the task pane.

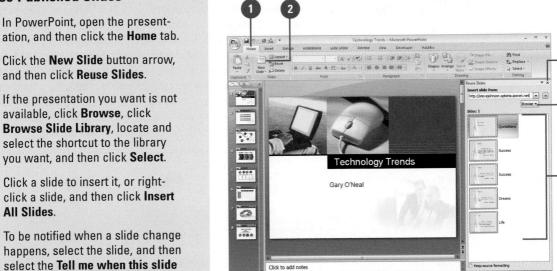

Check Reused Slides for Updates

1. In PowerPoint, open the presentation that contains reused slides.

2. In the Alert dialog box, click **Get Updates**.

   If the dialog box doesn't appear, right-click the reused slide in the Slide pane (Normal view), point to **Check for Updates**, and then click **Check This Slide for Changes** or **Check All Slides for Changes**.

3. If no slides in the presentation need to be updated, a message alert appears. Click **OK**.

4. If the Confirm Slide Update dialog box appears, click **Replace** to replace the local slide with the changed slide from the Slide Library, or click **Append** to add the changed slide after the outdated one in your presentation.

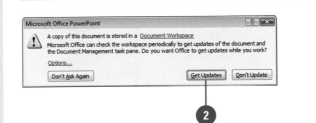

Saving a Presentation to a Document Management Server

You can save workbooks to a Document Management Server, such as a Document Library on an Office SharePoint site, or another Web location in a similar way that you save workbooks on your hard disk. After you save the workbook for the first time using the Document Management Server command, you can click the Save button on the Quick Access Toolbar as you do for any workbook to update the document on the site. If you save a file to a library that requires you to check documents in and out, the SharePoint site checks it out for you. However, you need to check the document in when you're done with it. If the site stores multiple content types, you might be asked to specify the content type.

Save a Presentation to a Document Management Server

1. Open the presentation you want to save to a Document Management Server.

2. Click the **Office** button, point to **Publish**, and then click **Document Management Server**.

3. Navigate to the network folder location on the SharePoint server where you want to save the file.

4. Type a presentation file name.

5. If necessary, click the **Save as type** list arrow, and then click **PowerPoint Presentation**.

6. Click **Save**.

Did You Know?

You can access SharePoint resources from PowerPoint. After you save or publish a presentation to a SharePoint Server site, you can click the Office button, and then point to Server to access other server related commands: View Version History, View Workflow Tasks, and Document Management Information.

Point to access online SharePoint document resources

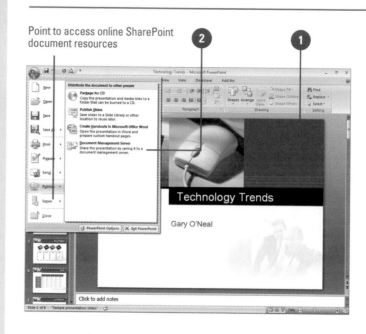

SharePoint server location

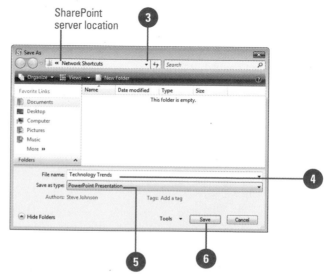

Customizing the Way You Work

13

Introduction

Once you've become familiar with Microsoft Office PowerPoint and all the features it contains, you might want to customize the way you work with PowerPoint. You can change your view settings so that your PowerPoint window looks the way you want it to. PowerPoint comes with set defaults, such as opening all documents using a certain view, showing the vertical ruler, or how many files you've recently opened, which you can change to a new default.

Some of the other PowerPoint customization features allow you to set a default font and related attributes to use when you are typing text in text boxes. Other defaults might be the color or line style of a shape object that you create. You can change the location of the Ribbon, and the configuration of the Quick Access Toolbar to include commands not available on the Ribbon.

When you want to scan one or more documents or faxes and recognize the text using an **Optical Character Recognition (OCR)**, Microsoft Office Document Scanning and Document Imaging gives you the tools you need to quickly and easily scan and recognize text for use in PowerPoint. All you need is scanner hardware.

When you need to manage all the pictures on your computer, Microsoft Office Picture gives you a flexible way to organize, edit, and share your pictures. With Picture Manager, you can view all the pictures on your computer no matter where you store them. If you need to edit a picture, you can use Picture Manager to remove red eye and to change brightness, contrast, and color. You can also crop, rotate and flip, resize, and compress a picture.

What You'll Do

Set General PowerPoint Options

Customize the Way You Create Objects

Access Commands Not in the Ribbon

Scan and Image Documents

Manage Pictures

Use Multiple Languages

Setting General PowerPoint Options

You can customize the performance of many PowerPoint features including its editing, saving, spelling, viewing, printing and security procedures. Each person uses PowerPoint in a different way. PowerPoint Options allows you to change popular options to personalize what appears in the PowerPoint window (**New!**). When you change these options, PowerPoint uses them for all subsequent PowerPoint sessions until you change them again.

Change Popular Options

1 Click the **Office** button, and then click **PowerPoint Options**.

2 In the left pane, click **Popular**.

3 Select the Top options for working with PowerPoint you want:

- ◆ **Show Mini Toolbar on Selection** (**New!**). Select to show a miniature semi-transparent toolbar that helps you work with selected text.

- ◆ **Enable Live Preview** (**New!**). Select to show preview changes in a presentation.

- ◆ **Show Developer tab in the Ribbon** (**New!**). Select to access developer controls, write code, or create macros.

- ◆ **Color Scheme** (**New!**). Click the list arrow to select a Windows related color scheme.

- ◆ **ScreenTip style** (**New!**). Click the list arrow to select a screentip option: Show enhanced ScreenTips, Don't show enhanced ScreenTips, or Don't show ScreenTips.

4 Type your name and initials as you want them to appear in Properties, and review comments.

5 Click **OK**.

Change Advanced Options

1. Click the **Office** button, and then click **PowerPoint Options**.

2. In the left pane, click **Advanced**.

3. Select the display options you want:

   - ◆ **Number of documents in the Recent Documents list**. Enter the number of document you want available on the Office menu. Set to 0 to turn off the recent documents display.

   - ◆ **Show all windows in the Taskbar**. Select to show a window button for each presentation in the taskbar.

   - ◆ **Show shortcut keys in ScreenTips (New!)**. Select to show shortcut keys in ScreenTips.

   - ◆ **Show vertical ruler (New!)**. Select to show the vertical ruler along with the horizontal ruler.

   - ◆ **Open all documents using this view**. Click the list arrow to select a default view when you open a presentation.

4. To make a sound when an error appears, select the **Provide feedback with sound** check box.

5. Click **OK**.

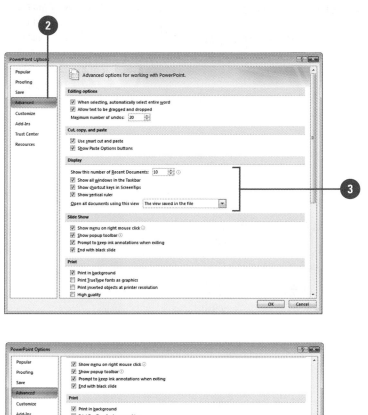

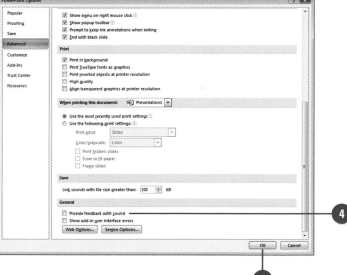

Did You Know?

You can change the appearance of Office programs in Windows. The appearance of the ribbon, toolbars, menus, and dialog boxes in Microsoft Office programs follows the theme or color scheme you set up in the Windows control panel.

Customizing the Way You Create Objects

When you create a text box, PowerPoint applies a set of default text attributes. Some examples of PowerPoint's font default settings include font style, size, and formatting options, such as bold, italic, and underline. When you draw an object, PowerPoint applies a set of default object attributes. Examples of object default settings include fill color, shadow, and line style. To find out the current default settings for your presentation, you can draw an object, or create a text object and check the object's attributes. If you change a default setting, PowerPoint will use the new setting for all subsequent PowerPoint sessions until you change the setting again.

Customize the Way You Create Text Objects

① Create a text box.

② Change the text attributes, including font type, style, and size.

③ Right-click the shape, and then click **Set as Default Text Box**.

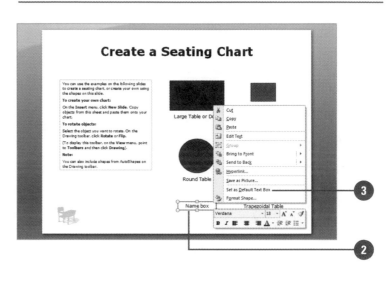

Customize the Way You Create Shape Objects

① Create a shape.

② Change the shape attributes, including fill color or effect, text color, outline color and style; and font type, style, and size.

③ Right-click the shape, and then click **Set as Default Shape**.

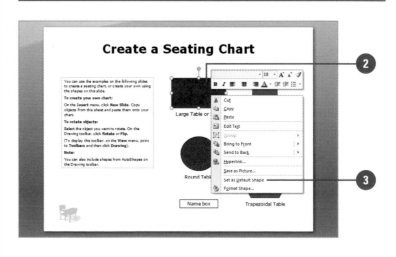

Accessing Commands Not in the Ribbon

If you don't see a command in the Ribbon that was available in an earlier version of PowerPoint, you might think Microsoft removed it from the product. To see if a command is available, check out the Customize section in PowerPoint Options. The Quick Access Toolbar gives access to commands not in the Ribbon (**New!**), which you can add to the toolbar. For example, you can add the following commands: Create Microsoft Office Outlook Task, Replace Fonts, Send to Microsoft Word, and Web Page Preview.

Add Commands Not in the Ribbon to the Quick Access Toolbar

1. Click the **Customize Quick Access Toolbar** list arrow, and then click **More Commands**.

2. Click the **Choose command from** list arrow, and then click **Commands Not in the Ribbon**.

3. Click the **Customize Quick Access Toolbar** list arrow, and then click **For all documents (default)**.

4. Click the command you want to add (left column).

   TIMESAVER *Click <Separator>, and then click Add to insert a separator line between buttons.*

5. Click **Add**.

6. Click the **Move Up** and **Move Down** arrow buttons to arrange the commands in the order you want them to appear.

7. Click **OK**.

Did You Know?

You can rest the Quick Access Toolbar to its original state. In the PowerPoint Options dialog box, click Customize in the left pane, click Reset, and then click OK.

Scanning and Imaging Documents

With Microsoft Office Document Imaging, you can scan and manage multiple page documents using the TIFF file format and recognize text in image documents and faxes as editable text by using Optical Character Recognition (OCR). You can copy scanned text and images into Microsoft Office programs as well as e-mail or fax the document over the Internet. If you need to add information to a document, such as a fax, you can add text as a note or comment, apply highlighting, draw shapes, and insert pictures by using the Annotation toolbar (**New!**).

Scan a Document Image

1 Click the **Start** button, point to **All Programs**, click **Microsoft Office**, click **Microsoft Office Tools**, and then click **Microsoft Office Document Imaging**.

2 Click the **Scan New Document** button on the toolbar.

3 Click **Scanner**, select your scanner hardware, and then click **OK**.

4 Click a preset scanning option.

5 Click the scanner options you want.

6 Click the **Scan** button.

The document is scanned.

7 Click the **Save** button on the toolbar, specify a name and location, and then click **Save**.

8 When you're done, click **Close**.

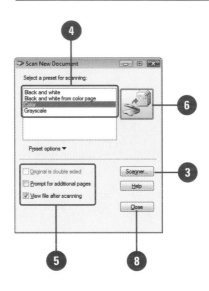

Did You Know?

You can open Microsoft Office Document Scanning program separately. Click the Start button, point to All Programs, point to Microsoft Office, point to Microsoft Office Tools, and then click Microsoft Office Document Scanning.

Perform OCR on a Document Image

1. Click the **Start** button, point to **All Programs**, point to **Microsoft Office**, point to **Microsoft Office Tools**, and then click **Microsoft Office Document Imaging**.

2. Click the **Open** button on the toolbar.

3. Click the **Look in** list arrow, and then navigate to the file.

4. Click the document image you want to open, and then click **Open**.

5. Click the **Recognize Text Using OCR** button on the toolbar.

6. To add annotations and comments, use the pen, highlighter, and comments buttons on the Annotation toolbar.

7. Select the text in the document. It appears with a red rectangle around it.

8. Click the **Edit** menu, and then click **Copy**.

9. Save and close the document.

10. Open or switch to PowerPoint, and the place the insertion point where you want to paste the text.

11. Click the **Paste** button on the Home tab.

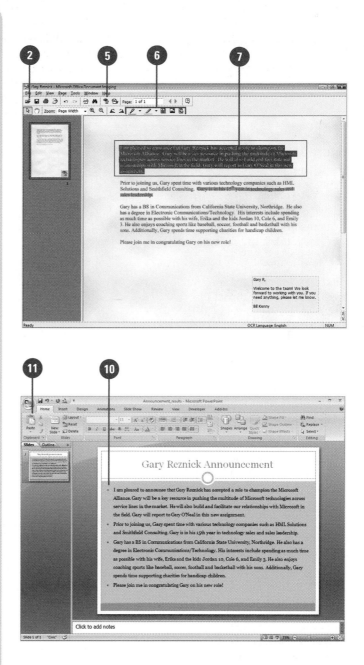

Managing Pictures

With Microsoft Office Picture Manager, you can manage, edit, and share your pictures. You can view all the pictures on your computer and specify which file type you want to open with Picture Manager. If you need to edit a picture, you can use Picture Manager to change brightness, contrast, and color, and to remove red eye. You can also crop, rotate and flip, resize, and compress a picture.

Open Picture Manager and Locate Pictures

1. Click the **Start** button, point to **All Programs**, click **Microsoft Office**, click **Microsoft Office Tools**, and then click **Microsoft Office Picture Manager**.

   The first time you start the program, it asks you to select the file types you want to open with Picture Manager. Select the check boxes with the formats you want, and then click **OK**.

2. If necessary, click **Add Picture Shortcut**.

3. Click **Locate Pictures**.

4. Click the **Look in** list arrow, and then click a drive location.

5. Click **OK**.

6. Use the **View** buttons to view your pictures.

7. When you're done, click the **Close** button.

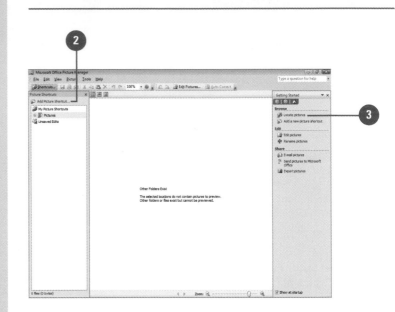

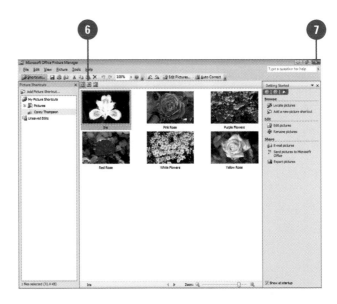

> ### Did You Know?
>
> **You can export a folder of files with a new format or size.** In Picture Manager, click the File menu, click Export, specify the folder with the pictures you want to change, select an export file format or select a size, and then click OK.

Edit Pictures

1. In Picture Manager, select the picture you want to edit.

2. Click the **Edit Pictures** button on the Standard toolbar.

3. Use the editing tools on the Edit Pictures task pane to modify the picture.

   ◆ Brightness and Contrast

   ◆ Color

   ◆ Crop

   ◆ Rotate and Flip

   ◆ Red Eye Removal

4. Use the sizing tools on the Edit Pictures task pane to change the picture size.

   ◆ Resize

   ◆ Compress Pictures

5. Click the **Save** button on the Standard toolbar.

6. When you're done, click the **Close** button.

Did You Know?

You can discard changes to a picture.
If you don't like the changes you make to a picture, click the Edit menu, and then click Discard Changes to restore the picture.

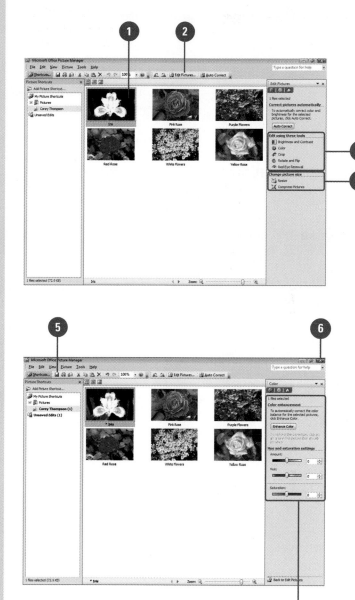

Color enhancing options

Using Multiple Languages

International Microsoft Office users can change the language that appears on their screens by changing the default language settings. Users around the world can enter, display, and edit text in all supported languages—including European languages, Japanese, Chinese, Korean, Hebrew, and Arabic—to name a few. You'll probably be able to use Office programs in your native language. If the text in your document is written in more than one language, you can automatically detect languages or designate the language of selected text so the spelling checker uses the right dictionary.

Add a Language to Office Programs

1. Click **Start** on the taskbar, point to **All Programs**, click **Microsoft Office**, click **Microsoft Office Tools**, and then click **Microsoft Office 2007 Language Settings**.

   TIMESAVER *In PowerPoint, click the Office button, click PowerPoint Options, click Popular, and then click Language Settings.*

2. Select the language you want to enable.

3. Click **Add**.

4. Click **OK**, and then click **Yes** to quit and restart Office.

Did You Know?

You can check your keyboard layout. After you enable editing for another language, such as Hebrew, Cyrillic, or Greek, you might need to install the correct keyboard layout so you can enter characters for that language. In the Control Panel, double-click the Regional And Language icon, click the Language tab, and then click Details to check your keyboard.

Expanding PowerPoint Functionality

14

Introduction

An add-in extends the functionality of Microsoft Office programs. An add-in is typically a third-party program you can purchase—some are shareware—and download from the Web. You can find a list of add-ins for Microsoft Office on the Microsoft Office Online Web site. Before you can use an add-in, you need to load it first. After you load an add-in, the feature may add a command to a Ribbon tab or toolbar.

If you want to customize Microsoft Office PowerPoint 2007 and create advanced presentations, you'll need to learn how to work with the Microsoft Office 2007 programming language, **Microsoft Visual Basic for Applications (VBA)**. VBA is powerful and flexible, and you can use it in all major Office applications. To create a VBA application, you have to learn VBA conventions and syntax. Office 2007 makes VBA more user-friendly by providing the Visual Basic Editor, an application that includes several tools to help you write error-free VBA applications. The Visual Basic Editor provides extensive online Help to assist you in this task.

A practical way to use VBA is to create macros. Macros can simplify common repetitive tasks that you use regularly in PowerPoint. Macros can reside on the PowerPoint Quick Access Toolbar for easy access. If a macro has a problem executing a task, the Visual Basic Editor can help you debug, or fix the error in your macro. VBA may be a difficult language for the new user, but its benefits make the effort of learning it worthwhile.

An ActiveX control is a software component that adds functionality to an existing program. An ActiveX control supports a customizable, programmatic interface for you to create your own functionality, such as a form. Excel includes several pre-built ActiveX controls—including a label, text box, command button, and check box—to help you create a user interface.

What You'll Do

View and Manage Add-ins

Load and Unload Add-ins

Enhance a Presentation with VBA

View the Visual Basic Editor

Set Developer Options

Simplify Tasks with Macros

Control a Macro

Add a Digital Signature to a Macro Project

Assign a Macro to a Toolbar

Save and Open a Presentation with Macros

Insert ActiveX Controls

Use ActiveX Controls

Set ActiveX Control Properties

Play a Movie Using an ActiveX Control

Change the Document Information Panel

Viewing and Managing Add-ins

An add-in extends functionality, such as smart tags, to Microsoft Office programs (**New!**). An add-in can add buttons and custom commands to the Ribbon. You can get add-ins for PowerPoint on the Microsoft Office Online Web site in the Downloads area, or on third-party vendor Web sites. When you download and install an add-in, it appears on the Add-Ins tab of an Office program depending on functionality and includes a special ScreenTip that identifies the developer. You can view and manage add-ins from the Add-in area in PowerPoint Options.

View Installed Add-ins

1. Click the **Add-Ins** tab.

   Add-ins with buttons and controls appear on the Ribbon.

2. Point to a button or control to display a ScreenTip.

3. Click the **Office** button, and then click **PowerPoint Options**.

4. In the left pane, click **Add-Ins**.

   The installed add-ins appear in the list by category.

   ◆ **Active Application Add-ins.** Lists the registered and running add-ins. A selected check box for a COM add-in appears here.

   ◆ **Inactive Application Add-ins.** Lists the installed add-ins, but not currently loaded. A cleared check box for a COM add-in appears here.

   ◆ **Document Related Add-ins.** Lists template files currently open in a document.

   ◆ **Disabled Application Add-ins.** Lists automatically disabled add-ins causing Office programs to crash.

5. Click an add-in to display information about it.

6. Click **OK**.

Add-ins

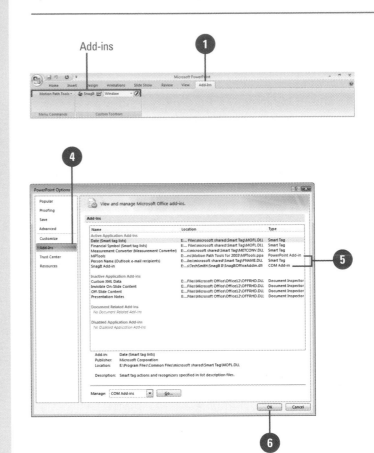

Manage Installed Add-ins

1. Click the **Office** button, and then click **PowerPoint Options**.

2. In the left pane, click **Add-Ins**.

3. Click the **Manage** list arrow, and then click the add-in list you want to display:

   - **COM Add-ins.** Opens the COM Add-Ins dialog box and lists the Component Object Model (COM) add-ins.

   - **PowerPoint Add-ins.** Opens the Add-Ins dialog box and lists the currently installed PowerPoint add-ins.

   - **Smart Tags.** Opens the AutoCorrect dialog with the Smart Tags tab and list the installed smart tags.

   - **Disabled Items.** Opens the Disabled Items dialog box and lists the disabled items that prevent PowerPoint from working properly. If you want to try and enable an item, select it, click Enable, click Close, and then restart PowerPoint.

4. Click **Go**.

5. Click **OK**.

Did You Know?

You cannot use the presentation broadcast add-in with PowerPoint 2007. Instead, Microsoft Office Live Meeting can provide you with the features you need to collaborate online and share presentations with individuals or groups in different locations.

PowerPoint Add-ins

Add-in	Descriptions
Microsoft Producer	Use to capture, synchronize, and publish audio, video, slides, and images for PowerPoint presentations.
Project Report Presentation	Create a PowerPoint presentation containing selected information from Project.
Template Creation Wizard	Create a templates using a wizard.
Desktop Language Settings	Change language, keyboard, and regional setting for Office, Internet Explorer, and Windows at the same time.
International Character Toolbar	Insert international characters in 26 languages.
Latin and Cyrillic Transliteration	Convert text from Cyrillic script to Latin script or vice-versa.

Loading and Unloading Add-ins

Add-ins are additional programs, designed to run seamlessly within PowerPoint or Office. There are two main types of add-ins: PowerPoint and **Component Object Model (COM)**. PowerPoint add-ins are custom controls designed specifically for PowerPoint, while COM add-ins are designed to run in one or more Office programs and use the file name extension .dll or .exe. Some add-ins are installed when you run the Setup program, while others can be downloaded from Microsoft Office Online or purchased from third-party vendors. To load or unload add-ins, PowerPoint provides commands you can access from an added button on the Quick Access Toolbar or the Add-in area in PowerPoint Options.

Load or Unload a PowerPoint Add-in

1 Click the **Add-Ins** button on the Quick Access Toolbar.

If necessary, use the Customize pane in PowerPoint Options to add the button to the Quick Access Toolbar.

2 Click the add-in you want to load or unload.

TROUBLE? *If the add-in is not available in the list, click Add New, locate and select the add-in you want, and then click OK.*

3 Click **Load** or **Unload**.

4 To remove the selected add-in, click **Remove**.

5 Click **Close**.

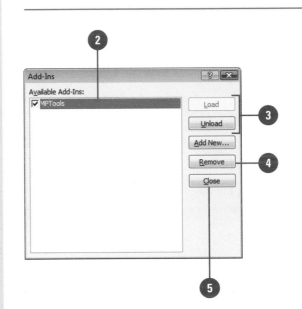

Did You Know?

You can open an add-in dialog box from PowerPoint Options. Click the Office button, click PowerPoint Options, click Add-ins, click the Manage list arrow, click PowerPoint Add-ins or COM Add-ins, and then click Go.

Load or Unload a COM Add-in

① Click the **COM Add-Ins** button on the Quick Access Toolbar.

If necessary, use the Customize pane in PowerPoint Options to add the button to the Quick Access Toolbar.

② Select the check box next to the add-in you want to load, or clear the check box you want to unload.

TROUBLE? *If the add-in is not available in the list, click Add, locate and select the add-in you want, and then click OK.*

③ To remove the selected add-in, click **Remove**.

④ Click **OK**.

Did You Know?

You can can get more information about COM online. Visit *www.microsoft.com/com.*

See Also

See "Working with Toolbar" on page 6 for information on adding a button to the Quick Access Toolbar.

For Your Information

Dealing with an Add-in Security Alert

When there is a problem with an add-in, PowerPoint disables it to protect the program and your data. When a problem does occur, a security alert dialog box appears, displaying information about the problem and options you can choose to fix or ignore it. You can choose an option to help protect me from unknown content (recommended), enable this add-in for this session only, or enable all code published by this publisher. See "Setting Add-ins Security Options" on page 352 for more information about setting options that trigger the Add-in security alert.

Enhancing a Presentation with VBA

Office 2007 applications like PowerPoint, Access, Excel, Word, and Visio share a common programming language: Visual Basic for Applications (VBA). With VBA, you can develop applications that combine tools from these Office 2007 products, as well as other programs that support VBA. Because of the language's power and flexibility, programmers often prefer to use VBA to customize their Office applications.

Introducing the Structure of VBA

VBA is an object-oriented programming language because, when you develop a VBA application, you manipulate objects. An object can be anything within your presentation, such as a shape, text box, picture, or table. Even PowerPoint itself is considered an object. Objects can have properties that describe the object's characteristics. Text boxes, for example, have the Font property, which describes the font PowerPoint uses to display the text. A text box also has properties that indicate whether the text is bold or italic.

Objects also have methods, actions that can be done to the object. Deleting and inserting are examples of methods available with a record object. Closely related to methods are events. An event is a specific action that occurs on or with an object. Clicking a button initiates the Click event for the button object. VBA also refers to an event associated with an object as an event property. The form button, for example, has the Click event property. You can use VBA to either respond to an event or to initiate an event.

Writing VBA Code

A VBA programmer types the statements, or **code**, that make up the VBA program. Those statements follow a set of rules, called **syntax**, that govern how commands are formulated. For example, to change the property of a particular object, the command follows the general form:

Object.Property = Expression

W here **Object** is the name of a VBA object, **Property** is the name of a property that object has, and **Expression** is a value that will be assigned to the property. The following statement sets the ViewType property of the ActiveWindow to Slide View:

ActiveWindow.ViewType = ppViewSlide"

You can use Office and VBA's online Help to learn about specific object and property names. If you want to apply a method to an object, the syntax is:

Object.Method arg1, arg2, ...

Where **Object** is the name of a VBA object, **Method** is the name of method that can be applied to that object, and **arg1**, **arg2**, ... are optional **arguments** that provide additional information for the method operation. For example, to exit all running slide shows, you could use the Exit method as follows:

SlideShowWindows(1).View.Exit

Working with Procedures

You don't run VBA commands individually. Instead they are organized into groups of commands called **procedures**. A procedure either performs an action or calculates a value. Procedures that perform actions are called **Sub procedures**. You can run a Sub procedure directly, or Office can run it for you in response to an event, such as clicking a button or opening a form. A Sub procedure initiated by an event is also called an **event procedure**. Office provides event procedure templates to help you easily create procedures for common events. Event procedures are displayed in each object's event properties list.

A procedure that calculates a value is called a **function procedure**. By creating function procedures you can create your own function library, supplementing the Office collection of built-in functions. You can access these functions from within the Expression Builder, making it easy for them to be used over and over again.

Working with Modules

Procedures are collected and organized within **modules**. Modules generally belong to two types: class modules and standard modules. A **class module** is associated with a specific object. In more advanced VBA programs, the class module can be associated with an object created by the user. **Standard modules** are not associated with specific objects, and they can be run from anywhere within a database. This is usually not the case with class modules. Standard modules are listed in the Database window on the Modules Object list.

Building VBA Projects

A collection of modules is further organized into a **project**. Usually a project has the same name as a presentation. You can create projects that are not tied into any specific presentation, saving them as PowerPoint add-ins that provide extra functionality to PowerPoint.

Using the Visual Basic Editor

You create VBA commands, procedures, and modules in Office's **Visual Basic Editor**. This is the same editor used by Excel, Word, and other Office programs. Thus, you can apply what you learn about creating programs in PowerPoint to these other applications.

The Project Explorer

One of the fundamental tools in the Visual Basic Editor is the Project Explorer. The **Project Explorer** presents a hierarchical view of all of the projects and modules currently open in PowerPoint, including standard and class modules.

The Modules Window

You write all of your VBA code in the **Modules** window. The Modules window acts as a basic text editor, but it includes several tools to help you write error-free codes. PowerPoint also provides hints as you write your code to help you avoid syntax errors.

The Object Browser

There are hundreds of objects available to you. Each object has a myriad of properties, methods, and events. Trying to keep track of all of them is daunting, but the Visual Basic Editor supplies the **Object Browser**, which helps you examine the complete collection of objects, properties, and methods available for a given object.

Viewing the Visual Basic Editor

The Project Explorer displays a hierarchical list of all open projects and modules.

The Modules window allows you to enter VBA commands.

VBA projects

Currently selected module

The Properties window displays properties for selected objects.

A VBA statement

Method

Properties

Objects

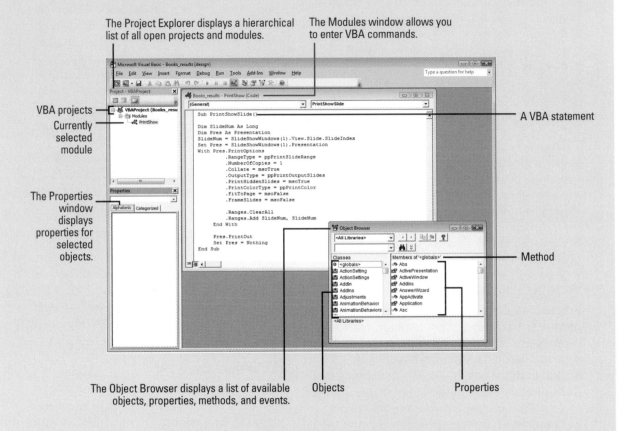

The Object Browser displays a list of available objects, properties, methods, and events.

Setting Developer Options

The Developer tab (**New!**) is a specialized Ribbon that you can use to access developer controls, write code, or create macros. You can set an option in the Popular section of PowerPoint options to show or hide the Developer tab. As a developer, you can also set an option to show errors in your user interface customization code.

Set Developer Options

1. Click the **Office** button, and then click **PowerPoint Options**.

2. In the left pane, click **Popular**.

3. Select the **Show Developer tab in the Ribbon** check box.

4. In the left pane, click **Advanced**.

5. Select the **Show add-in user interface errors** check box.

6. Click **OK**.

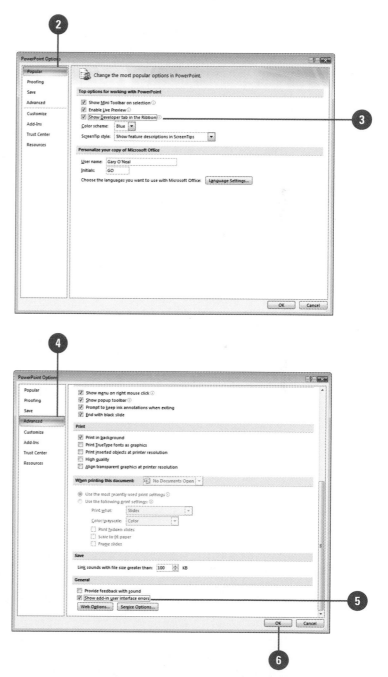

Simplifying Tasks with Macros

If you find yourself repeating the same set of steps over and over or if you need to add new functionality to PowerPoint, you could create a macro. Macros can run several tasks for you at the click of a button. You create macros using a programming language called Microsoft Visual Basic for Applications (VBA) (**New!**). With VBA, you create a macro by writing a script to replay the actions you want. The macros for a particular presentation are stored in a macro module, which is a collection of Visual Basic codes.

Create a Macro

1. Click the **View** or **Developer** tab.

2. Click the **Macros** button.

3. Type a name for the macro.

4. Click the Macro in list arrow, and then click **All open presentations** or the presentation to which you want the macro stored.

5. If you want, add a macro description in the Description box.

6. Click **Create**.

   The Microsoft Visual Basic window opens.

7. Click the Module window, and then type new Visual Basic commands, or edit existing ones.

8. When you're done, click the **File** menu, and then click **Close and Return to Microsoft PowerPoint**.

Did You Know?

You can use macros from earlier versions of PowerPoint. If you created a macro using the Macro Recorder in an earlier version of PowerPoint (97-2003), you can use VBA to edit the macro. The Macro Recorder actually writes a program in VBA to create a macro.

Object Browser helps you insert commands.

Run a Macro

1 Click the **View** or **Developer** tab.

2 Click the **Macros** button.

   TIMESAVER *Click the Marcos button on the Status bar.*

3 Click the name of the macro you want to run.

4 Click **Run**.

Did You Know?

You can stop a macro. Press Ctrl+Break to stop a macro before it completes its actions.

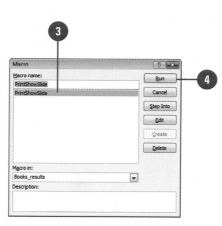

Delete a Macro

1 Click the **View** or **Developer** tab.

2 Click the **Macros** button.

3 Click the macro name.

4 Click **Delete**.

5 Click **Delete** to confirm the macro deletion.

Did You Know?

You can set up a macro to run during a slide show. In Normal view, click the text or object you want to use to run a macro, click the Insert tab, click the Action button, click the Mouse Click tab or the Mouse Over tab, click the Run Macro option, click the list arrow, select the macro you want, and then click OK.

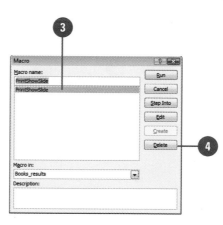

Controlling a Macro

If a macro doesn't work exactly the way you want it to, you can fix the problem using Microsoft Visual Basic for Applications (VBA). VBA allows you to **debug**, or repair, an existing macro so that you change only the actions that aren't working correctly. All macros for a particular presentation are stored in a macro module, a collection of Visual Basic programming codes that you can copy to other presentation files. You can view and edit your Visual Basic modules using the Visual Basic editor. By learning Visual Basic you can greatly increase the scope and power of your programs.

Debug a Macro Using Step Mode

1 Click the **View** or **Developer** tab.

2 Click the **Macros** button.

3 Click the name of the macro you want to debug.

4 Click **Step Into**.

The Microsoft Visual Basic window opens.

5 Click the **Debug** menu, and then click **Step Into** (or press F8) to proceed through each action.

◆ Use other commands like **Step Over** and **Step Out** to debug the code.

6 When you're done, click the **File** menu, and then click **Close and Return to Microsoft PowerPoint**.

7 Click **OK** to stop the debugger.

Did You Know?

You can display the Debug toolbar. In the Visual Basic editor, click the View menu, point to Toolbars, and then click Debug.

Edit a Macro

1 Click the **View** or **Developer** tab.

2 Click the **Macros** button.

3 Click the name of the macro you want to edit, and then click **Edit**.

4 Click the Module window containing the Visual Basic code for your macro.

5 Type new Visual Basic commands, or edit the commands already present.

6 Click the **File** menu, and then click **Close and Return to Microsoft PowerPoint**.

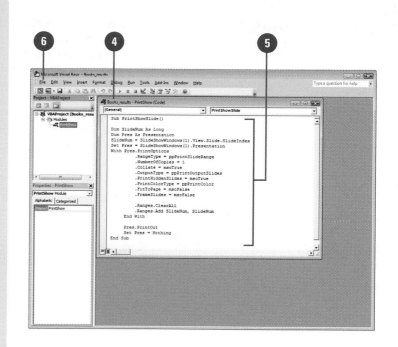

Copy a Macro Module to Another Presentation

1 Open the presentation files you want to copy the macro from and to.

2 Click the **Developer** tab.

3 Click the **Visual Basic** button.

4 Click the **View** menu, and then click **Project Explorer**.

5 Drag the module you want to copy from the source presentation to the destination presentation.

6 Click the **File** menu, and then click **Close and Return to Microsoft PowerPoint**.

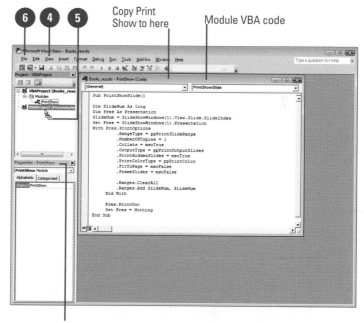

Copy Print Show to here

Module VBA code

Properties

Adding a Digital Signature to a Macro Project

If you want to add a digital signature to a presentation with a macro, you need to add it using the Visual Basic editor. If you open a presentation that contains a signed macro project with a problem, the macro is disabled by default and the Message Bar appears to notify you of the potential problem. You can click Options in the Message Bar to view information about it. For more details, you can click Show Signature Details to view certificate and publisher information. If a digital signature has problems—it's expired, not issued by a trusted publisher, or the presentation has been altered—the certificate information image contains a red X. When there's a problem, contact the signer to have them fix it, or save the presentation to a trusted location, where you can run the macro without security checks.

Sign a Macro Project

1. Open the presentation that contains the macro project, and then click the **Developer** tab.

2. Click the **Visual Basic** button to open the Visual Basic window.

3. Click the **Tools** menu, and then click **Digital Signature**.

4. Click **Choose**.

5. Select a certificate in the list.

6. To view a certificate, click **View Certificate**, and then click **OK**.

7. Click **OK**.

8. Click **OK** again.

9. Click the **Save** and **Close** button in the Microsoft Visual Basic window.

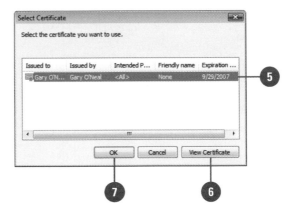

Did You Know?

You can create a self-signing certificate for a macro project. Click the Start button, point to All Programs, point to Microsoft Office, point to Microsoft Office Tools, click Digital Certificate for VBA Projects, enter a name, and then click OK. Office programs trust a self-signed certificate only on the computer that created it.

Assigning a Macro to a Toolbar

After you create a macro, you can add the macro to the Quick Access Toolbar for easy access (**New!**). When you create a macro, the macro name appears in the list of available commands when you customize the Quick Access Toolbar in PowerPoint Options. When you point to a macro button on the Quick Access Toolbar, a ScreenTip appears, displaying Macro: *presentation name!macro name*.

Assign a Macro to a Toolbar

1. Click the **Customize Quick Access Toolbar** list arrow, and then click **More Commands**.

2. Click the **Choose command from** list arrow, and then click **Macros**.

3. Click the **Customize Quick Access Toolbar** list arrow, and then click **For all documents (default)**.

4. Click the macro you want to add (left column).

5. Click **Add**.

6. Click the **Move Up** and **Move Down** arrow buttons to arrange the commands in the order you want them to appear.

7. Click **Modify**.

8. In the Display name box, type a name for the button.

9. Click an icon in the symbol list.

10. Click **OK**.

11. Click **OK**.

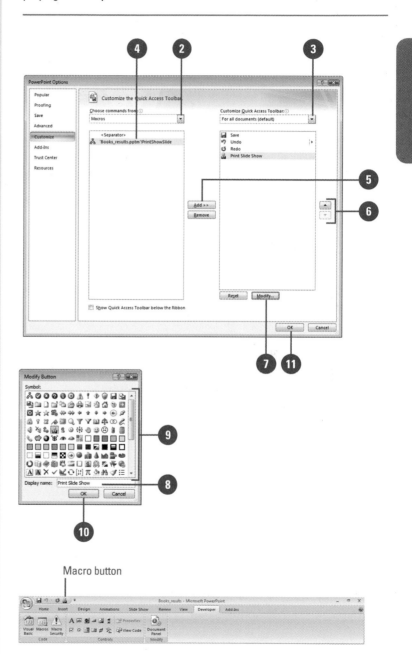

Macro button

> ### See Also
>
> See "Working with Toolbars" on page 6 and "Accessing Command Not in the Ribbon" on page 395 for information on using the Quick Access Toolbar.

Saving a Presentation with Macros

Macros are created using Visual Basic for Applications (VBA) code. If you add a macro to a presentation, you need to save it with a file name extension that ends with an "m" (**New!**), either PowerPoint Macro-Enabled Presentation (.pptm), PowerPoint Macro-Enabled Show (.ppsm), or PowerPoint Macro-Enabled Design Template (.potm). If you try to save a presentation containing a macro with a file name extension that ends with an "x" (such as .pptx, .sldx, or .potx), PowerPoint displays an alert message, restricting the operation. These PowerPoint file types are designated to be VBA code-free.

Save a Presentation with Macros

1. Click the **Office** button, and then click **Save As**.

2. Click the **Save in** list arrow, and then click the drive or folder where you want to save the file.

3. Type a presentation file name.

4. If necessary, click the **Save as type** list arrow, and then click one of the following:

   ◆ **PowerPoint Macro-Enabled Presentation.** A presentation (.pptm) that contains VBA code.

   ◆ **PowerPoint Macro-Enabled Show.** A presentation slide show (.ppsm) that includes preapproved macros.

   ◆ **PowerPoint Macro-Enabled Design Template.** A template (.potm) that includes preapproved macros.

5. Click **Save**.

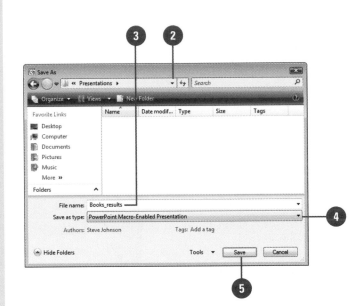

Opening a Presentation with Macros

When you open a presentation with a macro, VBA, or other software code, PowerPoint displays a security warning (**New!**) to let you know the presentation might contain potentially harmful code that may harm your computer. If you know and trust the author of the presentation, you can change security options to enable the macro content and use the presentation normally. If you don't trust the content, you can continue to block and disable the content and use the presentation with limited functionality. If you don't want a security alert to appear, you can change security settings in the Trust Center in PowerPoint Options.

Open a Presentation with Macros

1. Click the **Office** button, and then click **Open**.

2. Click the **File as type** list arrow, and then click one of the following presentation types with macros:

   ◆ **PowerPoint Macro-Enabled Presentation.** A presentation (.pptm) that contains VBA code.

   ◆ **PowerPoint Macro-Enabled Show.** A presentation slide show (.ppsm) that includes preapproved macros.

   ◆ **PowerPoint Macro-Enabled Design Template.** A template (.potm) that includes preapproved macros.

3. If the file is located in another folder, click the **Look in** list arrow, and then navigate to the file.

4. Click the presentation with macros you want to open, and then click **Open**.

5. Click **Options** in the Security Warning.

6. If you trust the presentation content, click the **Enable external content** option to open it. If you don't trust it, click the **Help protect me from unknown content** option to block and disable the macros.

7. Click **OK**.

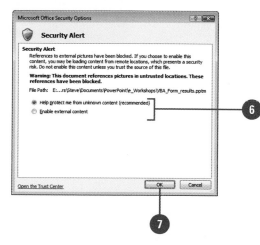

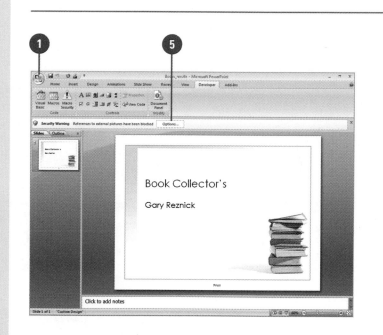

Inserting ActiveX Controls

An ActiveX control is a software component that adds functionality to an existing program. An ActiveX control is really just another term for an OLE (Object Linking and Embedding) object, known as a Component Object Model (COM) object. An ActiveX control supports a customizable, programmatic interface. PowerPoint includes several pre-built ActiveX controls (**New!**) on the Developer tab, including a label, text box, command button, image, scroll bar, check box, option button, combo box, list box, toggle button, and more controls. To create an ActiveX control, click the control you want in the Developer tab, and then drag to insert it with the size you want. If there is a problem with an ActiveX control, PowerPoint disables it to protect the program and your data. When a problem does occur, a security alert dialog box appears, displaying information about the problem and options you can choose to leave it disabled or enable it.

Insert ActiveX Controls

1. Click the **Developer** tab.

2. Click the button with the ActiveX control you want to use.

   See the next page for a list and description of each ActiveX control.

3. Display the slide where you want to place the ActiveX control.

4. Drag (pointer changes to a plus sign) to draw the ActiveX control the size you want.

5. To resize the control, drag a resize handle (circles) to the size you want.

Deal with an ActiveX Control Security Alert

1. Click the **Office** button, and then click **Open**.

2. Click the **File as type** list arrow, and then click the presentation type that contains the Active X control.

3. If the file is located in another folder, click the **Look in** list arrow, and then navigate to the file.

4. Click the presentation with the ActiveX control you want to open, and then click **Open**.

5. Click **Options** in the Security Warning.

6. If you trust the presentation content, click the **Enable external content** option to open it. If you don't trust it, click the **Help protect me from unknown content** option to block and disable the macros.

7. Click **OK**.

See Also

See "Setting ActiveX Security Options" on page 353 for more information about setting options that trigger the ActiveX security alert.

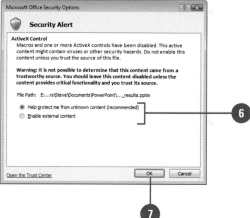

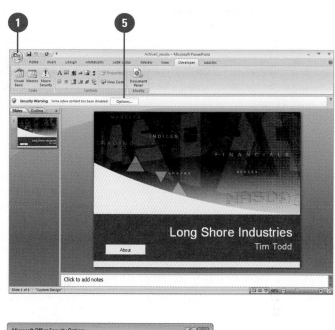

Using ActiveX Controls

ActiveX Controls

Button	Name	Description
	Label	This button creates a text label. Because the other controls already include a corresponding label, use this button to create labels that are independent of other controls.
	Text Box	This button creates a text box in which the user can enter text (or numbers). Use this control for objects assigned to a text or number data type.
	Spin Button	This button creates a box in which the user can click arrows to increase or decrease numbers in a box. Use this control assigned to a number data type.
	Command Button	This button creates a button that runs a macro or Microsoft Visual Basic function when the user clicks the button in the form.
	Image	This button inserts a frame, in which you can insert a graphic in your form. Use this control when you want to insert a graphic, such as clip art or a logo.
	Scroll Bar	This button creates a scroll bar pane in which the user can enter text (or numbers) in a scrollable text box. Use this control or objects assigned to a text or number data type.
	Check Box	This button creates a check box that allows a user to make multiple yes or no selections. Use this control for fields assigned to the yes/no data type.
	Option Button	This button creates an option button (also known as a radio button) that allows the user to make a single selection from at least two choices. Use this control for fields assigned to the yes/no data type.
	Combo Box	This button creates a combo box in which the user has the option to enter text or select from a list of options. You can enter your own options in the list, or you can display options stored in another table.
	List Box	This button creates a list box that allows a user to select from a list of options. You can enter your own options in the list, or can have another table provide a list of options.
	Toggle Button	This button creates a button that allows the user to make a yes or no selection by clicking the toggle button. Use this control for fields assigned to the yes/no data type.
	More Controls	Click to display other controls, such as Adobe Acrobat Control for ActiveX, Microsoft Forms 2.0, Microsoft Office InfoPath controls, and Microsoft Web Browser.

Setting ActiveX Control Properties

Every ActiveX control has **properties (New!)**, or settings, that determine its appearance and function. When you work with a control, you can open a property sheet that displays all the settings for that control in alphabetic or category order. The ActiveX controls appear in the Properties window in two columns: the left column displays the name of the control, and the right column displays the current value or setting for the control. When you select either column, a list arrow appears in the right column, allowing you to select the setting you want. After you set properties, you can add VBA code to a module to make it perform.

Set ActiveX Control Properties

1. Select the control whose properties you want to modify.

2. Click the **Developer** tab.

3. Click the **Properties** button to display the Properties window only, or the **View Code** button to open the Visual Basic Editor.

   If necessary in the Visual Basic Editor, click the **Properties Window** button to show it.

4. To switch controls, click the **Controls** list arrow (at the top), and then select the one you want.

5. Click the **Alphabetic** or **Categorized** tab to display the control properties so you can find the ones you want.

6. Click the property box for the property you want to modify, and then do one of the following.

   - Type the value or information you want to use.

   - If the property box contains a list arrow, click the arrow and then click a value in the list.

   - If a property box contains a dialog button (...), click it to open a dialog box to select options or insert an object, such as a picture.

7. When you're done, click the **Close** button on the Properties window.

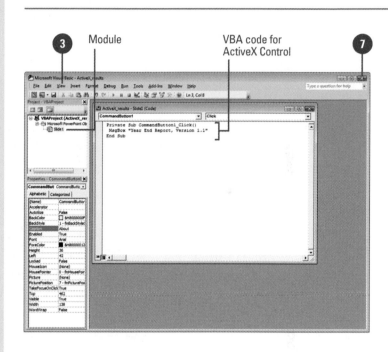

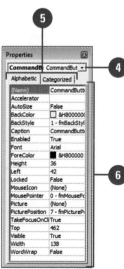

Playing a Movie Using an ActiveX Control

Although you cannot insert a Director or Flash movie into a PowerPoint 2007 presentation, you can play one in a presentation using an ActiveX control and the Shockwave or Flash players (**New!**). You can get these ActiveX controls at *http://activex.microsoft.com/activex/activex/*. To play the Director (.dcr) or Flash (.swf) movie, add the Director Shockwave or Shockwave Flash Object ActiveX control to the slide and create a link to the file. Before you can use the ActiveX controls, they need to be registered (available in More Controls) on the play back computer. If it's not registered, download and install the latest Shockwave or Flash player on your computer. If a movie doesn't play, check ActiveX security options in the Trust Center of PowerPoint Options.

Play a Director Movie

1. Save the Director movie to a Director Shockwave file (.dcr) using the Director software.

2. In Normal view, display the slide on which you want to play the Director movie.

3. Click the **Developer** tab.

4. Click the **More Controls** button.

5. Click **Shockwave ActiveX Control**.

6. Click **OK**.

7. Drag to draw the control.

8. Right-click the Shockwave ActiveX Object, and then click **Properties**.

9. Click the **Alphabetic** tab.

10. Click the **SCR** property, click in the column next to SRC, type full path and file name (c:\MyFolder\ Movie.dcr), or the URL to the Director file you want.

    TIMESAVER *If you place the .dcr file in the same folder as your presentation, you only need to type the file name.*

11. When you're done, click the **Close** button.

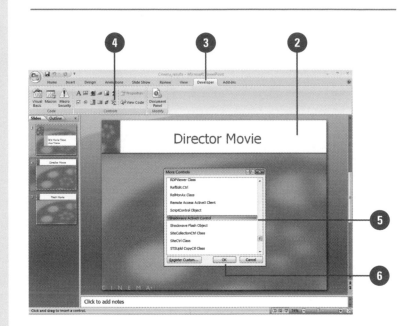

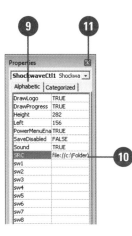

Play a Flash Movie

1. Save the Flash file to a Flash movie file (.swf) using the Flash software.

2. In Normal view, display the slide on which you want to play the Flash movie.

3. Click the **Developer** tab.

4. Click the **More Controls** button.

5. Click **Shockwave Flash Object**.

6. Click **OK**.

7. Drag to draw the control.

8. Right-click the Shockwave Flash Object, and then click **Properties**.

9. Click the **Alphabetic** tab.

10. Click the **Movie** property, click in the value column next to Movie, type full path and file name (c:\MyFolder\Movie.swf), or the URL to the Flash movie file you want.

    TIMESAVER *If you place the .dcr file in the same folder as your presentation, you only need to type the file name.*

11. To set specific options, choose any of the following:

    ◆ To play the file automatically when the slide appears, set the Playing property to True.

    ◆ To play the movie once, set the Loop property to False.

    ◆ To embed the Flash file, set the EmbedMovie property to True.

12. When you're done, click the **Close** button.

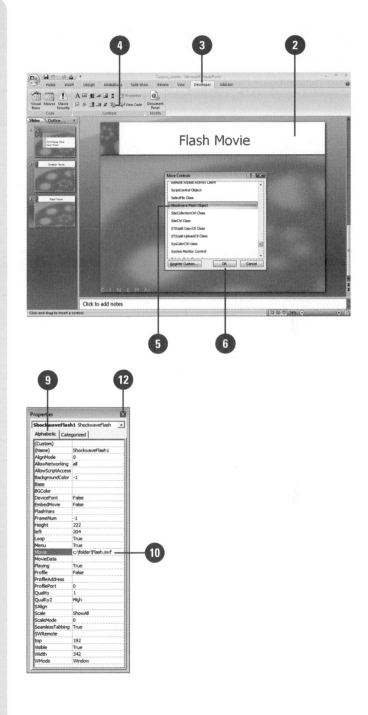

Changing the Document Information Panel

The Document Information Panel (**New!**) helps you manage and track document property information—also known as metadata—such as title, author, subject, keywords, category, and status. The Document Information Panel displays an XML-based mini-form using an InfoPath Form Template (.xsn) file developed in Microsoft InfoPath 2007. By using an XML InfoPath form, you can create your own form templates to edit the document property data and perform data validation.

Select a Document Information Panel Template

1. Click the **Developer** tab.

2. Click the **Document Panel** button.

3. Click **Browse**, locate and select the custom template you want, and then click **Open**.

   ◆ **URL.** Short for Uniform Resource Locator. The address of resources on the Web.

   http://www.perspection.com/index.htm

   ◆ **UNC.** Short for Uniform or Universal Naming Convention. A format for specifying the location of resources on a local-area network (LAN).

   \\server-name\shared-resource-pathname

   ◆ **URN.** Short for Uniform Resource Name.

4. Click the **Display by default** list arrow, and then select the default properties you want.

5. Select the **Always show Document Information Panel on document open and initial save** check box.

6. Click **OK**.

Workshop

Introduction

The Workshop is all about being creative and thinking outside the box. These workshops will help your right-brain soar, while making your left-brain happy; by explaining why things work the way they do. Exploring possibilities is great fun; however, always stay grounded with knowledge of how things work.

Getting and Using the Project Files

Each project in the Workshop includes a start file to help you get started with the project, and a final file to provide you with the results of the project so you can see how well you accomplished the project.

Before you can use the project files, you need to download them from the Web. You can access the files at *www.perspection.com* in the software downloads area. After you download the files from the Web, uncompress the files into a folder on your hard drive where you'll have easy access from your Microsoft Office program.

Project 1: Optimizing Presentations

Skills and Tools: PowerPoint options

PowerPoint comes with a varied set of features that allow you to create different kinds of presentations. However, not all features are created equal. Some features, such as hardware graphics acceleration, give you a little extra speed when you have the right hardware on your computer, but it also causes some movies not to display properly on the screen. Other features, like AutoFormat, are great when you want PowerPoint to automatically resize title or body text, but can be frustrating when you don't want text size to automatically change. If you take your presentations on the road, not having the right fonts installed on the presentation computer, missing linked movies and sounds, or showing a slow presentation can create big problems.

The Project

In this project, you'll learn how to set options to optimize PowerPoint and presentations for typical usage on any computer.

The Process

1 Open PowerPoint 2007, open **Optimize_start.potx**, and then save it as **Optimize_pres.pptx**.

> ➤ **Turn off or slow down hardware graphics acceleration.** To avoid movie display problems, either turn off or slow down hardware graphics acceleration.

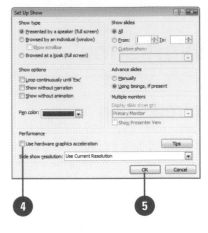

2 Click the **Slide Show** tab.

3 Click the **Set Up Slide Show** button.

4 Clear the **Use hardware graphics acceleration** check box.

5 Click **OK**.

6 To slow down hardware acceleration in Windows, right-click the desktop, click Properties, click the Settings tab, click Advanced, click the Troubleshoot tab, drag the Hardware acceleration slider one or two marks toward the None side.

> ➤ **Embed fonts.** To avoid fonts not showing up in a presentation on another computer, either use standard fonts, or embed the nonstandard fonts in the presentation. Embed only the fonts you need. When you embed a font in your presentation, the presentation may grow by as much as the size of the font file. Before you decide to embed, check the size of the font file. Some of the new Unicode fonts are enormous!

1 Click the **Office** button, and then click **PowerPoint Options**.

2 In the left pane, click **Save**.

3 Click the list arrow next to Preserve fidelity when sharing this presentation, and then select the presentation you want to embed fonts.

4 Select the **Embed fonts in the file** check box.

5 Click the option you want.

◆ **Embed only the characters used in the presentation (best for reducing file size)**.

◆ **Embed all characters (best for editing by other people)**.

6 Click **OK**.

> ➤ **Link sounds and movie.** To avoid a typical problem of linked sounds and movies not playing on a computer, place the sound and movie files in the same folder as your presentation file first, and then link the file to the presentation. PowerPoint always links movies to a presentation, and only links sounds when they are greater than a set size, which you can change in PowerPoint Options.

1 Click the **Office** button, and then click **PowerPoint Options**.

2 In the left pane, click **Advanced**.

W

3 Click the up and down arrows next to Link sounds with file size greater than *x*.

The larger the sound file size, the greater the overall presentation file size. If your presentation resides on the same computer, you can set a small size (the default is fine). However, if you plan to move the presentation to different computers, you should set a larger size. Check the sizes of your sound files and set the PowerPoint option accordingly.

4 Click **OK**.

> **Turn off AutoFormat.** To avoid PowerPoint automatically changing text size when you type or paste, turn off the three parts of AutoFormat: AutoFit title text in placeholder, and AutoFit body text to placeholder.

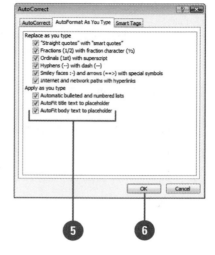

1 Click the **Office** button, and then click **PowerPoint Options**.

2 In the left pane, click **Proofing**.

3 Click **AutoCorrect Options**.

4 Click the **AutoFormat As You Type** tab.

5 Clear the **Automatic title text to placeholder** check box, and then clear the **Automatic body text to placeholder** check box.

6 Click **OK**.

7 Click **OK**.

> **Printing and showing a presentation.** To avoid problems printing a color presentation on a back and white printer, where the background, diagrams, or shapes might not look good, take the time to test your presentation in grayscale as you're working on it, instead of waiting until the end.

1 Click the **View** tab.

◆ Or, if in Print Preview, click the **Options** button, and then point to **Color/Grayscale**.

2 Click the **Pure Black and White** or **Grayscale** button.

3 On the Black and White or Grayscale tab, click the button with the specific color method you want to use.

4 When you're done, click the **Back To Color View** button.

> To avoid large presentation file sizes and increase performance, it's a good idea to compress and reduce image sizes in a presentation. In most cases, images don't need to be much larger than 1024 × 768 pixels. If your images are larger than this, your PowerPoint files are probably bigger than they need to be. It's actually alright to copy and paste images from one slide to another within PowerPoint. PowerPoint stores only one copy of the image no matter how many times you use it, so reusing an image can actually help keep your file sizes down.

① Click to select the pictures you want to compress.

② Click the **Format** tab under Picture Tools.

③ Click the **Compress Pictures** button.

④ Select the **Apply to selected pictures only** check box to apply compression setting to only the selected picture. Otherwise, clear the check box to compress all pictures in your presentation.

⑤ Click **Options**.

⑥ Select the **Automatically perform basic compression on save** check box, and then select the **Delete cropped areas of pictures** check box to reduce the file size.

⑦ Click the **Print**, **Screen**, or **E-mail** option to specify a target output.

⑧ Click **OK** to close the Compression Settings dialog box.

⑨ Click **OK**.

⑩ Click the **Save** button on the Quick Access Toolbar.

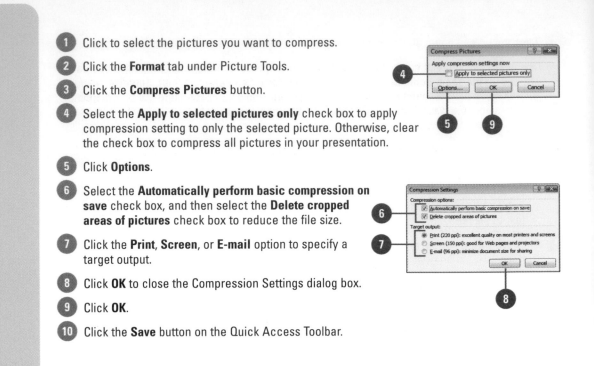

The Results

Finish: Compare your completed project file with the presentation **Optimize_results.pptx**.

Project 2: Creating Better Presentations

Skills and Tools: Designing a presentation

PowerPoint makes it easy to create consistent professional slides, but you need to come up with the content and determine the layout of the material. Here are 10 important techniques to help you create and deliver better presentations.

The Project

In this project, you'll learn how to creating a better presentation without spending more time and effort.

The Process

① **Be a presenter, not a reader.**

The audience has come to hear you give a presentation, share ideas, and communicate a message, not to look at you read information on a slide. PowerPoint can help you create slides, but it doesn't deliver the presentation. In many ways, you become a story teller. Create a presentation with a compelling introduction to catch the audiences attention, a powerful body of content to draw them in, and a unique ending the audience will remember.

2 Keep it simple.

Keep slides simple and to the point. If slides contain too much information, the audience can get confused and turn off. Remember less is more. Experts suggest no more than five words per line and no more than five lines per slide. Instead of putting more information on a slide, put it in speaker's notes for you to share. Don't crowd your slides, and only include elements that contribute to the points you want to make.

➤ In PowerPoint, add slides with specific layouts to avoid slide over crowding.

3 Stay visual.

A picture is worth a thousand words, or so they say. I think they are right. The world revolves around visuals, including billboards, traffic signs, and television to name a few. Insert an image, diagram, chart, or other visual to help get your point across to the audience. If you need to share statistics or other data, use a chart to convey the information. Visuals can promote an emotional response and interaction, instead of just information.

➤ In PowerPoint, use the Insert tab to add images, diagrams, charts, and other visuals.

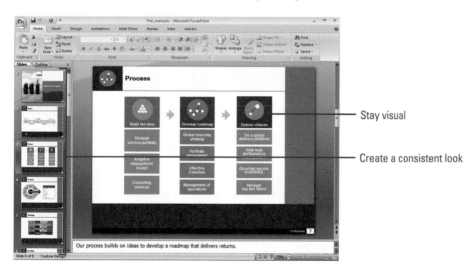

4 Insert other sounds and movies.

Use other sounds and movies for variety and visual appeal. Adding other media into a presentation re-enforces and supports your message. It provides validity to your message when someone else conveys the same thing.

➤ In PowerPoint, use the Insert tab to add sounds and movies.

5 Create a consistent look.

A colorful background and unique look can make your presentation stand out. However, it may also be a distraction to the audience from hearing your message. Know your audience and create a consistent look for your presentation that complements your message.

➤ In PowerPoint, use slide masters to create a consistent look.

6 **Add the unexpected.**

When you want to make a strong point during a presentation, a unique slide or a blank screen can help you get your point across to the audience. It's useful when you want your audience to remember a certain point or concept.

➤ In PowerPoint, use Slide Master view to create another slide master with a different look, or use slide controls in Slide Show view to display a white or black screen.

7 **Review, Review, Review.**

Review your slides for correctness, accuracy, and content. Use the spell checking and proofing tools to avoid spelling errors and accidental mistakes, which can make you look bad. Check the accuracy of your content to make sure it's correct. Make sure your slide content contributes to your main point. If some content doesn't add to your message, then take it out.

➤ In PowerPoint, use the Review tab to access spell checker, thesaurus, and other text-related proofing tools.

8 **Practice, Practice, Practice.**

Practice your presentation over and over again. The more comfortable you are delivering the material, the easier it will be to focus on the message instead of the mechanics of the presentation. Your PowerPoint presentation slides are here to add to your message. Let your message take center stage and use your PowerPoint slides, speaker's notes, and handouts to support your cause.

➤ In PowerPoint, use the Slide Show tab to practice your presentation in Slide Show view with slide timings.

9 **Keep time.**

I don't think anyone ever minded if a presentation ended early. However, going long can detract from your message. Determine how long you want your presentation to take and stay on time. The best way to stay on time is to rehearse with slide timings. Seems like everything takes longer than you think, so practicing your delivery from start to finish will keep you on time.

➤ In PowerPoint, use the Slide Show tab to practice your presentation in Slide Show view with rehearse slide timings.

10 **Distribute minimal handouts.**

In many situations, the audience may need to take notes during your presentation. I believe it's better to provide minimal handouts with only slide content to avoid distraction during the presentation. You want the audience to focus on you and your message instead of the handout. If you need to provide more detailed information for the audience, distribute it at the end of the presentation, where they can take it with them for later review.

➤ In PowerPoint, use the Handouts Master view to create supplemental handouts for the audience.

The Results

Finish: Open the example project file with the presentation **Pres_example.pptx**.

Project 3: Creating Custom Animations

Skills and Tools: Custom animations

You can use animation to introduce objects onto a slide one at a time or with special animation effects. For example, a bulleted list can appear one bulleted item at a time, or a picture or chart can fade gradually into the slide's foreground. You can design your own customized animations, including those with your own special effects and sound elements. You can also control the animation of each object, in what order each object appears, specify how long to wait between animation effects, and remove unwanted animations.

The Project

In this project, you'll learn how to create a custom animation with multiple effects, and control the order and appearance of each animation effect.

The Process

1. Open PowerPoint 2007, open **CustomAnimation_start.potx**, and then save it as **CustomAnimation_pres.pptx**.

2. In Normal view, go to slide 2, and then select the text object on the slide.

3. Click the **Animations** tab, and then click the **Custom Animation** button.

4. Click the **Add Effect** button, point to **Entrance**, and then click **More Effects**.

5. Scroll down, and then click the **Light Speed** effect to preview the effect.

6. Click **OK**.

7. Click the double-arrow below the animation in the Custom Animation task pane to expand and display the multiple animations for the text object, and then click the double-arrow again to collapse the multiple animations.

8. Click **Play**.

9. Click the **Add Effect** button, point to **Exit**, and then click **More Effects**.

   Note: The Add Effect button changes to Change after you create an animation effect.

10. Scroll down, and then click the **Faded Zoom** effect to preview the effect.

11. Click **OK**.

12. Click **Play**.

13. Click the second set of animations in the Custom Animation task pane.

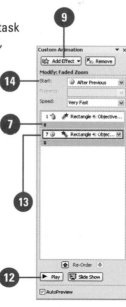

14 Click the **Start** list arrow, and then click **After Previous**.

15 Click the **Slide Show View** button, click through the animation effects for slide 2, and then press Esc to stop the show.

16 In Normal view, go to slide 10, and then select the QA image.

17 Click the **Add Effect** button, point to **Motion Paths**, and then click **More Motion Paths**.

18 Click the **Equal Triangle** effect to preview the effect.

19 Click **OK**.

20 Click the **Speed** list arrow, and then click **Slow**.

21 Click the **Path** list arrow, and then click **Reverse Path Direction**.

A green arrow on the path indicates the direction of the animation.

22 Click the **Path** list arrow, and then click **Edit Points**.

23 Drag the bottom middle size handle up about a 1/4 inch.

24 Click **Play**.

25 Click **Slide Show**, click through the animation effects for slide 10, and then press Esc to stop the show.

26 Click the **Save** button on the Quick Access Toolbar.

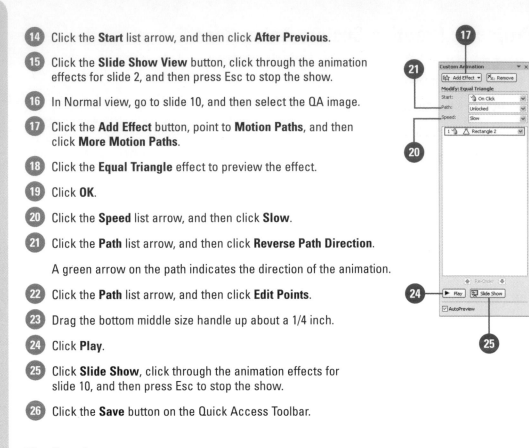

The Results

Finish: Compare your completed project file with the presentation **CustomAnimation_results.pptx**.

Project 4: Creating a Self Running Presentation with Narration

Skills and Tools: Record narration and create a self running presentation

Self-running slide shows are a great way to communicate information without needing someone to run the show. You might want to set up a presentation to run unattended in a kiosk at a trade show or place it on your company's Intranet to run at the user's convenience. The slides will advance automatically, or a user can advance the slides or activate hyperlinks. Instead of creating a silent presentation, you can record a narration to convey your message.

The Project

In this project, you'll learn how to add sound narration to a presentation, and make the presentation self running.

The Process

1 Open PowerPoint 2007, open **SelfRun_start.potx**, and then save it as **SelfRun_pres.pptx**.

➤ Add sound narration.

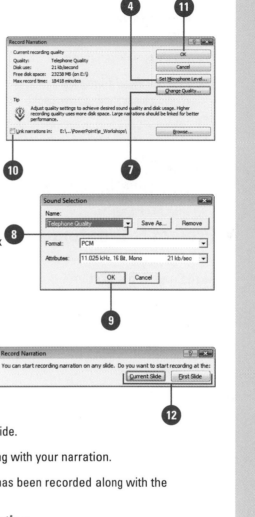

2 Click the **Slide Show** tab.

3 Click the **Record Narration** button.

4 Click **Set Microphone Level**.

5 Set the microphone level you want.

6 Click **OK**.

7 Click **Change Quality**.

8 Click the **Name** list arrow, and then click the recording quality you want.

9 Click **OK**.

10 If necessary, select the **Link narrations in** check box to insert the narration as a linked object.

11 Click **OK**.

12 If necessary, click **Current Slide** or **First Slide**.

As you record narration, you can pause and resume it at any time. To pause narration, right-click on the screen, and then click Pause Narration. To resume it, right-click on the screen, and then click Resume Narration.

13 Speak clearly into the microphone attached to your computer and record your narration for each slide.

14 Click **Save** when prompted to save slide timings along with your narration.

15 Rerun the slide show and verify that your narration has been recorded along with the automatic timings.

➤ Create and start a self running presentation.

1 Click the **Slide Show** tab.

2 Click the **Set Up Show** button.

3 Click the **Browsed at a kiosk (full screen)** option.

The *Loop continuously until 'Esc'* option is selected and grayed out.

4 Select the **Using timings, if present** option, where you can advance the slides automatically.

5 To show a presentation with narration on a computer without sound hardware installed, select the **Show without narration** check box to avoid problems running the presentation.

6 Select additional show options check boxes as appropriate.

7 Click the **Slide show resolution** list arrow, and then select the display resolution you want, such as 640x480, 1024x768, or User Current Resolution (**New!**).

8 Click **OK**.

9 Click the **From Beginning** button to start the self running slide show. Press Esc to stop it.

10 Click the **Save** button on the Quick Access Toolbar.

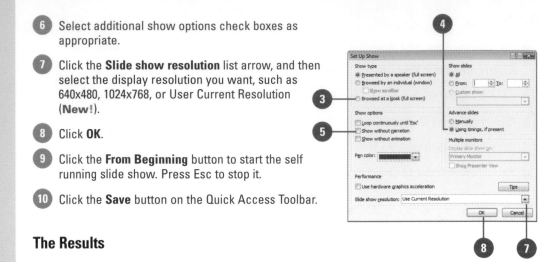

The Results

Finish: Compare your completed project file with the presentation **SelfRun_results.pptx**.

Project 5: Creating a VBA Form in a Presentation

Skills and Tools: ActiveX controls and Visual Basic for Applications (VBA) form

An ActiveX control is a software component that adds functionality to an existing program. An ActiveX control supports a customizable, programmatic interface using VBA, which you can use to create your own functionality, such as a form. Excel includes several pre-built ActiveX controls—including a label, text box, command button, and check box—to help you create a user interface.

The Project

In this project, you'll learn how to create a form using VBA that allows users to apply a template to the active presentation. You'll also learn how to insert a picture from a selected folder, and show the active presentation in Slide Show view.

The Process

1 Open PowerPoint 2007, open **VBA_Form_start.potm**, and then save it as **VBA_Form_pres.pptm** (macro-enabled presentation).

> ➤ **Create a form.**

2 Click the **Developer** tab.

3 Click the **Visual Basic** button.

4 Click the **Insert** menu, and then click **UserForm**.

A new form, UserForm1, opens and the Toolbox appears, displaying controls.

5 Click the **Label** button in the Toolbox.

Label

Combo Box

6 Position the mouse pointer in the upper-left corner of the form, and then click the mouse button.

A label appears selected on the form with the default caption, Label1.

7 Click the **ComboBox** button in the Toolbox.

8 Position the mouse pointer below the Label1 control, and then click the mouse button.

The ComboBox button appears selected on the form.

9 Repeat steps 5 through 8 to add Label2 control, and second ComboBox control to the form, and then repeat steps 5 through 6 to add Label3 control to the form.

10 Click the **CommandButton** button in the Toolbox.

11 Position the mouse pointer below the second ComboBox, and then click the mouse.

The CommandButton1 button appears selected on the form.

12 Repeat steps 10 through 11 to add CommandButton2 and CommandButton3 to the form.

13 Resize the form and any of the controls to match the illustration to the right.

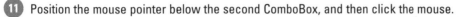

➤ Set control properties.

1 Click the Label1 control on the form.

2 Click the **View** menu, and then click **Properties Window**, if necessary, to display the Properties window.

3 In the Properties window, click **Caption** on the Alphabetic tab.

4 Double-click the Label1 caption, type **Select a template**, and then press Enter.

5 Change the caption of Label2 to **Select a picture**, change the caption of Label3 to **Select a folder**, change the caption of CommandButton1 to **Apply**, change the caption of CommandButton2 to **Show**, and change the caption of CommandButton3 to **Browse**.

6 Resize the width of the two ComboBoxes to stretch across the form. The height remains the same.

➤ Add VBA functionality to the form.

1 Click the **Insert UserForm** button arrow on the Standard toolbar, and then click **Module**.

A new module, Module1, opens.

2 Type the VBA code that appears in the following illustration:

```
VBA_Form_results - Module1 (Code)

(General)                                           createpresentationcompany

' A comment begins with an apostrophe (') at the beginning and appears in green.
'
' Create Presentation Procedure
'
' Creates a dialog box that allows you to apply a template to the active presentation
' and insert a picture from a selected folder, and then show the presentation in
' Slide Show view.

Sub createpresentationcompany()
    UserForm1.UserForm_Initialize
    UserForm1.Show
End Sub
```

3 Select **UserForm1** in the Project Window, and then click the **View Code** button.

4 Type the initialize form procedure VBA code that appears in the following illustration:

```
VBA_Form_results - UserForm1 (Code)

UserForm                                            Initialize

Sub UserForm_Initialize()
' Purpose: Initialize the drop down list
    ComboBox1.Clear
    ComboBox2.Clear
    ComboBox1.AddItem "ROI Pres"
    ComboBox2.AddItem "ROI Logo"
        ' You can add more items to the list
End Sub
```

5 Click the **Object box** arrow at the top of the Code Window, and then click **CommandButton1**.

6 In the Procedure box, type the VBA code that appears in the following illustration:

```
VBA_Form_results - UserForm1 (Code)

CommandButton1                                      Click

Private Sub CommandButton1_Click()
' Purpose: Applies a template and inserts a picture on slide 1
    TemplateName = ComboBox1.Text & ".potx"
    Application.ActivePresentation.ApplyTemplate MyPath & TemplateName
    Set PictureSlide = Application.ActivePresentation.Slides(1)
    With PictureSlide
        .Shapes.AddPicture MyPath & ComboBox2.Text & ".png", True, True, 47
        ' .Shapes.AddPicture(FileName, LinkToFile, SaveWithDocument, Le
    End With
End Sub
```

Repeat steps 5 through 6 to add VBA code for CommandButton2 and CommandButton3 to the form that appears in the following illustration:

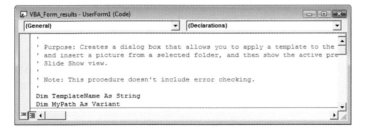

```
VBA_Form_results - UserForm1 (Code)
CommandButton2                          Click

    Private Sub CommandButton2_Click()
    ' Purpose: Shows the active presentation in slide show
        ActivePresentation.SlideShowSettings.Run
        Unload UserForm1
    End Sub
```

```
VBA_Form_results - UserForm1 (Code)
CommandButton3                          Click

    Private Sub CommandButton3_Click()
    ' Purpose: Select the folder location with the template and picture files
        Dim dlgFolder As FileDialog
        Set dlgFolder = Application.FileDialog( _
            Type:=msoFileDialogFolderPicker)
        With dlgFolder
            .Show
                For Each MyPath In .SelectedItems
                ' MsgBox "Selected item's path: " & MyPath
                ' Take off the apostrophe off above statement to display
                ' current path
                Next
        End With
    End Sub
```

8 Click the **Object box** arrow at the top of the Code Window, and then click **(General)**.

9 Type **Dim TemplateName As String**, press Enter, type **Dim MyPath As Variant**, and then press Enter.

Compare your screen to the following illustration:

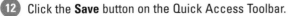

```
VBA_Form_results - UserForm1 (Code)
(General)                               (Declarations)

    '
    ' Purpose: Creates a dialog box that allows you to apply a template to the
    ' and insert a picture from a selected folder, and then show the active pre
    ' Slide Show view.
    '
    ' Note: This procedure doesn't include error checking.
    '
    Dim TemplateName As String
    Dim MyPath As Variant
```

10 Click the **Save** button on the Standard toolbar.

11 Click the **Close** button on the Visual Basic Editor window to return to PowerPoint.

12 Click the **Save** button on the Quick Access Toolbar.

➤ **Add a button on the Quick Access Toolbar to run the form.**

1 Click the the **Customize Quick Access Toolbar** list arrow, and then click **Customize Quick Access Toolbar**.

2 Click the **Choose command from** list arrow, and then click **Macros**.

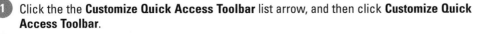

3 Click the **Customize Quick Access Toolbar** list arrow, and then click **For all documents (default)**.

4 Click the VBA form macro (left column).

5 Click **Add**.

6 Click the **Move Up** and **Move Down** arrow buttons to arrange the commands in the order you want them to appear.

7 Click **Modify**.

8 In the Display name box, type **CompanyPres**.

9 Click an icon from the symbol list.

10 Click **OK**.

11 Click **OK**.

12 Click the **Save** button on the Quick Access Toolbar.

13 Click the **CompanyPres** button on the Quick Access Toolbar, and then test out the form.

14 When you're done, click the **Close** button on the form.

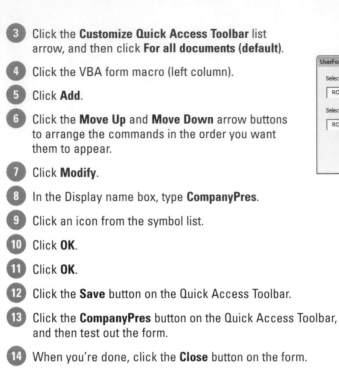

Completed form

The Results

Finish: Compare your completed project file with the presentation **VBA_Form_results.pptx**.

Want More Projects

You can access and download more workshop projects and related files at *www.perspection.com* in the software downloads area. After you download the files from the Web, uncompress the files into a folder on your hard drive where you'll have easy access from your Microsoft Office program.

Get Everything on CD

Instead of downloading everything from the Web, which can take a while depending on your Internet connection speed, you can get all the files used in this book and much more on the Microsoft Office 2007 On Demand CD. The CD contains task and workshop files, tips and tricks, keyboard shortcuts, transition helpers from 2003 to 2007, and other goodies from the author.

To get the Microsoft Office 2007 On Demand CD, go to *www.perspection.com*.

New! Features

n

Microsoft Office PowerPoint 2007

Microsoft Office PowerPoint 2007 is a presentation graphics program that helps you create and deliver slide shows either in person or online. With enhancements to the user interface and the addition of SmartArt graphics and Quick Styles for text, shapes, tables, and pictures, you can create high-impact presentations more easily in PowerPoint 2007.

Only New Features

If you're already familiar with PowerPoint 2003, you can access and download all the tasks in this book with Microsoft Office PowerPoint 2007 New Features to help make your transition to the new version simple and smooth. The PowerPoint 2007 New Features as well as other 2003 to 2007 transition helpers are available on the Web at *www.perspection.com.*

What's New

If you're searching for what's new in PowerPoint 2007, just look for the icon: New!. The new icon appears in the table of contents and throughout this book so you can quickly and easily identify a new or improved feature in PowerPoint 2007. The following is a brief description of each new feature and it's location in this book.

Office 2007

◆ **Ribbon (p. 4)**   The Ribbon is a new look for PowerPoint 2007. It replaces menus, toolbars, and most of the task panes found in PowerPoint 2003. The Ribbon is comprised of tabs with buttons and options that are organized by task.

◆ **Live Preview (p. 4, 118-119)**   A gallery displays graphical options on the Ribbon. When you point to a gallery on the Ribbon, Office programs display a live preview of the option change so that you can see exactly what your change will look like before committing to it.

◆ **Quick Access Toolbar and Mini-Toolbar (p. 6, 59, 395, 415)**   PowerPoint includes its most common commands, such as Save and Undo, on the Quick Access Toolbar. The Mini-Toolbar appears above selected text and provides quick access to formatting tools.

- **Dialog Box Launcher (p. 8, 106)**   Dialog Box Launchers are small icons that appear at the bottom corner of some groups on the Ribbon. When you point to a Dialog Box Launcher, a ScreenTip with a thumbnail of the dialog box appears to show you which dialog box opens when you click the Dialog Box Launcher.

- **Status bar (p. 9)**   The Status bar displays the on/off status of features, such as signatures and spelling, and determines what information appears on the bar.

- **Spotlight (p. 12)**   The Spotlight section under the Featured category in the New Presentation dialog box, highlights new PowerPoint content from Microsoft Office Online.

- **Office button and menu (p. 13)**   The Office button and menu replaces the File menu with a revised list of commands and options, such as the Recent Documents list.

- **Compatibility mode (p. 13, 22-23)**   When you open a presentation from PowerPoint 97-2003, PowerPoint 2007 goes into compatibility mode where it disables new features that cannot be displayed or converted well by previous versions.

- **Save in XML-based file format (p. 22-23, 265)**   PowerPoint 2007 saves files in an XML (Extensible Markup Language) based file format (.pptx). The XML-based format significantly reduces file sizes, provides enhanced file recovery, and allows for increased compatibility, sharing, reuse, and transportability.

- **Diagnose problems (p. 28)**   The Diagnose command improves performance by diagnosing and repairing problems, such as missing files from setup, corrupted file by malicious viruses, and registry settings.

- **SmartArt graphics (p. 190-202, 308)**   SmartArt graphics allow you to create diagrams that convey processes or relationships. PowerPoint provides a variety of built-in SmartArt graphic types, including organization charts, graphical lists, process, cycle, hierarchy, relationship, matrix, and pyramid.

- **Common spell checking and dictionary (p. 275-279)**   Microsoft Office 2007 programs share a common spell checker and dictionary, so you only need to make additions and changes once.

- **English Assistant (p. 282)**   The English Assistant is a Microsoft Office Online service that helps people for whom English is a second language write professional English text.

- **Document Information Panel (p. 286-287, 424)**   You can view or edit standard document properties or create advanced custom properties by using the Document Information Panel, which is an XML-based Microsoft InfoPath 2007 form hosted in PowerPoint.

- **Check compatibility (p. 288)**   The Compatibility Checker identifies the potential loss of functionality when you save a PowerPoint 2007 presentation in the PowerPoint 97-2003 Presentation file format.

- **Create a PDF or XPS (p. 291-292)**   You can now save a presentation as a PDF or XPS file, which is a fixed-layout format that retains the form you intended on a computer monitor or printer.

- **Document Inspector (p. 340-341)** The Document Inspector uses inspector modules to find and remove any hidden data and personal information specific to the modules that you might not want to share with others.

- **Information Right Management (p. 344-345)** If you want to view or change the permissions for a presentation, you can use the Change Permission button on the Message Bar or the IRM icon button on the Status bar.

- **Trust Center (p. 350-356)** The Trust Center is a place where you set security options and find the latest technology information as it relates to document privacy, safety, and security from Microsoft. The Trust Center allows you to set security and privacy settings, including Trusted Publishers, Trusted Locations, Add-ins, ActiveX Settings, Macro Settings, Message Bar, and Privacy Options.

- **Microsoft Office safe mode (p. 358-359)** Microsoft Office 2007 uses two types of safe modes—Automated and User-Initiated—when it encounters a program problem. Safe mode only loads minimal features to help start the Office program.

- **Mark a document as final (p. 360)** The Mark as Final command makes a PowerPoint 2007 presentation read-only and disables or turns off typing, editing commands, and proofing marks.

- **Microsoft Office Groove (p. 363-386)** With Office Groove 2007, you can bring a team, tools, and information together from any location to work on a project.

- **Microsoft Office Document Imaging (p. 396-387)** With Microsoft Office Document Imaging, you can now add annotations to a scanned document image, such as a fax.

PowerPoint 2007

- **Slide Layout gallery (p. 32)** PowerPoint provides a gallery of slide layouts to help you position and format slides in a consistent manner.

- **Indent markers (p. 50)** You can now set different indent markers for each paragraph in an object.

- **Align text (p. 54)** You can now align text vertically to the top, middle, or bottom within a text object.

- **Kerning (p. 56)** Kerning is the amount of space between each individual character that you type. You can adjust the character spacing in PowerPoint the same way you do in word processing and desktop publishing programs.

- **Stack letters (p. 57)** You can now stack letters on top of one another.

- **Additional formatting options (p. 58)** PowerPoint includes new formatting options, such as strikethrough or double strike-through, all caps or small caps, and double or color underline.

- **Clear all formatting (p. 58)** If you no longer like your text formatting, you can quickly remove it.

- ◆ **Create columns (p. 68)**   You can now create text columns within a text box.

- ◆ **Reuse Slides task pane (p. 72, 388-389)**   With the Reuse Slides task pane, you can view a miniature of each slide in a presentation and then insert only the ones you select. If you only want to reuse the theme from another presentation, the Reuse Slides task pane can do that too. If you have access to an Office SharePoint Server site, you can publish slides on a team site for other project members to reuse.

- ◆ **Slide master layouts (p. 80)**   Each slide master includes a standard set of slide layouts. However, you can modify a slide master layout using different types of placeholders, such as Text, Picture, Chart, Table, Diagram, Media, and Clip Art.

- ◆ **Themes (p. 89-99)**   A theme is a set of unified design elements that provides a consistent look for a presentation by using color themes, fonts, and effects, such as shadows, shading, and animations. You can use a standard theme or create one of your own.

- ◆ **Text and Shape Quick Styles (p. 110, 118-119, 128, 140, 176-180)**   You can quickly add different formatting combinations to text using WordArt Quick Styles or to a shape using Shape Quick Styles. You can also change individual styles by applying shadows, reflections, glow, soft edges, bevels, and 3-D rotations.

- ◆ **Add a gradient to a line (p. 126)**   You can now add a gradient fill to a line.

- ◆ **3-D Effects (p. 132-134)**   You can add the illusion of depth to your slides by adding a 3-D effect to a shape. Create a 3-D effect by using one of the preset 3-D styles, or you can use the 3-D format tools to customize your own 3-D style.

- ◆ **Selection pane (p. 142)**   With the Selection task pane, you can now select individual objects and change their order and visibility.

- ◆ **Apply theme to photo album (p. 162)**   You can now customize a photo album by applying themes.

- ◆ **Picture Quick Styles (p. 164)**   The Picture Quick Style gallery provides a variety of different formatting combinations.

- ◆ **Apply a shape to a picture (p. 165-166)**   You can now select a picture and apply one of PowerPoint's shapes to it.

- ◆ **Picture effects (p. 167)**   You can now change the look of a picture by applying effects, such as shadows, reflections, glow, soft edges, and 3-D rotations.

- ◆ **Best scaling for slide shows (p. 168)**   You can make sure your pictures keep the same relative proportions as the original and provide the best scaling size for a slide show on a specific monitor size.

- ◆ **Recolor Picture Quick Styles (p. 172-173)**   The Recolor Picture Quick Style gallery provides a variety of different formatting combinations.

- ◆ **Microsoft Excel used to create charts (p. 204)**   PowerPoint now uses Microsoft Excel to embed and display a chart instead of Microsoft Graph.

- ◆ **Added chart types (p. 214)** PowerPoint added more built-in chart layouts and styles to make charts more appealing and visually informative.

- ◆ **Chart template (p. 220)** You can now create a chart template (.crtx) to save a chart style for use in other presentations.

- ◆ **Large tables (p. 222)** You can now organizes information in a table up to a maximum of 75 rows by 75 columns.

- ◆ **Table Quick Styles and effects (p. 226-230)** The Table Quick Style gallery provides a variety of different formatting combinations. You can change the look of a table by applying effects, such as shadows, reflections, glow, soft edges, 3-D rotations, and transformations.

- ◆ **Wide screen slide sizes (p. 268)** You can now set the slide size to fit computer monitor with ratios of 16:9 (wide screen HDTV's), or 16:10 (wide screen laptops).

- ◆ **Transition Quick Styles (p. 300)** The Transition Quick Style gallery provides a variety of different transition effect combinations you can add between slides.

- ◆ **Add-ins and ActiveX controls (p. 402, 418, 421-422)** PowerPoint includes several pre-built ActiveX controls, including a label, text box, command button, image, scroll bar, check box, option button, combo box, list box, and toggle button that you can insert into your presentations to add functionality.

- ◆ **Macros (p. 410, 416-417)** Macros are created using Visual Basic for Applications (VBA) code instead of the Macro Recorder. If you add a macro to a presentation, you need to save it with a file name extension that ends with an "m", either PowerPoint Macro-Enabled Presentation (.pptm), PowerPoint Macro-Enabled Show (.ppsm), or PowerPoint Macro-Enabled Design Template (.potm).

What Happened To . . .

- ◆ **Allow Fast Saves** The Allow Fast Saves option is not available in PowerPoint 2007 to provide enhanced performance, security and recovery.

- ◆ **AutoContent Wizard** The AutoContent Wizard is not available in PowerPoint 2007. Instead, you can create a presentation using a template, which gives you a professional looking starting point where you can add your own content.

  ➤ Click the **Office** button, click **New**, click one of the templates installed on your computer or available on Microsoft Office Online, and then click **Create**.

- ◆ **Check presentation styles** The Check Style check box and Style Options button are not available in PowerPoint 2007. Instead many of the options are incorporated into the Proofing section of the PowerPoint Options dialog box, which the spelling checker uses to check a presentation.

  ➤ Click the **Office** button, click **PowerPoint Options**, and then click **Proofing**.

- ◆ **Comparing and merging presentations** The Compare and Merge Presentations feature is not available in PowerPoint 2007.

◆ **Detect and Repair**   The Detect and Repair command has been replaced by Microsoft Office Diagnostics, which provides additional detection and repair capabilities.

➤ Click the **Office** button, click **PowerPoint Options**, click **Resources**, and then click **Diagnose**.

◆ **File menu**   The File menu has been replaced by the Office button and menu with a revised list of commands and options.

◆ **Macro recorder**   The macro recorder is not available in PowerPoint 2007. Instead, you can use Visual Basic for Applications (VBA) to create and edit macros. If you created a macro in an earlier version of PowerPoint using the macro reader, you can use Visual Basic to edit it.

➤ Click the **View** or **Developer** tab, and then click the **Macro** button, type a name for the macro, click the template or presentation you want to store in the macro in, type a description, and then click **Create** to open Visual Basic.

◆ **NetMeeting**   NetMeeting is not available in PowerPoint 2007. Instead you can use Microsoft Office Live Meeting. Check out the Microsoft Web site for more details.

◆ **Presentation Broadcast**   Broadcast is not available in PowerPoint 2007. Instead you can use Microsoft Office Live Meeting. Check out the Microsoft Web site for more details.

◆ **Scanner or Camera option**   The From Scanner or Camera option for adding pictures to a presentation or photo album is not available in PowerPoint 2007. Instead, you can download the pictures from your camera or scanner, or use the Microsoft Office Document Imaging program that comes with Office 2007, and then insert or paste them into PowerPoint.

◆ **Send for Review**   The Send for Review command is not available in PowerPoint 2007. Instead, you can attach your presentation file to an e-mail message and send it to a reviewer. The reviewer can add comments and send the marked-up presentation back to you in an e-mail message.

If you use PowerPoint 2003 or earlier to send your presentation for review, reviewers who use PowerPoint 2007 can view and add comments, but you cannot merge their comments into your presentation.

◆ **Summary slide**   The summary slide is not available in PowerPoint 2007. Instead, you can create a summary slide by copying slide titles onto a slide.

◆ **Title master**   The title master is not available in PowerPoint 2007. Instead, PowerPoint 2007 uses layouts to define the same slide content.

➤ Click the **Home** tab, click the **Layout** button, and then click the **Title Slide layout** from the gallery.

◆ **Web Toolbar**   The Web toolbar is not available in PowerPoint 2007, Word 2007, or Excel 2007. However, you can still use some of the commands on the toolbar. You can add the Back and Forward buttons to the Quick Access Toolbar.

Microsoft Certified Applications Specialist

About the MCAS Program

The Microsoft Certified Applications Specialist (MCAS) certification is the globally recognized standard for validating expertise with the Microsoft Office suite of business productivity programs. Earning an MCAS certificate acknowledges you have the expertise to work with Microsoft Office programs. To earn the MCAS certification, you must pass a certification exam for the Microsoft Office desktop applications of Microsoft Office Word, Microsoft Office Excel, Microsoft Office PowerPoint, Microsoft Office Outlook, or Microsoft Office Access. (The availability of Microsoft Certified Applications Specialist certification exams varies by program, program version, and language. Visit *www.microsoft.com* and search on *Microsoft Certified Applications Specialist* for exam availability and more information about the program.) The Microsoft Certified Applications Specialist program is the only Microsoft-approved program in the world for certifying proficiency with Microsoft Office programs.

What Does This Logo Mean?

It means this book has been approved by the Microsoft Certified Applications Specialist program to be certified courseware for learning Microsoft Office PowerPoint 2007 and preparing for the certification exam. This book will prepare you for the Microsoft Certified Applications Specialist exam for Microsoft Office PowerPoint 2007. Each certification level has a set of objectives, which are organized into broader skill sets. Throughout this book, content that pertains to a Microsoft Certified Applications Specialist objective is identified with the following MCAS certification logo and objective number below the title of the topic:

Microsoft Certified Application Specialist	PP07S-1.1 PP07S-2.2

PowerPoint 2007 Objectives

Objective	Skill	Page
PP07S-1	**Creating and Formatting Presentations**	
PP07S-1.1	**Create new presentations**	
PP07S-1.1.1	Create presentations from blank presentations	11
PP07S-1.1.2	Create presentations from templates	12
PP07S-1.1.3	Create presentations from existing presentations	13
PP07S-1.1.4	Create presentations from Microsoft Office Word outlines	48-49
PP07S-1.2	**Customize slide masters**	
PP07S-1.2.1	Apply themes to slide masters	74-75, 88-89
PP07S-1.2.2	Format slide master backgrounds	92-93
	Add background graphics to slide masters	99, 160
	Apply Quick Styles to backgrounds	99-101
	Change font theme	94
PP07S-1.3	**Add elements to slide masters**	78, 80, 84
	Add slide numbers, add footers and headers	85-87
	Add placeholders and graphic elements	82-84
	Add date and time, and set to update automatically	86-88
PP07S-1.4	**Create and change presentation elements**	
PP07S-1.4.1	Change presentation orientation	268-269
PP07S-1.4.2	Add, change and remove transitions between slides; needs to be applied to all slides at the presentation level	300-301
PP07S-1.4.3	Set slide size	268-269
PP07S-1.5	**Arrange slides**	
	Insert or delete slides	32-33
	Use the slide sorter to organize slides	70-71
	Arrange slides: cut, paste, and drag in Normal view	70
PP07S-2	**Creating and Formatting Slide Content**	
PP07S-2.1	**Insert and format text boxes**	
PP7S-2.1.1	Insert and remove text boxes	66-67
PP07S-2.1.2	Size text boxes	34-35, 44-45
PP07S-2.1.3	Format text boxes	58, 64, 118-119
	Select fill, border, and effects	120-129
PP07S-2.1.4	Select text orientation, direction, and alignment	54-55, 57

PowerPoint 2007 Objectives *(continued)*

Objective	Skill	Page
PP07S-2.1.5	Set margins	66-67
PP07S-2.1.6	Create columns in text boxes	68
PP07S-2.2	**Manipulate text**	
PP07S-2.2.1	Cut, copy and paste text	40-41
	Drag and drop, copy, cut and paste text	40-41
	Cut and paste special	232-233
PP07S-2.2.2	Apply Quick Styles from the Style Gallery	118-119, 178
PP07S-2.2.3	Format font attributes	58-59
	Change text size, font, and color	58-59
PP07S-2.2.4	Use the Format Painter to format text	64, 80
PP07S-2.2.5	Create and format bulleted and numbered lists	38-39
	Add bullets and numbered lists	5, 50
	Format bullets and numbered lists	54-55, 6- 61
	Promote and demote bullets and numbering	50-51
PP07S-2.2.6	Format paragraphs	58-59
	Align text	54-55, 58-59
	Change line spacing and indentation	50-51, 54-55
PP07S-2.2.7	Insert and modify WordArt	180-181
	Create and format WordArt	176-179
	Apply Quick Styles to WordArt	178-179
	Change WordArt shape	181
PP07S-2.3	**Add and link existing content to presentations**	
PP07S-2.3.1	Reuse slides from an existing presentation	72, 389
	Apply current slide masters to content	78-83
PP07S-2.3.2	Copy elements from one slide to another	116-117
	Copy elements within presentations	116-117
	Copy elements between presentations	116-117, 232-233
PP07S-2.3.3	Insert hyperlinks	246, 248, 250
PP07S-2.3.4	Insert media clips	152
	Insert movies and sounds	182-183
PP07S-2.4	**Apply, customize, modify, and remove animations**	
PP07S-2.4.1	Apply built-in animations	302-303

PowerPoint 2007 Objectives *(continued)*

Objective	Skill	Page
PP07S-2.4.2	Modify animations	304-307
	Change and Remove animations	307
PP07S-2.4.3	Create custom animations	304-308
	Insert entrance, emphasis, and exit effects	306-307
	Change start settings and effect speeds	306-307
PP07S-3	**Working With Visual Content**	
PP07S-3.1	**Create SmartArt diagrams**	
PP07S-3.1.1	Create a SmartArt diagram (Relationship, Workflow, Cycle, and Hierarchy)	190-191, 200-201
PP07S-3.1.2	Create SmartArt diagrams from bullet points	190-191
PP07S-3.2	**Modify SmartArt diagrams**	
PP07S-3.2.1	Add text to SmartArt diagrams	192-193
PP07S-3.2.2	Change theme colors	196-199
PP07S-3.2.3	Add effects by using Quick Styles	196-199
PP07S-3.2.4	Change the layout of diagrams	196-197
PP07S-3.2.5	Change the orientation of charts	195-196
PP07S-3.2.6	Add or remove shapes within SmartArt	194
PP07S-3.2.7	Change diagram types	196-197
PP07S-3.3	**Insert illustrations and shapes**	
PP07S-3.3.1	Insert pictures from file	160
PP07S-3.3.2	Insert shapes	106-108
	Insert line, polygon, and arrow	110-115
PP07S-3.3.3	Insert clip art	152, 156
PP07S-3.3.4	Add text to shapes	109
PP07S-3.4	**Modify illustrations**	
PP07S-3.4.1	Apply Quick Styles to shapes and pictures	164, 166-167
	Apply fill to shapes	120-129
	Remove borders from shapes	166
PP07S-3.4.2	Add, change and remove illustration effects	172
	Remove background (transparencies)	172-173
	Modify brightness and contrast	171

PowerPoint 2007 Objectives *(continued)*

Objective	Skill	Page
PP07S-3.5	**Arrange illustrations and other content**	
PP07S-3.5.1	Size, scale, and rotate illustrations and other content	144, 168-169
	Adjust size, scale, and rotation	168-169, 174
PP07S-3.5.2	Order illustrations and other content	143
	Bring to front and send to back	143
PP07S-3.5.3	Group and align illustrations and other content	138-139, 146
PP07S-3.5.4	Use gridlines and guides to arrange content	136-137
PP07S-3.6	**Insert and modify charts**	
PP07S-3.6.1	Insert charts	204
PP07S-3.6.2	Change chart types	214, 216
PP07S-3.6.3	Format fill and other effects	216
PP07S-3.6.4	Add chart elements: legend and title	218
PP07S-3.7	**Insert and modify tables**	
PP07S-3.7.1	Insert tables in a slide	222
PP07S-3.7.2	Apply Quick Styles to tables	228
PP07S-3.7.3	Change alignment and orientation of table text	224-225
PP07S-3.7.4	Add images to tables	226
PP07S-4	**Collaborating on and Delivering Presentations**	
PP07S-4.1	**Review presentations**	
PP07S-4.1.1	Insert, delete and modify comments	336, 338, 339
PP07S-4.1.2	Show and hide markup	336
PP07S-4.2	**Protect presentations**	
PP07S-4.2.1	Add digital signatures to a presentations.	346-347, 414
	Add lines for a digital signatures	346-347
	Set passwords on presentations	342-343
PP07S-4.3	**Secure and Share Presentations**	
PP07S-4.3.1	Identify presentation features not supported by previous versions	288
PP07S-4.3.2	Remove inappropriate information using Document Inspector	286-287, 340-341
PP07S-4.3.3	Restrict permissions to a document using Information rights management (IRM)	344-345
PP07S-4.3.4	Mark presentations as final	360

C

Objective	Skill	Page
PP07S-4.3.5	Compress images	170
PP07S-4.3.6	Save presentations as appropriate file types	22-25
	Save files in .pps format so that they open as a slide show	320
	Save presentations for Web viewing (.html format)	254-255
	Save slides as images (.jpg, .gif, tif, etc.)	257, 289
PP07S-4.4	**Prepare printed materials**	
PP07S-4.4.1	Customize handout masters	82-83
	Add headers, footers, and page numbers	85-87
	Apply Quick Styles to handout masters	82-83
PP07S-4.4.2	Print a presentation in various formats	296-297
	Print slides, handouts, outlines, notes	296-298
PP07S-4.5	**Prepare for and rehearse presentation delivery**	
PP07S-4.5.1	Show only specific slides in presentations	314
	Hide specific slides	315
	Create custom slide shows	316
PP07S-4.5.2	Rehearse and time the delivery of a presentation	310-313
PP07S-4.5.3	Use presentation tools	324-327
	Use a pen and highlighter, add annotations, etc	326-327
	Navigate to specific slides	324-325
PP07S-4.5.4	Package presentations for a CD	330-331
PP07S-4.5.5	Set slide show options	314
	Set presentations to loop continuously	318
	Show presentation with or without narration	312-315
	Select presentation resolution	314-315

C

Preparing for a MCAS Exam

Every Microsoft Certified Applications Specialist certification exam is developed from a list of objectives based on how Microsoft Office programs are actually used in the workplace. The list of objectives determine the scope of each exam, so they provide you with the information you need to prepare for MCAS certification. Microsoft Certified Applications Specialist Approved Courseware, including the On Demand series, is reviewed and approved on the basis of its coverage of the objectives. To prepare for the certification exam, you should review and perform each task identified with a MCAS objective to confirm that you can meet the requirements for the exam.

Taking a MCAS Exam

The Microsoft Certified Applications Specialist certification exams are not written exams. Instead, the exams are performance-based examinations that allow you to interact with a "live" Office program as you complete a series of objective-based tasks. All the standard ribbons, tabs, toolbars, and keyboard shortcuts are available during the exam. Microsoft Certified Applications Specialist exams for Office 2007 programs consist of 25 to 35 questions, each of which requires you to complete one or more tasks using the Office program for which you are seeking certification. A typical exam takes from 45 to 60 minutes. Passing percentages range from 70 to 80 percent correct.

The Exam Experience

After you fill out a series of information screens, the testing software starts the exam and the Office program. The test questions appear in the exam dialog box in the lower right corner of the screen.

◆ The timer starts when the first question appears and displays the remaining exam time at the top of the exam dialog box. If the timer and the counter are distracting, you can click the timer to remove the display.

◆ The counter at the top of the exam dialog box tracks how many questions you have completed and how many remain.

◆ If you think you have made a mistake, you can click the Reset button to restart the question. The Reset button does not restart the entire exam or extend the exam time limit.

◆ When you complete a question, click the Next button to move to the next question. It is not possible to move back to a previous question on the exam.

◆ If the exam dialog box gets in your way, you can click the Minimize button in the upper right corner of the exam dialog box to hide it, or you can drag the title bar to another part of the screen to move it.

Tips for Taking an Exam

◆ Carefully read and follow all instructions provided in each question.

◆ Make sure all steps in a task are completed before proceeding to the next exam question.

◆ Enter requested information as it appears in the instructions without formatting unless you are explicitly requested otherwise.

◆ Close all dialog boxes before proceeding to the next exam question unless you are specifically instructed otherwise.

◆ Do not leave tables, boxes, or cells "active" unless instructed otherwise.

◆ Do not cut and paste information from the exam interface into the program.

◆ When you print a document from an Office program during the exam, nothing actually gets printed.

◆ Errant keystrokes or mouse clicks do not count against your score as long as you achieve the correct end result. You are scored based on the end result, not the method you use to achieve it. However, if a specific method is explicitly requested, you need to use it to get credit for the results.

◆ The overall exam is timed, so taking too long on individual questions may leave you without enough time to complete the entire exam.

◆ If you experience computer problems during the exam, immediately notify a testing center administrator to restart your exam where you were interrupted.

Exam Results

At the end of the exam, a score report appears indicating whether you passed or failed the exam. An official certificate is mailed to successful candidates in approximately two to three weeks.

Getting More Information

To learn more about the Microsoft Certified Applications Specialist program, read a list of frequently asked questions, and locate the nearest testing center, visit:

www.microsoft.com

Index

A

abbreviations in AutoCorrect, 42
Account Configuration Wizard, 364
action buttons. *See* Web presentations
Action Settings dialog box, 246-247
Activation Wizard, 2
active application add-ins, 402
ActiveX controls, 265. *See also* Trust Center
    Director movies, playing, 422
    Flash movies, playing, 422-423
    harmful attacks and, 348-349
    inserting, 418
    for movies, 182, 422-423
    properties, setting, 421
    registering, 422
    security
        alerts, 419
        options, setting, 353
    toolbox buttons for, 420
adding/removing. *See also* Clip Organizer;
    deleting
    borders on pictures, 166
    bullets from text, 60
    clips, 153
    custom themes from gallery menu, 97
    gradient fills, 127
    guides, 137
    hidden information, 340-341
    legend data series from charts, 209
    numbering from text, 60
    passwords, 342-343
    personal information, 340-341
    Quick Access Toolbar, items from, 7, 395
    smart tags, 47
    status bar, items on, 9
    table, lines from, 227
    WordArt text, 176

add-ins, 25. *See also* COM add-ins
    list of, 403
    loading/unloading, 404-405
    managing, 403
    security
        alerts, 405
        options, 352
    viewing, 402-403
adjustment handles on shapes, 106
Adobe
    Acrobat Reader, 291
    Director movies, 182, 422
    Flash movies, 422
    Photoshop, bitmap graphics from, 152
    Type Manager fonts, kerning with, 56
    Type 1 PostScript font, 319
advanced options, setting, 393
adware, 348
AIFF format, 182, 186
alerts. *See* Groove; security
aligning. *See also* aligning text
    other objects, aligning objects with, 139
    shapes, 138-139
    SmartArt graphic, shapes in, 195
    texture fills, 125
aligning text, 54-55
    horizontal text alignment, 55
    in organization chart, 240
    in tables, 225
    vertical text alignment, 55
Align or Distribute command, 138-139
Align Selected Objects command, 138
all caps formatting, 58, 59
angles
    rotating shapes to, 144
    shadows, setting for, 130, 131
    WordArt text angle, adjusting, 176-177

animation
bulleted lists, animating, 304
in charts, 218, 305
customized animation, applying, 303
deleting animation, 307
dimming text after, 305
multiple animations, coordinating, 306-307
order, modifying, 306
previewing, 302
SmartArt graphic, animating, 308-309
sound, adding, 303
specialized animations, 304-305
standard animation, adding, 302
time between animations, setting, 307
Web page, showing slide animation in, 258
in Web presentations, 260
Animations tab, Slide Sorter view, 17
annotations, 396-397. *See also* slide shows
antivirus software, 349
appearance of programs, changing, 393
Apple. *See also* TrueType fonts
QuickTime movies, 182
arguments in VBA, 406
arrows. *See also* lines or arrows
Counterbalance Arrows, 192
up/down arrows, 8
ASF format, 182, 186
attachments
Groove meeting documents, 375
harmful attacks and, 349
photo album attachments, 163
audio file formats, 186
AU format, 182, 186
AutoCorrect, 30
for foreign languages, 284
for numbering or fractions, 62-63
spell-checking, 276
for text, 42-43
AutoFit Options, 44
for specific objects, 45
turning off, 44
AutoFormat
changing options, 63
for organization chart layout, 240
typing, text while, 62-63
Automated Safe mode, 358-359

Automatic Updates, 349
AutoNumbering lists, 63
AutoRecover feature, 27
AutoShapes
Clip Gallery, inserting from, 148-149
grouping/ungrouping in, 146
similar AutoShapes, locating, 149
averages, working with, 218
AVI format, 182, 186
avoiding attacks, 348-349
axis. *See* charts

B

backgrounds. *See also* background styles; color themes
adding graphics, 84
chart backgrounds, changing, 219
hiding on slides, 84
resetting, 99
shapes, fill for, 120
tables, adding to, 229
background styles
adding, 99
gradients, creating, 101
modifying, 100-101
pictures for, 100
solid fill background style, 101
textures for, 100
backwards compatibility. *See* OLE (object linking and embedding); compatibility mode
Ballpoint Pen option for slide show, 326
Banded Row/Banded Column options, 226
banner slide size
bevel effect, 128
adding, 129
for SmartArt graphics, 198-199
tables, applying cell bevel to, 230
3D effects, 133
to WordArt text, 180
bitmaps, 152
device independent bitmaps, 161
fonts, bitmapped, 319
for Groove pictures, 380
modifying images, 173
black and white
converting pictures to, 172

print preview, 294-295
black-out screens for slide shows, 329
blank presentations, 10, 11
blur, shadows with, 130, 131
boldfacing hyperlinks, 253
borders
    pictures, applying to, 166
    shapes, color outlines for, 121
    for SmartArt graphics, 198
    tables, applying to, 229
    to WordArt text, 179
brightness, 171
    in photo album pictures, 163
    Picture Manager, adjusting in, 399
Bring to Front command, 143
    for SmartArt graphic, 195
Browsed at a Kiosk option, 318
browsers, animation with, 307
browsing
    in photo albums, 163
    presentations, 18-19
bulleted lists
    adding/removing bullets, 60
    animating, 304
    character of bullets, changing, 61
    distance between bullets and text,
        changing, 60
    objects, 36
    placeholders, 33
    shapes, adding to, 109
    text, entering, 39
buttons. *See also* specific types
    in dialog boxes, 8
    on Ribbon, 4

C

Calendar tool in Groove, 374
cascading windows, 14
case
    finding and replacing by, 69
    in spell-checking, 275
CDs
    inserting audio CDs, 184
    Package for CD feature, 330-331
cells. *See* charts; tables
Cell Styles button, 213
certification authority (CA), 346

Character Code box, 65
characters. *See also* case
    direction, changing, 57
    international character toolbar, 403
    spacing, changing, 56
    symbols, inserting, 65
chart area, 216
Chart Elements list arrow, 216
charts. *See also* OLE (object linking and
        embedding); organization charts
    advanced analysis techniques, 218
    animation in, 218, 305
    AutoFit, column width with, 212
    automatic complete, turning on/off, 207
    axis, 205
        changing, 219
        titles, 218
    backgrounds, changing, 219
    cells, 204
        automatic complete, turning on/off,
            207
        hidden or empty cells, 209
        inserting, 213
    creating, 204
    data labels, 218
    data tables for, 218
    default, setting template as, 221
    deleting, 214
    drawing objects in, 218
    editing
        data source, 209
        worksheet data, 208
    embedding charts, 235-236
    empty cells in, 209
    entering data in worksheets, 207
    floor of chart, showing/hiding, 219
    formatting
        objects in chart, 216-217
        resetting formatting, 214
        worksheets, 213
    hidden cells in, 209
    horizontal series, editing data in, 208
    importing data into, 210-211
    inserting, 204
        cells, rows and columns, 213
    labels, changing, 218
    layouts
        applying layouts, 215

charts *(continued)*
    changing, 214
    labels, changing, 218
    legend series, 205
        adding/removing, 209
        editing data in, 208
        labels, 218
    modifying worksheets, 212-213
    moving in, 209
    objects
        formatting, 216-217
        shape styles to object, applying, 217
        style, changing, 217
        zooming on, 216
    opening, 205
    pasting data into, 211
    pictures in, 218
    placeholders, 33
    plot area, 216
        showing/hiding, 219
    ranges of data, 206
    saving templates, 220-221
    selecting worksheet data, 207
    shapes
        inserting, 218
        objects, applying styles to, 217
    styles
        applying, 215
        object style, changing, 217
    switching data series in, 211
    templates
        applying, 221
        creating custom template, 220
    3D view, changing, 219
    title labels, 218
    trendlines, adding, 218
    type of chart, changing, 214
    viewing
        data in, 205
        imported data, 210
    wall of chart, showing/hiding, 219
    width of column, changing, 212
Charts folder, 221
Chart Type button, 221
chatting in Groove, 383
check boxes, 8
Check for Updates button, 26

Check Office documents, 349
Chinese, support for, 400
circles, drawing, 106
class modules in VBA, 407
ClearType options, 392
Clip Art, 151, 152
    downloading, 159
    keyword, locating by, 156
    placeholders, 33
    slide layout, inserting clip art with, 157
    on Web, 158-159
Clip Art task pane
    inserting clip art with, 157
    picture fills from, 122-123
    properties of clip, changing, 155
Clipboard
    picture fills, pasting, 122-123
    shapes, copying, 117
Clip Gallery for AutoShapes, 148-149
Clip Organizer, 152
    adding/removing
        clips, 153
        shapes to, 150
    categories, organizing clips into, 154-155
    Clips Online button, 158-159
    movie, inserting, 182
    new collection, creating, 154
    properties of clip, changing, 155
    sound, inserting, 182
clips, 148-149. *See also* Clip Art; Clip
    Organizer
    adding/removing, 153
    downloading, 159
    multimedia clips, 152
    properties of clip, changing, 155
Clips Online, 158-159
Close Master View button, 75
closing
    presentations, 30
    Task panes, 15
    Window panes, 15
collaborative workspaces. *See* Groove
Collapse Dialog button, 208, 209
collapsing slides, 71
color fills
    customizing attributes, 394
    shapes, adding to, 120-121
    for WordArt, 178-179

colors. *See also* background styles; color themes
    for gradient fills, 127
    for menus (palettes), 98
    of organization charts, 203
    Picture Manager, adjusting in, 399
    properties of, 92, 93
    for reviewers, 338
    scheme options, 392
    for shadows, 130, 131
    SmartArt graphic colors, changing, 197
    tables, adding to, 229
    underlining text, 58, 59
color themes, 89
    creating, 92-93
    custom colors, adding, 92, 93
    deleting, 93
    editing, 93
    six accent themes, 89
    for WordArt, 178-179
columns and rows. *See also* charts; tables
    text columns, 67
Column Width command, 212
COM objects, 418
COM add-ins, 403
    loading/unloading, 404-405
Co-Manager chart layout, 239
command-line switches, 333
commands. *See also* voice commands
    buttons on Ribbon, 4
    Diagnose command, 28
    from Office menu, 5
    Quick Access Toolbar, adding to, 395
    from shortcut menus, 5
comments
    adding, 336
    copying text of, 339
    deleting, 339
    editing, 338-339
    merging, 337
    reading, 337
Compatibility Checker, 288
    for Internet faxes, 362
Compatibility mode
    opening, 13
    opening, macros in, 417
    saving, 22-24

Compatibility Pack for Office 2007, 266
Compressed Windows Enhanced Metafile, 161
compression
    of embedded objects, 235
    of pictures, 170
    in XML presentations, 264
connecting shapes, 140-141
connection status, 21
consistency of presentation, 74
contacts. *See* Groove
contents of document, 287
contextual spelling, 275
contextual tabs on Ribbon, 4
continuously playing
    movies, 186
    slide shows, 314, 315
    sounds, 187
contour effects, 133
contrast, 171
    in photo album pictures, 163
    Picture Manager, adjusting in, 399
converting
    linked objects, 235
    presentations from PowerPoint 97-2003 to PowerPoint 2007, 22-24
    XML presentations, converters for, 266
copying
    CD, slide shows on, 330-331
    comment text, 339
    existing presentation, 10
    macros, 413
    objects from slide, 35
    shapes, 116-117
    slide shows on CDs, 330-331
    smart cut and paste, 41
    text, 40
Counterbalance Arrows, 192
Create Microsoft Office Outlook Task command, 395
cropping pictures. *See* pictures
curves, 112
Custom Animation task pane, 306
Custom Dictionaries dialog box, 278
Customize Quick Access Toolbar list arrow, 6
customizing, 268. *See also* slide shows
    advanced options, setting, 393
    personal options, setting, 392-393

customing *(continued)*
  Quick Access Toolbar, 6, 7
  shadows, 131, 394
  text objects, creating, 394
  themes from files, 97
cutting
  objects from slide, 35
  slides, 70
  smart cut and paste, 41
cycle purpose, SmartArt, 191

D

dashes, replacing, 62-63
data markers, 205
data series, 204
date and time
  animations, setting time between, 307
  Handout Master, Date placeholder in, 82
  slide show, setting timings for, 310-311
  text, inserting in, 88
debugging macros, 412
Debug toolbar, 412
Decrease List Level button, 50
Delete Cropped Areas of Picture setting, 170
deleting. *See also* adding/removing; Groove
  animation, 307
  charts, 214
  color themes, 93
  comments, 339
  digital signatures, 347
  freeform vertex, 115
  hyperlinks, 253
  macros, 411
  movies, 183
  objects, 35
  organization chart box, 240
  passwords, 343
  shapes, 106
  Slide Master, 78
  slides, 33, 48
  slide shows, 317
  sounds, 183, 185
  table columns and rows, 224
  Text pane, lines in, 193
  theme effects, 95
depth effects, 133
deselecting. *See* selecting/deselecting

Design Templates, 25
desktop language settings, 403
destination file, defined, 231
destination program, defined, 231
developer options, setting, 409
Developer tab, 409. *See also* macros
  for ActiveX controls, 418-419
  general options, setting, 392
device independent bitmaps, 161
diagnosing problems, 28-29
dialog boxes. *See also* specific types
  navigating in, 8
  options, choosing, 8
Dialog Box Launcher, 3, 8
dictionaries. *See also* spell-checking
  exclusion dictionaries, 278-279
digital signatures, 243, 346-347
  creating digital IDs, 346
  deleting, 347
  document, adding to, 347
  macros, adding to, 414
  viewing, 347
dimming text after animation, 305
direction
  of characters, 57
  of WordArt text, 181
Director movies, playing, 422
Director Shockwave files (.dcr), 422
DirectShow, Microsoft, 186
disabled application add-ins, 402
disabled items, 403
  viewing, 359
Discussion tool in Groove, 368, 372
distance setting for shadows, 130, 131
distributing objects, 138
Document Information Panel, 286-287
  changing, 424
Document Inspector, 340-341
document properties, 286-287
  advanced properties, displaying, 287
  Compatibility Checker, 288
  customizing, 287
Document Recovery task pane, 27
documents
  add-ins related to, 402
  digital signatures, adding, 347
  imaging, scanning, 396-397

inspecting, 340-341
dotted lines in organization charts, 202
double strikethrough formatting, 58, 59
double underline formatting, 58, 59
downloading
    add-ins, 402
    clips, 159
    harmful attacks and, 349
    PowerPoint Viewer, 332
    SharePoint information, 384
    template packs, 12
    updates, 26
drag-and-drop
    Clip Art pictures, 157
    text, 41
    into Text pane, 191
drawing. *See also* shapes
    charts, drawing objects in, 218
    straight lines or arrows, 110
    tables, 222
    ungrouping/regrouping, 147
Draw Table button, 227
duplicating slides, 33, 49
DVDs
    movies from, 188
    slide shows on, 330-331

E

Edit Data Source button, 209
Edit Data Source dialog box, 208
editing. *See also* charts; Groove; slide shows
    calendar, 374
    color themes, 93
    comments, 338-339
    hyperlinks, 246, 253
    lines or arrows, 111
    linked objects, 234
    macros, 413
    marked as final presentations, 360
    photo albums, 163
    in Picture Manager, 399
    presentation properties, 286
    SharePoint files, 385
    SmartArt graphics, 195
    text, 40-41
    text boxes, 66

WordArt text, 177
Edit Master, renaming in, 78
Edit Pictures button, 399
Edit Sound Object Dialog Box Launcher, 242
effects. *See also* specific types
    individual effects, adding, 129
    pictures, adding to, 167
    preset effects, adding, 128
    shapes, adding to, 128-129
    tables, applying to, 230
    theme effects, 95
    WordArt text, applying to, 180
e-mail. *See also* attachments
    Groove, address for, 364
    hyperlinks for sending, 251
    photo album attachments, 163
    review, sending presentation for, 361
embedding. *See also* OLE (object linking and embedding)
    defined, 231
    fonts, 319
Encapsulated Postscript files, 161
English Assistant, 282
Enhanced Windows Metafile, 161
entire word, selecting, 41
equalize character height, 59
Eraser button, 227
event procedures in VBA, 407
Excel. *See* Microsoft Excel
exclusion dictionaries, 278-279
existing presentations
    copying, 10
    opening, 13,
    opening, macros with, 417
Expand Dialog button, 208, 209
expanding slides, 71
exporting. *See* importing/exporting
extensions. *See* file extensions

F

fading out effects, 300
fax, sending presentations by, 362
    imaging, scanning, 396-397
Featuring categories
    for blank presentations, 11
    list of, 10
    for templates, 12

file encryption, 343
file extensions, 265
    for macros, 416
    showing/hiding, 24
file permissions
    restricted presentations, 344-345
    for SharePoint files, 384
files. *See also* movies; SharePoint; synchro-
        nizing files; specific formats
    audio file formats, 182
    hyperlinks to, 248
    movies from file, inserting, 183
    OLE (object linking and embedding) for,
        232
    pictures from file, inserting, 160
    sounds from file, inserting, 183
Files of Type list, 13
Files tool in Groove, 368, 371
FileZ, 349
fills. *See also* color fills; gradient fills; tex-
        tures
    table, adding fill to, 229
    WordArt, text fills for, 178-179
finding and replacing text, 69
first-line indents, 60
Fit To Window button, 9
Flash movies, 182
    playing, 422-423
flipping. *See* rotating
folders
    Groove Folder Synchronization (GFS),
        385
    Picture Manager, exporting folders in,
        398
    for presentations, 331
    synchronizing local folders, 386
Font Color button, 89, 93, 98
fonts. *See also* characters; TrueType fonts
    CDs, slide shows on, 330-331
    differences between, 319
    embedding fonts, 319
    entire presentation, replacing fonts for,
        59
    formatting text fonts, 59
    for headers and footers, 85
    for hyperlinks, 253
    kerning with, 56
    printing options, 293

Ribbon, changing font with, 58
    in slide shows, 319
    for symbols, 65
    for text boxes, 66
    theme fonts, 94, 95
Footer placeholder, 82
footers. *See* headers and footers
foreign languages, 277
    adding to programs, 400
    designating, 284
    French spellings, 275
    international character toolbar, 403
    marking text as language, 284
    thesauruses, 281
    translating text to, 283
Format Painter, 64
    slides, applying themes to, 89
Format Shape dialog box
    for color fills, 120
    for effects, 128
    for gradient fills, 126
    for texture fills, 124
    undoing changes in, 120, 122, 124
formatting. *See also* charts; formatting text;
        SmartArt graphics
    connector lines, 141
    curves, 113
    freeforms, 113
    Handout Master, 270
    hyperlinks, 253
    organization charts, 240-241
    placeholders, 83
    tables, 226-227
    Text pane, text in, 193
    WordArt text, 178-179
formatting text. *See also* AutoFormat; fonts
    with Mini Toolbar, 59
    with Ribbon, 58
    showing/hiding, 51
    styles, applying, 64
forms. *See* Groove
Forms tool, Groove, 376-377
fractions, correcting, 62-63
frames
    in photo albums, 162
    on printed slides, 271
freeforms
    angle of vertex, modifying, 115

deleting freeform vertex, 115
polygons, drawing, 112
vertex in freeform, modifying, 114-115
FTP (File Transfer Protocol), 262
adding/modifying locations, 262
sites, accessing, 262
function procedures in VBA, 407

G

Get External Data button, 210
GIF format, 161
slides, saving, 257
glow effect, 129
to pictures, 167
for SmartArt graphics, 198-199
to WordArt text, 180
gradient fills, 126-127
background style gradients, creating, 101
in charts, 218
custom gradient fills, 127
with presets, 126
tables, adding to, 229
tiling options, 127
for WordArt, 178-179
graphics. *See also* Clip Art; pictures;
SmartArt graphics
background graphics, adding, 84
slides saved as, 289
Web graphics, saving slides as, 257
Graphics Interchange Format. *See* GIF
format
grayscale
converting pictures to, 172
print preview, 294-295
gridlines in table, showing/hiding, 227
grids and guides
adding/removing, 137
aligning objects to, 136-137
snapping objects into, 136
turning on/off, 136
Groove, 363. *See also* SharePoint; synchronizing files
action items for meetings, 375
active contacts, 381
adding tools to workspace, 373
agenda for meetings, 375
alerts, 370

chat message postings, 383
managing, 371
options, setting, 370
tools, setting for, 379
attachments for meeting documents, 375
attendees of meetings, 376
calendar appointments, setting, 374
chatting in, 383
configuring, 364
contacts
adding, 381
messages to contacts, sending, 382
creating workspace, 368
deleting
calendar appointments, 374
files, 371
forms, 377
issue record, 379
pictures, 380
tools, 373
workspace, 368
Designer Access privileges, 376
design sandbox, managing, 376-377
Discussion tool, 368, 372
editing
calendar, 374
issue tracking, 379
pictures, 380
SharePoint files, 385
exiting, 365
exporting pictures, 380
Files tool, 368, 371
forms, 376-377
Response form, 378-379
Forms tool, working with, 376-377
general preferences, setting, 367
guests on, 369
InfoPath tool, 373
inviting users to workspace, 369
Issue Tracking, 378-379
launching, 365
managers on, 369
manage tools in, 371
meetings, managing, 375
messages, sending, 382
microphone, chatting with, 383
navigating

Groove *(continued)*
    in calendar, 374
        meeting options, 375
    offline contacts, 381
    online contacts, 381
    opening files, 371
    participants on, 369
    picture library, creating, 380
    Preferences dialog box, 367
        alerts, setting, 370
    renaming
        pictures, 380
        tools, 373
    Response form, 378
    roles of users, 369
    searching issues, 379
    sorting issues, 379
    synchronizing SharePoint files, 385
    template, saving workspace as, 368
    tracking issues, 378-379
    updating assignments, 379
    window, 366
    workspace properties, setting, 365
Groove Folder Synchronization (GFS), 385
Groove InfoPath Forms tool, 363
Groove Workspace Explorer, 368
grouping
    drawings, ungrouping/regrouping, 147
    on Ribbon, 4
    shapes, grouping/ungrouping, 146
    SmartArt graphic, shapes in, 195
    tables, ungrouping, 146
Guest role for Groove, 369
guides. *See* grids and guides

H

hackers, 342
Handout Master, 76
    formatting, 270
    placeholders in, 82, 270
    viewing, 77
handouts, 267
    headers and footers in, 270-271
    preparing, 270-271
    printing, 271
handwriting text, 396-397
hanging indents, 60

hard-to-select objects, selecting, 142
Header placeholder in Handout Master, 82
Header Row option, 226
headers and footers
    adding, 85
    changing look of, 85
    in handouts, 270-271
    placeholders, 82
    on speaker notes, 274
help, 20-21
    command help, 6
    contacting Microsoft Help, 26
    with Microsoft Excel, 206
    searching for, 21
Help Viewer, 20-21
    connection status, 21
hidden information, managing, 340-341
hiding. *See* showing/hiding
hierarchy purpose, SmartArt, 191
Highlighter Pen option for slide show, 326
homographs, 348
horizontal alignment, 55
    of WordArt text, 181
HSL color mode, 92
HTML (Hypertext Markup Language), 243, 254
    with XML, 264
hue, 92, 93
hyperlinks
    action buttons activating, 244
    autoformatting, 62-63
    color themes for, 89
    deleting, 253
    destinations for, 250
    between documents, 251
    editing, 246, 253
    for e-mail messages, 251
    to external objects, 248-249
    to files, 248
    formatting, 253
    highlighting click or mouse over, 246
    inserting, 250-251
    inside of presentation, 250
    mouse over for, 249
    to other presentation, 248
    to programs, 249
    relative links, 250
    slide object, adding to, 246

sound, adding, 247
    using, 252
    to Web page, 249
hyphens, replacing, 62-63

I

icons
    objects inserted as, 233
    Pin icon, 13
Imaging, scanning, 396-397
Import Data Options dialog box, 210
importing/exporting
    chart data, importing, 210-211
    Groove pictures, exporting, 380
    Microsoft Excel charts, importing, 237
    Microsoft Word, exporting notes to, 273
    Picture Manager, exporting folders in, 398
    rotating imported objects, 145
inactive application add-ins, 402
Increase List Level button, 50
increasing/decreasing list level text, 50-51
indenting text
    for bulleted lists, 60
    level of indent, changing, 50
    modifying indent, 51
    Text pane, lines in, 193
InfoPath Forms tool, 373, 376
InfoPath Form Template, 424
InfoPath tool, 373
initials of reviewer, changing, 336
ink annotations on slide shows, 320
Ink button, Language bar, 397
Insert Cells button, 213
Insert Movie dialog box, 188
Insert Shape button list, 239
inspecting documents, 340-341
international character toolbar, 403
Internet. See also Web pages; Web presentations
    Clip Art on, 158-159
    fax, sending presentations by, 362
    FTP (File Transfer Protocol), using, 262
    Microsoft Office online information, 263
    photo albums, sharing, 163
Internet Explorer download monitoring, 349
invisible on-slide content, 341

IRM (Information Rights Management), 335, 344-345
ISO paper side size, 268
Issue Tracking, 373, 378-379
italicizing hyperlinks, 253

J

Joint Photographic Experts Group format. See JPEG format
JPEG format, 161
    for Groove pictures, 380
    slides, saving, 257
jumps. See hyperlinks

K

kerning, 56
keyboard
    browsing slides with, 18
    grid settings, overriding, 137
    nudging drawing object with, 117
    objects, moving, 35
    window panes, resizing, 15
KeyTips, 4
keywords for Clip Art, 156

L

labels in chart, changing, 218
landscape orientation, 268-269
languages. See also foreign languages
    adding to programs, 400
LAN (local-area network), 424
layouts. See also charts; slide layouts
    organization chart layout, changing, 202-203, 240
    SmartArt graphic layout, changing, 197
left indents, 60
legend series. See charts
letter paper slide size, 268
libraries
    Groove picture library, creating, 380
    SharePoint libraries, 384
lines or arrows
    in charts, 218
    connector lines, 140-141
    Counterbalance Arrows, 192
    customizing attributes, 394
    editing, 111

lines or arrows *(continued)*
    modifying, 111
    Quick Style to line, adding, 110
    straight lines or arrows, drawing, 110
line spacing, 54
linking. *See also* hyperlinks; OLE (object linking and embedding)
    defined, 231
list boxes, 8
list purpose, SmartArt, 191
lists. *See* bulleted lists; numbered lists
Lists and Galleries, 3
live preview, 4. *See also* tables
    general options, setting, 392
    of organization charts, 202
    with Picture Shape gallery, 165
    for SmartArt graphics, 199
    themes, 90
    of transitions, 300
Lock Aspect Ratio check box, 224
luminosity, 92, 93

M

Macro-Enabled Design Template, 25
Macro-Enabled Show, 25
macros, 265, 401. *See also* Trust Center
    controlling, 412-413
    copying to other presentations, 413
    creating, 410-411
    debugging, 412
    deleting, 411
    digital signatures on, 414
    earlier versions, macros from, 410
    editing, 413
    file extensions for, 416
    harmful attack sand, 248-249
    running, 411
    saving presentations with, 416
    security settings, 354
    self-signing certificates for, 414
    stopping macros, 411
    toolbar, assigning macro to, 415
    VBA macros, 265
maintenance, performing, 29
Manager role for Groove, 369
margins
    tables, changing cell margins in, 224
    for text boxes, 66
    wrapping and adjusting, 67
Margins button, 224
Marks as Final command, 360
Master Layout, 80
masters. *See also* Handout Master; Notes Master; Slide Master
    placeholders in, 74-75
    viewing, 76-77
    working with, 74-75
matrix purpose, SmartArt, 191
maximizing/minimizing
    windows, 14
McAfee, 349
meetings, Groove, 375
menus. *See also* shortcuts
    colors, adding, 98
    Office menu, 5
    for slide shows, 323
merging
    comments, 337
    tables, cells in, 225
Message Bar
    macros, signatures on, 414
    security options, 355
metadata, 340
    Document Information Panel tracking, 424
methods in VBA, 406
MHTML format, 256
microphones.
    with Groove, 383
Microsoft. *See also* Clip Organizer; organization charts; TrueType fonts
    DirectShow, 186
    help from, 26
    Paint, bitmap graphics from, 152
    Producer, 403
    Windows Explorer, 2
    Wordpad for playlists, 334
Microsoft Excel. *See also* charts; OLE (object linking and embedding)
    embedding charts, 235-236
    help, 206
    importing charts, 237
    tables, inserting, 223
    themes for, 90
Microsoft.Net Passport, 255

for IRM (Information Rights Management), 344-345
Microsoft Notepad, 264
   for playlists, 334
Microsoft Office. *See also* Clipboard
   Communicator 2007, 363
   Document Imaging, 396-397
   Document Scanning, 396-397
   Live Meeting, 403
   online information, 263
   SharePoint Server 2007, 363, 387-390
Microsoft Outlook
   for faxing presentation, 362
   IRM (Information Rights Management) in, 344-345
   review, sending presentations for, 361
Microsoft Word
   embedding documents, 238
   notes exported to, 273
   slides exported to, 273, 285
   speaker notes exported to, 285
   themes for, 90
minimizing. *See* maximizing/minimizing
Mini-Toolbar, 6
   buttons on, 5
   formatting with, 59
   general options, setting, 392
mirror type for texture fills, 125
modules in VBA, 407
monitors for slide shows, 328-329
mouse. *See also* slide shows
   for handwriting text, 396
   hyperlinks, mouse over for, 246, 249
   increasing/decreasing list level text with, 51
   objects, moving, 35
   slide timings, controlling, 310
movies, 152
   ActiveX controls, playing with, 182, 422-423
   Clip Organizer movie, inserting, 182
   delaying start of, 188
   Director movies, playing, 422
   files
      formats, 186
      inserting movie from, 183
   Flash movies, playing, 422-423
   inserting, 182-183

   new slide, inserting movies on, 183
   non-supported movies, playing, 182
   placeholders, 33
   playing movies, 186 187, 188
      options, setting, 186
      problems with, 188
   slide, inserting on, 183
   supported file formats, 182
   from video DVDs, 188
moving. *See also* navigating
   in charts, 209
   comments, 336
   grids and guides, 137
   objects, 35
   Quick Access Toolbar, 6
   shapes, 116-117
   text, 40
   Text pane, 192
   windows, 14
MPG/MPEG format, 182, 186
MP3 format, 182, 186
multimedia clips, 152
Multiple Manager chart layout, 239
My Templates, 10, 12
   chart templates, saving, 220-221

N

names
   for presentation, 296
   reviewer name, changing, 336
   Slide Master, renaming, 78
narration, 185, 312-313
navigating. *See also* Groove; moving
   dialog boxes, 8
   self-running slide shows, 318
   slide shows, 324-325
   in Web browser, 260
New Comment button, 336
New Presentation dialog box, 10
new presentations. *See also* blank presentations; templates; themes
   options, 10
Normal view, 1, 16-17. *See also* text
   movies playing in, 186, 188
   sounds playing in, 186, 188
   speaker notes in, 272
   text, working with, 36

notes. *See* comments; speaker notes
Notes Master, 76
    formatting, 273
    placeholders on, 274
    viewing, 77
Notes Page view, 1, 272
Notes pane, Normal view, 272
numbered lists
    adding/removing numbers, 60
    AutoCorrect Options with, 62-63
    character of numbers, changing, 61
    shapes, adding to, 109
    text, entering, 39
numbering. *See* numbered lists; slide numbering

O

Object Browser, 407
objects, 34-35. *See also* animation; AutoFit Options; backgrounds; charts; OLE (object linking and embedding); shapes; text
    aligning, 138-139
    deleting, 35
    hard-to-select objects, selecting, 142
    icons, inserting objects as, 233
    moving, 35
    on Notes Master, 273
    resizing, 34
    selecting/deselecting, 34
    stacking order, changing, 143
    VBA objects, 406
Office button, 3
Office menu, 5
Office Theme format, 25
off-slide content, managing, 340-341
OLE (object linking and embedding), 189, 231
    broken links, reconnecting, 235
    charts
        importing Excel charts, 237
        inserting Excel charts, 235-236
    compressing embedded objects, 235
    converting linked objects, 235
    editing linked objects, 234
    files, inserting, 232
    icons, inserting objects as, 233
    Microsoft Word documents, embedding, 238
    modifying linked objects, 234-235
    new object, inserting, 232
    organization charts, embedding, 239
    paste linking objects, 232-233
    sounds, linking and embedding, 242
    source of linked object, changing, 234
    updating source of linked object, 234
    working with embedded objects, 233
Online templates, 10
on-screen show slide size, 268
opening
    charts, 205
    default view, selecting, 393
    password-protected presentations, 343
    Picture Manager, 398
    presentations, 13
    presentations, macros with, 417
    presentations, PowerPoint 97-2003 in compatibility mode, 13
    Task panes, 15
    Web pages, 259
    XML presentations, 266
OpenType fonts, 319
Optical Character Recognition (OCR), 396-397
option buttons, 8
ordinals with superscript, 62-63
organization charts
    assistant shape object, 239
    colors, changing, 203
    coworker shape object, 239
    creating, 200
    deleting chart box, 240
    dotted lines in, 202
    embedded object, creating with, 238
    layout, changing, 202-203, 240
    methods for creating, 200-201
    modifying, 240-241
    rearranging chart box, 241
    selecting/deselecting chart boxes, 240
    shapes, adding, 201
    style, changing, 241
    subordinate shape object, 239
    text, aligning, 240
Organization Chart Style gallery, 241
Org Chart button, 203
orientation

slide orientation, 268-269

    SmartArt graphics and, 196

outline fonts, 319

Outline pane, Normal view, 16-17

    browsing slides in, 19

    collapsing slides in, 71

    expanding slides in, 71

    formatting, showing/hiding, 51

    rearranging slides, 71

    slides, working with, 48-49

    text, entering, 36, 37, 48

outlines. *See also* borders; Web
    presentations

    another program, inserting outlines
      from, 49

    document, saving text as, 290

    printing, 298

    text, entering, 48

overhead transparency slide size, 268

P

Package for CD feature, 330-331

Page Number placeholder, Handout Master,
    82

page setup options, 268-269

Paint Shop Pro, 152

parental controls, 356-357

Participant role for Groove, 369

passwords, 335

    adding to presentation, 342-343

    changing/removing passwords, 343

    for Groove, 364

    opening presentations with, 343

    for slide shows on CDs, 331

    strong passwords, 342

paste linking, 232-233

    Microsoft Word, exporting notes and
      slides to, 285

    for notes, 273

Paste Options button, 41

Paste Special command, 232-233

pasting. *See also* paste linking

    charts, data into, 211

    objects from slide, 35

    slides, 70

    smart cut and paste, 41

PDF documents, 1, 25

    creating, 24, 291

e-mail attachments, 361

pen. *See* slide shows

permissions. *See also* file permissions

    presentations, permission-restricted,
      344-345

personal information, managing, 340-341

PFCMedia, 188

phishing, 348

    privacy options and, 356

photo albums

    editing, 163

    new album, creating, 162

    sharing, 163

Picture Effects gallery, 167

picture fills

    custom picture fills, applying, 123

    to shapes, 122-123

    tables, adding to, 229

    tiling pictures, 123

Picture Manager, 398-399

    exporting folders in, 398

    red eye removal, 399

Picture Quick Style gallery, 164

pictures, 152. *See also* brightness; Clip Art;
    contrast; picture fills

    background style pictures, creating, 100

    borders, applying, 166

    on bullets, 61

    changing pictures, 160

    in charts, 218

    compressing, 170

    cropping, 174-175

      in Picture Manager, 399

    Delete Cropped Areas of Picture setting,
      170

    effects, adding, 167

    file, inserting from, 160

    file formats for, 161

    Groove picture library, creating, 380

    on numbers in lists, 61

    photo albums, 162-163

    Picture Manager, 398-399

    placeholders, 33

    precisely cropping pictures, 175

    precisely resizing pictures, 168

    Quick Style, adding, 164

    recoloring, 172-173

    red eye removal, 399

pictures *(continued)*
    redisplaying cropped pictures, 174
    resizing, 168-169
    rotating, 175
    in Picture Manager, 399
    scaling pictures, 169
    shapes, applying, 165
    tables, adding to, 227
    transparent background, setting, 173
Picture Shape gallery, 165
Pictures tool, Groove, 380
Pin icon, 13
pinning/unpinning documents, 13
placeholders, 32
    default, resetting to, 33
    entering information in, 33
    formatting, 83
    in Handout Master, 270
    for headers and footers, 82
    in masters, 74-75
    modifying, 83
    on Notes Master, 274
    showing/hiding, 82
    in slide layouts, 81
    in SmartArt graphics, 191
    text placeholders, 38
    title placeholders, 33, 82
playlists for multiple presentations, 334
plot area. *See* charts
PNG format, 161
    pictures, saving, 164
    slides, saving, 257
pointer options in slide shows, 326
points, 54
polygons, drawing, 112
Portable Network Graphics Format. *See* PNG format
portrait orientation, 268-269
.pot file format, 25
.potx file format, 25
PowerPoint Macro-Enabled Design Template (.potm), 416
PowerPoint Macro-Enabled Presentation (.pptm), 22, 25, 265, 320, 416
PowerPoint Macro-Enabled Show (.ppsm), 416
PowerPoint Options dialog box, 26
PowerPoint Show format, 25

PowerPoint Viewer
    customizing, 333
    Run command with, 333
    showing presentation on, 332
.ppt file format, 22, 25
Preferences dialog box. *See* Groove
presentation broadcast add-in, 403
presentation graphics software, 1
Presentation window, 3
Presenter view, 328-329
preserving Slide Master, 79
presets
    gradient fills with, 126
    for SmartArt graphics, 198-199
previewing. *See also* live preview
    animation, 302
    in black and white/grayscale, 294-295
    in dialog boxes, 8
    presentations, 294-295
    in Presenter view, 329
    print preview, 294-295
    Web pages, 260-261
Preview Synchronization dialog box, 385
Previous/Next Slide buttons, 17
Print dialog box, 270-271
printing
    changing options, 293
    custom shows, 297
    handouts, 271
    outlines, 298
    presentations, 296-297
    previewing, 294-295
    range of slides, 297
    scaling slides for, 298
    single slides, 297
Privacy dialog box, 2
privacy options
    parental controls, 356-357
    setting, 356
    statement, 348, 350
problems, 28-29
    macro problems, 412
    movies, playing, 188
    objects, arrangement of, 147
    recovering presentations, 27
procedures in VBA, 407
process purpose, SmartArt, 191

programs
    appearance, changing, 393
    hyperlinks to, 249
    shortcut, creating, 2
    Slide Show view, switching in, 324
program tabs, Ribbon, 4
Project Report Presentation add-in, 403
projects. *See also* macros
    in VBA, 407
publishing presentations as Web page, 255
pyramid purpose, SmartArt, 191

Q

Quick Access Toolbar, 1, 3, 391
    adding or removing items from, 7, 395
    buttons on, 5
    customizing, 7
    macros, adding, 415
    moving, 6
    resetting, 6
    resetting to default, 395
    Save button, 22
Quick Print command, 296
Quick Style
    lines, adding to, 110
    pictures, adding to, 164
    shapes, adding to, 118-119
    to SmartArt graphics, 196
    tables, adding to, 228-229
    Transition Quick Style gallery, 300
quitting PowerPoint, 30
quotation marks, 62-63

R

ranges. *See also* slides
    of data, 206
reading comments, 337
read-only presentations, 360
Recent Documents list, 13
    options, setting, 393
recently used documents, opening, 13
recoloring pictures, 172-173
Recolor Picture Quick Style gallery, 172
recording
    sounds, 185
    voice narration, 185, 312-313
recovering presentations, 27

red eye removal, 399
redoing actions, 43
reference books, searching, 280
reflection effect, 129
    in pictures, 167
    for SmartArt graphics, 198-199
    tables, applying to, 230
    to WordArt text, 180
regression analysis trendlines, 218
rehearsing slide show timings, 310-311
relationship purpose, SmartArt, 191
relative links, 250
removing. *See* adding/removing; deleting
renaming. *See also* Groove
    Slide Master, 78
repairing problems. *See* problems
repeated words, flagging, 275
Replace All option, 69
Replace Fonts command, 395
replacing text, 69
research, parental controls for, 356-357
Research task pane, 280
    for translating text, 283
Reset Picture button, 171
resizing. *See also* AutoFit Options
    movies, 186
    objects, 34
    panes in windows, 15
    pictures, 168-169
    shapes, 106-107
    SmartArt graphics, 194
    tables, 224
    Task panes, 15
    text boxes, 66
    Text pane, 192
    text while typing, 44
    windows, 14, 15
restricting presentation access, 344-345
Reuse Slides task pane, 72
reviewing presentations, 335
    changing reviewers, 338
    e-mail, sending presentations by, 361
    initials, changing, 336
rewinding movies, 186
RGB (red, green, blue) color mode, 92, 93
Ribbon, 1, 3, 391. *See also* add-ins;
    Developer tab; masters
    adding commands not in, 395

Ribbon *(continued)*
    Chart Elements list arrow, 216
    font changes with, 58
    formatting text with, 58
    for Microsoft Word documents, 238
    working with, 4
Right Management account, 360
rotating. *See also* 3D rotation effects
    characters, 57
    gradient fills, 127
    photo albums, pictures in, 163
    picture fills in shapes, 123
    in Picture Manager, 399
    pictures, 175, 399
    precisely rotating objects, 145
    preset increments, rotating objects to, 144-145
    shapes, 144-145
    SmartArt graphic, shapes in, 195
    texture fills, 125
    3D rotations, 128
    WordArt text, 181
RTF (Rich Text Format) documents, 25
    saving text as, 290
ruler. *See also* tabs
    showing/hiding, 50
    vertical ruler, showing, 393
Run command, 333

S

safe modes, 358-359
    disabled items, 359
saturation, 92, 93
Save As command, 243
Save As dialog box, 22
Save button, Quick Access Toolbar, 22
Save dialog box, 22
Save Template button, 220
saving. *See also* slide shows; Web presentations
    for different formats, 24-25, 289
    Groove workspace, 368
    macros, presentations with, 416
    options, setting, 23
    PowerPoint 97-2003 format presentations, 23
    presentations, 22-23

    presentations, PowerPoint 97-2003 in compatibility mode, 22-24
    smart tags, 46
    templates, 102-103
    voice narrations, 313
    Web graphics, saving slides as, 257
    Web page, presentations as, 254-255
    XML presentations, 264
scalable fonts, 319
scaling pictures, 169
schemas, 264
screen resolution, choosing, 314
ScreenTips
    shortcut keys in, 393
    showing/hiding, 6
scribbles, 113
scrolling in presentation, 18
searching
    for Clip Art, 156
    for clips on Web, 159
    Groove issues, 379
    for help, 21
    Research task pane, 280
    for text, 69
    for themes, 90, 91
security, 335. *See also* ActiveX controls; add-ins; digital signatures; passwords; Trust Center
    avoiding attacks, 348-349
    macro security options, 354
    Message Bar security options, 355
    parental controls, 356-357
    read-only presentations, 360
    restricting presentation access, 344-345
    safe modes, 358-359
    viruses, avoiding, 348-349
selecting/deselecting
    bulleted text, 61
    numbered text, 61
    objects, 34
    organization chart boxes, 240
    text, 40
selection boxes, 34
Selection pane, 142
self-running slide shows, 318
Send to Back, 143
    for SmartArt graphic, 195
Send to Microsoft Word command, 285,

290, 395

sepia, converting pictures to, 172

servers, 254

    Windows SharePoint Server, 373

Set Transparent Color command, 173

Set Up Show dialog box, 316-317

    for self-running slide shows, 318

Shading button, 229

shadows, 129

    customizing, 131, 394

    to pictures, 167

    preset shadows, adding, 130

    for SmartArt graphics, 198-199

    tables, applying to, 230

    to WordArt text, 180

Shape Effects button, 198

Shape Effects gallery, 128

Shape Fill button, 89, 198

Shape Outline button, 89, 120, 121, 198

Shape Quick Style gallery, 118-119

shapes, 105. *See also* AutoShapes; charts; freeforms; lines or arrows; SmartArt graphics

    adjusting shapes, 107

    basic shapes, drawing, 106

    bulleted lists, adding, 109

    Clipboard task pane, copying objects with, 117

    Clip Organizer, adding to, 150

    color fills, applying, 120-121

    color outline, applying, 121

    connecting shapes, 140-141

    converting to freeforms, 112

    copying objects, 116-117

    curves, 112

    customizing attributes, 394

    deleting, 106

    distributing objects, 138

    effects, adding, 128-129

    gradient fills, 126-127

    grids and guides, aligning objects to, 136-137

    grouping/ungrouping shapes, 146

    hard-to-select objects, selecting, 142

    for hyperlinks, 253

    multiple shapes, inserting, 108

    nudging, 117

    numbered lists, adding, 109

    one step, copying/moving in, 116

    organization charts, adding to, 201

    other shapes, changing shapes to, 108

    picture fills, applying, 122-123

    pictures, applying shapes to, 165

    precision, moving object with, 117

    Quick Style, adding, 118-119

    replacing shapes, 107

    resizing shapes, 106-107

    rotating, 144-145

    scribbles, 113

    Selection pane, selecting with, 142

    shadows, adding, 130-131

    for SmartArt graphics, 198-199

    snapping objects into grids and guides, 136

    stacking order, changing, 143

    text

        adding, 67, 109

        Quick Style to text, adding, 119

    for text boxes, 66, 67

    texture fills for, 124-125

    3D effects, adding, 132-135

    transparency, shape color with, 121

    two shapes, connecting, 140

SharePoint, 1, 363, 373, 387-390

    checking in/out files, 385

    publishing slides, 388-389

    synchronizing files, 385

    Windows SharePoint Server, 373, 387-390

sharing. *See also* Groove; OLE (object linking and embedding)

    documents, information among, 231

    Groove Folder Synchronization (GFS), 385

    photo albums, 163

    XML data, 264

Shockwave players, 422

shortcuts

    adding/removing, 289

    choosing commands from menus, 5

    for command-line switches, 333

    objects, resizing, 34

    program shortcut, creating, 2

    ScreenTips, shortcut keys in, 393

    Slide Show view navigation shortcuts, 325

showing/hiding. *See also* turning on/off
    background objects on slide, 84
    charts, elements in, 219
    Close button and, 30
    file extensions, 24
    movies, 186
    placeholders, 82
    Ribbon, 4
    ruler, 50
    ScreenTips, 6
    slide shows, hiding slides in, 315
    sound icon, 187
    spelling errors, 275
    status bar, checking on/off status with, 9
    tables, gridlines in, 227
    Text pane, 192
    Web presentation outlines, 255
Show Markup button, 337
signatures. *See* digital signatures
size. *See also* resizing
    shadows, setting for, 130, 131
    slide size, controlling, 268
Size Dialog Box Launcher
    pictures, scaling, 169
    for shapes, 106
sizing handles, 66
slide files, 25
slide layouts
    changing, 83
    charts, creating, 205
    Clip Art, inserting, 157
    existing slide layout, creating from, 81
    gallery, 32
    new slide layout, inserting, 80
    placeholders, inserting, 80
    saving template, 102
Slide Master, 73, 75
    background objects, hiding, 84
    deleting, 78
    new Slide Master, inserting, 79
    preserving/not preserving, 79
    renaming, 78
    saving template, 102
    viewing, 76
slide numbering
    different number, starting numbering with, 87
    on every slide, 87

specific slides, inserting on, 86
slides. *See also* backgrounds; placeholders; printing; slide numbering
    action buttons for specific slides, creating, 245
    CD audio, inserting, 184
    collapsing slides, 71
    cut and paste, moving with, 70
    deleting, 48
    duplicating, 33, 49
    expanding slides, 71
    exporting to Microsoft word, 285
    graphic image, saving as, 289
    hyperlinks, adding, 246
    landscape orientation, 268-269
    layouts to existing slides, applying, 32
    Microsoft Word, exporting to, 273, 285
    movie on slide, inserting, 183
    new slides, creating, 32
    from other presentations, 72
    in Outline pane, Normal view, 48-49
    portrait orientation, 268-269
    proportions, customizing, 269
    range of slides
        printing, 297
        in slide show, 314
    rearranging slides, 70-71
    recording sounds on, 185
    size of slide, controlling, 268
    text, entering, 37
    themes to other slides, applying, 89
    transitions, creating, 300-301
    voice narration, recording, 185, 312-313
    Web graphics, saving as, 257
slide shows, 299. *See also* animation; PowerPoint Viewer
    advanced options, 323
    annotations
        ink annotations on slide shows, 320
        pen, using, 326
        pointer options, changing, 326
        saving, 327
        showing, 336
    black-out screens, 329
    black slide, ending with, 323
    CD, packaging for, 330-331
    continuously playing, 314, 315
    custom slide shows, 316-317

navigating to, 325
deleting custom slide show, 317
editing
    custom slide show, 317
    timings, 311
fonts, working with, 319
hiding slides, 315
macros running in, 411
manually showing, 314
minutes of meetings, 375
monitors, multiple, 328-329
mouse pointer
    options, changing, 326
    pen, changing to, 327
multiple monitors for, 328-329
multiple presentations, showing, 334
navigating, 324-325
options, setting, 323
Package for CD feature, 330-331
pen
    mouse pointer, changing to, 327
    using, 326
presenting, 321
range of slides, showing, 314
rehearsing timings, 310-311
saving
    annotations, 327
    presentation as slide show, 320
screen resolution, choosing, 314
second monitor, running on, 328-329
self-running slide shows, 318
setting up, 314-315
speaker notes, 324
    in Presenter view, 329
speed of transition, setting, 301
starting, 322-323
timings between slides, setting, 310-311
transitions, creating, 300-301
turning on/off annotations, 327
Slide Show view, 1, 17
movies playing in, 186, 188
navigation shortcuts, 325
sounds playing in, 186, 188
speaker notes, adding, 324
switching between programs in, 324
Slide Sorter view, 1, 17
animation, viewing, 302

rearranging slides, 70
transitions, viewing, 301
Slides pane, Normal view, 17
browsing slides in, 18 19
rearranging slides in, 70
small caps formatting, 58, 59
SmartArt graphics, 108, 189. *See also*
    organization charts; Text pane
adding shape to, 195
animating, 308-309
blanket graphics, creating, 191
changing shapes in, 195
colors, changing, 197
converting text to, 190-191
creating graphics with, 190
customized animation, applying, 309
fills with, 198
formatting
    orientation, changing, 196
    Quick Style, applying, 196
    shapes, 198-199
layout, changing, 197
orientation, changing, 196
outlines, applying, 198
placeholders, 33
purposes in, 191
Quick Style, applying, 196
removing shapes from, 193
resizing, 194
reversing order of animation, 309
smart cut and paste, 41
smart tags, 403
accessing information with, 47
changing options, 46
saving, 46
security and, 352
snapping objects into grids and guides, 136
soft edges effect, 129
to pictures, 167
for SmartArt graphics, 198-199
solid fill background style, 101
sorting issues in Groove, 379
sounds, 152
action button to sound, creating, 247
animation, adding to, 303
CD audio, inserting, 184
Clip Organizer sound, inserting, 182
file, inserting sounds from, 183

sounds *(continued)*
  hyperlink, adding sound to, 247
  inserting, 182-183
  linking and embedding, 242
  playing sounds, 186, 188
    options for, 187
  recording sounds, 185
  supported file formats, 182
  for transitions, 300-301
  voice narration, 185, 312-313
source file object, defined, 231
source program, defined, 231
spacing
  line spacing, 54
  text columns, 68
spam, 348
speaker notes, 267. *See also* slide shows
  exporting to Microsoft word, 285
  formatting, 273
  headers and footers, adding, 274
  Normal view, entering notes in, 272
  in Presenter view, 329
special characters, inserting, 65
speed of transition, setting, 301
spell-checking. *See also* foreign languages
  all-at-once spell-checking, 276
  as-you-type, 277
  contextual spelling, 275
  custom dictionaries, using, 278-279
  exclusion dictionaries, 278-279
  foreign language words, 277
  Groove chat messages, 383
  options, changing, 275
splitters, 15
splitting cells in tables, 225
Spotlight, 10
  for templates, 12
spyware, 348
squares, drawing, 106
stacking
  changing stacking order, 143
  characters, 57
standard modules in VBA, 407
standard tabs on Ribbon, 4
starting
  Groove, 365
  PowerPoint, 2

slide shows, 322-323
Start menu, 2
  Groove, starting, 365
statistics of document, 287
status bar, 3, 9
stop position for gradient fills, 127
strikethrough formatting, 58, 59
styles. *See also* background styles; charts
  format styles, applying, 64
  galleries, 1
  organization chart style, changing, 241
sub procedures in VBA, 407
subscript, 59
summary of document, 287
superscript, 59
  for ordinals, 62-63
surface for 3D effects, 133
switching
  views, 16
  windows, 14
Symantec, 349
Symbol dialog box, 65
symbols, 65
synchronizing files
  Groove Folder Synchronization (GFS), 385
  SharePoint files, 385
synonyms, finding, 30, 281
syntax for VBA code, 406

T

Tab key
  objects, selecting, 35, 146
  tables, navigating, 222-223
Table button, 222
Table Effects button, 230
Table Effects gallery, 230
Table Quick Style gallery, 228-229
tables
  aligning text within, 225
  backgrounds, adding, 229
  bevel effect, adding, 230
  borders, applying, 229
  deleting columns and rows, 224
  drawing, 222
  effects, applying, 230
  fills, adding, 229

formatting, 226-227
   clearing, 228
height of row, adjusting, 225
inserting
   columns and rows, 224
   tables, 222-223
lines, adding/removing, 227
live preview
   of effects, 230
   of style, 228
margins of cells, changing, 224
merging cells in, 225
Microsoft Excel table, inserting, 223
outlines, applying, 229
pictures, adding, 227
placeholders, 33
Quick Style, adding, 228-229
resizing, 224
showing/hiding gridlines, 227
splitting cells in, 225
Tab key for navigating, 222-223
text
   aligning text, 225
   entering in, 223
textures in, 227, 229
ungrouping, 146
width of column, adjusting, 225
Table Size button, 224
Tablet PC, 396
tabs, 52-53
   clearing tabs, 53
   in dialog boxes, 8
   distance between stops, changing, 53
   on Ribbon, 4
   setting tabs, 52
Tabs dialog box, 52
tags. See XML presentations
taskbar options, setting, 393
Task panes, 15
Template Creation Wizard, 403
templates, 1, 73. See also charts
   creating presentations with, 12
   Document Information Panel template, 424
   existing design templates, changing, 103
   Groove workspace as, 368
   macro-enabled design templates, 416
   saving, 102-103

text. See also aligning text; animation; characters; color themes; comments; dictating text; formatting text; indenting text; shapes; spell-checking; tables; WordArt
   columns, 68
   copying, 40
   customizing attributes, 394
   date and time, inserting, 88
   developing text, 36-37
   dimming text after animation, 305
   editing text, 40-41
   entering text, 37-39
   finding and replacing, 69
   handwriting text, 396-397
   inserting text, 38
   kerning, 56
   modifying, 40
   moving, 40
   numbering on specific slides, inserting, 86
   options for editing, setting, 41
   organization chart, aligning text in, 240
   in outlines, 36, 37, 48
   placeholders, 38
   resizing while typing, 44
   ruler, showing/hiding, 50
   selecting, 40
   slide, entering text on, 37
   SmartArt graphic, converting text to, 191
   symbols, inserting, 65
   3D rotation effects for, 135
   typing, correcting while, 42-43
   undoing
      corrections, 43
      options, 41
   WordArt, text fills for, 178-179
   wordiness of, 31
   wrapping text, 67
text boxes, 8
   in charts, 218
   creating, 66
   objects, 36
   shapes, adding text to, 67
Text Effects gallery, 180
Text Import Wizard, 210
Text pane
   drag-and-drop into, 191

Text pane *(continued)*
   red "x" in, 192
   showing/hiding, 192
   working with text in, 193
textures, 124-125
   background style textures, creating, 100
   in charts, 218
   in tables, 227, 229
   Tile picture as texture check box, 123
   for WordArt, 178-179
Theme Colors button, 89
themes, 1, 73. *See also* background styles;
   color themes
   applying, 90
   create a new presentation, 89
   custom themes, 96-97
   effects, 95
   fonts, 94, 95
   other slides, applying to, 89
   for photo albums, 162
   saving template, 102
   searching for, 90, 91
   slides, applying to, 72
   viewing, 90
      effects, 95
      fonts, 94
Thesaurus, 30, 281
.thmx file format, 25
3D effects, 128. *See also* 3D rotation effects
   custom effects, adding, 133
   to pictures, 167
   shapes, adding to, 132-135
3D rotation effects, 129
   custom effects, adding, 135
   to pictures, 167
   shapes, adding to, 134-135
   for SmartArt graphics, 198-199
   to WordArt text, 180
3D view of charts, 219
thumbnails of slides, 329
tick marks in charts, 205
TIFF format, 161, 396-397
tiling gradient fills, 127
time. *See* date and time
Title bar, 3
titles
   chart title labels, 218
   placeholders, 33, 82

text objects, 36
toolbars. *See also* Language bar; Quick
   Access Toolbar
   choosing commands with, 6
   Debug toolbar, 412
   international character toolbar, 403
   macros, adding, 415
   for slide shows, 323
Total Row option, 226
transform effects for WordArt text, 180
Transition Quick Style gallery, 300
transitions, creating, 300-301
translating text, 283
transparencies
   backgrounds for pictures, 173
   for gradient fills, 127
   for picture fills, 123
   shadows, setting for, 130, 131
   shape color fill with, 121
trendlines to charts, adding, 218
troubleshooting. *See* problems
TrueType fonts, 293
   CDs, slide shows on, 330-331
   kerning with, 56
   in slide shows, 319
Trust Center, 348-349. *See also* privacy
   options
   Message Bar security options, 355
   viewing, 350
trusted lists, 351
trusted publishers/locations, 350, 351
TuCows, 349
turning on/off. *See also* showing/hiding
   annotations in slide show, 327
   AutoFit Options, 44
   cell entries, automatic completion of,
     207
   grids and guides, 136
   sound narration, 185
two shapes, connecting, 140
Type 1 PostScript font, 319

U

UNC (Uniform/Universal Naming
   Convention), 424
underlining
   hyperlinks, 253
   text, 58, 59

undoing. *See also* text
    Format Shape dialog box changes, 120, 122, 124
uninstalling Microsoft Office 2007, 29
updating
    Automatic Updates, 349
    linked object, source of, 234
    PowerPoint, 26
up/down arrows, 8
uppercase words, spell-checking, 275
URLs (uniform resource locators), 251
    on Document Information Panel, 424
URN (Uniform Resource Name), 424
User-Initiated Safe mode, 358-359

V

VBA (Visual Basic for Applications), 265, 401. *See also* Visual Basic Editor
    for ActiveX controls, 421
    arguments, 406
    class module, 407
    event procedures, 407
    function procedures in, 407
    harmful attacks and, 348-349
    methods, 406
    modules in, 407
    objects in, 406
    procedures in, 407
    projects, 407
    standard modules, 407
    structure of, 406
    sub procedures in, 407
    syntax for code, 406
    working with, 406-407
    writing code for, 406
vertex in freeform, modifying, 114-115
vertical alignment, 55
    of WordArt text, 181
Vertical chart layout, 239
vertical ruler, showing, 393
video. *See* movies
View buttons, 3
viewing. *See also* charts; themes
    add-ins, 402-403
    calendar appointments, 374
    clips online, 158
    digital signatures, 347

disabled items, 359
    document properties, 286
    PowerPoint window, 3
    presentation properties, 286-287
    transitions, 301
    Trust Center, 350
    Visual Basic Editor, 408
    XPS documents, 292, 361
views, 16-17. *See also* Normal view; Slide Show view; Slide Sorter view
viruses
    add-in security options, 352
    antivirus software, 349
    avoiding, 348-349
Visual Basic Editor, 407
    macro problems, correcting, 412
    viewing, 408
Visual Basic for Applications (VBA). *See* VBA (Visual Basic for Applications)
voice narration, 185, 312-313
volume
    for movies, 186
    for sounds, 186

W

washout, converting pictures to, 172
WAV format, 182, 186
    embedded WAV files, 242
Web Page Preview command, 260, 395
Web pages
    addresses, understanding, 251
    appearance, changing, 259
    formats for, 25
    full-screen mode, viewing in, 260-261
    hyperlinks to, 249
    individual slides, viewing, 260-261
    opening, 259
    options, changing, 258
    previewing, 260-261
    publishing presentation as, 255
    saving presentations as, 254-255
    single file Web page, saving presentation as, 256
Web presentations, 243. *See also* hyperlinks; Web pages
    action buttons
        inserting, 244
        sound, creating button to, 247

Web presentations *(continued)*
 specific slide, creating buttons for, 245
 animation, showing, 260
 full-screen mode, viewing in, 260-261
 individual slides, viewing, 260-261
 navigation bar for, 260
 outlines
  browser, viewing in, 261
  showing/hiding, 255
 Return action button, inserting, 245
 single file Web page, saving as, 256
 square action buttons, creating, 245
web servers, 254
 Windows SharePoint Server, 373
Web site spoofing detection, 349
wide screen slide size, 268
width
 chart column width, adjusting, 212
 table column width, adjusting, 225
windows
 switching, arranging windows, 14
 panes, 15
Windows Firewall, 349
 with Groove, 365
Windows Media Player, 152, 186
Windows Metafile (WMF), 161
 compression with, 235
Windows SharePoint Server, 373
Windows custom dictionaries, 279
WMA format, 182, 186
WMV format, 182, 186
WordArt, 151
 angle of text, adjusting, 176-177
 different style to existing text, applying, 178
 direction of text, changing, 181
 editing text, 177
 effects, applying, 180
 formatting text, 178-179
 for hyperlinks, 253
 inserting WordArt text, 176
 outlines to text, applying, 179
 rotating text, 181
 for text boxes, 66
WordArt Quick Style gallery, 119, 176
WordArt Styles group, 178
worksheets. *See* charts

wrapping text, 67

X

x-axis in charts. *See* charts
XML documents, 1
 inspecting, 340-341
 saving PowerPoint 2007 presentations, 22
XML presentations, 264
 benefits of XML, 264
 converters for XML, 266
 damaged files, opening, 264
 Microsoft Office support, 264
 opening, 266
 opening, macros with, 417
 saving, 265
 schemas, 264
 sharing XML data, 264
 transforms, 264
 well-formed data, 264
XPS documents, 1, 25
 creating, 24, 292
 e-mail attachments, 361

Y

y-axis in charts. *See* charts

Z

ZIP format, 264
zooming, 3
 on chart objects, 216
 for freeforms, 115
 presentation view, 19